Poetics, Plays, and Performances

Poetics, Plays, and Performances

The Politics of Modern Indian Theatre

VASUDHA DALMIA

OXFORD
UNIVERSITY PRESS

OXFORD
UNIVERSITY PRESS

Oxford University Press is a department of the University of Oxford.
It furthers the University's objective of excellence in research, scholarship,
and education by publishing worldwide. Oxford is a registered trademark of
Oxford University Press in the UK and in certain other countries.

Published in India by
Oxford University Press
2/11 Ground Floor, Ansari Road, Daryaganj, New Delhi 110 002, India

First Edition published in 2006
Oxford India Paperbacks 2008
Fifth impression 2015

ISBN-13 (print edition): 978-0-19-569505-2
ISBN-10 (print edition): 0-19-569505-4

ISBN-13 (eBook): 978-0-19-908795-2
ISBN-10 (eBook): 0-19-908795-4

Contents

For Gert, who once helped me get my act together,
and for my sister Ila, who watched over it to the last

Photographs

Acknowledgements

The genesis of the present work goes back a good two decades and a half, when I first launched upon dissertational research for a PhD at the Centre for German Studies in Jawaharlal Nehru University. Of the many friends and colleagues who have been part of my engagement with theatre since then, and whom I would here like to remember, though none can be held accountable for what I have finally produced, I should like to begin with Anil Bhatti, R.P. Jain, and Rekha Kamath, who provided warm support and encouragement through the many ups and downs of the dissertational process. In the field itself, I had the good fortune to view plays and to interview most of the main participants in the enterprise: Ebrahim Alkzai, Amal Allana, Fritz Bennewitz, B.V. Karanth, M.K. Raina, M.S. Sathyu and Habib Tanvir granted me extensive interviews and allowed me access to much first-hand information that would not have been accessible otherwise. Shyamanand Jalan of Anamika, Kolkata, took time off from a rushed trip to Delhi to talk to me. Kartik Awasthi, Anil Chaudhury, Amitava Das Gupta, Satish Gupta and Vijay Kashyap responded patiently to cross-questioning and discussion. Safdar Hashmi, with his characteristic generosity, came over to my house to talk about the politics of theatre.

Anuradha Kapur opened up the world of theatre aesthetics for me, Rati Bartholomew provided sustained intellectual guidance, tactfully balancing many a rashly formed thesis. Karin Pfotenhauer of the Brecht Archive in what was then East Berlin, O. Varkey of the Sangeet Natak Akademi Library and B. Leela Sivaramayya of the National School of Drama Library, were generous with their help and cooperation.

Friends and family helped, as always: S.H. Vatsyayan's *Ajneya* whetted my curiosity for Asian theatre outside India and directed my attention to readings in Chinese and Japanese theatre, Barbara von Reibnitz made possible the discovery of the East Berlin Brecht, accompanying me to performances of his plays at the Schiffbauerdamm theatre. Gert Luederitz helped to finally think through and prune the dissertation which had become a wild outgrowth. Manjari Dingwaney rushed with me to Nai Sarak in the Walled City, to get the many pages of prose which still remained bound in time to meet the set deadline. In the years after the labours of dissertation writing were over, of the friends who were present at theatre visits, conferences and discussions and from whose insights I have endlessly profited, I would like to specially mention: Amal and Nissar Allana, of whose warmth and friendship I have very affectionate memories, particularly at the conference in post-wall Berlin, and Roland Beer, also at Berlin, who always managed to get tickets, often at the last minute, for the most talked-about performances in town; Darko Suvin, whom I first met at the Hong Kong Brecht conference in the late 1980s, whose writings have continued to provide the most succinct analysis of Brecht's theatrical practice and political thought; Rustom Bharucha for his brilliant writings on theatre and conversations at various venues —a whole chapter in the book is devoted to my engagement with his work; Kumkum Sangari, for her incisive analysis of people and politics, Henry von Stietencron for theatre visits through the 1990s and the discussions thereafter; Francesca Orsini for her friendship and words of warm encouragement, and finally, Anuradha Kapur and Geetanjali Shree for generously making available all the material—script, photographs, recollections—connected with the production of Tagore's *Gora*, on which the last chapter in this volume is based.

In the Berkeley years, George Hart, Sylvia Tiwon and Joanna Williams have given me their warm friendship and intellectual support.

Raka Ray has stood staunchly by my side through the turbulent process of settling down in the new academic environment. I am also greatly indebted to Huma Dar, Dhananjay Kapse, Layne Little, Joyce Lu, Sujata Mody, Shobna Nijhawan, Gita Pai, Vasudha Paramasivan, Rae Perigoe, Scott Schlossberg and Archana Venkatesan, participants of my graduate seminar on modern Indian theatre in fall 2001, for questioning every easy supposition and turning it upside down, in order to view it from the most varied angles. I am especially grateful to Sujata Mody, this time in her capacity as my research assistant, for her careful reading of each chapter in the book, for being my most stringent critic and not shirking the responsibility of posing a range of uncomfortable questions, many of which have remained unanswered.

The book was written at many venues. I thank all those who offered me their hospitality at different periods: Henry von Srietencron in Tuebingen and Ronco, Srilata Raman and Christoph Emmrich in Heidelberg, and finally, Monika and Wolfgang Boehm-Tettlebach, who made it possible for me to work undisturbed in their beautiful house in Gaiberg in summer 2004, as I struggled to get the manuscript ready for print. Grateful thanks to the Oxford University Press for not giving up on me in the meantime and my editor for seeing a complicated manuscript through the press.

No words of gratitude can suffice to thank my immediate family: Gert who drove for hours on coastal roads in Greece so that we could be in time to witness a performance of Euripides' *Iphegenia in Tauris* in the spectacular amphitheatre in Epidaurus; my daughter Damini and my son Taru, whose theatre visits started very early in life, I remember particularly the eight-hour passion play in Esparreguera, the little township outside Barcelona, to which they promptly offered to go again the next day; my mother, ever a source of inspiration, my sister Ila, who kept up a steady supply of books, essays, ideas and photocopies to the last, and my sisters Sheela and Yashodhara, who helped in a myriad thoughtful ways.

I do not know how to convey what I owe Anuradha Kapur. Without her intellectual and emotional support, I could not have written this book.

Introduction

The political and aesthetic concerns of this volume have emerged from an engagement with modern Indian theatre which began in the late 1970s. Propelled by the urban interest in folk theatre and the manifest popularity of Brecht in connection with this, I had embarked on dissertational research which focused on 'Brecht in Hindi'. In those years, Brecht's theory and practice of theatre held out the promise of widening the scope of middle-class concerns, of questioning the politics of received notions of theatre, past and present, and of overcoming the bounds of the proscenium stage, by turning to the more flexible performance traditions of the many forms of folk theatre still current in the country.

In trying to gauge the role Brecht played in the process, there was no way to avoid confrontation with the larger issues being thrown up by theatre practitioners and critics, by dramatists and audiences, in those heady decades of self-discovery and national self-projection. It seemed natural to have turned to Hindi, at this stage still destined to be the national language, as the language of production for plays staged in the capital of the nation. What theatrical practice could this newly realized 'national' theatre invoke? Was there dramatic composition in modern Hindi, did it have any theatrical tradition? Of the print languages of the subcontinent, Hindi belonged rather to the late starters; it had come into literary existence only from the late 1860s on. It was self-conscious about the Sanskritic heritage it claimed and the social standing it therewith wished to attain. From the start, then, playwriting in modern Hindi had sought to distance itself from the commercial Parsi stage, which also used colloquial Hindustani but with scant regard for matters of correct usage in one direction or another, whereas these were issues to which Hindi in its modern print form reacted very sensitively.

What kind of continuity did this self-consciously literary Hindi dramatic canon have with post-Independence decisions regarding the constitution of national theatre? This prompted the research into the past, a journey which took me back to the plays of Bharatendu Harishchandra in 1870s Banaras, and forward from there to Jayshankar Prasad and Mohan Rakesh, landmark figures in the history of modern Hindi drama. But these figures did not lead to Brecht. To understand why he was important I had to turn to the counter currents, the socially committed theatre spawned by Indian People's Theatre Association (IPTA), which took recourse to folk theatre. But these issues formed merely the context for the main focus of my research: the transmission of Brecht's theatre to north India. The use and misuse of 'folk' theatre were of significance primarily because they helped in the analysis of Indian theatre makers' understanding of Brecht.

However, the close association with theatre in those years of intense activity where current rose against counter current, would lead to a long-term engagement with issues which acquired other urgencies with time. I had the good fortune to view plays and interview most of the main participants in the years when folk theatre was in ascendancy and freshly written plays from all parts of the subcontinent converged in Delhi. The late B.V. Karanth, then director of the National School of Drama, himself an avant-garde explorer of the uses of folk theatre for urban drama, supported my work generously, making available the scripts of the Brecht plays translated into Hindi. I saw his scintillating production of *Barnam Vana*, *Macbeth* in the Yakshgana style, in 1980; the script was written by well-known Hindi poet Raghubir Sahay. I interviewed Ebrahim Alkazi extensively. He had retired from active participation in the theatre world, but his had been the most formative influence in the creation of the modern Indian theatre canon. I could watch the late Fritz Bennewitz of the Weimar theatre rehearse *A Midsummer Night's Dream* with second-year students in the National School of Drama and hear him explain how his years of training with Helene Weigel would make him rethink his original Stanisklavskian training and equip him to work in India and Indonesia. I met and interviewed Amal Allana and her husband Nissar Allana and saw her brilliant production of *Aurat Bhali Ramkali*, an adaptation of *The Good Woman of Sezuan*, in the front court of the National School of Drama. Anuradha Kapur, who was later to be in the vanguard of the experimental theatre of the 1990s, was just revising her important monograph on the Ramlila of Ramnagar. It was in speaking to her that I was first emboldened to delve into the complexities of classical Sanskrit aesthetics, to try and understand the shifts which had occurred when these were invoked by modern practitioners of the dramatic arts. I spoke to M.K. Raina about his production of Brecht's *Mother* and heard him delineate his views on the use of folk theatre. M.S. Sathyu told me about his early production of *The Good Woman of Sezuan* and Habib Tanvir shared his views about what urban actors could learn from folk players. I could watch Tanvir Sahib rehearse with his players in Ber Sarai, the quarters they occupied near the Jawaharlal Nehru University campus, and record the songs sung in their most popular plays. Safdar Hashmi spoke about his street theatre; his group had just performed in the cellar theatre of Sri Ram Centre for Peter Brook, who was on the verge of completing his production of the *Mahabharata*. It was apparent that worlds separated Brook's *Mahabharata* from Indian street reality; he himself admitted that he hesitated to bring his production to India.

Apart from these intense encounters, I could also conduct archival research at many sites. Since I lived partly in Germany, I could go to the Brecht Archives in East Berlin and watch the productions of the Berliner Ensemble, frozen into some kind of 'Modellbuch' political correctness, but interesting nevertheless as museum pieces. I could juxtapose this Brecht to the West German Brecht, in the belligerent, iconoclastic reinterpretations of a Peter Zadek or a Claus Peyman, and then compare and contrast with these figurations the Brecht known to us in India. Brecht's theatre had passed its peak years in Germany and was becoming more important outside Europe.[1] It was a privilege to be able to traverse both worlds, the German and the Indian, and encounter the many figurations of Brecht, the waning and the waxing.

The present work has retained just a part of that dissertation, and that too, much revised and extended over the years. I was to go on to work on Bharatendu Harishchandra and write a monograph on his formative role in the constitution of modern Hindi and modern Hinduism, *The Nationalization of Hindu Traditions*, which became so voluminous that most of the work on Harishchandra's theatre had to be kept out of it, for which at least one reviewer severely reprimanded me. The chapter on Harishchandra is surely overdue, but it fits much better in the present project with its focus on the politics of modern Indian theatre, and I offer it here, as the result of a long engagement with the nineteenth-century concern with and construction of the past. The chapters which follow often have a kernel which goes back to the dissertation but the changing political situation and my own engagement with the politics of language and religion in modern India have made for major shifts in my perspective. The years of faith in the national project had receded rapidly after the late 1970s and the terms employed then—'folk', 'epic', 'naturalistic theatre'—themselves took on another cast. The essays which have emerged—sometimes referred to as essays rather than chapters, because they can also be read independently—now bear little resemblance to the original dissertation chapters. They are still concerned with tracing the genealogy of modern Hindi theatre; Brecht's theatre is still a presence, though it now plays a different role; it is part of an extended essay on the changing relationship of urban theatre makers to folk-traditional theatre through more than a century of rejection, discovery, and fresh appropriation of 'folk'. The overall focus of the volume is on the politics of modern Indian theatre, particularly the action and reaction inspired by official policy making in the capital of the country, and, in an essay devoted to just that, its international representation. The last chapter, in focusing on a politically significant production of the early 1990s, maps some of the routes taken by avant-garde women directors of the last decade of the twentieth century, as they questioned and dismantled the categories of dominant discourse.

Before undertaking a quick survey of the individual chapters in the sequence which has offered itself, I should like to discuss briefly the notion of national theatre as it emerged in the 1960s and 1970s and its link with Hindi.

THEATRE IN THE CAPITAL OF THE NEW NATION

The 1960s and 1970s were witness to a surge of theatrical activity in the metropolitan cities of India. There was widespread conviction that the spate of new plays being written and performed in these first post-Independence decades in many parts of the subcontinent, from Calcutta to Bombay, from Bangalore to Delhi, at long last brought to fruition the promise of the long overdue Indian national theatre. Not only was there a birth of new realism, emerging from the problems and issues of a rapidly industrializing India, urban theatre seemed to be on the verge of being able to successfully turn to new use the myriad folk forms which were being 'discovered'. As a retrospective essay by the Marathi theatre historian and critic Kumud Mehta was to put it:

By the sixties this realisation assumed concrete shape in the works of four playwrights writing in four different languages. Their experience was shared to such a degree by theatre practitioners all over the country that productions of their plays came to be considered a national theatre movement.

Typical of this period was the Hindi play *Adhe Adhure* by Mohan Rakesh, where the clash between a working wife and her unsuccessful husband, coupled with the frustrations of their children, pointed to the slow disintegration of the family as a viable social unit. (1981: 89)

Besides Mohan Rakesh, the other playwrights of national stature whom Mehta went on to consider in her article were Badal Sircar who wrote in Bengali, Girish Karnad writing in Kannada, and Vijay Tendulkar, in Marathi. These were the 'Big Four' of the new upsurge in theatre and their names would be invoked again and again. But they were also part of a much larger network in their own cultural-linguistic centres.[2] Several trends and movements seemed to flow together with a vibrancy last witnessed on the commercial Parsi stage in the first decades of the twentieth century. The time seemed now ripe to link past and present, rural and urban, to address contemporary issues with a new confidence. Conventions from classical Sanskrit dramaturgy and the many regional folk traditions burst asunder the constrictions of the proscenium stage. Delhi, the site of the Sangeet Natak Akademi, the National Music and Drama Academy founded in 1953, and the newly instituted National School of Drama[3] as also of national and international funding agencies, became an important centre of exchange and interaction and Hindi, ever poised on the threshold of achieving recognition as the 'national language', became one important medium through which these encounters took place. Apart from officially sponsored activity, the theatre workshops and festivals generated by the National School of Drama, other institutional frames, part professional, part amateur, also emerged: new auditoria, theatre groups, and at least two Delhi-based journals devoted entirely to theatre, which, though privately funded, managed to sustain themselves over several decades; they accompanied, critiqued, and helped to consolidate the burgeoning theatre activity. The Hindi journal *Natrang*, edited by Nemichandra Jain, published essays on the major themes of the day, interviews, reviews, and play scripts in Hindi, as well as translations of scripts from other Indian languages into Hindi. Rajinder Paul edited the English-language journal *Enact*, which published English translations of plays, as also interviews, reviews of plays, and reports from various regional centres.[4] As Paul noted in the May 1971 *Enact* editorial:

By all available accounts, Indian theatre is passing through a very significant phase. A phase which is continually providing it with maturity.... Their plays [the reference is once again to the Big Four: Rakesh, Sircar, Tendulkar, Karnad] have become nationally known, crossing the rigid regional barriers. Obviously, this couldn't have happened but for the enthusiastic, almost altruisitic, efforts of the translators. A new Sircar play is available in Hindi the moment it is scripted. So is the case with Tendulkar's and Girish's plays. Through Hindi, their plays are translated into other regional languages.

Paul was to write in a later survey of these years:

To the language writers, a Hindi production of their play was the thing. Every important playwright—be it Girish Karnad in Kannada, Badal Sircar in Bengali or Vijay Tendulkar in Marathi—sought the company of Hindi theatre directors, both in their respective regions and in Delhi. Three or four translators served as the important links: B.V. Karnath for Kannada, Pratibha Agrawal and Santwana for Bengali, and Vasant Dev for Marathi. Hindi theatre groups in regional language-dominated areas thus became good sounding boards. They operated in a small, unostentatious manner to present unestablished contemporary plays; while Hindi theatre groups in Delhi like Dishantar, Abhiyan and the National School of Drama helped in inter-regional translation of these plays: Kannada plays into Bengali and Bengali plays into Marathi. Sometimes the availability of these plays in English translation accelerated the process of cross-fertilization. Thus, when in 1969 *Enact* started publishing the full-length plays of these important playwrights in English translation, it helped satisfy the appetite of most new converts to theatre, who couldn't read the script in the original or in its Hindi version. English formed the necessary link. (1991: 8)

Even if the plays were read in English, they were produced in Hindi or the language of a given cultural region. Playwrights in Calcutta and Bombay sought the Hindi-language theatre groups in Delhi but also in their own cities, since this was an obvious step towards reaching yet wider audiences as well as national visibility.[5] In a recently published study of this almost feverish translation activity, Aparna Dharwadker has shown that not surprisingly, given its position at the centre, Hindi was the target language of most translations. Thus, for instance, of 69 key productions of 17 major post-Independence plays in Hindi, Bengali, Marathi, and Kannada, as many as 43 were in Hindi (Dharwadker 2002: 18–19). Hindi has indeed become a link language of sorts, not the 'official' Sanskritized Hindi which was imposed from above and inspired almost universal resentment, but the 'heteroglot, hybrid language which has absorbed the semantic resources of many traditions',[6] whether in the Bombay film, in the popular press, or indeed in the many spoken idioms which proliferated and prospered without official sanction or support. Though both English and Hindi continue to share the honour of being the two most important target languages of translation—English being the more important when it comes to print, making as it does for national visibility—Hindi outpaces English when it comes to performance and the issue of audience appeal:

This dual paradox suggests that in Indian writing, the naturalization of English has been effective when the *radical of presentation* is the printed word, but not when the radical of presentation is the acted or spoken word. In this respect,

Indian drama and theatre are very similar to Indian film, television, video, and music. India has the largest film industry in the world, but virtually no English-language cinema; one of the largest television audiences in the world, but little original English-language programming besides news, news programs, and documentaries; and a gigantic popular music industry, but little original English-language music....

The reason for this preference is the idea that a language corresponds to a structure of experience in the world: theatre has the quality of lived experience when the language is the 'natural' language of the characters it represents. (Dharwadker 2002: 23)

The adoption of Hindi as the language of theatre production of the National School of Drama, under the dynamic and inspiring directorship of Ebrahim Alkazi, was thus a strategically important decision. As Reeta Sondhi was to write of Alkazi's major contribution in this regard in the *Enact* issue devoted to the National School of Drama: 'It was entirely due to him that Hindi playwrights became stage worthy and a language which was an imposition earlier started becoming interesting and eminent' (1981: np).

This decision could not, and indeed did not, remain uncontested. But this choice of language was one part of a larger vision. Alkazi came to the School in 1962 as a young man of thirty-seven; he was to head it for fifteen years. He figured in manifold capacities in the project of creating a national theatre school as it evolved over the next years: he was simultaneously director, charismatic teacher, and skilled administrator, who carved out theatre space, both metaphorically and materially, in a city which had been created primarily for administrators and bureaucrats, as it struggled to establish itself as the cultural capital of the new nation. New Delhi as the capital of British India had, we need to recall, been formerly inaugurated only in 1928; the links with the past cities that surrounded it—particularly with Shahjahanabad, the Mughal Delhi ('Old' Delhi)—had been deliberately severed.[7] Any new cultural activity would have to establish new links with the past, not only of the nation, but also of the city.

Alkazi created a firm institutional foundation for the theatre of the new nation in Delhi. He founded the Repertory Company of the School within two years of taking over the directorship and such was the close connection between Repertory and School in those years that no distinction was observed between public performances put up by the School and the Repertory. He constructed a Studio Theatre and the open-air Meghdoot Theatre on the premises of Rabindra Bhavan, the building complex which housed the national academies (Indianized as Akademi) of arts and letters, and he used the space provided by the historical monuments of Delhi to stage spectacular productions which are still remembered today. His productions recalled the links with older history and the older Delhis. Three plays with historical themes were presented in Purana Qila, the Old Fort, in 1974; these would become landmarks in the history of modern Indian theatre.[8] Not only did he create star actors in the process, he also created a modern theatre sensibility in the capital. Each new play generated fresh interest and excitement. He went to colleges on the Delhi University campus for readings and talks. Graduates and undergraduates alike would rush to see his plays, whether Greek drama, Shakespeare, Ibsen or a new Mohan Rakesh. Little wonder that the corpus of Indian plays which the School performed laid the foundation for the newly constituting canon of modern Indian theatre.[9]

Alkazi had come to the School with a clear agenda: 'I wanted to work on a national scale, in the national language, and in the intervening years had, to some extent, equipped myself for the task.'[10] On his way to England for training at the Royal Academy of Dramatic Arts in London in 1947, he had written to Nissim Ezekiel that 'if theatre in the country had to amount to anything significant, it had to be performed in Hindi/Hindustani'.[11] The plays performed in the School were indeed in Hindi, though they were not confined to plays written originally in Hindi. Alkazi commissioned translations into Hindi from the Sanskrit, from other Indian languages, and from the European classics. The Hindi of these translations was not restricted to the Sankritized Hindi being 'officially' propagated; it opened its gates wide to accommodate the idiom needed to express a wide range of social and cultural issues. But in a nation torn by identity politics as rooted in the non-Hindi states, this adoption of Hindi as the sole language of theatre was bound to face opposition, then and later.[12]

There were constant attempts by Hindi-purists to restrict 'Hindi' theatre to plays written in Hindi alone. When Shyamanand Jalan's theatre group Anamika organized a Hindi drama festival in Calcutta in autumn 1974, the Bombay director Satyadev Dubey was told that only plays written originally in Hindi were being invited to the festival. Dubey responded by observing that what he did in Hindi, he considered to be part of Hindi theatre. The *Enact* editorial which reported this event, championed the cause of a 'hybrid' and open Hindi passionately:

The texture of Hindi theatre has undergone a great change in the last decade. It has acquired a new link role and playwrights like Sircar, Tendulkar, Karnad and others have come to be performed all over the country after they have been translated into Hindi. In the process these translations have also influenced playwrights in Hindi like Surendra Verma, Mudra Rakshash, Lakshmi Narayan Lal and even Rakesh (and vice-versa, even though the regional gods wouldn't accept it). What has emerged out of this cross-fertilization is of [an] all-India nature. People in the Hindi producing centres like Delhi, Jaipur, Kanpur, Allahabad, Calcutta and elsewhere have not flocked to a Tendulkar or Sircar play to notice the Marathi or Bengali inflections in speech or dress, but the identifiable streak of an Indian middle class ethos. Contemporary Indian theatre, as we understand it today and have been talking about for over a decade, does not consist of Bharatendu, Jaishankar or some playwrights or plays that *Anamika* is inviting.... The main thing is Hindi drama in performance—I think *Anamika* will be dealing out only half a measure by not projecting Hindi theatre as it is today—with an all-India character. It is like trying to recarve out an island as it once was, nostalgically, a few hundred years after it has become one with the great sea. (Paul 1974: np)

Though not entirely just to Bharatendu Harishchandra's multi-faceted agenda, for he himself had envisaged theatre as offering a public forum for thrashing out social and political issues, or even that of Jayshankar Prasad who for all his traditionalism remained deeply concerned with investigating history, the names Bharatendu and Prasad did conjure up visions of a narrow Hindi/Hindu agenda which attempted to cordon off Hindi from all alien influences.

Given this trajectory of Hindi and Hindu, it needs to be clarified at the outset of this volume, that Hindi theatre as discussed here is seen at no stage as concomitant with Indian theatre at large, though the title of the book carries the term 'Indian' and the chapters forming the major portion of it indeed deal largely with theatre in Hindi. Why I still seem to be speaking of both in one breath, though with all due qualifications and reservations, is based on two grounds:

1) Hindi-language theatre does form one central segment of modern theatre in post-Independence India, and thus can be seen as participating formatively in larger theatrical trends. Hence, though I myself begin this study with precisely Bharatendu and Prasad, the two playwrights seen as narrowing the scope of Hindi theatre, what I go on to consider in the subsequent chapters is not constrained or determined by their agendas, for the situation itself changes constantly. In pre-Independence India, however, I focus on their aspirations, since they were indeed the primary figures in Hindi language theatre as it sought to create a genealogy for itself and win performative space apart from the vibrant commercial Parsi theatre. These were the very decades when 'Hindi' as a print language was trying to put forth and substantiate its claim to the status of the 'national' language of the nation-to-be. As we now know, it was a claim which was never to find full official recognition; it was foiled by the chauvinism of those who pushed these claims to absurd lengths. Alok Rai has written of these self-defeating efforts with eloquence and conviction.[13] But Hindi, in its status as the 'official' language of the nation (along with English) did remain a link language, and as we have seen, it performed this function particularly in the performative media.

2) Post-Independence theatre in Hindi did not remain confined to plays originally written in Hindi. Apart from the fact that translation activity opened up endless possibilities for mutual expansion, and particularly so for Hindi, the concerns articulated in the work of Hindi playwrights themselves, specially of the stature of Mohan Rakesh, merged and meshed with those writing in the other major Indian languages at the same period, as the *Enact* editorial of November 1974 cited here points out, to form, together with them, what theatre viewers and reviewers of the time, saw as coming together in a veritable national theatre.

In the latter part of the book, then, I focus on theatre activity in Delhi, since official policy was created and implemented here and the

Monumental Reality: Alkazi's production of Dharmvir Bharati's *Andha Yug* (1970s) (National School of Drama)

experimental theatre which sprang up alongside the officially sponsored activity, also sought recognition here. This is not to suggest that all major theatrical ventures were created in Delhi or indeed that Delhi was the only place where this happened. However, it *was* the national capital and it sought to actively pull together and provide a forum, however selectively, for other segments of theatre in the Indian subcontinent. It thus became the site of two trends which could be seen as contradictory but which complemented each other: 1) officially patronized and sponsored theatre, such as the festivals of folk-theatre-inspired plays in the late 1980s, 2) but alongside, and precisely because Delhi had no long theatre history to pre-set the stage, avant-garde or experimental theatre, particularly in the decades when folk theatre lost whatever political edge it once possessed.[14] The Hindi which rose to the occasion and indeed performed the task of absorbing 'the semantic resources of many traditions', and thus the Delhi centred Hindi theatre that I speak of in this study, could not but maintain open, porous boundaries. It could not be the Hindi of the purists; certainly not in the years of the folk-theatre boom of the 1970s and early 1980s. Even when transposed to the urban stage, these forms perforce brought with them some of their own vocabulary. It was a Hindi, then, which was shot through with various dialect forms which the folk forms brought with them. It was far removed from standard Hindi. Though this movement in language seems to have provoked little opposition at the time, its earlier incarnation in the so-called *anchalik* or regional novel in Hindi, which had large stretches of dialogue in 'dialect' form, had inspired an almost vicious rejection of what was seen as tampering with the 'standard' form which had only recently stabilized.[15] The point to be made here is that theatre in Hindi could not and did not remain 'pure'; it was simply no consideration at the time.

This intense urban interaction with folk-theatre forms, its politicization in the 1940s and later in the 1970s, which was to crystallize at least partly through the contact with Bertolt Brecht's epic theatre, and its subsequent exploitation for cultural purposes in the international festival circuit, forms the focus of the second section of this volume.

The step to 'intercultural' theatre, Indian theatre as represented in the international arena, the official face of the national, seemed an inevitable corollary to the considerations which had first been mooted by the Orientalists in the late eighteenth and early nineteenth centuries, and which had informed nationalist notions as they evolved in the subsequent decades. Had we come full circle? What then was 'Indian' in the international arena? The classical, as mediated through the newly discovered 'folk'? In what terms was it projected, how was it received? Could it be Hindu alone? And finally, what could being 'Hindu' mean in the years which saw the destruction of the Babri Masjid? The answers to this could hardly be located in the officially sponsored theatre. It was the vibrant new experimental theatre, largely dominated by women directors, many of them based in the north, which rose to meet the challenges of the times in which we still find ourselves. It faced squarely the questions that it raised, as I discuss in the last chapter in the volume, even if it offered no pat answers.

IN SEARCH OF A NATIONAL THEATRE

The first section will focus on the works of the major literary figures who participated in the effort to create a 'high' tradition in theatre in literary Hindi, in an idiom which at least initially deliberately distanced itself from the rural and set out to cater to the emerging urban intelligentsia. The three essays in this section focus respectively on Bharatendu Harishchandra (1850–85), pioneer in the field of modern Hindi drama, Jayshankar Prasad (1889–1937) who wrote a series of historical plays while coining a new language of subjectivity, and Mohan Rakesh (1929–72), with whom realism in urban drama reached a new climax.

The first chapter, '"The National Drama of the Hindus": Harishchandra of Banaras and the "Classical" Traditions in Late Nineteenth-Century India' explores the links between the Hindi language theatre as it develops in Banaras under the aegis of Harishchandra with the Orientalist views of the newly 'discovered' Sanskrit drama in the early and mid-nineteenth century. It traces the evolution of Harishchandra's dramaturgy and practice, analyses the social and political direction his major plays sought to set, and discusses the long essay on drama, 'Natak', wherein he developed what were to be his finally formulated views on the history and aesthetics of the newly configured drama which could rise to meet the demands of the new age.

The aesthetics of Jayshankar Prasad, as against the more comprehensive frame Harishchandra sought to create, were developed with deliberate recourse to the aesthetics of classical Sanskrit drama ('*rasa*') though with a clear consciousness of the need to come to terms with 'conflict' in the modern world. The second chapter in this section, 'Twentieth-Century Projections of the Past: Jayshankar Prasad and the New Subjectivity' focuses, then, on the contradictions of what was an essentially modernist enterprise which yet sought to contain itself in a relatively conservative frame. Prasad's attempts to create modern Hindi theatre in classical format coincided with efforts to recreate music and dance as secular art forms, outside the temple and the royal court with its attendant feudal culture, away from priests and courtesans, thus Bharat Natyam in the south and, in the north, Kathak and Khayal *gayaki*, which were yet to be contained in a frame that turned incessantly to the classical Sanskrit treatise on drama, the *Natyashastra*, to create a genealogy for themselves and to find their aesthetic vocabulary. What Prasad had at his disposal as a visual model was the living commercial theatre of the Parsis, their melodrama, and their fine acting. Though he distanced himself from the Parsis almost violently, his aesthetics and his playwriting took recourse to both 'classical' and Parsi models. The essay concludes with an analysis of Prasad's best-known play, *Dhruvasvamini* (1933), a historical narrative shot through with the romanticism and individualism of the Chhayavadi movement in Hindi poetry, in which he himself was a prime player. A modernist play concerned with psychological reading of character, it has yet a distinct Hinduistic reading of the past which has made for a revival of its popularity in the late 1990s.

If Prasad was seeking to create 'whole' characters, in the plays of the 1950s the self has begun to be viewed as fragmented, as itself in search of wholeness. The third chapter, 'Neither Half nor Whole: Mohan Rakesh and the Modernist Quest' focuses on these attempts. Mohan Rakesh began his writing career in the years immediately after Independence. In his reflections on drama, he did not even attempt to establish a link with classical Indian aesthetic theory; he did not consider that Prasad had developed the directions indicated by Bharatendu or, for that matter, provided any new orientations. Rakesh maintained that he did not seek ideals in the past; though his plays were set in the past, he endeavoured to endow with flesh and blood the well-known figures with whom he chose to people his plays. His plays first became widely known when produced by Ebrahim Alkazi in the newly founded National School of Drama. Alkazi played a major role in bringing about the realization of this theatre as well as giving it direction; Rakesh was the first of the playwrights discussed here to evolve his dramaturgy in constant interaction with performance. His was a realism of a new sort, as it set out to recreate the politics of urban interiors as they evolved in a new and extremely conflicted repositioning of gender roles. Rakesh's later, shorter plays were to focus more sharply on the fragmentation of the self even as he experimented with new post-realist forms.

THE NATION AND ITS FOLK

The second section of the volume is concerned with the rising importance of 'folk' theatre forms and the politicization of theatre which prompted renewed urban interest in traditional forms from the 1940s on. The first chapter in this section, 'Folk Theatre and the Search for an Indigenous Idiom: Brecht in India' deals at some length with the relationship of urban theatre makers to the folk idiom. I go on to discuss the politicization of folk forms during the last days of the British Raj, as the newly formed Indian People's Theatre Association (IPTA) made good its promise of taking theatre to the 'masses'. I then discuss the rediscovery and renewed use of folk forms in the 1960s and 1970s which made for a particularly productive partnership with Brecht's theatre. I conclude with the developments in the era of liberalization, which were to make for an appropriation of folk forms for international presentation, thus changing the very nature of the inner Indian relationship to folk traditional forms. I discuss what I see as the four stages of the urban relationship to 'folk theatre': 1) the distancing from folk theatre by dramatists such as Bharatendu Harishchandra in the effort to create respectable urban theatre and running parallel to this, the work of the folklorists who became active in India from the late nineteenth century on; 2) the rediscovery, less on the aesthetic plane, more on the performative, in the 1940s in the work of IPTA; 3) the use of folk for the urban stage and partial politicization in the 1960s and 1970s: large-scale adaptation and modification of the aesthetics and conventions of Brecht's theatre; and finally 4) the appropriation of folk forms by 'official culture' accompanied by widespread depoliticization of theatre.

With this depoliticization in view, the second chapter in the second section, 'Brecht in Hindi: The Poetics of Response' consists of a juxtapostion and critical appraisal of the politics of Brecht's theatre aesthetics with that of Sanskrit drama (the rasa syndrome!) as also of 'folk' theatre in its twentieth-century incarnation, since Brecht's theatre was often uncritically equated with the latter two. The final chapter in the section, '"To be More Brechtian is to be More Indian": On the Theatre of Habib Tanvir', is a presentation and discussion of Habib Tanvir's folk theatre as it has evolved in the urban environment, in interaction with Brecht's theatre, but going beyond Brecht to create its own idiom.

WHAT IS INDIAN?

Yet, if it was more Brechtian to be more Indian, the question as to what constituted 'Indian' still remained to be answered, even if in the festival circuit, it seemed to be find an easy answer in the loosely assembled assortment of 'folk', 'classical', and 'folk' made urban, which was now to constitute an unreflected Indianness.

The third section of the volume then has to do with notions of 'Indian' theatre as represented in the 'international' context by both non-Indian and Indian theatre people, but also as queried in the aesthetically and politically vibrant north Indian feminist theatre of the 1990s. The first chapter, 'Encountering the Other, Accosting the Self', will be in dialogue with the views of prominent theatre and cultural historian, Rustom Bharucha. Western theatre practitioners have, with remarkable consistency, restricted their interest in Indian theatre to what they have regarded as classical theatre, or, at most, they have extended their patronage to the kind of theatre which has also come to be regarded as traditional, the 'folk' theatre variously referred to in the preceding discussion. Traditional sources have, then, inevitably been seen as repositories of ancient wisdom. Whereas taking resort to these sources in itself seems a legitimate enough undertaking, it has seldom been accompanied by any serious attempt to understand the historical, social, aesthetic, and, most of all, religious context of the performance tradition thus abstracted. Once extracted from the respective setting, however, it has been easy enough to see any given aspect of the performing arts as exemplifying and representing the essence of Indian culture. Yet, for all its essentialism, the engagement with traditional Indian theatre has inevitably been partial, eclectic, restricted often to a preoccupation with technique, with little sense of history, of differences within the traditions thus set up as single and linear. This has been a practice that the Indian culture industry has equally colluded in and indulged. Yet, if theatre is to remain an open forum for the enactment and querying of cultural difference, of issues of community and belonging which so plague the subcontinent, can it afford to relapse into complacency?

The final chapter, 'I Am a Hindu: Assertions and Queries', will consist of the exposition of the Hindi dramatization of Tagore's early-twentieth-century novel *Gora*, in 1991 and the translation into English of an entire key scene. The script of the Hindi play was written by well-known Hindi author Geetanjali Shree in cooperation with Anuradha Kapur, the director of the play, and indeed with the cast of the play. As Kapur has noted, the novel

brings several debates centre stage: debates about the meaning of nation, nationalism and national identity. The dramatization of the novel rehearses a re-enactment of these ideas in late modernity. While the audience knows that Gora is a white man, Gora himself struggles with the question 'who am I' posed in tandem with the question 'what makes a nation'.[16]

With this chapter, which takes up the theme of cultural and political identity, of the search for Indian-ness in late modernity, I hope to have come full circle and back to my beginning, since the volume began with a discussion of the efforts to create an Indian national theatre.

The issues discussed at the beginning of this Introduction, about how Hindi theatre is to be defined, still remain a concern; the debates conducted in the 1970s have not died out. There are still voices which complain of the dearth of original drama in Hindi, bewailing the loss of once promising writers, mourning the fact that most scripts are now worked out from already existing novels, short stories, Indian and foreign, by directors in collaboration with writers (Bardola 1999: 15). But surely this points to the very vitality of the non-commercial Delhi stage, which refuses to die out. If there is as yet no commercially viable Hindi theatre which can live off its box-office earnings or get subsidies which are not attached to strings of one kind or another, why should Hindi playwrights feel the need to write plays in Hindi? It does indeed make much more sense to write scripts for TV soaps rather than for the two or three night productions of plays, which, however exciting, have to look for funding in order to at least cover the costs of production. Does that not make us pause to consider: what makes for the vitality of the theatrical form, six decades after Independence, still struggling to make ends meet, but producing some of the most exciting theatre in the world? It is a miracle that it still exists, on this slim financial basis, and has yet to show any sign of extinction.

I am aware that the discussions pieced together here can only form a partial account, in all senses of the word, of the vast enterprise that is Indian theatre. Much remains unresolved. Much remains to be questioned again. But through these decades of viewing and reviewing theatre, Brecht has remained a teacher and a guide, a constant warning against the solutions too easily found:

Whenever we seemed
To have found the answer to a question
One of us untied the string of the old rolled-up
Chinese scroll on the wall, so that it fell down and
Revealed to us the man on the bench who
Doubted so much.

I, he said to us
Am the doubter. I am doubtful whether
The work was well done that devoured your days.
Whether what you said would still have value for anyone if it were less well said.
Whether you said it well but perhaps
Were not convinced of the truth of what you said....

But above all
Always above all else: how does one act
If one believes what you say? Above all: how does one act?[17]

Notes

[1] For there had also been a surfeit of Brecht in both East and West Germany; people were beginning to speak of Brecht fatigue. The Swiss dramatist 'Max Frish coined the phrase that soon became a slogan, asserting that Brecht had attained "the penetrating ineffectiveness of a classic"' (Voelker 1987: 427). There were radical reappropriations of the Brecht frozen into immobility by his heirs, most famously in the work of Heiner Mueller, Brecht's iconoclastic successor to fame in East Berlin. Mueller was tampering radically with the Brecht of the Berliner Ensemble. 'Mueller incorporates Brecht's blend of the political, the personal and the aesthetic. His communism combines with postmodern aesthetics and psychoanalytic subtexts for his persona. Both Brecht and Mueller seek to create a theatre of the future, as Mueller noted "Brecht—an author without a present, a work between past and future. I hesitate to propose this as a criticism: the present is the age of industrial nations and our future, I hope, won't be formed by these nations. If it is, I fear that it will become dependent on their politics." This statement implies that perhaps, outside of Germany, the new Brecht will appear somewhere in the Third World' (Voelker 1987: 433).

[2] 'However, these [the Big Four] were not the only playwrights who were translated into various Indian languages. Others like Mahesh Elkunchwar, Achyut Vaze, and C.T. Khanolkar in Marathi, Adya Rangacharya, Chandrashekar Kambar, and P. Lankesh in Kannada, Arun Mukerji, Utpal Dutt and Mohit Chattopadhyaya in Bengali, were also translated and staged by various amateur groups in the country' (Paul 1991: 85).

[3] The School came into being in 1958, with the aid of UNESCO, on the basis of the recommendations made in 1956 and then again by the Drama Seminar organized by the Sangeet Natak Akademi in 1956. Nehru himself was the president of the Akademi. Initially known as the Asian Theatre Institute, it was renamed National School of Drama and Asian Theatre Institute in 1959, operating initially under the aegis of the Sangeet Natak Akademi, to become an autonomous registered society, known henceforth as the National School of Drama, in 1975.

[4] *Natrang* came into existence as early as 1962. Nemichandra Jain remains associated with it even today, though it has formally been taken over by Natrang Pratisthan, the trust founded by him. The bimonthly *Enact* was edited by Rajinder Paul from 1967 to 1983.

[5] 'For the production of his plays in Hindi, Badal Sircar depended on Rajinder Nath of Abhiyan, Om Shivpuri and Karanth of Dishantar in Delhi, Satyadev Dubey of Theatre Unit in Bombay and Shyamanand Jalan of Anamika in Calcutta. Original Bengali groups like Nandikar and Bohurupee also took up the challenge; but had there been no translation into Hindi and from Hindi into other languages, there would have been no impact all over India' (Paul 1991: 82).

[6] Neeladri Bhattacharya in editorial preface to Rai (2001: vii).

[7] See Gupta (1981) for the history of this transfer of power from the old to the new city.

[8] See Sharma (1995: 9) for a critique of Alkazi's gigantic productions.

[9] Canon-formation brings its own problems: 'A consequence of Alkazi's working through and towards the canon is that the classics were played straight. Rarely interrogated, let alone subverted, these were at best merely personalized, and that too in a manner which tip-toed around the ideological and the political. Playing the ancient and the modern classics for their "intrinsic meaning", valuing them for what they teach us rather than taking from them what we wish to learn, he gave his productions a thinness that was redeemed primarily by the resonances of the acting. To be fair, we must remember that our alertness to hegemonic deployments of the canon was not a concern in the 60s here' (Arora 2003: 40).

[10] Interview with Sondhi (1981) as cited by and conveniently available in Arora (2003: 25), whose insights I refer to repeatedly in this brief documentation of the long and influential career of Ebrahim Alkazi.

[11] Reeta Sondhi in *Enact* issue on National School of Drama, Part I, 1981, as cited in Arora (2003: 25–6).

[12] As Sharma notes (1995: 10): 'NSD has repeatedly been accused of a bias towards Hindi-speaking students. This has created a lot of tension within and outside the campus. This language problem—the dominance of Hindi over other "regional" languages—has its roots in the role played by language in Indian politics in the sixties and later.'

[13] See Rai (2000) as also my review essay (2003).

[14] An insight I owe to Anuradha Kapur. The artistic subversion thus practised seeks to overturn hierarchies which are as political and social as they are aesthetic. For, as Bourdieu has pointed out: 'Specifically, aesthetic conflicts about the vision of the world—in the last resort, about what deserves to be represented and the right way to represent it—are political conflicts (appearing

in their most euphemized form) for the power to impose the dominant definition of reality and social reality in particular. On the right, reproductive art constructed in accordance with the generative scheme of "straight", "straightforward" representation of reality, and social reality in particular, i.e. orthodoxy (e.g., *par excellence*, "bourgeois theatre") is likely to give those who perceive it in accordance with these schemes the reassuring experience of the immediate self-evidence of the representation, that is, of the necessity of the mode of representation and of the world represented. This orthodox art would be timeless if it were not continuously pushed into the past by the movement brought into the field of production by the dominated fractions' insistence on using the powers they are granted to change the world view and overturn the temporal and *temporary* hierarchies to which "bourgeois" taste clings' (1995: 101–2).

[15] See Dalmia (2003: 1381) for the reaction of the canonically accepted Hindi writers to the changes being thus brought about in the hierarchy of acceptable 'Hindis'.

[16] Kapur in the director's note in the brochure of the play.

[17] English translation of Brecht's poem 'Der Zweifler' from *Poems 1913–1956*.

REFERENCES

Arora, Keval. 2003. 'Ebrahim Alkazi', *Theatre India*, May, 22–46.

Bardola, V.M. 1999. 'Post-1980 Plays: Hindi', *Theatre India*, November, 13–18.

Bourdieu, Pierre. 1995. *The Field of Cultural Production: Essays on Art and Literature*. Edited and introduced by Randal Johnson. New York: Columbia University Press

Brecht, Bertolt. 1976. *Poems 1913–1956*. Edited by John Willet and Ralph Mannheim with the co-operation of Erich Fried. New York: Methuen.

Dalmia, Vasudha. 2003. 'The Locations of Hindi', review essay of Rai (2000), *Economic and Political Weekly*, 3 April, 1377–84.

Dharwadker, Aparna. 2002. 'Translation and Translators', *Theatre India*, November, 15–29.

Gupta, Narayani. 1981. *Delhi between Two Empires 1803–1931: Society, Government and Urban Growth*. Delhi: Oxford University Press.

Kapur, Anuradha. 1990. *Actors, Pilgrims and Gods: The Ramlila of Ramnagar*. Calcutta: Seagull (Paperback, 2004).

Mehta, Kumud. 1981. 'Indian Theatre Today—Grappling with New Realities', *Marg*, Special Issue on Aspects of the Performing Arts of India, 34.3, 84–95.

Paul, Rajinder. 1971. *Enact* editorial. May.

———. 1974. *Enact* editorial. November.

———. [1989] 1991. 'Whatever Happened to Modern Indian Theatre?', *India International Centre Quarterly*. Spring [first published in *Seminar*, 359].

Sharma, Biren Das. 1995. 'How Apolitical is Cultural Policy? The NSD example', *Seagull Theatre Quarterly*, 6, August, 8–12.

Sondhi, Reeta. 1981. 'Impressions: National School of Drama', *Enact*, Special Issue on National School of Drama II, April–May–June, n.p.

Rai, Alok. 2001. *Hindi Nationalism*. Tracts for the Times 13, Delhi: Orient Longman.

Voelker, Klaus. 1987. 'Brecht Today: Classic or Challenge', *Theatre Journal*, 39.4, December.

I

In Search of a National Theatre

'The National Drama of the Hindus'
Harishchandra of Banaras and the 'Classical' Traditions in Late Nineteenth-Century India

Viewing the beginnings of literary creation in the modern languages of India in the nineteenth century, it is easier today to see the breaks with tradition rather than the continuities. The formal analogies with European models seem obvious, the connections with a Sanskritic drama tradition tucked away in a remote past seem tenuous at best. Yet to the progenitors of this new literature, writing under colonial rule, in constant interaction with a dominant, still very 'foreign' culture, with which it was also essential to establish equivalences, it was of vital importance to set up clearly identifiable national characteristics, with a distinct historical tradition. Though Western Orientalists were most often quoted as authorities as to what constituted the Indian classical tradition, and who seemed even here to serve as mediators, their views were clearly moulded to suit nationalist purposes.

In the first section of this essay I review the contribution of British Orientalists to the aesthetics and nationalist orientation of theatre in the nineteenth century. I then go on to trace the shifts in emphasis and orientation that accompanied the indigenous appropriation and recasting of this Orientalist reading. I focus on the work of Harishchandra in his pioneering attempt to create modern theatre in the Hindi region, limiting myself thereby to tracing and analysing the dominant trends and directions in his drama, supplemented by his own statements in the theoretical treatise, 'Natak' (1883); there is no attempt here to provide a comprehensive survey of his work.[1] In a final section I consider the possible reasons why Harishchandra's vision of theatre as a public forum remained unfulfilled in the period following his death.

THE ORIENTALIST LEGACY AND THE CONSTITUTION OF NATIONAL DRAMA

William Jones, in the preface to his translation of the Sanskrit drama *Shakuntala* ([1789] 1979: vol. 9) had announced the discovery of the national drama of the Hindus to the Occident. 'Dramatic poetry must have been immemorially ancient in the Indian empire...' (367), he had speculated, and further: 'The play of Sacontala must have been very popular when it was first represented; for the Indian empire was then in full vigour, and the national vanity must have been highly flattered by the magnificent introduction of those kings and heroes in whom the Hindus gloried; the scenery must have been splendid and beautiful; and there is good reason to believe, that the court in Avanti was equal in brilliancy during the reign of Vikramaditya, to that of any monarch in any age or country' (370). Jones had been the first to identify the genius of Kalidasa with that of Shakespeare, and while drawing up a list of the dramatist's available works, he had expressed immense regret 'that he has left only two dramatick poems, especially as the stories of his *Raghuvamsa* would have supplied him with a number of excellent subjects' (369).

Jones formed his ideas of the monolith which he termed Hindu theatre based on indigenous Brahminical sources, rather than from his own observation of the performative traditions which abounded in the region. Jones tells us that after several vague answers to his enquiries concerning the variety of literature known as 'natac' (*sic*) one 'very sensible Brahmen, named Radhacant' had been persuaded to give the information he was seeking. Radhacant had enlightened him regarding the nature of these compositions and when asked 'which of the natacs was the most universally esteemed', had answered without hesitation, 'Cakuntala [*sic*]' (366). Jones' deductions, however, were novel in the Indian context; they went farther than those of the Brahmins in that they set up chronologies in the new historical mode. They were to have manifold and far-reaching implications.

First, Jones maintained that the Hindus had a national theatre, an Indian drama, which bore testimony to the glory of the old Indian empire, to whole genealogies of kings who had reigned of old, 'before the conquest of it by the Savages of the North...' (365). Jones' notion of Indian drama was then related intimately to the collective national history of the Hindus; it had suffered a decline when the Muslims reached the subcontinent. Jones equated Hindu and Indian without second thought, though he was himself trained as a Persianist and it was these skills which had initially been seen as his special qualification for being sent to India.

The concept of a national theatre as a singular, and as a constitutive feature of the nation was itself a comparatively late development in Europe. In Germany it had gained ground around 1750, in Italy and France a little earlier in the century, and in the Eastern European countries only in the early nineteenth century. The original impetus was variously constituted. However, very generally and with inevitable simplification, it could be maintained that by the early nineteenth century, romantic-national political concepts tended to overlay or even supplant the enlightened, cosmopolitan impetus of the eighteenth century (Bauer and Werthheimer 1983).

Second, Kalidasa was for Jones the Indian Shakespeare, he was both the poet and chronicler of kings, as well as of the people's national pride in their kings. The comparison with Shakespeare served at once to elevate Kalidasa to national status, as well as provide key critical concepts in matters of playwriting and appreciation. For Shakespeare in the eighteenth century had increasingly come to be identified as 'the poet of the English people' (Bate 1989: 8). His morality, his broad social canvas, his characterization, as multifaceted as nature itself, were considered to create standards at once unique and universal. A new interest in psychology, increasingly concerned with the subtleties of characterization, had been thrust into the foreground by the Shakespeare criticism in the latter half of the century, which continued at the same time to maintain, in conformity with the theoretical expectations of the age, that dramatic characterization be consistent, a coherent whole, as well as that it fulfil a moral purpose (Vickers 1981: 12, 16). By the time we come to the English Romantic poets, to Coleridge, as one of the most authoritative interpreters of Shakespeare, we are confronted with the firm conviction that apart from the morality of his vision, it was Shakespeare's uncanny perception of character, which defied imitation: 'The interest in the plot is always in fact on account of the characters, not vice versa, as in almost all other writers the plot is a mere canvas and no more' (Vickers 1981: 435). For Coleridge, as for all later critics in the century, Shakespeare was a thoroughly English genius and he assumed that '(a)ssuredly that criticism of Shakespeare will alone be genial which is reverential. The Englishman, who, without reverence, a proud and affectionate reverence, can utter the name of William Shakespeare, stands disqualified for the office of critic' (430).

H.H. Wilson, the next British Orientalist to concern himself in any sustained fashion with Indian drama, in his *Select Specimens of the Theatre of the Hindus* (1835), writing forty years after Jones, whose enthusiasm he regarded with some caution and qualified in various ways, further confirmed the national status of Hindu drama, though he did not see it as confined to depicting the glories of the Indian empire, for just as 'the dramatic literature of every nation...the Hindu theatre affords examples of the drama of the domestic, as well as of heroic life; of original invention as well as of legendary tradition' (1835: vol. 1, x). He also made the following qualification: 'The theatrical representations of modern Europe, however diversified by national features, are the legitimate offspring of the classical drama' (xi). 'Classical' stood for ancient Greek drama. The Hindu theatre had its own origin, and belonged to a division of dramatic composition that modern critics had termed *romantic*, in opposition to the variety known as *classical*.[2] Hindu theatre could then occasionally measure up to Shakespeare. However, the heights of ancient Greek drama remained largely out of reach.

Yet if the Orientalists had merely projected the national theatre into a collective past, the need of the day, as felt by contemporary Indian patrons and theatre enthusiasts, was to establish links with a collective present. What they did take over from Occidental Orientalism was the notion of theatre as Hindu and as originating with Sanskrit drama, with no question of non-Hindu influence or admixture. Thus, though the Orientalist enthusiasm for the classical Sanskrit past was to wane and become diffuse after the anglicization of education in 1835, for the Indians initially activated by Orientalist readings of ancient Indian theatre, it was a question of furthering this past tradition in new directions. The formulation and articulation of a new programme was thereafter an entirely indigenous affair.[3]

Classical in the understanding of nineteenth-century Indian literati was to mean the ancient Sanskrit as filtered through their understanding of Shakespeare. The intimate association between the national theatre of the Hindus and Shakespeare was one of the major impulses in the creation of urban literary theatre in the nineteenth century, as the histories of the period testify.[4] After the first stiff translations and adaptations from Sanskrit and Shakespeare, Indian drama as envisaged by the modernizers did indeed proceed to make creative use of the traditions thus canonized. If it was the historical grandeur of a thus concretized past which proved to be most significant and which was repeatedly emphasized, with Shakespeare, the depiction of the 'meaner' characters of Sanskrit plays acquired a renewed significance. At the onset of the second half of the nineteenth century, the range of plays widened to include social satire, which was to establish itself as a popular form. Developments in Calcutta were so rapid that in 1872 it became commercially viable to establish a 'National' Theatre in the city. Bombay had a somewhat different trajectory, though here too by the second half of the nineteenth century, the hugely popular Parsi theatre not only consolidated itself in the city, but soon began to tour the length and breadth of the subcontinent.[5] The establishment of publicly accessible theatres in Calcutta and Bombay has parallels in Europe, where the metropolis played a decisive role in the development of the kinds of drama that later could lay claim to the status of 'national'. The Hindi–Urdu belt of north India could boast of no such metropolis. The fledgling theatre of Wajid Ali Shah in Lucknow expired after the demise of that city as the capital of Awadh in 1857. The scene of action, as far as modern Hindi, the newly emerging literary idiom, was concerned, shifted to Banaras. It was here that the combination of Hindi with a tradition that was constructed as explicitly 'Hindu' brought about yet another set of aspirations for the creation of a national theatre.

STRUCTURES OF AUTHORITY IN THE NORTH WEST PROVINCES
AND THE INVOCATION OF TRADITION

Hindi drama, as it came into being in the late nineteenth century, was largely the creation of Harishchandra (1850–85), born into a merchant family of Banaras, a city of central commercial significance. By the end of the eighteenth century, Banaras had established its position as one of the most important trading and banking centres in northern India. Harishchandra belonged to the city's commercial aristocracy, the Naupatti Mahajans, bankers who rose to prominence in the troubled period before the final collapse of the Awadh *nawabi* and the formal takeover of the province by the East India Company. If on the one hand the Naupattis were arbitrators in disputes within the merchant classes, they also mediated between the British and the people of the city. They maintained close relations with the Maharaja and participated in the festive-ritual life of the city. Harishchandra was on terms of easy friendship with the Maharaja and it is said that he contributed greatly to the expansion of the Ramlila of Ramnagar by devising the dialogues of the *lila*. He took a leading role in the cultural life of the city and there are accounts of the gathering of poets and the musical evenings that he organized. He was an honorary magistrate of the city until his voluntary resignation, and he was not only in contact with the local British officials and Orientalists, he also maintained relations with the Asiatic Society of Bengal in Calcutta, kept track of their publications—the lectures and essays published in the august *Asiatick Researches* by the major British Orientalists of the day—and knew and corresponded with the Society's secretary, Rajendralal Mitra, venerable scholar and ardent Vaishnava. This was in addition to the societies and school he founded and the three journals he edited. Though Harishchandra made full use of the privileges of his special status in the city, his habits were too extravagant and every now and then, too uncomfortably radical and subversive, for him to be acknowledged undisputedly as a leading voice within his community.[6]

While the nature of the authority which emanated from his person and standing in the social fabric of 'polite society' in the North West Provinces remains crucial for the 'model' character of his literary work and for the easy authority in his voice when he addressed his readers, it by no means necessarily determines the 'elite' status of his theatre, which in fact distances itself explicitly from the courtly tradition of classical Sanskrit theatre of 'raja-maharajas', and addresses a heterogeneous audience and reading public—traditional Brahmins, manifold merchant formations, upwardly mobile artisans and modernizing professional classes—even then in the process of organizing itself and forming a politically and socially operative public sphere.[7] Even though he distances himself from the low and the vulgar, in order to establish the respectability and desirability of the theatre he wishes to create and cast off the stigma attached to theatre, it would be an oversimplification to take him at his word and classify his theatre as elitist alone. It is true that, in order to forge links with the past, he himself resorts to Sanskrit classificatory categories to designate his plays. At the same time, he takes recourse to popular forms and to popular music, to strike a familiar note but also as framing devices to explicate contemporary issues. And in the prefaces to his plays, he maintains repeatedly that it is his intention to create theatre in Hindi, which he conceives of as a *sabha*, forum, as formerly, for those seeking aesthetic pleasure, but also for edification and as a social and political corrective.[8]

Harishchandra's early plays consist largely of translations from the Sanskrit, from Prakrit, from Bengali, and from Shakespeare. In his later plays, he experiments freely with the most diverse conventions.

In the following I begin with a consideration of the theoretical and historical treatise entitled 'Natak', 'drama' (1883) written towards the end of Harishchandra's life, in order to provide a frame for the analyses which follow. I then backtrack to trace Harishchandra's own trajectory as a playwright, the early beginnings which consisted of translations and adaptations from the Sanskrit and from Shakespeare. These were to provide the grounds for historical 'musical' drama and the widening of classical tradition by means of the social and political comedy, which, following the Sanskritic tradition, he called Bhana, but also by popular 'folk' themes which were elevated by various means so that they could be incorporated into the canon Harishchandra was attempting to set up. However, his lively religious, social, and political satires were to coexist with a future vision of the nation-to-be which fell back upon old Rajput models. His radical critique of existing structures of authority was tempered by the very structures of authority of which he was also a part: the merchant–Rajput nexus, which could so easily link up with romantic Orientalist visions of the past such as that of Edwin Arnold. I discuss this in a final section in the course of an analysis of *Nildevi* (1881), the historical political drama on a Rajput theme adapted from a poem by Edwin Arnold, and conclude with a discussion of the theatre in Hindi in the period after Harishchandra.

OCCUPYING STRATEGIC POSITIONS: MEDIATIONS AND NEW ORIENTATIONS IN 'NATAK' (1883)

Harishchandra's theoretical writing which culminated in his long essay *Natak* (1883), the summation of views evolved over a good two decades of writing, explicate and analyse his own practice.[9] I focus here on this last essay, which can be reviewed under three broad thematic clusters: 1) forging links with the past by invoking Sanskrit theatre, re-functionalizing it and assimilating thereby the new, 2) expunging and expanding the traditional goals and conventions of drama in the interests of contemporary politics and aesthetics, and 3) considering the progress as well as the prospects of *bhasha natak*, vernacular drama, and the knotty questions of patronage in the creation of the incipient national theatre

Links with the past could be forged by means of translation from the Sanskrit and by the adaptation of Sanskrit aesthetic terms. Harishchandra had, according to his own opening statement, first considered writing a theoretical and historical treatise on drama while working on the translation of *Mudrarakshasa* in the mid-1870s. The project took shape as an attempt to come to terms with the conventions and requirements of classical Sanskrit drama in its new function as progenitor of the new. When he finally assembled his views many years later, his own work had matured and emancipated itself from its early models and it was possible to classify and integrate the most diverse varieties of theatre, ancient and modern, Eastern and Western, by a combination of analytic strategies which he saw as framing his own work.

He first reviews contemporary theatre practice by undertaking a synchronic classification, according to aesthetical and social functions. Once this is accomplished, he introduces a diachronic perspective that allows, within the structural logic of the hierarchy he creates, Sanskrit drama to retain its authoritative status, as the older, more comprehensive genre, which in some ways contains the seeds of the newer, western developments, thus ensuring the status of the ancient Indian as predominant, both chronologically and qualitatively.

'Natak' is by definition *drishya kavya*, 'visual poetry' and its authors were Brahma, Shiva, Bharata, Narada, Vyasa, and Valmiki, though its first exponent was Bharata (*Granthavali 1*: 749). Having established this genealogy, Harishchandra proceeds to freely improvise his own account which is very loosely based on Bharata and later unspecified Sanskrit treatises on drama. According to Harishchandra, drama has three divisions: 1) Poetry-mixed or Poetical (*kavya mishra*), 2) Pure Spectacle or Curiosity (*shuddha kautuk*), and 3) Corrupt (*bhrashta*). In the second category, which he does not reject entirely, he includes puppetry, mime, feats of skill, and other forms of civilized entertainment. In the third category, from which he distances himself, the forms included are those that originally possessed theatricality, but which have since degenerated; no recognizable dramatic quality is any longer to be found in them (*natakatva shesha nahim rah gaya hai*) and they have become devoid of poetry (*kavyahin*). Under this third category he includes not only the popular forms, *bhand, Indar sabha, tamasha,* and *yatra,* but also, suprisingly given his pious bent, forms explicitly rooted in religious traditions such as rasa, lila, and *jhanki*. Less surprisingly, he adds the theatre of the Parsis to the list of the corrupt (750). Thus his attempt at a synchronic classification of the drama of his age. However, in spite of his theoretical stand on the subject, as we shall see when we consider his trajectory as a playwright, he will be found using the conventions of many, if not all, of these corrupt forms in his own dramatic works.

It is the first category, the poetical, which Harishchandra then proceeds to discuss at length and where he introduces the diachronic subdivisions: ancient (*prachin*) and modern (*navin*). The ancient theatre of the Hindus was, of course, Sanskrit drama. The Aryas were the first in world history to propagate drama and the rest of the world undoubtedly followed suit in learning the art of theatre from them. In fact, where the others merely partook of pleasure in the music and literature of theatre, the Aryas worshipped their gods in the very pleasure that they found in it (775). That drama was never considered lowly entertainment is demonstrated by the practice of the ancients, for it was performed not only by professional *nat*s, but also by great personages themselves, royal princes and princesses, for women also performed on the ancient Indian stage (776). While expounding the traditionally accepted ten divisions of the ancient, though he does indeed rely primarily upon the definitions laid down in the classical Sanskrit texts, he extends them into the present, for his examples are drawn largely from modern *bhasha* texts, which at this early stage of Hindi-language theatre, amounts to drawing examples from his own corpus of plays; he has by then written copiously enough to cover a broad range. It becomes apparent then, that unlike the Orientalists, his purpose in the essay is not merely to recount the classical tradition, but to stretch it into the present, wherever it is possible, by giving contemporary examples. He feels free to modify definitions, where contemporary practice seems to call for it, as in the case of *prahasan*. He amends the classical precedent of confining the whole to a single act, by allowing a sequence of several scenes. As examples he offers his own *Vaidiki himsa himsa na bhavati* and *Andher nagari* (750–2).

Within the modern variety, he states forthrightly enough, are to be counted the plays modelled on European drama, of which several already exist in Bengal. The chief characteristic of the modern is the repeated change of scene, a narrative segmentation that is implemented by the recurrent shift of the painted backdrop. This backdrop thereby becomes the organizing principle of each scene. Modern plays are further subdivided into two: *natak*, drama, and *gitirupak*, musical drama, the former when narrative predominates, gitirupak when narrative is highlighted by song and itself recedes into the background, a genre which since the early 1880s, he himself was in the process of adopting. His own recent play *Nildevi* serves as an example here. Both kinds can have either a happy or a tragic end; a third variety has a mixed ending, where some characters fare well and others suffer. Thus the integration of Western categories: tragedy, comedy, and tragi-comedy. But in keeping with his practice of expanding the potential of modern bhasha natak, or navin natak, he offers no examples from the West, preferring to list instead the Indian adaptations of Western plays, thus Lala Shri Nivasdas' *Randhir premmohini* (1878), the Hindi adaptation of *Romeo and Juliet*, serves an example of a play with a tragic end (753–4).

Traditional categories need re-interpretation and expansion if they are to remain comprehensive and serve new needs. The chief goals/designs, *uddeshya*, of theatre demonstrate the heterogeneity—the mixture of aesthetic with socially oriented goals—which is an indication of the categories that are replacing and supplementing the older classifications; *rasa*, for example, is still a consideration, but has a much reduced significance. The goals of theatre are fivefold: 1) comic, 2) erotic, 3) spectacular, 4) social reform, and finally 5) patriotism. The first three are barely discussed. It is the last two which call for remark: these are to be created by the reinterpretation of old tales, by the creation of a public forum where social issues can be discussed, and where the love of the country is to be generated (754).

The plays of the time were written as much to be read as to be performed, and Harishchandra never tires of pointing out that they were to be educative, corrective—politically, historically, ethically—in the widest possible sense. At a later stage in his essay, when the rasas come up for discussion again, he allows that some knowledge of *Nayika bhed* (classification of the types of romantic heroines) is necessary, as also of the figures of speech, but it is no coincidence that once again he emphasizes that the play should have an elevating goal and that reading or seeing the play should lead to the acquisition of some kind of a moral education (*koi shiksha mile*) (773). *Satya Harishchandra*, thus, points to the truthfulness of the Arya *jati* and *Nildevi* serves to generate patriotism. If in some play the character of the chief protagonists proves to be contrary to these aims, then they are to be shown suffering a downfall. His own father had followed this practice in showing the fall of the Raja Nahush in the play of the same name (774).

While deploring the fact that today drama is looked down upon in the country, he once again makes the explicit point that it carries important social functions. He cannot, he says, express what freedom (*svacchandata*) of expression there is in playing drama. The country is being devoured by the forest fires of corruption, and no single person, by means of private critique, can alone hope to better the situation. If a king, or a wealthy man, or some pandit is engrossed in evil deeds, it is not possible to effect individual correction publicly, in assembly (sabha). Yet collectively, when the performance of plays becomes practice, then it will be possible to make the aforesaid people aware of their faults by injuring them publicly, in the course of aesthetic enjoyment, by the mere dramatization of the word (778). It is in this sense that plays such as *Shakuntala* and *Ratnavali* are educative and contemporary. They offer a mine of information about the social and political conditions of the period. A veritably Shakespearean world is seen to reveal itself in the play, *Mricchakatika*. He cites the testimony of Shivaprasad Singh at length, who sees the play as disclosing a myriad details of daily life, the great and the lowly, the pious and the fraudulent, the romantic and grotesque (779–80).

Finally, there is a serious attempt to determine the chronological order of the Sanskrit plays available; in drawing up a list of classical Sanskrit plays he chooses to add plays by contemporary playwrights, such as by his friend Damodar Shastri. Sanskrit plays thus constitute a tradition which is not to be seen as confined to the past alone (785–7).

In considering the uddeshya of drama, Harishchandra locates older Sanskrit drama firmly in the past. It was created for the amusement of the cultivated and was performed in the theatres of kings or royal personages. The poets of old created for the amusement of the people of old, it was legitimate to cater to the needs of the time, but to merely recreate in the old mould would now be inappropriate, and Harishchandra distances himself expressly from this mode of playwriting. It is not necessary to totally discard anterior practice but it is advisable only to retain those conventions which meet the needs of Hindi play composition today. The cultivated in the contemporary world show a preference for natural, *svabhavik*, composition.

He proceeds to review those conventions of Bharata which retain meaning and serve a contemporary social function (754–6). According to Harishchandra, there have been some shifts of emphasis since Bharata's day; costume, for instance, has become an indication of character and state of mind. But Harishchandra also reads some present theatre practice into the past: significant are his reinterpretations of stage conventions, so that he can authorize the all important backdrop and the drop-scene as conventions firmly located in the past. This doubtlessly implies a reduction of the flexibility possible in the older theatre, which could shift scenes swiftly, use words to paint landscapes, and involves some belaboured justification, yet here Harishchandra is caught in the practice of the times, of English models but most of all, of the popular Parsi theatre (754–9). But he allows for some innovation and some modification of Sanskritic convention. He has no hesitation in dropping some of the initiatory introductory conventions, since these have been replaced by printed programme notes; printing has, according to him, in any case, revolutionized communication and heralded a new age. He discusses this at length in a long note (761–3).

Natural, svabhavik, is also the key term as regards play composition. Psychological states of mind should be expressed as naturally as in real life, wordiness being the chief fault of bad plays. The dialogues should be composed without inflated figures of speech and with such economy, that it becomes possible to gauge the character of the persons concerned on the basis of their utterances. The plot should be so constructed as to seem self-generating, and it be possible to read all action as the expression of internal states of mind. It is for this reason that Kalidasa, Bhavabhuti, and Shakespeare, that *Shakuntala*, *Hamlet*, and *Macbeth* were the objects of such veneration and such world fame.[10] In playwriting, intellect alone is of no avail. It is the study of characters from the most diverse walks of life, the exchange of dialogue with the lowest and the meanest, and knowledge of the most diverse disciplines—politics, ethics, jurisprudence, and so on—that form the essential preconditions for successful composition of plays (767–72).

In considering bhasha natak, he is compelled to admit ruefully, that the practice of writing in Hindi is no older than the last twenty-five years; it began with a play written by his father, *Nahush natak*, on a Puranic theme. His father was a man with vision, and sent his daughters to school at a time when this was considered novel and scandalous. Harishchandra is clearly aware of the twofold allegiance of present theatrical activity, classical Sanskrit, and Shakespearean, the classical in its reinterpretation as programme for the future, the Shakespearean criticism of the nineteenth century as further colouring this interpretation and providing it with contemporary psychology and social purpose (787–8).

Given the lack of a metropolitan centre in the Hindi–Urdu belt, there is the vexed problem of which Harishchandra is also acutely aware, for he deplores the present lack of interest in poetical drama, of who should provide the patronage for the creation and staging of plays in Hindi. It is obvious that patronage needs to be discerning if it is to be effective. He asks explicitly for the financial support as well as good wishes of government; this is, however, to exclude guidance in matters of taste or appropriateness. Government had no hesitation in providing ample grants for a project such as Fallon's Hindi–English dictionary, which overstepped the bounds of decorum by including a whole series of socially unacceptable terms, but then, how far can one function check and control instance under the government of '*andhere sahib*', of blind, undiscriminating masters? A number of books were written under the financial support and encouragement of William Muir, which also led to the sorry translation of *Ratnavali* into Hindi by the Bareilly Sanskrit Professor Pandit Devdatta Tiwari, as sorry and coarse as the performance of Sanskrit plays by the visiting commercial Parsi theatre. This is followed by an oft-quoted description of a performance of *Shakuntala* by a visiting Parsi company:

When the Parsi theatrical company performed *Shakuntala natak* in the Dance Hall in Kashi and the brave and noble hero Dushyanta began to dance salaciously with his hand on his waist like a dancing girl and sing 'Watch my slim waist gyrate', Dr Thibaut, Babu Pramadadas Mitra and several other learned scholars came away, saying: 'We can't stand to watch this any longer; these people are putting the knife to Kalidasa's throat.' This is precisely what happens to bad translations. Translating without first merging with the poet's heart means not only to indulge in babble but also to put the soul of the departed poet to hellish torture. [789]

Clearly, there was little to be expected of the Parsis. According to Harishchandra, however, in spite of misguided government and lack of public patronage, there was some ground for hope, since a dozen plays had been written independently in Hindi, though much remained to be gained and to be drawn upon from the wealth of Hindi's knowledgeable elder sister, Bengali (790). Some Hindi plays had also been performed, but there was no regular theatre company for the pleasure of the cultivated in the North West Provinces (791). Thus, at present there was no support either from government or from the affluent. All the same, Harishchandra took it upon himself to draw up an inventory of the available Hindi plays, some fifty-two of them, original and translated, of which nineteen stemmed from his own pen, the rest from those of his friends and acquaintances (791–2).

In this groundbreaking essay, Harishchandra has sought then to produce a new aesthetics of drama, which draws upon the old while integrating the new. The base is still to be provided by the Sanskritic tradition, its conventions, however, are to be judiciously modified to meet the needs of the times and its goals distinctly re-oriented towards the socially corrective and politically progressive. At the same time, Harishchandra is sifting through the prevalent theatrical modes to extract the grain and discard the chaff, so as to create genealogies which will allow him not only to find a frame for his own dramatic work but also to draw up guidelines for others in the field. He is setting up a canon for Hindi drama, and writing thereby a first comprehensive, if necessarily sketchy, history of theatre in modern Hindi.

How had he himself traversed the grounds he laid out in his essay? We turn now to a consideration of his trajectory as a playwright.

THE PAST AS FRAMED BY THE CLASSICAL SANSKRIT TRADITION AND SHAKESPEARE

Though his translation activity had begun by 1867–8, and his first original play published in 1872, it was really only in the mid-1870s that Harishchandra undertook lengthier works, both by way of translations as well as original creation. His language had by then acquired an easy conversational tone, a supple, mellifluous prose and verse style; even in the more solemn passages, the sonorous Sanskritized words were interspersed with lively colloquialisms. The verse passages were almost entirely in Brajbhasha, which had the musicality characteristic of religio-erotic Krishna-bhakti poetry. The lower characters, when they versified and when he wished to establish distance from them, spoke an Urdu/Khariboli, emulating the style made popular by Amanat in his *Indar sabha* (1853).[11]

Harishchandra's most ambitious venture was the translation of the Sanskrit play *Mudrarakshasa*, an almost entirely political play, which he chose to publish as instalments in the years 1875–7, in *Balabodhini*, the women's journal of which he was proprietor and editor.[12] The play had been translated by H.H. Wilson and included in his *Select Specimens of the Theatre of the Hindus* ([1835] 1977). In the learned introduction to the work, Wilson had offered historical data, diligently collected from all the possible sources, the various versions in the ancient literature of the Hindus, complemented and historically corroborated by the reports of the Greeks. Wilson was writing history and every word was weighted with significance, for it amounted to nothing less than an investigation of national history and an evaluation of the national character. Wilson's admiration for past achievements was offset by the kind of alienation expressed generally for Asiatic statecraft. If Chanakya's dexterous manipulations and foresight excited respect; the remarks appended to the play stated in no uncertain terms:

It is a historical or political drama, and represents a curious state of public morals, in which fraud and assassination are the simple means by which inconvenient obligations are acquitted, and troublesome friends or open enemies removed.... The principle is one which has long pervaded Asiatic courts, and has proved no unimportant instrument in working their downfall. (Wilson, Volume 2: 253)

Wilson, however, allowed that the delineation of character invested even the treacherous with interest and dignity, and the devoted fidelity to an employer was a redeeming feature in the delineation of Chanakya's character.

As Edward Said has shown, the beginning of a work marks its point of departure: 'A beginning immediately establishes relationships with works already existing, relationships of either continuity or antagonism or some mixture of both' (1975: 3). Harishchandra prefaces his play with historical information, the *purvakatha*, or preceding narrative. In this prose introduction to the play he is concerned primarily with telling a tale, citing the various versions in the Puranas and the story literature in Sanskrit, in order to highlight facets of character, which he sees as inherent to the plot. He skillfully builds up the conflict between the two protagonists, Chanakya and Rakshasa. But if the subtleties of character delineation are thus regarded implicitly as essential for the understanding of the play, he also takes obvious pleasure in the political magnitude of the state of Magadha. Its downfall comes about because kings are too often vulnerable to the advice of their ministers and followers who cause strife and infighting (*Granthavali 1*: 384). However, as against the explicatory model created by Wilson, the discussion of the Greek sources is reserved for the appendix. Here, though he is obviously indebted to Wilson for his information and cites him by name, he can cap the authority of both the Greeks and Wilson by citing Raja Shivaprasad Singh's *Itihas Timirnashak* (1866), which, as he proclaims at the outset, will clarify many issues of the times. Thus indigenous historiography, even when following European precedent, is seen as being more reliable on issues relating to genealogy and the determination of the exact location of the political arena.[13]

Yet these are not the only alterations Harishchandra undertakes. He offers his own introductory verses to the several acts, as well as his own conclusion. These are all composed in a mix of musical modes today classified as classical and semi-classical—*dhrupad*, *thumri*, *purabi*—which constitute a familiar plane for contemporary audiences. The moral which can be abstracted from each act, which relates the text to the present, whether it be ethical or political, echoes themes which are repeated incessantly in the literature of the period: it is dissension within their own ranks which makes for the political downfall of the Aryas. The obvious examples are the battle of Mahabharata and Jaychand's fatal call to the *yavana*s for help which led to the downfall of Prithviraj, the last Hindu ruler of Delhi, the consequences of which the Aryas must bear up to this day, for they continue to remain slaves of a foreign power. Pressed somewhere in between, there is also express demonstration of loyalty to the ruling power, symbolized by the far-off Empress Victoria, with her assurance, from across the seven seas, of fair dispensation of justice for all. Yet, at the end of the play, the poet calls upon the people of India to cast off sloth and the servitude, to rise and be industrious, to worship Hari, the one god, and to take their rightful place as the equals of all the other peoples of the world.

The introductory essay, containing as it does the study of narrative sources in the ancient Sanskrit literature, serves to establish temporal continuity; the interspersed verse, the moral dictums, relate the text to the present; the detailed historical evaluation in the appendix integrates Orientalist research into the historical narrative while offering indigenous historiography as conclusive evidence. The cumulative effect is that of a reorganization of forces, historical and moral, which back the call, with which the play concludes, to cast off the foreign yoke (*Granthavali 1*: 496–8).

If *Mudrarakshasa* was serialized in a journal for women, the next play, *Satya Harishchandra*, written in the same year in response to the request of a friend, and serialized in the *Kashi patrika* in the following year (1876), was designed expressly as an educational text for boys, in fact the pedagogical and moral dimensions of the theme dictated the choice of the play. The theme had been dramatized by Arya Kshemishvara in the Sanskrit play *Chandakaushika* (Das Gupta 1962), and it had also been adapted into Bengali. It was a perpetuation as well as a widening of tradition that Harishchandra now undertook, for the full-length play is no longer a translation alone, rather it is a free improvisation of *Chandakaushika*, which comes to be firmly grounded in the experience of nineteenth-century Banaras. There are structural correspondences with his treatment of *Mudrarakshasa*, for in the introduction he narrates the previous treatments of the story in the epics and Puranas. But the ancient roots of the story, its ramifications through the ages, have a clear function in the present, for as he clarifies at the outset, 'Maharaj Harishchandra was born in the very same Bharatvarsha we know today, and he was our very own ancestor' (*Granthavali 1*: 253). Thus his fate foreshadows the course present history will take.

The past is also tempered by the present in the handling of time and place as also in the delineation of character and situation. The innovations Harishchandra introduces consist in 1) the contemporarization of the framework brought about by locating the play in the city of Banaras, constituted of sites familiar to contemporaries but projected as existing since time immemorial, and 2) the psychological elaboration of character and scene.

The contemporizing framework: The structure inherited from Sanskrit plays and fully exercised in the *Mudrarakshasa* translation is essentially retained. The play is classified as a *rupak*, that is, a full-fledged play in four acts with *karuna* (the pathetic) as its central rasa, though it also claims to contain *bhayanak* (the terrible) and *vir* (the heroic) rasas. The *prastavana*, prologue, is both programmatic and personal. It is spoken by the *Sutradhar*, director, and the *Nati*, his wife and partner; their apparel, as described by the playwright, is characteristic of contemporary 'popular' street performers.[14] The state of the dramatic art, they proclaim, is dismal; there is no appreciation of it amongst the cultivated, who remain ignorant as to what kind of a 'beast' drama is, though the present company is to be blessed, for it wishes to see a new *Hindi* play. Sutradhr chooses a play by an author whom his friend Pandit Shitalaprasad had lately compared to Raja Harishchandra.[15]

The framing story seems to be entirely of Harishchandra's making, though the pattern is well established in the Puranas as well as in folklore: There is a dialogue in heaven between Indra, the irascible sage Vishvamitra, and that irrepressible wanderer between the worlds, Narada. Vishvamitra and Indra, for their several ends, plot Harishchandra's downfall. Narada's asides serve as comments, his voice is proverbially mischief making, but it also speaks with the wisdom of a people who see through the machinations and stratagems of the mighty. And it is he who provides a political link with the contemporary world, as casting forth a shadow from the past into the future which has now become the present: 'It is as if Harishchandra is the very personification of Truth. Doubtlessly, the sheer thought of such persons being born on this soil, will keep the head of Bharata high, even at such times when she will have been subjected and have reached a state of degradation' (259). The *Bharata-vakya*, the benediction with which plays traditionally close, consists in this case of a summation of all the wishes, literary, religious, social, and political, of the playwright for the future well-being of the country:

May the gentle not be plagued by rogues, may devotion to Hari hold sway, may all the sub-varieties of religion lose their hold, may Bharat have access to her own substance, may the burden of taxes flow away, may the wise abandon sloth, women become the equals of men, all the world attain happiness, all abandon rustic song and speak with the voice of the cultivated poet. (308)

But within this classical frame, the details of plot and character are handled with a new ease and flexibility. Thus, though Varanasi is the legendary locus of the final scenes of Harishchandra's story—since it is balanced on Shiva's trident it is outside the bounds of any earthly empire, and it is depicted as such in *Chandakaushika* and in the opening scene of the play—the poet Harishchandra's treatment of the city to which the action shifts in the last two acts, contemporizes the play and creates an intimacy and immediacy. The long lyrical description by the exiled king on his arrival there offers the portrait of an ideal city, which make it possible for the four varnas to live in accordance with their status and stage of life. Brahma has constructed a city of incomparable beauty so that it stands out as the very rose of cities, poised as it is on the banks of the divine river which it lines with such renowned temples as Bindu Madhav and Visheshwar and with sites as famous as Panch-Ganga and Manikarnika.[16] The quartrains are followed by fourteen gay, tripping couplets, describing the divine river Ganga. Knowing Kashi to be her beloved, she had leapt so eagerly to join the city that now she keeps it locked in her embrace and would not dream of ever parting from it. Boats with their tall masts, sunshades, and gleaming white houses with flags aflutter, decorate its banks. The sweet sounds of the *naubat*, the ceremonial kettledrum, and of temple bells, the song of men and women, and the chanting of the Veda float in its air. On its banks are yogis sunk in meditation but, most of all, there are beautiful women sprinkling themselves with water, their fine-looking faces cleansed by the river and glowing in the pure stream as if the moon itself were being washed clean of its blemishes (275–6).

The slave market scene in the city, in spite of the seriousness of Harishchandra's plight, communicates a raucous gaiety and liveliness—the *Banarasipan*, which Nita Kumar has remarked upon as being typical of the city on public occasion and festivity (1988: 165ff.). The allegorical characters *Dharma*, right order, and *Satya*, truth, appear as lowly *dom*s and *chandala*s who serve at the cremation grounds; they are looking to buy new slaves and purchase Raja Harishchandra. They are dark, with curly hair and red eyes, their bodies are bare save for loin cloths, and they sing a jaunty *Amad* or introductory verse in Urdu, invoking thus the genre made popular by *Inder Sabha*:

Ham Chaudhary dom sarkar,
amal hamara donom par.
We are the chiefs of the doms,
We operate on both sides, the here and the beyond.

These colloquial, almost comic tones alternate with scenes at the cremation gounds which hover between the mythical and the realistic, consisting as they do of elaborate descriptions of the horror and desolation of death and dying. They seem initially to have been sparked by a similar description about the temporality of human existence in the Sanskrit play (Das Gupta 1962: 90) but they also have Harishchandra philosophize in a vein so Hamlet-like ('Alas, poor Yorrick...') that it is impossible to overlook the echoes and parallels:

> King and subject, no difference to be sighted,
> Their time is reckoned with the same strokes.
> Fortunate or flawed, mixed as nectar with poison,
> Knocked off at the same price today.
> Puru or Dadhichi, they exist no more,
> Save as names in books.

Ah, observe that head there, which was anointed once with *mantras*, adorned with the nine-gemmed-crown, which prided itself such, that it regarded even Indra as inferior, which was filled with the ambition to conquer great kingdoms; today it has become the play-ball of pishachas, and people disdain to touch it even with the tip of their toes. (*Granthavali 1*: 289)

Within this web woven of Shakespearan echoes—the everyday world of doms and chandals who inhabit the *ghats* of the city and the everyday needs of the merchant who purchases the queen and her son—are placed characters whose emotional state the play telescopes upon with an ease derived from handling diverse sites and states of mind.

The psychological elaboration of character and scene: Though their sense of duty finally overweighs personal considerations, the scenes draw their power from the depiction of the psychological suffering of the king and queen. The play proper opens with the queen caught in a state of unease and foreboding, reminiscent of similar scenes in Shakespeare. She has just woken from a spine-chilling dream of her husband in a desolate state, his hair in wild tresses, and his body smeared with ash; her son has been bitten by a snake. The king seeks to console her, but he has himself arisen from a similarly disturbed sleep, and from a dream sequence in which he gifts away his empire to an unknown Brahman, whom the king had tried to rescue from distress but whom he only manages to enrage instead, and who demands an enormous recompense. Raja Harishchandra is distraught, so real was the dream that he now resolves to rule in the name of that Brahmin, since he can no longer be king in his own empire. The dream glides effortlessly into real life, as the unknown Brahmin, who turns out to be none other than the famous–infamous sage Vishvamitra, appears in person to demand his due. It is as if, in fact, the line separating the dreaming from the waking state has become non-existent, and the promise given in the dream holds true in the world of wakefulness and daylight. The sequence is finely wrought, depicting various shades of emotions and responses.

The concluding scene, which also forms the emotional climax of the play, is a similar elaboration of feeling, when the desolate king and the lamenting queen accost each other across the dead body of their son Rohitashva. He has, as forecast, indeed been bitten by a snake and his mother has carried his corpse to the cremation grounds, with one-half of her own garment covering his bare limbs. It is the practice of the cremation ground watchman to demand half of this cover as the price for using the place, a task that Harishchandra now feels compelled to carry out. But before the pathos of this scene can finally unfold, the husband and wife have to recognize each other, so bedraggled are they that it takes time for them to do so. Harishchandra hears her lamenting wildly, driven almost to lunacy by her despair:

What's been happening? Where have you gone, son, come back quickly. Oh, I feel so scared here in these cremation grounds, oh, who brought me here? Come quickly, son. What are you saying? That you had gone to fetch flowers for the guru and there a black snake bit you? Alas, alas, alas! Oh, where did it bite you? Oh, go call a healer someone, so that my son can be brought to life again. Oh, where did that snake go? Why didn't it bite me? Bite, oh bite, did you have to bite that delicate child alone? Bite me. Alas, it refuses to bite me. Oh, there is no snake here. Since when has my darling learnt to lie? I keep calling out to you but you refuse to stop playing.

The king-turned-slave tries to hang himself from a tree when he realizes who mother and son are. But he has still to fulfil his duty. It is this commitment to truth which will secure him everlasting fame. He steps forward to demand half of the cloth which covers the child. She also recognizes him. Gone is the high-flown speech of court and ritual; husband and wife speak the simple language of despair, till such time as the irate sage and the gods themselves appear, accompanied by the allegorical figures of truth and dharma, a modern variation of the *deus ex machina*, who restores the universe to its rightful order.

As Yagnik (1933: 221 ff.) has observed, the presence of Shakespeare in the handling of scene and plot is subtle and pervasive, to insist on parallels would be pedantic, so intertwined has this other 'classical' heritage of the nineteenth century become with the notion of drama.

Interestingly, *Durlabh bandhu,* Harishchandra's translation of *The Merchant of Venice* (1880), is a lacklustre, pedestrian affair, an academic exercise, which has none of the usual sparkle of his language; in fact, there have always been doubts, as to how much of it is the work of his pen (Cf. Brajratnadas 1967: 20 ff.). Not surprisingly, this has been the fate of most literary adaptations of Shakespeare, in spite of the efforts of enthusiastic critics (Yagnik 1933; Mishra 1970) to detect merit in stray versions.[17] Shakespeare's influence, apart from literal echoes, is subterranean. It is present much more as a view of history, character, and morality as interpreted by the Romantic poets and nineteenth-century criticism, and further propagated in British India through his decisive place in the colonial educational curriculum (Vishwanathan 1989).

As we saw in the Hindi dramatization of *Mudhrarakshasa* and *Satya Harishchandra,* both of which were treated as historical plays, it was possible to establish the historicity of the national past, seen primarily in Hindu terms, as contained and perpetuated within the frame and conventions of classical Sanskrit drama, and as filtered through the various influences of the times. This flexibility and refunctionalization of Sanskrit drama for the present, the vitality and contemporaneity of translations and adaptations, were uses obviously not foreseen by the Orientalists when they had first posited the existence of the classical theatre of the Hindus. Ranajit Guha's observations regarding Bankimchandra's call for an autonomous historiography hold true in a special sense for indigenous dramaturgy:

It insisted on self-representation as the very condition of that autonomy. But the right of self-representation was not for a subject people to claim: it was not supposed to represent itself; it was merely to be represented. To insist on self-representation, even in terms of the past, was, therefore, for such a people, already a signal of its impatience with the state of subjection. Considered thus, the urge for an autonomous historiography could be understood as a symptom that it really was of an urgent, insistent, though incipient nationalism. (Guha 1988: 57)

Dramatic representation, even if largely confined to the printed page in the Hindi region, made possible a mapping out of areas of experience not filled in by historical narrative. In a sense it was an escalation, a heightening of the kind of self-representation possible through historiography. We shall return to history-making in theatre in the section following the next, to view the emergence of the new stereotypes which would ultimately tilt the balance of the political history of the subcontinent, with Hindus and Muslims regarded as monolithic communities ranged in perpetual antagonism against each other.

THE TRADITION OF SOCIAL AND POLITICAL POLEMICS

It would, however, narrow the range of the traditional forms available as resources, were we to regard mainstream Sanskrit drama mediated through its propagation by the Orientalists, by Shakespeare, and by the Bengali precedence (Satyendra 1976: 276), as the only source of inspiration for contemporary drama. There was also a tradition of radical polemics available within the canons of tradition. Harishchandra was an ardent Vaishnava, with a firm grounding in traditional Vaishnava literature.[18] For the creation of his own most vital plays, with social and political themes, nationalist and anti-colonial, it was the eleventh-century Sanskrit drama *Prabodhachandrodaya* and the satirical sketches he published in his own journals that provided the most potent models. Polemical, irreverent, satirical, with characters allegorical as well as drawn from professedly pious ranks, and with a definite Vaishnava bias, the *Prabodhachandrodaya* discloses the pretensions and hypocrisy of the various orders of mendicants and ascetics in the subcontinent. The play had maintained a strong vernacular tradition by way of translation through the centuries, so that in undertaking yet another act of assimilating and adjusting the text by translating its third act

Harishchandra was setting forth a tradition which needed no laboured justification.

Krishna Mishra's *Prabodhachandrodaya* was an allegorical play, which depicted the conflict engendered by the destructive forces under the leadership of the virulent *Mahamoha*, Grand Delusion,[19] who were consolidating their ranks in order to wipe out the fast spreading influence of the virtuous Raja *Viveka*, Discrimination. Raja Viveka had the support of *Vishnu bhakti* and was ultimately to triumph, but not before there had been many false scares and skirmishes and the Raja, thanks to the felicitous union with the divine *Upanishad*, become the progenitor of *Prabodha*, Spiritual Awakening. Since the play is by express intention the generator of the pacificatory *shanta* rasa, there were no scenes of violence, the final battle being merely recounted in the fifth *anka*. It had been translated several times.[20] With the verse translation into Brajbhasha in 1760 by Brajvasidas, who was as Harishchandra himself, a member of the Vallabha *sampradaya*, the play had become securely ensconced within the Vallabha tradition. Harishchandra was familiar with Brajvasidas's version, since he makes explicit mention of it in his essay 'Natak'.

Harishchandra's translation of this third act of *Pakhanda vidambana* in the lively idiom particular to him, was made relatively early in his career in 1872. The act depicts the two women, *Shanti* and *Karuna*, Peace and Compassion, respectively, in search of their mother *Shraddha*, Faith. They belong to the forces of Viveka. Krishna Mishra uses the occasion to arrange a series of encounters with a Buddhist monk, a Jaina mendicant, and a Shaiva *kapalika*. With the help of wine and two women summarily beckoned from his domain of power, the kapalika is easily able to persuade the other two holy men to share in his ecstasy and abandon their faith. Shanti and Karuna observe these proceedings with consternation, and at the end of the act, overhearing that their mother is safe by the side of Vishnu bhakti, rush away to join her. Of the six acts of the play, it is the merriest, the most raucous, and at the same time the most polemical exposure of the non-Vedic faiths. Harishchandra delights in this disclosure; by substituting certain letters in the words of the Buddhist and the Jaina he produces a kind of pseudo-Apabhramsha and pseudo-Pali in the verse portions of their speech.[21] He can make dexterous use of sound to imitate and caricature speech. Though he protests in the dedication of the play that he agitates against no sect, in fact, as is to be expected, there is a definite Vaishnava bias, though to some extent he is indeed able to subsume the sectarian character of the work under cover of the goal that he projects as a shared one: working against the diversity of the many paths which divide the Hindu faiths and for the propagation of the one true way (*Granthavali 1*: 673).

This polemical, irreverent satire was to remain his most sustaining model in the following decade. In the same year, he wrote a similar piece: *Vaidiki himsa himsa na bhavati* (1873), 'Vedic slaughter is no slaughter', which has the barest of narrative lines—a lascivious, meat-devouring king with a sycophant *mantri*, minister, and *purohita*, house priest, who obligingly minister to his needs, deeds which catch up with the trio in the world beyond. In announcing the completion of the play, Harishchandra made the following statement:

Let it be known that the play appeals to people of a kindly nature, for it is completely against Vedic sacrifice, *karma kanda* and animal sacrifice, as well as against tantric chakra worship and alcohol-intake. This is indeed the first work in Hindi by the pen of a Hindu, which mocks at some aspects of Hinduism in that it takes a stand against these; but be that as it may, it aims to lift the practice of violence and alcohol-intake from Hindustan. (*Kavivachansudha* 3.21, 21 June 1872)

The play is advertised, then, as treating of the Hindu religion, in order to cleanse it of malpractice, by criticizing some corrupt offshoots of it. The body of the play consists of hilarious encounters and word-mongering with a Bengali (a Brahmo with dubious notions of social reform), a Vedantin, a Vaishnava, and a Shaiva. The Purohit supplies on demand (mis)quotations from the Shastras to support any and every kind of vagrant practice, with the result that absolute chaos reigns, which in the fourth anka or act of the play is put in order by Yama himself. Practically all of the main characters are consigned remorselessly to the special hells they deserve. In the end only the Shaivas and the Vaishnavas can be elevated to the heavens to which they have so righteously acquired a claim:

It is through your genuine bhakti that Ishvara has ordained that you inhabit Kailasha and Vaikuntha, so be pleased to go and partake of the fruits of your good deeds.... Delighted by your good deed Ishvara grants you redemption, so that you can ever remain in his vicinity. So you see, you have attained the highest state. (*Granthavali 1*: 26)

The play then transformed the polemics and sectarian bias of *Pakhanda vidambana* into an original composition which satirized contemporary divisions of the one faith, which was viewed as Hindu with a firm Vaishnava core.

Alongside this, Harishchandra was developing a kind of social satire which attempted realist portraiture at the same time; it was stylistically closely affiliated to the *Panch* skits that he was writing as regular columns for his journal *Kavivachansudha*. *Prem jogini* (1874–5) was to exhibit the same social satire, comment, and sparkling wit.[22] In spite of the occasional hyperbole, however, within the social comedy a core of hard realism seemed to have consolidated itself. Under what rubric could such pieces be subsumed? As we have seen, conscious as he was of the need to create High Literature in Hindi at this stage, Harishchandra had begun to use the classificatory categories of Sanskrit drama to designate his plays. However, when *Prem jogini* was published in book form, he chose to caption the scenes which together constituted the play as *Kashi ke chhayachitra ya do bhale bure fotograf*, reflections of Kashi or a couple of good and bad photographs. Thus he was aware that every now and then, there was no traditional precedence for the form he was creating, and in choosing the word 'photograph' he both indicated the modern character of his undertaking—he was considered a good amateur photographer—as well as the reality of the individual in social situations that the photograph as a medium sought to capture and hold fast. The main and the subtitle represented the dual intentions of the scenes. The central focus was obviously to be on the character of *Prem jogini* or Ramchandra, the *nayak* or hero of the play, in his capacity as lover but also as *bhakta* or devotee, who placed himself in the position of the beloved woman in relation to Krishna. But situated within the framework of the photograph, he was to be viewed with wide-angle lens and in soft focus, rather than in any kind of close-up. This meant that it was in the public places of the city that he was viewed and in the social milieus in which his reputation was the topic of discussion. If in the one good photograph he was glorified, along with others of his kind, in the bad photographs he was observed from below, that is, he was depicted in the terms that the riff-raff of the city saw him: self-indulgent and pleasure loving. Harishchandra had come a long way from the dialogue situation of the Panch pieces. In *Prem jogini* it was a concert of voices he orchestrated, while, in effect, documenting the life of the city. It is not surprising that the play remained confined to the four scenes written in the first rush of creativity. It was apparently difficult to sustain the momentum and to find an adequate framework for a longer composition.[23]

Bharat durdasha (1876) is an allegory, which more obviously follows the pattern of *Prabodhachandrodaya*, set as it is in an explicitly political context. It is structured as an impending confrontation between two antagonistic forces, around the symbolic image of *Bharat*, a tottering figure resting on a stick for support, in tattered clothes, with a worn out crown. After an initial invocation of past glory and a desperate call for help to the Queen Empress beyond the seas, Bharat lies prostrate on the stage through the course of the play.[24]

The chief antagonist is *Bharat durdev*, Bharat's Misfortune, who, to judge by the description of his apparel as half-Muslim and half-Christian, stands for alien rule, both past and present. The battle is half lost even before it can begin; Bharat durdev has viciously potent forces at his command. The scenes alternate between elegiac lyric and satiric dialogue. The play could bear extensive analysis. Here I shall focus on one key scene, the fifth act, where a committee of seven gentlemen has collected in a library to consult on strategies to cope with the impending disaster—the library along with debating clubs, book clubs, British Indian Associations, where the educated gathered for consolidation and organization of opinion, is the typical scenario for such discussions in the second half of the nineteenth- century.[25] The chairman, for all his obvious vacillations, is to be the chief organizer of resistance. He opens the meeting with the proclamation that the country is under attack; it is obvious that Bharat durdev is, in fact, the foreign presence in the country, though he is nowhere explicitly referred to as British. The other six members are a Bengali, a Maharashtrian, a newspaper editor, a poet, and two 'native' gentlemen. What follows then is the sum of the response that the country can muster up in the face of such a threat.

The Bengali says, with some claim to self-satisfaction, that in Bengal there is a forum for protest, there is the British Indian Association and there are the newspapers which can pressure government.[26] The two native gentlemen show signs of unease. The poet has the most preposterous suggestion: Just follow, he says, what in the times of Nadir Shah's invasion, the buffoons of the Mughal emperor Muhammad Shah had suggested, that a canvas wall be put up on this side of the river Yamuna, behind which soldiers dressed as women position themselves. Once the invading army were to appear on this side of the river, a bangled wrist could be stuck out from behind the wall, wag its fingers, and say: 'Don't come here you beasts, there are only women here'. The British forces, mindful of their masculine code of honour, would not dare attack women.

The assembled gentlemen meet the poet's suggestion with equanimity, though the Bengali has doubts regarding the propriety to be expected of enemy forces, what if they show no respect for our women? The editor, not unexpectedly, proposes that he write about the impending attack, that one fire with the armoury of newspapers and with the canon-balls of speeches. The two native gentlemen fear that the local officials might take affront. Wherefore, asks the Bengali, after all we merely desire that English rule not be borne. For the first time the Maharashtrian speaks: Could it be that the officials themselves might eventually align themselves with Bharat durdev? It is a provocative and incendiary insinuation, that the very officials who proclaim that they rule the country for its own benefit, are allied with contrary forces, whatever finally the identity of Bharat durdev.

The Maharashtrian's suggestions are as radical as they are practically efficacious: constitute a public assembly, demand spinning machines, wear cloth spun in India.[27]

The discussion in the library, mixed generously with frivolous reflection, is abruptly terminated by the entrance of Disloyalty, dressed as a policeman, who proceeds forthwith to handcuff the present company. Protests are of no avail, Disloyalty disarms by himself protesting personal disinterest in the matter, what cause after all had he had to show some time ago, when the journal *Kavivachansudha* was similarly taken to task?[28] He merely acts under the Regulation known as 'English Policy', the paragraph number being 'Official Caprice'. Disloyalty merely acts as the arm of law, a law operating in the interest of Bharat durdev, if not expressly at his command.

The last act culminates not in the demise of Bharat, but in the suicide of *Bharat bhagya*, the Fortune of Bharat. Yet though it ends on a sombre note, the tenor of the play as a whole and of the last act in particular, is rousing rather than gloomy, for the long monologue of which it consists, though mourning the present fallen state, is in fact a song of glory, a most extravagant eulogy of the past. Before plunging the dagger into his breast, Bharat bhagya asks that he take birth again and again on the banks of the rivers Ganga and Yamuna, ever as the brother of Bharat. This recalls the challenge of the initiatory *Mangalacharan*, where the dramatist had offered his salutation to Krishna's *Kalki* incarnation, sword in hand, who would establish *Satyug*, the age of order, again and destroy the dealings of *Mlecchas*, thus rescuing earth from the burden of unrighteousness.

Drama has here, I suggest, acquired additional dimensions; besides the romantic–nationalist, it has claimed public space, where opinions are criticized as well as created. It has the function of a newspaper debating club, which it can at the same time caricature: it is invective, eulogy, a call for action as well as an arena to voice despair. It is worth remarking that of the seven plays classed as 'original' in Harishchandra's collected works, five can be regarded as social, political, religious satire.

The next play I want to consider is *Vishasya vishamaushadham*, poison is the antidote of poison, published in the journal *Harishchandrachandrika* in October 1876.[29] In the instance here dramatized, the Sanskrit proverb of the title provides both a pithy summing up of the political situation and the moral authority, as it were, for the condemnation of the Native Chiefs in general and the British colonial power at its most imperious. The genre chosen to articulate this social–political critique is *bhana*, a classical Sanskrit form for a monologue. In actual practice, Harishchandra could also have derived the form from the current *bhand-bahurupia* tradition of a single impersonator, enacting and overstretching a social role, with much impertinent commentary on contemporary events, in a way which would delight and amuse his

audience.[30] However, he chooses to classify the piece as a bhana, thereby
endowing it with the most respectable of genealogies.

The wrangle for power described in the piece took place in Baroda.[31]
After much infighting, intriguing, and counter-intriguing, Malharrav
Gayakvar, the third of the sons of the former chief of Baroda, managed
to ascend the throne in 1873. Malharrav had a sinister reputation,
since in 1863 he had tried to poison his brother. He had been placed
under house arrest at the time. He was known for his ill administration
of the state and in 1874 the British had seen fit to threaten that if
matters did not improve, he would be removed from the throne. Not
only did he pay no heed to this warning, he indulged in the most wanton
of excesses by marrying Lakshmibai, a married woman, in a ludicrously
lavish ceremony. Not content with this escapade, he tried to rid himself
of the British resident Mr Phayre, who had been appointed to this
position only in 1873, by poisoning him as well. This plot was discovered
and Malharrav was put under arrest in January 1874. A commission
of enquiry was appointed, consisting of three Englishmen and three
Indians—the Chiefs of Gwalior and Jaipur and Sir Dinkar Rao. The
evidence was conclusive, but the Indians did not wish to be implicated
in an action which would thus damn a brother chief. The Englishmen
had no such qualms and the Viceroy, Lord Northbrook, clinched the
matter and summarily removed Malharrav from the throne. The adoptive
son of the second brother Khanderav was installed in his stead. The
measure was received unfavourably by the vernacular press and there
were a number of dramatizations which chose to depict Malharrav as
the victim of the usual British intrigue for power. Harishchandra's
view was more balanced. He accepted the British verdict, but saw
behind the measure the arrogance of an imperial power which in the
end completely crippled Indian enterprise. It was at this level that he
opposed the deposition which amounted to little less than loss of
prestige for the country at large, but he could not overlook the
corruption and depravity of the Gayakvar.[32] Was poison then to be
the antidote of poison?

The monologue is spoken by the *bhandacharya*, the Maharaja's own
purohit, who is in a position to observe and comment on the affairs
of state in the most intimate manner. Yet he resorts to oblique comment
alone, since he has to continue to remain in favour and retain his own

position. Thus the first kind of poison, the revelry and corruption engaged in by Malharrav, is described with elegant restraint:

aur phir sukh to hindustan mem tin hi ne kiya, ek muhammad shah ne dusare wajid ali shah ne tisare hamare maharaj ne. muhammad shah ke zamane mem nadirshahi hui, wajidali se laknau chuta, ab dekhem inki kaun gati hoti hai. (Bharatendu natakavali, Dvitiya bhag: 32)

And then in Hindustan only three people really knew how to be happy, the first was Muhammad Shah, the second was Wajid Ali Shah, and the third was our own Maharaj. In the reign of Muhammad Shah, there was much wilful tyranny, Wajid Ali Shah had to abandon Lucknow, now we can keep watch to see what becomes of him here.

The bhandacharya himself can apparently see the impending disaster in no other light than as entirely befitting. Yet, as a loyal subject, he cannot but mourn the deposition when it comes, as also he cannot remain unaware of its consequences for the structure of power in the Native States.

Hay! hay! maharaj, are kya hue? gaddi se utare gaye? hay! maha anarth hua. maharaj nahim gaye hindustan gaya. (33)

O woe, o woe, what happened to Maharaj? He was removed from the royal throne? O woe, this was a great upheaval. It was not Maharaj who departed, it was [the prestige of] Hindustan which took leave.

For it was quite obvious that with that the British, who had entered the country as mere traders, now regulated the affairs of state with complete and unhampered authority. The native chiefs of the country were now no more than figures on a chessboard who moved when they were moved. When the native chiefs indulged in fighting, the British forcibly induced peace, though they sometimes had to suffer losing their good officers on the battlefields. As a reward for the pains they had to take to restore justice, the least they could do to compensate their loss was to take, now and then, some territory into their own possession. The British had, of course, given assurance in writing that no one, apart from the legal heirs of Khanderav and Malharrav, would be recognized in this royal line, so it seemed *tanik anuchit*, a little inappropriate, to keep the throne from the progeny of Malharrav. But the bhandacharya turns to take a closer look at the doings of Malharrav. His reputation is such that:

We have heard that when Maharaj visited the houses of the wealthy of the city, the women would be let down into wells (to hide).... Now, was Ravan bigger than he or was he bigger than Ravan? On one score he was definitely bigger than Ravan, since he indulged in such outrage at such times and under the nose of the British. Praise be the soil of Mother Bharat, that she brought forth such sons. Muhammad Shah and Wajid Ali Shah were after all Muslims, but how will the blemish of Malharrav be removed from the Hindus? Everyone is for widow remarriage, but he contrived marriage with a married woman. (38–9)

Whatever else one might say, the British knew how to dispense justice. If it had been some other ruler, he would have, according to the bhandacharya, used the occasion to take over control of the state himself. It was really only they who had the large-heartedness to let the state remain under the control of the Gayakvars. '*Dhanya angrez! ram aur yudhishthir ka dharmrajya is kal mem pratyaksha dikhaya, ahaha.*' (Praise be the English! They have shown us that the righteous rule of Ram and Yudhishthir can prevail in this age, hurrah, hurrah.) (39) And as for the fate of Malharrav, why poison is the only antidote of poison. If the event is to be viewed as a catastrophe then only because at present the country has native chiefs such as Malharrav.

Harishchandra's bhana, since it was eminently political in tone and content, was noted duly in the government record of the native press, *Selections from the Vernacular Newspapers*, for the week of 9 October 1876.[33] After the publication of Dinabandhu Mitra's *Nildarpan*, Indigo Planters' Mirror, in 1860 there had been a spate of plays which used *darpan* in their titles and which held up the mirror to expose, in one way or another, the exploitation practised by the British, whether as a class or as government servants, or simply in their capacity as white traders and planters.[34] From 1875 onwards there had been increasing agitation in official circles in Calcutta regarding the political tone of the plays printed and produced there. In 1876 the Dramatic

Performances Bill was passed prohibiting drama 'likely to excite feelings of disaffection to the Government established by law in British India' and laying down penalty for all those participating in the performance, including the spectators, of a prohibited play.[35] Though there was protest, the critical-political theatre of the Presidency towns suffered a heavy setback. The provinces were quieter and demonstrated less activity, though a few protest meetings were held in Lucknow and Kanpur.[36] Plays depicting social and political abuse receded noticeably; there was a proliferation instead of plays with Puranic or historical-romantic themes.[37] There was renewed glorification of the heroic Rajput past of the country—an almost collective fantasy, which consolidated itself in images that pitted themselves not so much against the present rulers of the country as against the past. Colonial oppression and racial discrimination were projected almost entirely onto past Muslim sovereigns but also onto the present Muslim population of the country.

The Dramatic Performances Act seemed to have acted as a brake on further explicitly political compositions by Harishchandra. It was only in 1881 that he was to write *Andher nagari*, which had a folktale-like character and lively lyrics, and revolved around the theme which most often concerned him, that is, the wilful tyranny of government. But the British were mentioned almost in passing and it was a folktale king who bore the brunt of the satire.

In a report in *Kavivachansudha* (2.5, 1870), entitled '*Levi pran levi*', 'The Levee as Life-levy', which was to expose him immediately to official displeasure, Harishchandra in describing a function, a levee, at the court of the Maharaja of Banaras to welcome Lord Mayo, had taken the liberty of calling the fawning, uncertain behaviour of the attendant dignitaries as typical of '*andher nagari*'. *Andher nagari*, the city of blind excess, of proverbial misguided management, has a special place in popular memory. In the land now known as Jhuosi, there once reigned a Raja Harbong, who was known for his dim-witted, whimsical, often cruelly unjust treatment of his people. He was finally trapped into pronouncing his own death sentence, his whimsy ably managed by the equally proverbial, wonder-working yogis, the gurus Gorakh and Machandar.[38] To describe the behaviour of loyal subjects thus was a double offence.

It was in much the same vein that Harishchandra wrote the play *Andher nagari* in the year 1881, reportedly an overnight composition, to be staged by amateur Bengali and Hindustani enthusiasts in their newly established National Theatre in Banaras. By the early 1880s, Harishchandra had, as mentioned earlier, started arranging the plays he wrote in a single sequence of short scenes. It has been suggested that this was in emulation of the Parsi model (Sinha 1969: 88; Rastogi 1986: 35). Be that as it may, at yet another structural level, it is possible to trace conceptual continuity. If in *Bharat durdasha*, action was confined to dialogue in a library, here it has reached the marketplace with a Banarasipan, a roguishness, a delight in disrespect, already referred to above. A wandering mendicant, who with the permission of his *mahant* enters the town, discovers that all goods cost just a *taka* for a whole *seer*, regardless of difference in content and quality. Vendors advertise their wares in verse.[39] Built into each jingle are caustic comments on the state of the country, leaving little doubt that it is the British Raj with its hangers-on and supporters, which is in its turn the prototype of this *andher nagari*. Ghasiram, the vendor of roasted peas, advertises his wares thus: 'Very high officials eat *chana*, those who impose double taxes on us all.' The *kunjari* sells her grocery with the quip: 'Here, take your pick of Hindustan's dry fruits, dissension and animosity.' The *pachakvala* sells his digestives with the remark: 'The Sahibs who eat *churan*, can digest all of the land of Hind. The police officers, when they eat their churan, can digest all legislation.' The most original vendor of goods is the one who offers *jatis*, castes, for sale. He is, of course, a Brahman, who is willing to write *vyavastha* to order, awarding the payee any varna that he asks for—a sweep at the upward mobilization, made possible by British insistence on classification of the varna status of castes—all available for a *taka* each. When the *mahant* hears of this dangerous state of affairs, he takes to his heels, advising the young mendicant to follow suit. But the young man is hopeful, and the Raja puts in an appearance and there follows one grotesque error of judgement upon another, manipulated by his officials, who in their turn cannot see beyond their noses and strike an uneasy balance between catering to their own needs and pandering to the wishes of the Raja. It is solemn nonsense which threatens at each stage to acquire dreadful reality. Such is the awful wisdom of this constellation of thieves and thugs who rule the chaotic state that the Raja finally allows himself to be hanged so that he can enter heaven before the rest of his populace. Such then was Harishchandra's rather malicious view of the 'native' princes, who could still claim their natural rights to direct the fate of the people of Hind.

The play was revived and became popular in the last century from the 1960s onwards; it was even suggested that it had been modelled on *nautanki*, folk theatre.[40] This has occasioned protest (Hansen 1989: 89), since the formal grounds for this comparison, if any, are thin. What, however, seems to have led to this identification, is a certain vision of 'folk' theatre, where the everyday voice of the people is heard on the stage, establishing an ironic distance to the larger gestures of the mighty.[41] With the alteration of some staging conventions, and the addition of some contemporary allusions, the play can acquire contemporary dimensions and become, in addition to a radical critique of colonial society, an equally damning exposure of neo-colonial politics.

Harishchandra could caricature the excesses of various religious denominations, as in *Vaidiki himsa himsa na bhavati*; he could poke fun at the vainglorious posturing of the would-be nationalists in *Bharat durdasha*, while registering acute distress at the state that the country had fallen into; he could protest the behaviour of Indian princes as much as that of the high-handedness of the British in *Vishashya vishamaushadham*; he could speak in the voice of the people, colloquial and irreverent, as in *Prem jogini* and *Andher nagari*. He cherished little illusion regarding the kind of action to be expected from the ruling classes, British or indigenous. It is important to bear this in mind, while we turn to yet other political and social dimensions of his dramatic oevre.

REGRESSIVE POLITICS: VISIONS PAST AND FUTURE

Who could bring order to the present disarray, what were the political models of state which history offered, which could inspire and direct change? Here there was a yawning gap in Harishchandra's vision, between a popular orientation represented by plays such as *Vishashya vishamaushadham*, *Prem jogini* and *Andher nagari*, and the elite models to which he resorted when it came to seeking new moulds for the ruling class, particularly its women. Structurally, he innovated: as we have seen. Once the theatrical edifice stood—he had, after all, himself opened the way for a series of dramatic genres—it was also possible to create new models which went beyond the frames offered by Sanskrit drama. In the early 1880s, Harishchandra had so far emancipated himself from the Sanskrit model and the social–political satire he had himself evolved, that he could attempt a historical play, *Nildevi* (1881), in a more Western mould consisting of a rapid scenic sequence, with none of the traditional Sanskritic framing devices. However, the vision of nation represented here restored to a purely Hindu reading of Indian history which viewed Muslims as foreigners and aggressors.

Nildevi, written in 1881, apparently at the same time as *Andher nagari*, was explicitly historical, and presented his reading of the history of the people of Aryavarta.[42] He termed it *aitihasik* gitirupak or historical musical drama. It did away with the conventions of Sanskrit drama. In the essay 'Natak', discussed earlier, Harishchandra had classified *navin* or modern plays, as being of two kinds, natak or drama proper and gitirupak, or musical drama, which last he defined simply as proliferating in song. The music obviously served to highlight the emotional quality of the play. He had classified *Bharat janani*, 1877, adapted from the Bengali, as an opera. But it is much more likely that he drew the inspiration for *Nildevi* from the much decried Parsi theatre which abounded in songs composed in the popular forms, today classified as semi-classical.

Each of the short scenes of *Nildevi* is so structured that it ends with a climax of some sort, which is then topped by a song in popular mode: whether *thumri*, ghazal or a rousing *rola*. The emotionality thus engendered lends life to the rather sketchy story and the barely etched characters. There is no attempt here at any kind of Shakespearean characterization, apart from one short scene wherein an apparently mad man makes an appearance which seems to have a Shakespearean model (the porter scene in *Macbeth*). The allegorical figure of the *devata*, divine being, who bemoans the lot of Bharat, evokes if anything the tradition of *Pakhanda vidamban*, elaborated in his social-political plays. That Harishchandra turns to an entirely new form—the quick shifts of scene, the dramaturgically central use of song—in order to contain his view of the ancient past is indicative that the past is indeed being viewed through a new prism.

The play is written for *matri bhagini sakhi-tulya arya lalanagana*, the Arya woman, respected as mother, sister, and companion. As earlier discussed, the political play *Mudrarakshasha* had early been serialized in the journal *Balabodhini,* which had ceased publication by this time. Thus it was not surprising that yet another political play should be addressed to women. The context of this address is made clear in the preface: the freedom enjoyed by Englishwomen is explicitly contrasted with the freedom that Arya women had once enjoyed, though they had utilized it for very different ends: 'It is Christmas day. There is no greater day of joy for Christians. But I am, paradoxically, much sadder today. The reason for this is the envy, which is natural to mankind. I am no ascetic [siddha], devoid of attachments and aversions.' He goes on to say that when he sees Englishwomen, artificially adorned, their hair piled high, their waists pulled in tightly, flitting about like butterflies on the arms of their husbands, he thinks of the inferior status of the women of his country and he becomes very sad. Not that he would even dream of wishing that Indian women follow the ways of this fair-limbed flock, who shamelessly prance about with their husbands:

But the matters of which these women are aware, the way they are educated, the care they take of household matters, impart instruction to their progeny, recognize the [worth of their] own being, the prosperity and problems of their people and country, and [the way they] help thereby and do not lose this rich life (which is full of prospects) for slaving in the house and with infighting, it is our desire that in a similar way, the goddesses of our homes overcome their inferior status and make some progress. The only obstacle in the way is none other than our own present family tradition. The entire Arya race believes this to be the case. It is to disprove all doubts on this score that this work has been composed and put into your lotus hands. It is our entreaty that you read and hear this *charita*, deeds, of these virtuous women and strive for your advancement to the best of your ability. (102–3)

For the role that the Aryan woman played and was to play in the future, Harishchandra's first reference point was the *Devimahatmyam* or *Durgashaptasati*.[43] In the *shlokas* cited as the first of the two mottos to the play, the Mother Goddess Durga calls out to the Buffalo Demon Mahishasura that she will slaughter him so that the Gods exist in triumph on the very spot where he rages now. And to the Demon pair Shumbha-Nishumbha, there is her fierce admonition to disappear from the face of the earth and return to the nether world. The third verse carries her assurance to mankind that she would be there to protect whenever there was threat of demonic obstruction and, finally, there is a fragment from a verse to establish that all women are part of the Mother. Nildevi is the Mother Goddess, destructive and protective, and the Muslims, as the plot makes clear soon enough, the inglorious demons. Her slaughter of these provides a reassuring vision of the past as well as a promise for the future.

The second of the two mottos stems from the poem 'The Rajpoot Wife' by Edwin Arnold,[44] from which the story of the play has been taken in its entirety. The verses cited from this poem seem to respond to the battle cry of the Sanskrit text. They describe the scene of the final encounter between the Rajput queen and the Muslim chief: the queen draws the Muslim chief's own sword to kill him:

> From his jewelled scabbard, drew the shureef's sword,
> Cut at vein the neck-bone of Muslim Lord,
> Underneath, the star light sooth a sight of dread!
> Like the Goddess Kali, comes she with the head.
> (Arnold 1882: 331)

Thus the dual lineage of the play: Puranic and Orientalist. Where others had resorted to James Tod's *Annals and Antiquities of Rajasthan* (1829) as the source of their information and inspiration for the celebration of Rajputhood and India's valorous past, Harishchandra drew upon Edwin Arnold, the popular Orientalist and publicist who was so admired in his own day.[45]

The plot of the play can be summed up in a few sentences: The Amir Abdussaraf Khan, Commander to the Delhi Sultan, plans to attack the Hindu camp of the valiant Raja Suryadev of Punjab by night, breaking all martial codes of honour, while Raja Suryadev, unaware of these plans, speaks to his Queen Nildevi and his courtiers of his intentions of fighting a fair battle for his faith, *dharmayuddha*. A lonely Rajput sentinel, singing wistfully of his wife and son, is overwhelmed by the brutal Muslim attack which follows and Raja Suryadev is taken prisoner. Imprisoned in an iron cage and lying in near faint, the Raja overhears a divine being sing a long lament about the downfall of the once proud Aryas and their land. A Rajput agent, dressed as a Muslim lunatic, reports the events leading to Raja Suryadev's death: When told that conversion to Islam would secure his release, the Raja could only spit his defiance and when attacked, break out of his iron cage with almost supernatural force, to die fighting valiantly. Nildevi is broken-hearted at the news of her husband's death. Her son and other Rajput chiefs vow desperate vengeance, but she has a plan, which she whispers into her son's ear. The plan is not disclosed. A foreign dancing girl is announced at the court of the Muslim Amir, where wine and song flow freely. The dancing girl sings and dances enticingly. When the Amir, totally won over, offers her a cup of wine and more intimacy, she suddenly stabs him. She is the valiant Rani Nildevi. Rajput soldiers burst into the camp and overpower the Muslims. Nildevi's last words are that she is now free to immolate herself with her husband.

In Arnold's poem, Shureef Khan 'was Sultan Mahmood's vassal, and wore an Amir's tassal', he was apparently one of the many who followed Mahmud in the conquest of the Panjab.[46] Arnold's description of Suraj Dehu identified him with the Vedic Aryans, nomads who lived in harmony with nature and were favoured by the gods (326). The poem espoused the cause of the Rajputs vigorously and uncritically. The Muslims were depicted entirely from the Rajput point of view, as assumed by Arnold. They were dastardly, heinous, and depraved, 'aflame with lawless wine', 'wagging their goatish chins' (330). Shureef Khan was called 'the hound', the Muslims who bait the caged Suraj Dehu were cowards (327). There was clear glorification of *sati*; the supreme self-negation of the sacrifice was to be read as supreme self-assertion. Ranee Neila manages to retrieve her husband's body in the confusion which follows her stabbing of the Amir, so that she can perform sati:

For where a Rajpoot dieth, the Rajpoot widows burn. (328)

Harishchandra adopted this narrative line, with some modifications and additions. Though he also celebrates past Rajput valour, Harishchandra allows Nildevi to play a much more active role. She is depicted as the brain behind the stratagem that turns the tide; she displays great mental and physical courage in carrying out the plan to kill the Amir and route out his men. She crowns her heroism with self-immolation. The great sati debates of the 1820s which had culminated in legislation against it had revolved around the voluntary or involuntary nature of the decision which led the woman to perform such a sacrifice. Nildevi expressly articulates the pleasure of the deed and thus the voluntary nature of her decision in her last words: *'sukhpurvak sati homgi'*, I shall commit sati with a sense of fulfilment (129). The only way to demonstrate the freedom, even defiance, which Harishchandra had wished to set up as a model for Arya women, came about by falling back upon old patterns of submitting to male dominance, though admittedly with a shift of emphasis, since it was the voluntary nature of the deed which was now foregrounded.[47]

Both Nildevi and the less successful Raja lead, then, what is depicted as collective resistance to Muslim rule, presumably by proxy also to colonial rule. But what is the form of the opposition and the model proposed as alternative to this rule? And for what kind of collective 'we' is Harishchandra speaking? The answers are discomfiting, whether we turn to Arnold's images or Harishchandra's own: 'they' are the Muslims, viewed as a homogeneous block, 'we', the Hindu Aryans. The stereotypes of nationalist historiography can here be observed in the very process of being frozen into generally accepted visions of the past: the dastardly Muslim chief, the valiant Rajput king as the epitome of Aryan bravery and resistance, and the faithful Rajput wife and queen, following her lord unto death. Harishchandra used these stereotypes to account for the course of the newly conceived nation's history: his main difference from Arnold's brand of romanticism lay in the patriotic, all-India framework with which he endowed his play, making of the tale an episode of significance in the history of the Muslim invasion of the subcontinent, as also a blueprint for the future. How does he bring this about?

In the very first scene in which he appears, Suryadev clarifies the nature of the battle to be fought: it is to be dharmayuddha, between Rajputs/Aryans who were defending their own land, *nijbhumi*, and the Muslims, who were *adharmi*, unrighteous, in a twofold sense: they were of alien faith and they observed no code of battle, they did not

fight the open but attacked from behind (*Granthavali 1*: 107). Not
bravery but treachery accounted for the capture of the valiant Rajput
king. Under this treacherous rule, the *dharmic* order could only be
thrown into disarray, as the allegorical figure of the devata in Scene 7,
points out. He forecasts that the four varnas would lose their calling,
they would all become Shudras, following *dasavritti*, slavishness.
Bharatbhuvbasi, the inhabitants of Bharat, would abandon their own
true religion. They would turn away from their own Hari, they would
disdain their own products, their own ways, and they would forget
that they had ever been *svadhin*, independent. The message was dismal:
'*ab tajahu birbar bharat ki sab asa*' (116). (O best of the brave! Now
abandon all hope for Bharat.)

Once Suryadev dies, all hope does indeed seem lost. As Miyam,
who is none other than the Raja's priest in disguise, mourns in a *pada*
at the end of Scene 8: the Krishna who had promised to appear in times
of distress seems to be slumbering in deep sleep even as the populace
of Bharat weeps in many ways ('*Kaham karunanidhi keshav soe! jagat
neku na yadapi bahut bidhi bharat basi roe!*') (120–1). Thousands of
his children are slaughtered, countless women made slaves, yet he
turns away? Has the sharp edge of his discus, the *sudarshana chakra*,
been blunted?

But all is not yet lost. The penultimate scene has a rousing rola,
sung by Suryadev's son, Somdev. If the Aryas unite, abandon *grhayuddha*,
infighting, the lowly Muslims could hardly be expected to withstand
the joint impact of their onslaught. Could dogs hold their own in
battle once the lions wakened? The blood of the *yavanas* would quench
the thirst of the Arya forefathers. In anticipation of the joyful event:
'*kahahu sabai bharat jay bharat jay bharat jay*' (124). (Call out, all of
you, victory to Bharat, victory to Bharat, victory to Bharat.)

Even as the singers in the Amir's court rejoice that the first Muslim
victory in the Punjab holds out hope of conquering all of Hind ('*fatah
e panjab se sab hind ki umid hui*') and enslaving Hindus (126), the
Rajputs are preparing to attack and overpower the camp. The play closes
heroically, terminating at a favourable moment for the Rajputs. Sudipta
Kaviraj has pointed out the importance of the moment of closure:
'By wiping out the beyond, erasing the historical sequel, the narrative

can alter the significance of events without actually telling an untruth. It remains a truthful distortion of the truth of history' (1995: 153). If disunity led to the fall of Arya Hindus, then unity could win back their territory for them again. This then is held up as the moment of truth. In doing so, the historical imagination is pointing not only to the past or even to the present, it seems to be pointing to a future course of action. This may lie in ousting foreign rule by throwing off the yoke of the British. However, it also preprogrammes antagonisms within Indian society by cementing the splits projected into the past.

Yet it is important to add a word of caution regarding Harishchandra's polemical depiction of the Muslims as the opponents of Hindudom in this play: as far as he is concerned, it is primarily in the readings of the past that Muslims become the other. In other contexts—historical, political, and religious—such as in his review of Shivaprasad's *History*, or in the biographical sketch of Mohammad, he can exhibit great solidarity with Muslim rule or even the original religious impulse wherein Islam originated. The contradictions of this position are self-evident; they reflect the complexity of the newly forming colonial public sphere and its apparent readiness to split into polarized interest groups.

The politics of *Nildevi*, especially if read along with the social political plays discussed earlier, contain, in a nutshell, the contradictions of the nationalist endeavour in the colonial context: the progressive and the regressive coexist in uneasy coalition. The emancipatory moment is prominently displayed in the sharp-eyed, sharp-tongued critique of contemporary power holders in political satire; it seems to be pleading for popular representation and democracy. But it is capped with a romantic vision of the past, which reinstalls king, priest and the rhetoric of caste and increasingly also of race ('Arya') which is associated with them and it operates with essentialist notions, with oppositions viewed in black and white, with Hindus and Muslims ranged in battle against each other. Dismal as this may seem in view of the politics of the Hindu Right today, it is important to remember that Harishchandra had clearly foreseen wide-ranging tasks for the theatre he was seeking to create and the theatre public he was seeking to educate. The emancipatory potential offset and balanced in some measure the romantic–nationalist thrust.

THE FUTURE OF DRAMA IN HINDI: RESERVATIONS AND RESTRICTIONS

Harishchandra had conceived of his fledgling national theatre as a public forum, firmly rooted in the national historical past, yet assimilating new techniques and tasks urgently and eagerly. A long way seemed to have been traversed since the initial Orientalist discovery of the national theatre of the Hindus. During his own lifetime, his example and encouragement initiated vigorous amateur theatrical activity in the city of Banaras. After he departed from the scene, the drama he had envisaged shrank to become confined to a literary medium alone. He achieved more enduring results as a publicist. There could hardly be hope of patronage for this new theatre from the colonial government, the very power it could and at times did indeed most centrally challenge. There were obvious political considerations that created barriers, and it was to stifle just this kind of critique and potential subversion of authority that the Dramatic Performances Act had been enacted and enforced in 1876.[48]

Under this kind of obvious political control and repression, there is the question of indigenous 'elites' and the kind of patronage to be expected of them. As Barun De pointed out, properly speaking, there could be no elites in colonial society, since they were always dependent for career advantage on the British, and had no control of the economy or government. At most, the urban intelligentsia of the times could be described as a 'dependent sub-elite'.[49] Patronage was inevitably linked with British patronage and the critique of the ruling power could only be articulated with certain reservations.

However, Harishchandra's theatre was not conceived of as a theatre for the traditional indigenous 'elite' alone, rather for this emerging 'dependent sub-elite' which was in the process of organizing itself as a social and political force, and was heterogeneous in its composition.[50] But for the kind of theatre he envisaged, in Banaras and the Hindi belt, the social space, the wide basis, the political momentum, the sustained and varied patronage available in the big metropolitan centres, were missing and it took longer to evolve than he had anticipated or possibly had the vision to foresee. The heritage of incipient 'enlightened' critique within Harishchandra's theatre retreated for the time being to vacate and thus make yet more place for the other dominant streak in his own drama, the romantic glorification of the national past.

Yet even for this kind of theatre to become a public institution, amateur activity hardly sufficed. Dhirendranath Singh in his edition of the first play to be performed in Banaras, *Janaki mangal* (1969: 6–25), has documented the kind of straggling amateur activity, which continued in the city of Banaras in one form or another right up to Independence. Even the ingenious Parsis established no permanent base and only had itinerant theatre companies in the north of India, though in the late nineteenth century, Parsi theatre establishments sprang up in Delhi. They catered increasingly to nationalist sentiment, but no serious critique of the prevailing configurations of power could be expected from commercially oriented companies. In the countryside, *nautanki* flourished as never before under the patronage of rich peasants and landowners, in fact more so in the British period than ever before. In industrialized Kanpur it crossbred with the Parsis.[51]

Further, with time, and an educational system geared to this purpose, even the sub-elite, which could have fostered a lively local tradition, underwent a sense of alienation from popular culture. Nita Kumar has documented this process in her study of the popular culture of the artisans of Banaras. However, this only became visible and audible in the 1920s, when in the name of the 'decency' and 'morality' propagated most fiercely by the nationalist press, the urban intelligentsia began to withdraw from the modes of entertainment and festivity practised by the artisans of the city (1988: 192–5). And literary drama, increasingly cut off from the local and the popular and for lack of any theatrical base and sustained urban patronage, trod a lonely path, and in fact carried on a monologue with itself. But I would hesitate to describe this as an entirely dormant tradition, for in the meanwhile, though cut off from wide interaction, it was perfecting, in the plays of Jaishankar Prasad, the potentialities of literary Hindi as a vehicle for self-expression. Admittedly, it had little public presence; Yagnik in his study of Indian drama in the 1930s, reserves four lines for Hindi literary theatre, which was more visible in its absence than in presence (1933: 102). In fact, Hindi drama could only come into its own after Independence when it became part of official cultural policy to support theatre.

But practically parallel to the withdrawal of the urban intelligentsia from popular forms of entertainment, in the 1920s *kisan* and *mazdur* sabhas were to become a political presence. When in the wake of the Progressive Writers movement, the Indian People's Theatre Association was founded in the 1940s, popular forms again acquired cultural and political significance, and were integrated into a tradition that had in the meantime increasingly distanced itself from the common 'folk'. It was only in the 1970s, however, in search of an alternate tradition and precedents, that Harishchandra's political and social satire again received attention and recognition. However, to project this awareness of a division of culture into 'elite' and 'popular' into the late nineteenth century, is to ignore the social and political configurations of the time and read consistency where there is still fluidity. In Harishchandra's theatrical concept with its radical reorganization of 'classical' traditions, the Sanskritic as read through present need and as incorporating nineteenth-century readings of Shakespeare, several possible future orientations remain inherent: historical spectacle with Orientalist readings of the past, but also realist portraiture and social and political satire. He offers thus the dramaturgical and social frame for the national theatre he envisions and he creates the linguistic space for it, in all its breadth and flexibility, with all its promise and its contradictions.

NOTES

[1] See my monograph on Harishchandra (1997) for a more detailed survey of his journalistic and other writings.

[2] Wilson quoted no less an authority than Schlegel: 'This has not escaped the observation of one of the first dramatic critics of any age, and Schlegel observes, "The drama of *Sakontala* presents, through its oriental brilliancy of colouring, so striking a resemblance, upon the whole, to our romantic drama, that it might be suspected the love of Shakespeare had influenced the translator, if other orientalists had not borne testimony to the fidelity of the translation"' (vol. 1: xii).

[3] As Ranajit Guha has shown for Indian historiography: 'For, by designating itself as "Indian", that alternative announced its organizing principle as if

one of distantiation from what was paradigmatically un-Indian, because British and colonialist' (1988: 3).

⁴ H.H. Wilson himself was responsible for the early staging of Indian classical plays in the Calcutta of the second quarter of the nineetenth century. Simultaneously the boys of the Hindu College performed Shakespearean plays under the enthusiastic direction of a Captain Richardson and H. Jeffrey of the Oriental Seminary (Yagnik 1931: 86). The process of creating modern drama in Bengali, as unfolding from the preoccupation with the classic, is best documented by a contemporary observer, Babu Kissory Chand Mittra, in a long article for the *Calcutta Review* (1873). He confirms that it originates in private space: 'The Modern Drama in Bengal is held not in the sangitasala or open space, but in theatres neatly and beautifully erected at the lower end of the drawing room, with scenic embellishments of considerable pretensions' (248). Mittra has obviously witnessed the performance of Bengali translations from the Sanskrit in these theatres; he provides a vivid account of the successive productions. He makes the two points I follow in this chapter. First, that this modern theatre is also indebted to the West for its presentational mode: 'The modern theatre is composite, combining the stage and scenic attractions of the European with the performance of the Indian classical dramas rendered into the vernacular language' (248). Second, that it is deeply affiliated to the concept of Shakespearean drama, for which it seeks affiliations in the past: 'The age of Kalidasa opens a new era in the annals of the dramatic literature of the Hindus. He has been justly called the Shakespeare of India, and his marvelous knowledge of human nature in all its varied and profound phases is almost Shakespearian' (249). Mittra remains largely indebted to the Orientalists for his evaluations, whom he repeatedly cites: Wilson, Schlegel, Monier Williams. Yet, while reporting the opening of a public National Theatre in Calcutta, he hopes that 'the modern Hindu theatre will, in the words of an intelligent critic, become to the spectators as it ought to be, not merely the pastime of an idle hour, but a place of study, a whetstone of the imagination and the sympathies, a revealer of secret springs of character and emotion, and the subtler beauties of our finest poetry. They would learn at the same time to appreciate the niceties and the difficulties of histrionic art; and by their knowledge be enabled to stimulate merit and rebuke defects of the careless, instead of encouraging (as audiences too often do at present) whatever is most false in conception and meretricious in style' (273).

Many of these theoretical concepts are repeated in Harishchandra's analysis, yet his classification is more comprehensive, since it both modifies the classical and creates space for the new as emerging from within the classical framework, which acquires explicitly political dimensions.

[5] See Kapur (1995 and 2003) and Hansen (2003) for the theatrical and linguistic history of Parsi theatre as it evolved through the nineteenth into the twentieth century.

[6] The personal communication to this effect, made to me by Professor Anand Krishna of the Banares Hindu University (March 1990), whose family were near relations and close associates of Harishchandra, is supported by the evidence of Harishchandra's own reading of the situation in his autobiographical play *Prem jogini* (1874), discussed briefly hereafter.

[7] Cf. Eagleton (1987: 9–27) for the notion of the 'public sphere' as a political force in English literary criticism. See Dalmia (1997) and Orsini (2002) for the history of the late-nineteenth-century and early-twentieth-century 'Hindi' public sphere.

[8] For social and political space, the middle ground wherein he sought to locate his readership, see my monograph (1997: 251–67).

[9] The text of this essay is available in *Granthavali 1* (1970).

[10] As an example of an exquisite depiction of natural emotion, Harishchandra cites the scene in Kalidasa's *Shakuntala*, when the heroine of the play takes leave of the forest and her foster-father, Kanva. Perhaps it is no coincidence, that it is this very scene that is cited by Robertson in his *Historical Disquisition*, as an example of the 'beauties of the piece', the dialogue being 'in a strain of sentiment and language perfectly suited to their pastoral character' (1804: 237).

[11] See Hansen (1998) for a discussion of Amanat's play.

[12] See my essay on *Balabodhini* in Blackburn and Dalmia (2003).

[13] For, notwithstanding his much-vaunted loyalty to the colonial government, Shivaprasad Singh himself saw his *History* as superseding English historiography, and he proclaimed as much in the Preface: 'I was not fully aware of the difficulty of my task when I promised to prepare a little work on the History of India in Hindi and Urdu, for the use of our village schools. I know how imperfect and full of errors the so-called histories are which have hitherto been written in the Vernacular, but I had not imagined for a moment that even so cautious a writer as Elphinstone was liable to commit such mistakes as to say that Firoz Tuglak was nephew of the "late king" (Muhammad Tuglak)....

Or that a talented author like Mr Marshman would forget the topography of the country so far as to write that "the greatest achievement of this [Firoz Tuglak's] reign was the canal *from the source of the Ganges* to the Sutlej, which still bears his name". Having thus no English book that would completely answer my purpose, I was obliged to have recourse to original Persian works. But Benares is not a place where Persian books can easily be procured, and there was no time to procure them from other quarters, so I was obliged to make the best of the means at my disposal.' (*History of India* 1863: 65)

[14] The Sutradhar wears embroidered satin shorts, the tassels of his belt swing down from his waist, a short waistcoat, close fitting around the neck and buttoned in the front, and various kinds of jewellery. He carries a basket on his head and a stick in his hands. The Nati is described as dressed in a Maharashtrian outfit (reminiscent of the female performers in Tamasha), with a belt pulling in her waist, or alternately, dressed in male attire but wearing the jewellery of females.

[15] When the Nati chooses *Satya Harishchandra*, the Sutradhar utters words which were prophetic and which were indeed to be oft repeated after Harishchandra's short lifetime: 'The world has not understood the true character of Harishchandra. What matter? They will tell of him afterwards with moist eyes, the tale of beloved Harishchandra will survive' (256). There are several instances, both before and during the play, where the identity of Harishchandra, the poet, and Harishchandra, the king, merge, especially when their proverbial generosity is invoked.

[16] Harishchandra thus puts into the king's mouth the four quatrains or *kavita*s composed by his father Gopalchandra, a poet in his own right, who wrote under the pseudonym Girdhardas.

[17] The plays of Shakespeare had a much more lively reception in Parsi melodrama; they were both translated and adapted, and remained a constant source of inspiration. To my knowledge, there exists no sustained study of this vital and vibrant intercultural encounter. There is a special issue on Shakespeare in India of the journal of the Sahitya Akademi: *Indian Literature* (1964) and a compilation of essays and translation and performance data in *A Tribute to Shakespeare* (1989), compiled and edited by Sunita Paul and Nissar Allana.

[18] See my monograph on Harishchandra for his role as religious leader and expounder of the Vaishnava faith (1997: 338–426).

[19] The translations of the names of the allegorical characters in the play are adopted from Nambiar (1971).

[20] Saroj Agraval (1962) in her study of the Hindi tradition of the play records as many as twenty translations all the way up to the present.

[21] For the prose parts he uses a childish lisp and a kind of Marwari respectively to caricature the pretensions of the two.

[22] The play was published in three instalments in *Harishchandrachandrika*, first as *Premyogini*, subsequently as *Premjogini*. Act I, Sc. 1 and 2 in 1. 11 (August 1874); Act I, Sc. 3, in 2. 3 (December 1874), and finally, Act I, Sc. 4 in 1. 7 (April 1875). With that he declared Act I to be complete. Further acts, however, were not to be published. The whole, with a *prastavana*, introductory scene, added was published as a booklet in 1876. The text is also accessible in *Granthavali 1* (195–230), whence the following quotations.

[23] For a discussion of the Panch skits and for an analysis of the four extended scenes of *Prem jogini*, see my monograph (1997: 251–60, 302–8).

[24] The appeals to the Queen Empress might appear ignominious today, yet they permeate the work of the period. In order to understand the nature of the antagonisms presented in the play, we must distinguish at least three dimensions in the contemporary references to all that the British stand for:

1) The actual British presence in India with its arrogance and obvious misrule, perpetrating economic exploitation, is the prime target of protest. There is also a lingering sense of belief in, to be increasingly replaced by a sense of betrayal by, the British sense of justice and fair administration (Chandra 1966: 1.55).

2) The final arbiter in the matter of just and fair administration at this stage is the figurehead of the monarch, Queen Victoria, with solemn proclamations of good faith in 1858, invoked again by her in 1887 as prefaced in the writings of Dadabhai Naoroji:

We hold ourselves bound to the Natives of our Indian territories by the same obligations of duty which bind us to all our other subjects, and these obligations, by the blessing of Almighty God, we shall faithfully and conscientiously fulfill.

And it is our further will that, so far as may be, our subjects, of whatever race or creed, be freely and impartially admitted to offices in our service, the duties of which they may be qualified, by their education, ability and integrity, duly to discharge (Naoroji 1901: 1).

3) Finally, there is the all pervading awareness of Western science and technology, '*vidya*', which inspires respect and calls for emulation ('*Dekho vidya*

ka surya paschim se udaya hua chala ata hai,' Bharat durdasha: 160; *Granthavali* 1: 467–97).

25 Harishchandra's friend and fellow journalist, Balkrishna Bhatt, with a pen which could be as biting as his, considered this fifth anka, to be the apex of his friend's achievements as a playwright. If Harishchandra could provide such exemplars for all the eighteen subcategories, *uparupaka*, of drama, then they could all be saved for posterity (*Hindi Pradip* 5.8, April 1881).

The same Balkrishna Bhatt wrote a piece on sabhas in his journal, which reads like a commentary to this scene. Entitled 'The Uselessness of Sabhas', *'Sabhaom ka vaiyarth'*, it laments the narrowness of vision and the wordiness of most such institutions, which have sprung up in astonishing numbers across the country. 'The welfare of the country can only be achieved by such associations and sabhas, which reflect over and conduct debates only on political issues, such as the Poona Sarvajanik Sabha. But the people here (of the North West Provinces) have not yet had the courage to constitute such assemblies. Of what use are other sabhas ?' (*Hindi Pradip* 3.6, February 1880).

26 According to a personal communication made by Stuart McGregor, *Bharat durshasha* is based on a short (25 pages) Bengali play, *Bharatoddhar* (1877) by Ramdas Sharma, a copy of which exists in the British Library. Harishchandra has taken over the satiric suggestion made during the library discussion in the play which recommends that Bengal would save India by offering armed resistance to British rule.

27 It is obvious that nationalist economy, represented most eminently by the person of the Maharashtrian economist Dadabhai Naoroji, has here entered and occupied theatrical space and the Maharashtrian's words echo Naoroji's even voice in his speeches of 1876, patiently dissecting the disparity between Britain's word and deed, turning the official rhetoric against itself: 'The drain of India's wealth on the one hand, and the exigencies of the State expenditure increasing daily on the other, set all the ordinary laws of political economy and justice at naught, and lead the rulers to all sorts of ingenious and oppressive devices to make the two ends meet, and to descend more and more to the principles of Asiatic despotism, so contrary to English grain and genius. Owing to this one unnatural policy of British rule of ignoring India's interests, and making it the drudge for the benefit of England, the whole rule moves in a wrong, unnatural, and suicidal groove.' (Naoroji 1901: 125)

28 The reference was to the official displeasure provoked by the

Kavivachansudha when it chose to indulge in an irreverent satire of the British insistence on pomp and ceremony, and yet more dangerously, question their monopoly of the trade in textile. This was to lead to the discontinuation of the life-sustaining government subscription of the paper in 1876, which in turn imposed such financial constraint upon Harishchandra that in the following year, he was forced to discontinue his editorship of the paper.

[29] It is available in *Granthavali 1* (196–230) whence the following citations.

[30] It has survived into the present, as documented by the Emighs (1986) for Rajasthan.

[31] The wrangle had inspired a number of plays in Bengali (cf. Zbavitel 1968: 38) and was the theme of one of the plays that was instrumental in provoking the Dramatic Performances Act of 1876.

[32] For details of the transactions in Baroda see Brajratnadas' introduction to his edition of Harishchandra's plays (*Bharatendu natakakavali, Dvitiya bhag* 1957: 13–20).

[33] One of the functions of *Selections from the Native Newspapers* was to register the shifts in public opinion, the attitudes towards particular government measures and the tensions within. Accordingly, the report on the bhana, while summing up the contents at some length, noted the subtle and not-so-subtle critique of the high-handedness of the British in deposing the Gayakvar, as well as the Hindu–Muslim tensions which also came to light in the process. A remark made in passing regarding the unfairness of the Muslim-ruled Native States was given much prominence:

> But it is a matter of regret that the Government is not always on the alert in reference to all its subjects. It has turned a deaf ear to the complaints of Hindus resident in the Rampur State. The Muhammadans are inexorable in their high-handed dealings towards them. They cannot perform their religious worship. The blowing of the conch is under strict prohibition. At the same time it must be borne in mind that this injustice goes on in territory which was once under British administration, and regarding which firm stipulations are in force. But what can mere stipulations do? The policy of the Government takes its taint and colour from the character and turn of mind of the administrator of the time being.

Another dig at the Muslims at the end of the bhana was also given due prominence: 'Widow-marriage, to be sure, has come into fashion of late, but Malhar Rao was the first to start the custom of marrying women whose husbands are alive. Had he been a Musalman, he could make his marriage legal with Luchmi Bai [*sic*] after procuring her divorce from her husband; but as she was a Hindu, her husband asserted his rights in the civil courts.'

[34] When the Viceroy, Lord Northbrook, read a translation of the play *Chakardarpan* which performed the same service for tea planters, he wrote to Sir Richard Temple to look into the matter, who advised prompt action, since he himself had read of the performance of an objectionable play on the proceedings in Baroda under the title *Gayakvardarpan*. This play was indeed fearlessly libellous and depicted the whole episode as a British plot to dethrone the Maharaja. Temple, in any case, had found *Chakardarpan* most unjust, since he considered that the most amiable relations existed between the planters and workers. The text of the plays *Gayakvardpan* and *Chakardarpan* in translation, as well as documentation of the correspondence around the framing and promulgation of the Act, along with the response in the native newspapers as gleaned from the *Selections*, are to be found in Pandhe (1978).

[35] An extensive article from *Mookerjee's Magazine*, June 1876, by Prannath Pundit, recording the public response to the Act in great detail, has been reprinted in Ray (1974).

[36] Prannath Pundit (ibid.) quotes an article from *The Englishman* of 9 May 1876, which reported on the Lucknow and Kanpur meetings.

[37] In 1876 the Great National Theatre staged the farce *Gajadananda o yubraj*, a satirical reaction to the visit of the Prince of Wales. This, along with the two plays mentioned earlier, was banned. After this the Theatre staged no more forbidden farces and advertised simple (*sadharan*) performances. If in 1875, 46 per cent of dramas dealt with contemporary subjects with only 25 per cent treating mythological themes, in 1879 only 16 per cent treated contemporary subjects while 70 per cent of them occupied themselves with mythological themes. Extensive documentation is available in Zbavitel (1968).

[38] The legends of the Raja were related in English by Elliot (1869: vol. 1, 261–9). Cf. Satyendra (1976: 285–6).

[39] This is a scene reminiscent of the *bazar* poetry of Nazir Akbarabadi, who may have served as model here.

[40] See Rastogi (1986: 35) for details. B.V. Karanth, director of the National School of Drama, noted for his experiments in adapting traditional theatre forms for the urban stage, was to direct the play in 1979.

[41] Habib Tanvir's extremely popular play *Agra Bazar* (1955), based on the life and poetry of Nazir Akbarabadi, with some affiliation to nautanki and

folk theatre in general, contains scenes which bear uncanny resemblance to the play, though Tanvir almost certainly did not know *Andher nagari*. See the essay on Tanvir Ch. 6 in this volume.

[42] The text of *Nildevi* is available in *Granthavali 1* (99–129).

[43] The *Devimahatmyam* (popularly known as the *Durgashaptasati*) is contained within the *Markandeya*, one of the early Sanskrit Puranas. It is one of the first Sanskrit texts to provide an articulation of the ultimate reality of the universe as feminine, and was probably composed in or around the Narmada river valley in the fifth or sixth century CE. For further information on the text, see Coburn (1985).

The lines cited by Harishchandra can be located in Ch. 3, verse 38; Ch. 8, verse 26; Ch. 9, verse 55, and Ch. 11, verse 6 of the Gita Press, Gorakhpur 1957 edition of the *Durgashaptasati*.

[44] Though the reputation of Edwin Arnold (1832–1904) has sunk in the last century (he is now regarded as a minor Victorian poet), in his own day, he was a widely read poet of a stature close to that of Tennyson. He had been principal of Deccan College (1857–60), where he played a leading role in the Anglicization of the curriculum. However, he took some pains to learn Marathi and Sanskrit. From 1860 to 1878 he was feature writer and editor of *Daily Telegraph*. The newspaper financed well-publicized expeditions by recognized scholars and explorers to many parts of the world. It is safe to assume that Arnold was well known in India and a recognized authority on historical and cultural matters, since his Indian connection was well established. He had translated the *Gita Govinda* and published it under the title *The Indian Song of Songs* in 1870. His verse biography of the Buddha, *The Light of Asia* (1879) had undergone several reprints in quick succession; it was even more widely known in the USA than in England. It was a household classic for over thirty years and was translated into five languages. The *Song Celestial*, his popular translation of the Bhagavad Gita, appeared in 1885. For further details of Arnold's career, see Wright (1956).

[45] See Sreenivasan (2002) for the significance of the Rajput theme in late nineteenth-century print literature, particularly in Bengali.

[46] Arnold (1882). Structurally, Arnold's ballad is a poem within a poem. There is a narrator, who is introduced at the beginning of the poem thus:

Sing something, Jymul Rao! For the goats are gathered now;
And no more water is to bring.... (325)

Harishchandra, intent upon scenic division, chooses to ignore the device of the narrator and bridges the time gap and the rapid change of scene by making it part of the structural division.

[47] See my essay (1992b) for a discussion of sati as a religious rite and the voluntary and involuntary nature of the deed as part of the validating process.

[48] Nikhat Kazmi (1990) has remarked on the potency of this Act through the twentieth century. Presently there is a Stage Performances Scrutiny Board in each state. According to www.indialawinfo.com, about the Dramatic Performances Act, 'This Act has been repealed in its application to Madras, to Andhra Pradesh, to Madhya Pradesh and to Andaman and Nicobar Islands by various State enactments and regulations. This Act has been repealed in the Union Territory of Delhi by Notification No. G.S.R. 850, dated 6 June 1964. The Act has been amended in Punjab by Punjab Act No. 48 of 1956.' I am indebted to Dhananjay Kapse for this information.

[49] The point De makes deserves extensive citation: 'The subjects of British India, even the urban intelligentsia, should not in the interests of precision, be called "elites". *Vis-à-vis* the poor or the petty bourgeois, some members of the more cultivated urban intelligentsia might have harboured a mentality which is called elitist in the simplistic sense of the term. But *vis-à-vis* the British *Herrenvolk*, they felt racially inferior or counterdependent, were discriminated against, even when possessed of equal talents for advancements in careers in official service, and faced metropolitan commercial protection when they sought to build up their fortunes in production or mercantile activity...they could not gain hegemony over the forms of production or government. To borrow a term from Antonio Gramsci, they could not be an "organic intelligentsia".... A dependent sub-elite could never take the "hegemonic" leadership of nationalism in a way which could lead to the War of Independence or to a Revolution. Elitism is a term which does not fit the nineteenth century trends of social and economic development in India.' (1977: 211)

[50] Of assessments in English of Harishchandra's dramatic works, mention must be made of King (1989), who offers a general survey, his analysis concentrating on the nationalist aspects of the works and the Hindu–Muslim polarization to be found in them. A detailed consideration of Hansen's essay (1990), where Harishchandra's theatre is seen as an elite ideological construct, conceived of primarily in opposition to the popular and folk forms of the day, is not possible within the limits of the present essay. Some important

points, however, do need to be raised. First, that Harishchandra while developing
the Orientalist conception of the national theatre of the Hindus, formulates
his programme over the years as counterpoint and counterweight to the
notion and practice of Western classical theatre and as a corrective to the
practices of the ruling colonial elite and indigenous elite. Though this theatre
does originate in the privacy of the reception halls of the affluent, it seeks
wider audience, and though it does seek to distance itself from the cruder
varieties of contemporary theatre practice, in the interest of making theatre
respectable, Harishchandra's programme is not formulated, in spite of occasional
polemics, against popular and folk theatre, nor does it have the effect of widening
a gulf, which as yet hardly exists, between elite and popular, as Kumar in her
study (1988) has demonstrated at some length. Harishchandra seeks to make
the elite popular, and it is in this that he does not ultimately succeed. Second,
a point also worth considering is the effect of the structure of folk and popular
Parsi theatre as a whole, which does not only subvert the given social order,
the 'inversions' and 'the debunking of authority' that Hansen refers to (1990:
73, 77), but which in the final run restores that very order, and though it
admittedly articulates the possibility of subversion, ultimately the subversions
are contained within it. In so far, the social critique can never become threatening
to possible addressees. Finally, the puritanism that Hansen refers to, which
she takes to be one of the reasons for the ultimate failure of Harishchandra's
theatre, makes only a sporadic appearance. At this stage, the puritanism of
the Arya Samaj was not a decisive factor, and Harishchandra himself was no
supporter of Dayanand Saraswati, as his writings repeatedly testify.

[51] See Hansen (1993) for a survey of nautanki theatre.

References

Agraval, Saroj. 1962. *Prabodhachandrodaya aur uski hindi parampara.*
    Allahabad: Hindi Sahitya Sammelan.

Arnold, Edwin. 1882. *The Poems of Edwin Arnold, containing The Light of
    Asia; Pearls of the Faith, or Islam's Rosary; and The Indian Song of Songs, to
    which is Added Indian Poetry: from the Sanskrit of the Gita Govinda of
    Jayadeva; Two Books from the 'Iliad of India' (Mahabharata); 'Proverbial
    Wisdom' from the Shlokas of the Hitopadesha, and Other Oriental Poems.*
    New York: Hurst and Company.

Bate, Jonathan. 1989. *Shakespeare and the English Romantic Imagination*. Oxford: Clarendon Paperbacks.

Bauer, Roger and Jürgen Werthheimer (eds.) 1983. *Das Ende des Stegreifspiels. Die Geburt des Nationaltheaters. Ein Wendepunkt in der Geschichte des Europäischen Dramas*. München: Wilhelm Fink.

Blackburn, Stuart and Vasudha Dalmia (eds.) 2003. *India's Literary History: Essays on the Nineteenth Century*. Delhi: Permanent Black.

Brajratnadas (ed.) 1967. *Bharatendu-natakavali. Dvitiya bhag*. Allahabad: Ramnarayan Lal. 2nd ed.

Chandra, Bipan. 1966. *The Rise and Growth of Economic Nationalism in India: Economic Policies of Indian National Leadership, 1880–1905*. Delhi: People's Publishing House. 2nd reprint. 1969.

Coburn, Thomas B. 1985. *Devi Mahatmya: The Crystallization of the Goddess Tradition*. Delhi and Columbia, MO: Motilal Banarasidass and South Asia Books.

Dalmia, Vasudha. 1997. *The Nationalization of Hindu Traditions: Bharatendu Harischandra and Nineteenth Century Banaras*. Delhi: Oxford University Press.

———. 2003. 'Genre Questions: Bharatendu Harishchandra and Women's Issues', in *India's Literary History: Essays on the Nineteenth Century*, Blackburn and Dalmia (eds.). Delhi: Permanent Black, 402–34.

Dalmia-Lüderitz, Vasudha. 1992a. 'Harishchandra of Banaras and the reassessment of Vaishnava bhakti in the late nineteenth century', in *Devotional Literature in South Asia: Current Research, 1985–1988*, R. S. McGregor (ed.). Cambridge: Cambridge University Press, 281–97.

———. 1992b. '"Sati" as a Religious Rite. Parliamentary Papers on Widow Immolation, 1821–30', in *Economic and Political Weekly*, January 1992, 58–64. Reprinted in *Orienting India: European Knowledge Formation in the Eighteenth and Nineteenth Centuries*. V. Dalmia, 2003. Delhi: Three Essays.

Das Gupta, Sibani (ed.) 1962. *The Chanda-kaushika of Arya Kshemisvara*. With Introduction, full Critical Apparatus of Manuscripts, English Translation & Indices. Calcutta: The Asiatic Society.

De, Barun. 1977. 'A Historiographical Critique of the Renaissance Analogues for Nineteenth Century India', in *Perspectives in the Social Sciences*, Volume 1. Calcutta: Oxford University Press, 178–218.

Durgashaptasati. 1957. Gorakhpur: Gita Press.

Eagleton, Terry. [1984] 1987. *The Function of Criticism: From the Spectator to Post-Structuralism*. London: Verso.

Elliot, Henry M. 1869. *Memoirs on the History, Folk-lore, and Distribution of the Races of the North Western Provinces of India*. Edited, Revised and Re-arranged by John Beames. 2 Volumes. London: Trübner & Co.

Emigh, John, and Ulrike. 1986. 'Hajari Bhand of Rajasthan', *Drama Review* 30. 1 (Spring): 101–30.

Guha, Ranajit. 1988. *An Indian Historiography of India: A Nineteenth Century Agenda and its Implications*. S.G. Deuskar Lectures on Indian History, 1987. Calcutta: Centre for Studies in Social Sciences.

Hansen, Kathryn G. 1989. 'The Birth of Hindi Drama in Banaras, 1868–1885', in *Culture and Power in Banaras: Community, Performance and Environment, 1800–1980*, Sandria B. Freitag (ed.). Delhi: Oxford University Press, 62–92.

_____. 1993. *Grounds for play: the Nautanki theatre of North India*. New Delhi: Manohar.

_____. 1998. 'The Migration of a Text: The *Indar Sabha* in Print and Performance', *Sangeet Natak*, 127–8, 3–34.

_____. 2003. 'Language, Community and Theatre Public: Linguistic Pluralism and Change in Nineteenth-Century Parsi Theatre', in *India's Literary History*, Blackburn and Dalmia (eds.). 60–86.

Harishchandra. 1954–1970. *Bharatendu Granthavali*. [Collected works in 3 Volumes] *Volume 1: Natak* (cited as *Granthavali 1*), Shivaprasad Mishra (ed.). Varanasi: Nagaripracharini Sabha. 2nd ed. 1975. *Volume 3: Prose Works* (cited as *Granthavali 3*), Brajratnadas (ed.), 1954. Varanasi: Nagari Pracharini Sabha.

_____. *Bharatendu natakavali*. 1936. *Pratham bhag*, Brajratnadas (ed.). Allahabad: Ramnarayanlal.

_____. *Bharatendu natakavali*. 1957. *Dvitiya bhag*, Brajratnadas (ed.). 2nd ed. Allahabad: Ramnarayanlal.

Indian Literature, Special Issue on Shakespeare in India, 8.1.1964.

Jones, William. 1979. *The Works of William Jones. With the Life of the Author by Lord Teignmouth. In Thirteen Volumes*. Volume IX. Reprint. Delhi: Agam Prakashan.

Kapur, Anuradha. 1995. 'The Representation of Gods and Heroes in Early Twentieth Century Drama', in *Representing Hinduism*, Vasudha Dalmia and H. von Stietencron (eds.). Delhi: Sage Publications, 401–19.

_____. 2003. 'Impersonation, Narration, Desire and the Parsi Theatre', in *India's Literary History*, Blackburn and Dalmia (eds.). 87–118.

Kaviraj, Sudipta. 1995. *Unhappy Consciousness: Bankimchandra Chattopadhyay and the Formation of Nationalist Discourse in India*. Delhi: Oxford University Press.

Kazmi, Nikhat. 1990. 'Obsolete theatre act stops the action'. *Times of India*, 15 April, 12.

King, Christopher R. 1989. 'Hindu Nationalism in the 19th Century U. P. and the Dramas of Bharatendu Harishcandra', in *Boeings and Bullock Carts*, Dhirendra Vajpeyi (ed.). Leiden: E. J. Brill, 179–93.

Kumar, Nita. 1988. *The Artisans of Banaras: Popular Culture and Identity, 1880–1986*. Princeton: Princeton University Press.

Mishra, Jagdish Prasad. 1970. *Shakespeare's Impact on Hindi Literature*. Delhi: Munshiram Manoharlal.

Mittra, Kissory Chand. 1873. 'The Modern Hindu Drama', *The Calcutta Review*, Vol. LVII, 245–73.

Nambiar, Sita Krishna (ed.) 1971. *Prabodhachandrodaya of Krishnamishra*. Sanskrit Text with English Translation, a Critical Introduction and Index. Delhi: Motilal Banarasidass.

Naoroji, Dadabhai. 1901. *Poverty and Un-British Rule in India*. London: Swan Sonnenschein & Co.

Orsini, Francesca. 2002. *The Hindi Public Sphere 1920–1940: Language and Literature in the Age of Nationalism*. Delhi: Oxford University Press.

Pandhe, Pramila (ed.) 1978. *Suppression of Drama in Nineteenth Century India*. Calcutta: Indian Book Exchange.

Paul, Suneeta and Nissar Allana. 1989. *A Tribute to Shakespeare*. Delhi: Theatre and Television Associates.

Pundit, Prannath. 1974. 'The Dramatic Performances Bill'. See Ray 1974: 200–245.

Rastogi, Girish (ed.) 1986. *Andher nagari caupatt raja*. Delhi and Patna: Rajkamal Paperbacks.

Ray, Alok (ed.) 1974. *Nineteenth Century Studies*. Calcutta: Bibliographical Research Centre.

Robertson, William. 1804. *An Historical Disquisition concerning The Knowledge which the Ancients had of India; and the Progress of Trade with that Country prior to the Discovery of the Passage to it by the Cape of Good Hope*. London: T. Cadwell and W. Davies, Edinburgh: E. Balfour. Fourth ed.

Said, Edward W. 1975. *Beginnings, Intention and Method*. New York: Basic Books.

Satyendra. 1976. 'Bharatendu ke natak', *Bharatiya natya sahitya*, Nagendra (ed.). Delhi: S. Chand & Co., 264–90.

Shivaprasad Singh. 1866. *Itihas timirnashak. A History of India in Three Parts*. Allahabad: Government Press. Sixth ed. 1891.

Singh, Dhirendranath (ed.) [1876] 1969. *Janakimangal natak* by Shitalaprasad Tripathi. Kashi: Nagari Pracharini Sabha.

Sinha, Satyavrat. 1969. '"Andher nagari" ki prastuti: nirdeshak ki dristi mem', in *Adhunik hindi natak aur rangmanch*, Nemichandra Jain (ed.). Delhi: Macmillan 1978, 88–91.

Sreenivasan, Ramya. 2002. 'Gender, Literature, History: The Transformation of the Padmini Story'. PhD thesis, Jawaharlal Nehru University.

Sudhir Chandra. 1984. 'Literature and the Colonial Connection', in *Social Transformation and the Creative Imagination*, Sudhir Chandra (ed.). Delhi: Allied Publishers. 145–99.

Vickers, Brian. 1981. 'The Emergence of Character Criticism, 1774–1800', in *Shakespeare Survey* 34, Cambridge: Cambridge University Press.

Viswanathan, Gauri. 1989. *Masks of Conquest: Literary Study and British Rule in India*. London: Faber & Faber.

Wilson, Horace Hayman. 1835. *Select Specimens of the Theatre of the Hindus*. Translated from the Original Sanskrit. 2 Volumes. London: Parbury, Allen, and Co.

Wright, Brooks. 1956. *Interpreter of Buddhism to the West: Sir Edwin Arnold*. New York: Bookman Associates.

Yagnik, R.K. 1933. *The Indian Theatre: Its Origins and its Later Developments under European Influence. With Special Reference to Western India*. London: George Allen & Unwin.

Zbavitel, Dusan. 1968. 'The Beginnings of the Modern Bengali Drama, 1852–1880', in *Archiv Orientální* 36: 29–66.

Twentieth-Century Projections of the Past
Jayshankar Prasad and the New Subjectivity

After Bharatendu Harishchandra, there was a period of indifferent production for the self-consciously literary Hindi theatre he had set out to create, though Parsi theatre flourished and expanded, irrespective of the derision reserved for it in literary circles. Literary envy in this period was reserved for Bengal instead, where theatre activity continued unabated, providing a forum for the historical-romantic plays of Girishchandra Ghosh (1844–1911) and Dwijendralal Ray (1863–1913) which attracted large audiences in the theatres of Calcutta.[1] Clearly, theatre with literary claims, given sufficiently acclimatized urban audiences, could be a commercially viable proposition.

Though these audiences continued to elude Hindi dramatists, with Jayshankar Prasad of Banaras (1886–1937), literary drama in Hindi acquired a new maturity and sophistication. Many threads connected him to Harishchandra, though he was not as flamboyant a personality. Prasad also stemmed from the merchant aristocracy of the city, which had provided patronage for the arts for well over a century and made for the reputation of the city as a cultural centre. Born into a well-known family of wealthy snuff and tobacco merchants, Prasad was initially educated at home, where he was taught Sanskrit, Persian, Hindi, and Urdu. He was enrolled in the prestigious Queen's College at the age of ten, to stay there for the brief span of two years; his formal education terminated abruptly with the death of his father. In spite of the financial hardship which followed, alongside the commercial activity called for by the snuff and tobacco business of which he now became involuntary head, and undeterred by the lack of a formal education, Prasad managed to lead the life of a scholar and cultivated man about town. He acquired knowledge of a wide range of Sanskrit texts, aesthetic, literary, religious, juridical, and commentarial, and though to all outward appearance, he remained bound to tradition, he evolved his own strategies to read modernist views into the past. His intellectual spirit of adventure was reflected also in the eccleticism of the sources that he drew upon for his literary and critical writings. He came from a family of Shaivites and he retained his devotion to Shiva, but he also developed a great sympathy for Buddhism, which opened avenues for quite another estimation of ancient India. But his knowledge was not confined to books alone. He was also a connoisseur of the arts. He had a deep love of music, the classical and the semi-classical for which Banaras was renowned; he was a regular patron of the celebrated courtesans of the city; he was known to have had a close relationship with Siddheshwari Devi, later known all over India for her rendition of *thumri*s. If his relationship to women could be seen as firmly bound by the patriarchal mould in which he was cast, in his literary work, he could also plead fiercely for the rights of women within the very traditional frame that he elected. He was a modernist who deliberately donned the mantle of tradition, a mantle which could both provide protective cover for the introduction of the new but which could also muffle it.

Prasad early acquired a reputation for innovation in the world of Hindi letters, still largely based in Banaras in the first decades of the twentieth century. He was known as a short story-writer and dramatist, but his enduring reputation was to be founded in his poetry. Though he wrote in chaste, Sanskritized Hindi, it was a language supple enough to express a tender lyricism when he was at his best; he was clearly coining a new poetic diction in Hindi. He came to occupy a position in the forefront of Chhayavad, the new romantic movement in modern Hindi poetry.

Prasad had grown up in an era that his group of young poets was later to reject vehemently: the so-called Dvivedi period, which spanned roughly the first two decades of the twentieth century. Named after Mahavir Prasad Dvivedi (1864–1938), the influential editor of the journal *Saraswati*, it was an age, as periodized in literary histories, which was concerned primarily with creating standardized Hindi prose and with creating a vocabulary large enough to contain and encourage scholarly enterprise in all manner of humanistic and scientific disciplines. The poetry of the period was nationalistic in tone and devoid of the kind of sensuality and eroticism considered characteristic of Brajbhasha poetry of the so-called *riti kal*, or manneristic age. Dvivedi's regime was regarded as puritanical by the generation that followed him. The radical new movement which gained a foothold in poetry from the mid-1920s onwards came to be known as Chhayavad: *chhaya* is reflection or shadow, *vad* is -ism. The very different poets who came to be associated with the movement had certain features in common: a romantic individualism, a new relationship with nature, and a subjective selection and understanding of natural phenomena, often seen as reflecting their own emotional experience.[2] Romantic love acquired an all-pervasive character, being equated in Prasad's own poetry with *jijivisha*, the will to life (Singh 1955: 50). Most importantly, this poetry created another space for women, who had figured till then as objects of desire: a new freedom for the articulation of emotion now became possible and a new dignity in the bearing of women towards men (Singh 1955: 52). Prasad would later be considered the senior member of the quartet which was to be recognized as representing the movement's most lasting achievements.[3]

Prasad wrote poetry from 1918 on; the collection of poems contained in the volume titled *Ansu* (Tears, 1925), a poignant lament over the loss of love, first established him as a poet of standing. There was much speculation about the personal experience which presumably lay behind such emotionally moving poems. But there was also widespread consensus that for the first time in Hindi poetry there entered a new intimacy of tone that was also reflected in his prose works and plays. Prasad's activities as a poet and as a dramatist were to remain inextricably intertwined: when his *dramatis personae* begin to reflect on their personal predicaments and their emotional state, they break into poetic prose, sometimes even into song, which makes use of the very sensibility, the very vocabulary he has evolved in his poems. The lyrics that intersperse his many plays are regarded as some of his finest.

In the following, I shall delineate briefly the concepts which underpinned Prasad's understanding of Chhayavad in poetry, they are important for understanding the poetic and historical sensibilities that Prasad carried into drama. I shall then focus upon the aesthetics of the Hindi theatre he projected and his assessment of modern Hindi drama and stage in its evolution since Bharatendu Harishchandra. I shall end with a discussion of *Dhruvasvamini* (1933) considered his most compact and mature drama, in order to evaluate it in the light of the dramaturgical principles he had set up.

New Interpretation of Traditional Aesthetics: Chhayavad and Hindi Dramaturgy

Prasad was to understand Chhayavad as setting forth the fine ideals that had once been available in Sanskrit literature. They had subsequently suffered a decline, become more crass and externalized in expression as in the Puranic corpus, but they had remained a resource to which the new poets of the 1920s could turn in their search for the terminology of feeling:

When in the field of poetry, as different from the external depiction of some incidence or of some beautiful woman, which was prevalent in the Puranic age, the self perception based on creative experience began to find expression, then in Hindi it was called Chhayavad.... These new emotions were shot through with the ecstasy of inner contact. Subtle, interior emotions appear bizarre once they assumed tangible external form. The verbal configurations current [in Hindi] did not suffice in order to express these fine interior forms; a new style, a new syntax had to be found for that. [It was then that] a new terminology came into currency for the description of interior desire in Hindi. (Prasad 2000: 80)[4]

The new expressions to represent these fine shades of emotion, culled then in the main from Sanskrit, were little understood in Hindi initially, but words, in Prasad's view, possessed the power to produce new meaning when used in new contexts and eventually Hindi poetry found it possible to carry and mediate subtle, interior emotions with such Sanskritic terminology. It is true that people were initially somewhat surprised when this literature first emerged in Hindi; ultimately they had no option but to accept it (80). Thus it came about that individual experience as inhering in internal mental and emotional states found a new vocabulary to express a new subjectivity and sensuality. The characters in Prasad's plays also used this new vocabulary of the interior in moments of great emotional intensity, both in introspection and in communicating with each other, particularly in matters of romantic love, which acquired an existential dimension as never before.

Perhaps surprisingly, considering the new subjective direction of this movement, Prasad saw Chhayavad as standing in polar opposition to the Yatharthavad or realism, current in the 1930s: 'There are two primary trends in the present age of Hindi, they are known as Yatharthavad (realism) and Chhayavad (reflection-ism) respectively' (75). He saw the genesis of this realism in the unfortunate history of the country: the political frustrations of colonial India and the disappointment in the deportment of the princes and the contemporary religious leadership of the country. Thus it came about that the suffering of the common man, the mundane trivialization of private experience, gained new prominence: 'The literature which touched the humanity suffused with this pervasive pain became realist. This realism is abundantly endowed with the sense of lack, decline, and suffering' (76). This realist literature dwelt on pain to the exclusion of all other mental states and it explored the various facets of suffering from innumerable perspectives and with an assortment of refined psychological tools developed specifically for the purpose. But there were differences of opinion on the ultimate worth of this enterprise:

There is some difference of opinion about the selection of matter for drama in the present age. The trend of presenting the narrative matter from innumerable perspectives has gathered force. Some people have begun to give more weight to characterization than to the ancient *rasa* theories. The group which is curious about the various mental operations of human beings has gone yet farther; it places great faith in individuation of character. (53)

This individuation of character, *charitra vaichitrya*, led to isolation from the rest of society, which was then held responsible for that particular individual's ills. Further, in so stressing individuation of character, this group of writers focused particularly on the frustrations of the man–woman relationship, viewed within the narrow confines of personal, physical fulfilment. Prasad vehemently resisted this reductivist trend, which would see woman only in her sexual relationship to man and all that obstructed this relationship as caused by hostile societal obstructions, which could in their turn be analysed with great subtlety. This tendency, of holding societal forces responsible for casting barriers in the way of the individual woman or man in his or her particular relationship to the other, had led to the exclusive focus on the petty and the mundane in Hindi literature, particularly in drama: a spate of one-act plays written for radio broadcast followed this trend tenaciously.

Prasad rejected this new brand of Yatharthavad, which he saw as clearly Western in origin and which, according to him, had been introduced in Hindi with the plays of Bharatendu Harishchandra. This realism was pessimistic in the extreme, and fatalistic in outlook. It concerned itself with *laghuta*, petty traits of character, and it exhausted itself in offering psychological justification for individual shortcomings and morally inferior natures, so that these could no longer be considered despicable but were viewed rather as objects of pity. 'By laghuta I mean the actual account of the pain and lack that is experienced in individual lives, that which lies outside the principles recognized by literature; principles which ask for depictions of greatness as moulded by the [poetic] imagination' (75).

This was the main problem with the newly popular realist theatre of Ibsen. 'It says secretly that we should not despise those who make mistakes, we should sympathize with them, and this is used to affirm individuation of character' (68). For Prasad, the characterization of particular individuals in this sense had far-reaching consequences—the sequence *vasana*, desire, leading to *kriti*, deed action, leading in its turn to *vyakti charitra* or individuation of character inevitably culminated in *samgharsha*, conflict.

As against this trivializing, pessimistic turn in theatre, which he saw as a vapid imitation of the West, Prasad sought to establish an Indian point of view in literary and dramatic criticism, which could cope with an Indian system of values, aesthetic as well as literary. For the creation of *rasa*, as seen by classical Indian aesthetics, the *manovritti* or mental states which exist in *vasana* or desire were generalized and created *ananda*, bliss, thus serving as a corrective for individual desire (55). The divisive tendency, which regarded conflict and struggle as intrinsic to human nature, was clearly borrowed from the West. He saw the Indian viewpoint as consisting in regarding the reality of a given person and his individuation as a medium for creating rasa, not as its goal (54). Literature was to depict historical reality, *yathartha*, but also ideality *adarsha*, for, as he pointed out, 'Yatharthavad is not only of the petty, it is also of the great' (77). There needed to be no split between reality and ideality: if the realist alone claimed to represent history, there were others who insisted that literature represent only the ideal. However, for Prasad, 'the littérateur is neither a historian nor a promulgator of social codes. The tasks of these last two are separate. Literature tries to fill the deficiencies of both. While showing the real state of the times, literature also tries to bring it in harmony with idealism' (77). Literature was not related to *vishleshan*, analysis, *vikalpa*, differentiation, or *vijnan*, systematized knowledge. The poet was a *rishi*, a seer, as in Vedic times, whose efforts were to combine both *shreya* and *preya*, be conducive to betterment and be pleasurable at the same time. Indian classical drama fulfilled these requirements most completely; *sadharanikarana*, generalization, lead to ananda, bliss, the transcendent joy experienced while partaking in the aesthetic experience of rasa. In classical drama there was a place reserved for *laghutama*, the most ordinary, but it also sought to create ideals: greatness could only be depicted through the great. Here sorrow did not provoke *nirasha*, hopelessness, but *daya*, kindness, and *sahanubhuti*, compassion (71). In the *abheda*, undivided, *nirvikara*, imperturbed, enjoyment of these and other emotional states, all three, the poet, the player, and the spectator, could partake of rasa (53) where philosophy and literature coalesced (51).

Prasad had similar reservations about the so-called natural and simple language to be used by the characters on stage. Simple or more difficult speech could naturally be awarded according to character, but not so that it resulted in a babble of tongues: he saw the unity of language destroyed by the use of idiolects and dialects: 'It is a major error to consider that drama should be written for a [given] stage. The effort should be to see that there is a usable theatre for drama' (69).

This was Prasad's central creed: the times had to be changed by forward-looking, model-building drama which radiated optimism; drama did not need to change in accordance with the fast-changing fads of the times.

Prasad did not, however, content himself just with counterposing a classical theory against the newly imbibed realism from the West. In thus classicizing, he was seeking to establish a link with that part of tradition with which his own position was to be in continuum but with modification (which he did not always specify). It was to provide the classificatory terminology he needed but set in a new context, which he derived from nationalist history and which he filled with the subjectivity of Chhayavad. He thus posited that the poet's *anubhuti*, creative experience, found its fullest expression in the depiction of *sukshma antarbhav*, subtle internal states. He did not explicitly establish an equivalence of these with the *sthayi bhava* or emotional states of Indian aesthetics, but apparently left them to the arbitrary definition of the individual poet, who would find images, *rupaka*, corresponding to the emotional states which led to the experience of rasa. He did not offer any explicit conceptual framework regarding the nature of the relationship of the poet's experience to the external world.[5] The insistence was on *atmanubhuti*, the creative experience of the self as being the soul of poetry, the models invoked were venerable older poets such as Surdas or Tulsidas: 'Where self-perception or experience is primary, only there will expression find its completion in a given field, only there will a given poetic corpus conjoined with skill or a specific verbal composition achieve beauty' (Prasad 2000: 30). Thus, in spite of Prasad's polemical rejection of individuation, the way was opened for subjectivity, both of the dramatist and of the characters he created in drama.

PRASAD'S PERSPECTIVE ON THE EVOLUTION OF THE MODERN HINDI STAGE

Prasad was not attached to any stage nor was there any substantial movement in urban theatre in north India, professional or amateur, of any literary aspirations, which he could find himself ready to acknowledge. The only theatre that continued to flourish through the

1920s and into the 1930s was the commercial Parsi theatre, which he rejected outright for its vulgar indulgence in sensation. However, as we shall see in the following discussion, dramaturgically, he remained largely bound to this very Parsi theatre when it came to imagining the visual frame of his plays. Since he could never descend to being actually connected with the Parsis, his plays were in effect written to be read rather than to be performed. He had demanded, as we have seen, that theatre accommodate itself to drama and not that drama be asked to adjust itself to the limitations of the existent stage.

At the end of his life, Prasad was to set out his views on theatre in Hindi in the essay '*Rangmanch*', theatre, written in 1936.[6] Though he was concerned with setting up an expressly Indian frame for the theatre he wished to bring into existence, he cited as model the practice of according space to multiple traditions, old and new, in Western theatre; he paid special tribute to the efforts made by Victorian actor-directors such as Charles Kean to undertake historical research in order to produce historically authentic plays, most of all Shakespeare.[7] He also paid some grudging respect to the earnest and grave theatre of Ibsen, which he understood to be realist at its root and thus of the kind that he most despised and discouraged. However, even this theatre contributed to the multi-dimensionality of the Western stage, which had always seen fit to reserve adequate space for tradition (Prasad 2000: 66). He has great admiration for the Bengali stage, which, as he saw it, always made tasteful use of the Western modes it had adapted for its purposes; most of all, it kept its scenic devices simple. Prasad strongly condemned the commercial Parsi stage of the subcontinent, which he saw as taking over Western technical innovations without having first reflected upon their use.

But the Parsi stage has never sought to put a stop to its dreadful (*bhayanak*) ways. Primarily, it piles scene upon scene and situation upon situation. However slack the subject matter, behind a given drop-scene, there is bound to be another sensational drop-scene—if nothing else, any stray, uncouth, hired hand will do the trick. (67)

Interestingly, Prasad did concede that the Parsi stage had possessed the potential of being further developed by Hindi dramatists of stature.

But it had the misfortune of being overtaken by talking pictures or films. The scene was dismal now: 'Hindi has no stage of its own. Just when it had the opportunity of evolving, there came into being the talking film with its cheap sentimentality, as a result of which the acting stage more or less went out of existence' (67). But cheap or not, the talkies did have one advantage, they allowed female acting, which had not been possible for the Parsi stage in its beginnings. At present, the greatest problem for the respectable Hindi stage was the lack of female participation. There was also little incentive to write. Every once in a while, at one annual function or another, when an amateur theatre group wanted to mount a production, the cry went up: why are there no plays in Hindi?

It is easy to find fault, no one has the courage to understand that there exists no stage. It is difficult to make the effort that Kean had once made. We indulge in the farce of following the trends of the times, we want to see realist plays performed in Hindi, we do not see that in the West, there are still efforts being made to bring ancient plays to life. To make spoken drama of historical plays, tons of makeup is applied to each actor who plays a historical part in such a way that he appears authentic. Overwhelmed by our own unrealized claim to contemporaneity, the ghost of Ibsen is conjured up to fill the gaps of realism. The West has tried to award space to all its concerns by trying to look farther back, beyond a large stretch of time. How will we evolve in the same sequential way, if we can look just at the West's 'today'?... The future is made by keeping the past and present in sight, we should not have one-dimensional aims in literature.... The West has also not found the new by taking leave of all else that it [once] possessed. (68)

The only playwright in Hindi Prasad acknowledged as worthy of note was Bharatendu Harishchandra, references to whose works are scattered through his essays, though his relationship to Harishchandra's dramaturgy remains, at best, ambivalent. He has strong reservations regarding Harishchandra's rasa theories, Gaudiya Vaishnava in origin. The Bhakti aesthetics of the Gaudiyas, stemming largely from Bengal and evolving their devotional aesthetics through the sixteenth century, and following them the Vaishnavas of Vallabhite provenance, awarded primacy to the rasa obtained in *dasya*, *sakhya*, and *vatsalya*, service, friendship, and parental love, rather than the old *hasya, karuna, vibbhatsa,* etc. (comic, pathetic, odious). Thus it came about that the new plays written in Hindi, as for example Harishchandra's highly emotional Vaishnava bhakti play *Chandravali,* were somewhat monotonous in mood,[8] as also the *shravya kavya* or plays meant to be read aloud, which were written first in Hindi. 'This flood [of plays] came in a rush but it did not possess the comprehensiveness of rasa. It remained somewhat mono-dimensional, both in principle and in actual practice' (Prasad 2000: 51). Prasad also has some doubts regarding the value of Harishchandra's brand of realism that essentially opened the way for the use to which it was being put today:

In the period of the resurgence of Hindi, Harishchandra once again reinstalled the significance of the rasa *anubhuti,* creative experience, of ancient drama and used suffering and contentment in the literary stream in a new way.... Harishchandra also depicted the realist aspect of life along with national suffering. *Premyogini* is the first effort of this kind in Hindi and I understand the poem '*Dekhi tumhari Kasi*', Have you seen your Kashi, as belonging in this category. Even if this order of representation was rather weak, the effort to express life [realistically] began in this period. [However] the form for expressing suffering realistically crystallized only gradually. (75)

But Prasad did express some grudging admiration for the variety and range of Harishchandra's experimentation and thus for the breadth of his theatre, which he would have liked to see followed in his own day:

It was while regarding the disarray of the stage of his time that Bharatendu had conjoined all these elements to create an independent Hindi theatre. There was the contribution of *Satya Harishchandra, Mudrarakshasha, Nildevi, Chandravali, Bharat-durdasha* and *Premyogini.* We should try to protect the independent consciousness of Hindi theatre in order to keep alive this tradition of Hindi theatre, so that the new Western trends do not become our only guides to the path we should follow. (68)

However, the model that most suited his own inclination was, as we have seen in the words of praise he reserved for it, the one evolved in modern Bengal. He was closely acquainted with the works of Bengali playwrights.[9] In the period from 1910 to 1933, Prasad wrote a total of thirteen plays. Just as Charles Kean, he undertook intensive forays into all possible sources for his plays, both Sanskrit texts and modern historical research. It is not surprising, then, that the themes of most of his plays were culled either from the Puranas or from ancient history; three were based on stories from the Puranas and as many as nine on the historical research he himself conducted.[10] This quest for history, for the socially progressive and politically powerful as located in it, was driven, and he cited the practice of the past as similarly motivated when taking recourse to the yet more ancient, by '*bal grahan karne ki pipasa*', the thirst for deriving strength from it, as he was to write in another context (Prasad 2000: 72). The results of his research and the use to which he put them were contained in long essays prefaced to his plays. As for the plays themselves, he tended to construct many-stranded plots with a variety of characters, though his chief protagonists were always of divine or noble origins. As a dramatist, then, he was thematically bound to a historical vision of the past that could be astonishingly progressive at times, given his multiple agendas, though the very fact that he needed to turn to the past, to what he defined as Indianness, could often defeat his own purpose and later lay his work open to misuse by would-be progressive conservatives.

FILLING THE GAPS IN HISTORY: *DHRUVASVAMINI*

Of Prasad's thirteen plays, the last, *Dhruvasvamini* (1933) is considered his most compact and mature composition.[11] It was written at the tail end of what is considered the most creative decade of his life, beginning in 1927 to last to the end of his life in 1937. In this relatively short span of time he was to produce his well-known poetry collections *Ansu* and *Lahar*, his epic poem *Kamayani*, the novels, *Kankal*, *Titli*, and *Iravati* (left incomplete), and his best-known plays, *Chandragupta*, *Skandagupta*, *Ek Ghunt*, and *Dhruvasvamini*.[12]

Dhruvasvamini is securely ensconced in the Hindi literary canon; it is part of the high school and university curriculum.[13] It has fewer characters than is usual for Prasad and the scenes do not shift with such rapidity from one location to another, as is the case with his earlier plays.[14] It has a very slender stage history. In his own time, Prasad's plays continued to wait for a stage that could provide the kind of space he sought. Later, the play seemed dated in its dramaturgy and in spite of its modernist thrust, too caught in its own contradictions to make for other than historical interest.[15]

As so often in his writing career, Prasad turns in this play to the Gupta period for his subject matter, a period long regarded as the golden period of ancient Indian history. The theme is the final Gupta conquest, under the leadership of Chandragupta, of the territories still controlled by the alien Shaka dynasty whose chief is merely designated Shakaraja. The event is located in a troubled and controversial spot in Gupta history: not only does Chandragupta come to power through fratricide, he marries his brother's beautiful wife Dhruvasvamini. The focus of the play is on the wife and her claim to life, love, remarriage, and political justice, and it is from her perspective that the struggle of the two men is viewed. The men in the play are, without exception, meaner in stature than she. As is Prasad's practice, the historical controversy surrounding the characters and the action in his play, the opposing views, the interpretation of Sanskrit sources, most of all of the law codes as enshrined in the older Dharmashastras and as pertaining to the practice of women's remarriage, are contained in a learned preface, which he entitles simply, *suchana*, information.

Prasad is concerned, on the one hand, with providing proof of the historicity of his material and, on the other, with the rights of women as sanctioned by Indian 'tradition', he focuses in particular on Dhruvasvamini's right to remarry, given that her husband, the Gupta emperor Ramagupta, is both cowardly and possibly impotent. To this end, Prasad quotes modern authorities, the well-known historians of ancient India—and it is worth noting that all of these scholars are Indian: Rakhaldas Bannerjee and Professors Altekar and Bhandarkar—but also takes direct recourse to Sanskrit sources: Kautilya's *Arthashastra* and the fragment of the Sanskrit play on the theme, *Devichandragupta* by Vishakhadatta, which had recently come to light. He does not invoke the authority of Western Indologists. His prime concern is to prove that the right of the woman to happiness and, as connected with this, her right to remarry, found codification in the oldest law books of the

Hindus; the proof of its practice he finds testified in history. He is of the firm opinion that the past was more generous in this regard than later practice would have us believe:

It is true that our manner of life and the practicability of the tradition found in the Dharmashastras have become severed from each other. We are quick to denounce as unIndian the reforms and the investigative experiments of social science we see performed in our own time, thinking them to be thoughtless and novel, but it is my belief that ancient Aryavarta had made investigative use of pretty much every societal tradition which has prevailed over a long span of time. These also led to changes which brought well being. Therefore it is not impossible that this [remarriage of women] happened fifteen hundred years ago. What ought to happen and how, these are matters upon which the legislators of conduct can reflect; however, this drama has been evolved on the basis provided by history from narrative material which actually occurred or could have. (Prasad [1933] 2001: ix)

True to the intent he spelt out so clearly in his essays, Prasad sets out to complement the work of the historian and the legislator, and to supplement the information available in history and in legal texts by literary intervention.[16] His play is based on history and on Kautilya's *Arthashastra*, but it takes an imaginative leap which makes it possible to cross the bounds of both. The evidence Prasad cites seems to prove beyond doubt that Dhruvasvamini was a historical personage, in all the beauty and vitality of her person, as was Ramagupta, whose cowardliness and meanness was the reason, according to Prasad, why history chose to erase him; it was willed amnesia. However, history provides no insight into the actual experience of their lives: thus, if they existed and if indeed Dhruvasvamini remarried, what was the nature of the relationship she, Ramagupta, and Chandragupta had with each other, and, even more importantly, what did Dhruvasvamini seek and find in the new relationship which was to lead to remarriage? This is the gap Prasad's play sets out to fill. In thus meshing historical 'fact' with a subjective quest for happiness, Prasad is making modernist moves which take him far beyond Harishchandra's early experiments with Orientalist narratives.

Dhruvasvamini has a relatively simple plot, contained in a single act divided into three long scenes. The narrative is linear and straightforward: the first scene is concerned with Dhruvasvamini wedded to and rejected by the heir of the Gupta empire, Ramagupta, who has acquired the throne by guile and who for reasons not clarified, though impotence is suggested, is at once attracted to and repelled by his consort. She is in love with Chandragupta, his brother and rightful heir, who is held in prison. Ramagupta is threatened by Shakaraja whom he, in a show of bravery, had once set out to defeat. This Shakaraja now demands Dhruvasvamini as ransom as well as the wives of other feudal lords. There is a perfidious plan to send Chandragupta who has beauty of person, disguised as Dhruvasvamini and accompanied by her, to Shakaraja, in the hope that this would lead to the annihilation of both. At the end of the scene, the victims of the plot are seen wending their way to what is considered their certain doom.

The second scene moves to the enemy camp. Here also there is a spirited maiden, Koma, who has been slighted in love by Shakaraja, who in his turn is attracted to Dhruvasvamini and has asked that she be sent to him. Shakaraja is a cowardly villain and with this request has managed to offend the clan guru Mihirdev, who has brought up Koma as his foster daughter. The guru predicts disaster, but is not able to prevail upon Shakaraja to change his mind. Chandragupta enters the scene disguised as Dhruvasvamini and defeats and kills Shakaraja in a fair duel.

The third scene opens again with Dhruvasvamini, alone and dejected, for she has no social standing as a rejected wife, even though the victory that has come about is largely due to her courage. Koma enters and asks for Shakaraja's body so that she can immolate herself with him. This wish is granted but both she and Mihirdev are murdered at the behest of Ramagupta who enters the fortress now. This heinous act causes a revolt amongst the feudal lords and, after some debate, Chandragupta, who till then had patiently waited, throws off his chains. Ramagupta is dethroned and by a special decree the marriage of Dhruvasvamini and Ramagupta is anulled, and she is free to marry Chandragupta, who is elected to the throne. At the last moment Ramagupta makes a desperate bid to stab Chandragupta in the back; he is discovered and killed. The play ends with the triumph of virtue.

Within this narrative of political intrigue and the transfer of power from one prince to the other, the real drama of the play takes place in the emotional lives of the two women who are at the centre of it, focusing more on Dhruvasvamini than on the equally vital Koma, who plays a secondary role in the life of her partner. Some space, however, is also reserved for the self-reflection, or the lack of it, of the men. The political activity is thus the frame for an interiority that seeks to ground itself and find fulfilment in romantic love, which thereby acquires new existential significance: the lavish backdrops are projections of these interior landscapes into nature, and are addressed as such by the protagonists. Not surprisingly, the expression of love remains essentially inward bound, finding expression in dejection and in solitude rather than in mutual affirmation or even in the consummation of love. Thus space is created for monologue, for self-introspection, as well as for some dialogue, even if this often borders on non-communication.

The three scenes focus on three important agendas, a feminist bid for independence, the exaltation of romantic love, and finally the challenge to constricting Brahminical orthodoxy, all three of which Prasad himself sabotages by the kind of closure he finally finds. In depicting and analysing the three scenes, I shall follow the plan the play itself suggests and focus upon the three agendas respectively.

FIERY FEMINISM: 'THERE IS RED BLOOD IN MY VEINS, THERE IS FIRE IN MY HEART'

All three scenes open with the presence of a solitary female character on stage and all three focus upon the emotions to which the woman concerned gives vent the moment she begins to speak. The wild beauty of the mountainous region which is the northern frontier of the Gupta empire forms the backdrop to the emotional intensity and violence felt—both received and returned—by the women in the play, who address nature as if it were as living and breathing as they or, as Prasad puts it, '*vishva sundari prakriti mem chetana ka arop*', the attribution of consciousness to universally beautiful nature (Prasad [1933] 2001: 44). The first lavish drop-scene depicts the mountain range, rampart-like, before which are pitched luxurious tents of cloth intricately embroidered with thick silk thread. Dhruvasvamini enters from one side of the tent and her first address is directed towards the mountains, whose phallic significance is unmistakable: 'Unrestrained mountain peak, straight and erect, piercing the skies in masterful hardness!' (1). Juxtaposed to this majesty is the impotence of Ramagupta and his entourage: 'Will one find no single evidence of intact humanity in this royal clan? Wherever one casts the eye, hunchbacks, dwarves, eunuchs, the dumb and the deaf' (2). If these characters are there to provide entertainment to the royal court, their deformity also stands for the slight stature, crooked nature, and physical impotence of Ramagupta. Once Dhruvasvamini finds out what fate Ramagupta plans for her, the sheer defiance that she hurls initially at him recoils into the misery of the constraints imposed on her by her royal stand:

I only want to say that the habit men have formed of regarding women as their animal possession and tyrannizing them will not work with me. If you cannot protect me, if you cannot save the honour of your own clan, the dignity of woman, then, you cannot sell me either. To protect you from that bother, I shall go away myself. (18)

She offers in her despair to cohabit with Ramagupta, something she has successfully managed to avoid until now. However, he is apprehensive about accepting this offer. It is then that she throws off all pretence of being under his protection and with that also implicitly of being bound by the marriage bond: 'There is red blood in my veins, there is fire in my heart and there is the glow of self-respect in it. I will protect it myself' (20).

These were tones reserved for men. For a married woman, suspected of being in love with another—Ramagupta confides to his following that he has long looked for the signs of her attachment to Chandragupta—reference to red blood, to fire, to her own sense of self, are nothing short of revolutionary. She draws a sword to kill herself. She is prevented from doing so by Chandragupta, who stammers out a half articulated declaration of love to her. It is only when she finds herself alone that, thinking back upon the scene where she had folded Chandragupta in her arms to declare before everyone that she would not let him go alone to Shakaraja, Dhruvasvamini reflects on the physical satisfaction of her embrace and the nature of her own feelings:

How emotional was that embrace of just one moment? How filled with satisfaction? It is as if fate had involuntarily allowed the earth, scorched by blistering winds, to meet the cool evening sky on the lonely horizon. (After a pause) Life had become intolerable in that airless region, where there was restriction, a bar, even on uneven breathing. But I shall not die. I will secure a few days of this world for myself in the Maker's ordinance. You unloosed just that, Kumar, which I have been trying to hold back all this while. I find myself drenched now with the goodwill and affection you poured on me. Oh (placing her hands on her heart) are there two hearts in this chest? When the inner self wants to do something, why does the outer self say 'no'? (26–7)

This is the very *jijivisha*, will to live or life force, which romantic love inspires and keeps alive. The first scene ends with a song about a lonely traveller on life's stony path, sung by Mandakini, Dhruvasvamini's companion. She is surrounded and finally engulfed by the storm which darkens the stage.

CELEBRATION OF ROMANTIC LOVE: 'HEAVENLY LIGHT RESIDES IN TWO HEARTS WHICH LOVE'

Dhruvasvamini's counterpart Koma is similarly venturesome and bold in her speech. But from the start she is in a weak position since her love is not reciprocated: she is placed in a barbaric environment and thus is condemned to becoming a sacrifice to the very ideals she craves to keep alive. The second scene also opens on a lavish set—a drop scene which depicts the interior of the Shaka fortress, a throne of carved Kashmiri wood placed at the centre of it, draped with Tibetan silk curtains. Flowering shrubs and climbing vines fill the courtyard before it. The sagging shrubs represent Koma's emotional state: 'They have to be watered, their dryness and wilt casts a veil on beauty' (29). Her encounter with Shakaraja confirms the effort needed to keep the relationship alive; though aware of the disappointment and hurt he has caused Koma, Shakaraja is taken aback at the intensity of her emotion. His easy declaration that he really loves her (37) cannot gainsay the fact that he is already seeking another woman. Koma's passionate resistance to this measure is not just personally motivated; she feels that women should not be trampled upon for purposes of political revenge. And yet, why is it not possible for her to break loose from the insecure bond of her relationship? As Guru Mihirdev says, great attachment can form even to being mistreated. His deep insight into the nature of Koma's love, its persistence in the face of obvious abuse, presages the action that she will ultimately take. For, once she realizes that there is no way to make Shakaraja change his course of action, she rebuffs him with: 'Don't speak of love. It was a pain which has now let go of me. The nagging ache of it will also leave slowly. Raja, I don't love you. I had adored the proud manliness of my own image of you' (42). Love that finds no adequate receptacle to hold it and that cannot be reciprocated, can be a mere projection of one's own desire. Not all women who think they love find true love. Not all men are capable of living up to the demands of love. But the sanctity of true love tolerates no disrespect, as Mihirdev warns Shakaraja. Romantic love finds its apotheosis in this pronouncement by an authoritative figure, a guru with his heart in the right place: in the very denial of a love that cannot come to fruition, there is the promise of the light which can be obtained, once it is truly found and reciprocated: 'You can make the mistake of thinking you are cunning by practising the common forms of political deceit and enjoying momentary triumph, but the greatest injury in this fearsome world is to lose a heart which loves. Shakaraja, heavenly light resides in two hearts which love' (39).

Shakaraja, who is blind to love that was his for the asking, is doomed to destruction, taking along with him those who have been unfortunate enough to be emotionally tied to him. Though the play will end happily, the dark, unfulfilled side of romantic love will cast its murky shadow on the light which shines on the happy couple.

THE CHALLENGE TO ORTHODOXY: 'WHAT IS THE TRUTH OF YOUR RITUAL TEXTS AND YOUR LAW BOOKS?'

The third scene opens with Dhruvasvamini seated pensively under a rose spotlight. Her passions and convictions will move the action along in this scene. Are there further impediments to her union with Chandragupta? There is some hesitation on his part, which he will, after some introspection, finally overcome: Chandragupta can become the true ruler of state after he has found the courage to claim

Dhruvasvamini. But both law and ritual will now need to be publicly challenged, if true justice is to prevail—both in the matter of personal right and state right; the two seem to be indissolubly linked. Hedged in from all sides, Dhruvasvamini is pushed into asking the *purohita*, the royal priest: 'What is the truth of your ritual texts and your law books, if women who need protection are compelled to come to this pass?' and when he recoils from this attack and wants to wave it off as mere rage, she responds passionately:

It is rage, yes, I am burning with rage. Such great mockery... in the name of dharma, such fiendish test of woman's obedience, extracted from me by force. Purohita, the celebration of the fiendish marriage that you performed for me proved to be so beautiful. Regard this mass murder, the blood soaked corpse of Shakaraja must still lie in that chamber. How many soldiers must be breathing their last! While I still breathe, floating in this bloodstream like an ogress. You think your benediction will bring me peace? (50)

Her companion Mandakini goes even further in her recrimination:

Arya, why don't you speak? Have you allowed for no countermeasure, no protective clause in your dharma, for the women you hold constrained in the bonds of dharma? You have snatched all their rights without first taking their consent. What rights have they retained, so that they can avail of them when in trouble? Can you be at peace after ordering them to remain satisfied with the mere fantasy of a future union? (50)

The purohita reassures her with the words: 'No, the mutual belief-filled protection of rights and cooperation between woman and man is called marriage. If this is not so, then dharma and marriage are mere play' (50–1). Yet, it is clear that there is little more than evasion in these words and that Dhruvasvamini has reached the limits of her resistance. Women who love are condemned to wilt in its fire. This in confirmed in the second important encounter in the scene, which takes place between Koma and Dhruvasvamini.

Koma: I have loved.
Dhruvasvamini: And what was your punishment for this terrible offence?

Koma: Just that which women often receive: disappointment, agony and derision. (51)

If in Harishchandra's *Nildevi*, the queen's self-immolation had formed the crowning act of freedom and glory, here, in a mid-twentieth century dramatization of a royal death, in the melancholy act of sacrificing a life for a love that was based on delusion, it can be viewed as none other than bitterly hollow and mistaken in the extreme. For all Prasad's enthusiasm for the past glories of Hindudom, this is one practice that his text refuses to sanction and that it condemns not just in this one instance but in its entirety. Once Koma departs with Shakaraja's corpse, Mandakini observes bitterly:

This sacrifice that women make has no value. What a helpless state it is. They fall at the feet of men, their weak hands groping for support, and the men favour them with the alms of disdain, abhorrence, and ill-use. But do these crazed women learn even then?

Dhruvasvamini: It's a slip; it's mere delusion (after a pause) but there is reason for this. Something like a tradition of dependence has entered each vein of theirs, their very consciousness, since who knows how many aeons. They feel compelled to make these slips even after they have understood. (52)

With sati thus devalued, with the authority of the Dharmashastras questioned, and the use men make of women roundly denounced, with so clear a validation of introspection, of the pleasurable sensuality women experience in union, the issue of personal suitability for a particular union and the fulfilment to be found in love that is reciprocated, we seem to have reached an impasse in the sequence of events. How can things be put right, ideals reinstated, when the moral frame refuses to give way? This is when Prasad begins to fit things back into neat moulds; he does a neat turnaround. We need to look once again at the Dharmashastras, as the priest says, departing hastily to do just that. The priestly stand can, if challenged, suffer a change of mind and of heart. At the climax of the dramatic activity, at the very end of the play, the priest makes an energetic intervention. He tells the blustering Ramagupta:

Political knave! Don't argue about the meaning of the Shastras. You Eunuch, do you know why Krishna called Arjuna a eunuch? A man who has no hesitation in sending his wife into the arms of another, who, if not he, should we pronounce impotent? I decree by the authority of the Dharmashastras that Ramagupta set Dhruvasvamini free from the marriage bond. (63)

The Dharmashastras, if consulted with an open mind, show the great flexibility of which they are capable. In the half century between the writing of *Nildevi* and *Dhruvasvamini*, there has come about a vast shift in sensibility. It allows for the free expression of sensuality in women other than courtesans, it makes possible the choice of another male partner, if the first partner fails to fulfil the duties expected of him. But it is a shift that still needs to invoke the sanction of scripture as proof of its validity, which is not slow in coming, at least in Prasad's reading of such texts: the Dharmashastras were generous to women, they recognized their need for meaningful partnership, they made possible 'true' marriage. The priest can therefore cite the authority of the Dharmashastras to sanction this public act of divorce and declare proudly, if somewhat unconvincingly that 'The Brahman is only afraid of dharma. He considers all other power to be petty. Your killers cannot stop me from pronouncing Dharmic truth. Call them, I am ready' (62).

THE MELODRAMATIC STAGE FRAME AND THE CONVOLUTIONS OF PRASAD'S MODERNISM

Structurally the play echoes the compromises that the narrative itself is ultimately compelled to make. Each scene is composed of many smaller units that are signalled by exits and entrances. Some manoeuvring is necessary to bring this about, for sometimes a character has to leave in order to allow another to hold a soliloquy, sometimes both have to leave for a new set of characters to enter and hold a short conversation to impart some necessary information. Stage directions assume great importance towards the end of these scenes, where action is too swift to allow for words.[17] There is frequent use of the device of one character, while entering, overhearing the last words of the character who had just spoken. At the end of each scene, there are sensational peaks of action, reminiscent of both of Harishchandra's *Nildevi* and the very

Hindu Romanticism: Jayshankar Prasad's *Dhruvasvamini* (late 1990s) (National School of Drama)

Parsi melodrama Prasad so despised. The device of the chorus used for song is also a borrowing from the Parsi stage. The first scene concludes with the main pair of lovers, Dhruvasvamini and Chandragupta, leaving for an uncertain destination, the disguise which plays a pivotal role already being plotted. The second scene ends with the disclosure of Chandragupta's true identity and the duel. The third with dethronement, enthronement, and Ramagupta's killing, which is preceded by Chandragupta breaking the iron chains binding him, reminiscent of a similar incident in *Nildevi*. Prasad has no hesitation in showing death on the stage; he is clearly following precedents prevailing on the commercialized stage though he may himself have wished to see it derived from Shakespeare.

However, within this melodramatic frame, the songs serve to underscore and make explicit the general emotional mood; the lyrics are clearly Chhayavad poetry, sung by the minor women characters, as for instance Koma's song about the passing of youth which is at the same time a lament about Shakaraja's neglect of and disregard for his former beloved, so also Dhruvasvamini's companion Mandakini's song about the untiring traveller on a hazardous road, as Chandragupta and Dhruvasvamini wend their way towards the enemy camp. The songs are not composed according to any musical mode of raga, as was still the case in Harishchandra's time, nor do they follow popular musical forms, as the Parsi stage so often did. They are lyrics, subjective emotions projected onto the landscape; even the chorus of dancing girls sings such lyrics. The beckoning youthful damsel is twilight, 'sandhya', personified, or as Prasad had himself put it and as already quoted: 'vishva sundari prakriti mem chetana ka arop', the attribution of consciousness to universally beautiful nature (Prasad 2001 [1933]: 44). The melodramatic frame and the cloak and dagger narrative provide an ill fit for the subjectivity of the female characters and the wistful or stormy nature lyrics that they embody.

This contradiction is reflected as well in the ideological resolution of the problems posed. Thus, in spite of attempting to establish a position which was to be seen as simply setting forth Indian classical aesthetics, Prasad works within the double heritage of a self-consciously 'Indian' system of values and those very concepts of character and conflict, the subjectivity and defiance of social norms that he resisted as being

'Western' and rejected most vehemently: the lyricism allowed to the woman characters and the scope given to other characters, for instance Chandragupta, to ruminate on their feelings make it possible for the reader/onlooker to enter into their innermost feelings. The discrepancy between Prasad's avowed aims and his actual practice is reflected formally and thematically in his work. Thus the social reforms Prasad seems to be proposing, the rights of woman to personal happiness, though developed with more consequence than Harishchandra before him, occur within a frame wherein these reforms are projected into the past and presupposed as already existent there. There is then little need to ask for social change in the present. Thus, though Prasad does depict, in spite of his protext, *yathartha*, reality, that is, the emotional rather than the social reality of human predicaments, since this reality is realized in a romantic-historic rather than contemporary setting, in high personages, kings, queens, and nobles and the high moral standards they are expected to fulfil instead of in the lives of ordinary, everyday people, it can finally only be ruled by the *adarsha*, ideality, projected similarly into the past. The characters are then caught in situations which seem more than a little stilted. The right to feel, the space to live these feelings, the denial of this space to women, the sacrifices they are expected to make for their men, the boundaries placed on marital bonds as applying to women alone, women's internalization of these and thus their willing compliance: in attempting to resolve these vexed issues, Prasad places his characters in situations which seem more than a little contrived. The solutions he offers are then no less contrived. In the process he validates Brahmins, the laws they make, and their—in the last instance—exemplary role as keepers of this law.

And yet, precisely because this capitulation to tradition seems to be so complete, there can be a tendency to overlook what Prasad, in fact, does accomplish with such finesse in the meantime, the psychological awareness of character, the deep introspection of his characters, the '*antarbhava*' demanded by Bharatendu. Prasad often uses this introspection to create a lyrical mood, as much in drama as in his poetry. This lyricism can at times sit uneasily in a dramatic frame which would seem to demand action. At other times it is this introspection which makes unusual action possible as when Dhruvasvamini's self-aware sensuality and passion inspire radical decisions which almost burst asunder the frame Prasad so carefully constructs: she develops enough character and energy to border on conflict, she stands in danger of completely overshadowing Chandragupta, who manages to save his honour just in time to be pronounced king-emperor. Prasad thus opens the way for more self-introspection, particularly for his women characters, more inner-life and the creation of unique individuals, as yet looking inwards and barely able to communicate with each other, but part of a modern quest, thwarted of its full expression by being capped with backward-looking idealization of person and situation.

When the progressive Marxist poet Gajanan Madhav Muktibodh (1917–64) came to engage with Prasad's famous epic poem *Kamayani* (1936) in a critical study he devoted entirely to the project, he was iconoclastic enough to see it as a 'modern poem, in which modern tendencies, realities and questions were presented'.[18] Entitled *Kamayani*: *ek punarvichar* (Kamayani, renewed reflection), Muktibodh's work was written around 1950 but could not be published until 1961, since it met with vehement ideological opposition. Instead of falling into the awe-filled reverence usually reserved for the treatment of this stately work, Muktibodh had dared to see Prasad's Manu, the mythic father of the human race, as the prototype of modern man, who reflected the contemporary change in value orientation and the identity crisis which inevitably followed: 'Manu is not the Manu of the Vedic ages, Manu is a type, a type of the class whose splendour and rule has run out' (Lotz 1999: 207). Muktibodh found that the technique that the history-loving Prasad used was mainly one of connecting the present with the past in order to throw a veil on modern problems. As Namwar Singh had pointed out: 'This is how the metaphor in *Kamayani* is ancient, the sentimental eternal and the problem modern.'[19] Muktibodh considered this a typical feature of the treatment of reality in Chhayavad sensibilities, where the realities of actual life were preferably presented in poetic abstractions. But, as Muktibodh saw it, the quest Prasad engaged in was real enough and the sensibility which registered it acute enough: '(T)he whole complex which is alive, restless and agitated in Prasadji's inner soul emerges in *Kamayani* with all its pain and knowledge, with all its anger and consciousness, and in the confusion of this consciousness' (Lotz 1999: 194). *Kamayani* set forth an approach that Prasad had evolved in his long tussle with the very modernity that he sought to subsume under his notions of 'tradition'. Just as in his drama, if on the one hand he fought for an individuation which inevitably thrust his characters into conflict-riddled situations that provoked rage at the barriers set up by so-called tradition, on the other hand, he ended by finding resolutions that covered up the very roots of the issues and problems he had raised. He looked backwards to effect change, not forward. It is not surprising then that modern productions of *Dhruvasvamini* continue to bear the burden of these contradictions. If Prasad's text is reproduced without any subtext on the modern stage today, can it be other than backward looking?

NOTES

[1] For older accounts of the work of these playwrights in English, see Sukumar Sen (1979: 229–33) and Priyaranjan Sen (1966: 189–202). For a more recent discussion, see the chapter devoted to Ghosh in Sudipto Chatterjee (forthcoming).

[2] See S.H. Vatsyanyan (1976: 64) and Sumitranandan Pant, one of the four famous Chhayavadi poets in his prefatory essay: 'Paryalokan,' in *Adhunik kavi* (1959: 8): '*Prakrti nirikshan se mujhe apni bhavanaom ki abhivyanjana mem adhik sahayata mili hai, kahim us se vicharom ki bhi prerana mili hai.*' (I have received great help in expressing my emotions by examining nature; at times I have even found inspiration for ideas therein.)

[3] The other three poets are Suryakant Tripathi Nirala (1899–1961), Sumitranandan Pant (1900–77), and Mahadevi Varma (1902–87).

[4] Prasad's essays on poetry and aesthetics were collected under the title *Kavya aur kala tatha anya nibandh*. All translations from the Hindi are mine, unless specified otherwise.

[5] Cf. Nandadulare Vajpeyi in his introduction to Prasad 2000 (18).

[6] Published first, according to a note by the editor of *Kavya aur kala* in *Hindustani* (7 March 1937), the journal of the Hindustani Academy.

[7] Charles Kean (1811–68), British actor and theatre manager who made a name for himself as a pedagogic manager and director. His production of classical plays was researched with great attention to historical accuracy of set design and costumes; this could involve extensive consultation of

architectural history or even of archaeological excavation reports. The production of his plays was accompanied by lengthy documentation of the historical sources used.

[8] For a discussion of the bhakti aesthetics of this play, see my essay (1992).

[9] See Maheswar (1974: 154–219) for an extensive discussion of Prasad's debt to Dwijendralal Ray.

[10] The recourse to Puranic and epic material cast in a historical frame was a practice followed by most contemporary and even later playwrights. For an important discussion of the imaginary 'ancient' Indian world thus created see Pandeya (1987). The titles of plays discussed in the work themselves provide a clear indication of the subject matter (272–5).

[11] Thus, for instance, Kumar (1978: 133) and Tarun (1976: 310). For a spirited, though nonetheless conventional analysis of *Dhruvasvamini*, see Anand (1998, vol. 1: 117–24). The edition of *Dhruvasvamini* used for this study and available for easy reference is (Delhi: Mayur Paperbacks, 2001).

[12] Cf. Shah ([1979] 2002: 25).

[13] A 'guide', notes and explications meant to serve as examination help for high school Hindi at Class 12 level, has several pages devoted to this play, with model examination questions-answers and a relatively sophisticated analysis of the play and its context. See Sharma, *Excellent Hindi Prabha* (2004: 216–84).

[14] Of the first act of Prasad's play *Ajatshatru* (1922), Peter Gaeffke notes: 'Even these four scenes are set in three different locations while the remaining five scenes of the first act will change the setting of action three times. With each different location more and more characters are added or dropped and nearly every scene or short sequence of scenes has its own climax and functions as a complete unit' (Gaeffke 1978: 97).

[15] Anand's lavishly produced two-volume study of the playwright Prasad, published by the National School of Drama, Delhi, is at pains to document all known productions of his plays. For *Dhruvasvamini*, Anand documents a student production in Osaka, Japan, in 1961, which was largely viewed by other students, according to the information he himself provides (1998: 279). There have been two National School of Drama productions in Delhi in recent years: a student production directed by Rabijita Gogoi in 1997, to be followed by a repertory production by the same director in 1998–9. These productions undertook a feminist rereading of the play, which remained caught in the contradictions with which Prasad himself tussled.

[16] Cf. N. Vajpeyi in his introduction to Prasad (2000): 'He [Prasad] has collated matter from the Shastras and only then subjected them to a double filter of the Puranas and psychology. It would take courage to pronounce this filtered matter incorrect or unproven' (42).

[17] Maheshwar (1974: 8) maintains that D.L. Ray of Bengal was the first in his own dramatic tradition, following the example of English plays, to incorporate lengthy stage directions into his plays. But this was also the practice of the Parsi stage, already partly adopted by Bharatendu.

[18] The following observations draw on the brilliant analysis of Muktibodh's efforts to come to terms with Prasad's complex work by Barbara Lotz (1998), which she also discusses in her 1999 Heidelberg PhD dissertation: 'Poesie, Poetik, Politik: Engagement und Experiment im Werk des Hindiautors Gajanan Madhav Muktibodh (1917–1964)'.

[19] Namvar Singh (1957: 113), as cited by Lotz (1998: 221).

REFERENCES

Anand, Mahesh. 1998. *Jayshankar Prasad: Rangdrishti*. 2 Vols. Delhi: National School of Drama.

Chatterjee Sudipto (forthcoming). *The Colonial Stage(d): Hybridity, Women and Nation in the 19th Century Bengal Theatre*. Calcutta: Seagull.

Dalmia-Lüderitz, Vasudha. 1992. 'Hariscandra of Banaras and the reassessment of Vaisnava Bhakti in the late nineteenth century', in *Devotional Literature in South Asia: Current Research, 1985–1988*, R.S. McGregor (ed.). Cambridge: Cambridge University Press, 281–97.

Gaeffke, Peter. 1970. *Grundbegriffe moderner indischer Erzählkunst aufgezeigt am Werke Jayasankara Prasadas (1889–1937)*. Leiden: Brill.

_____. 1978. *Hindi Literature in the Twentieth Century*. Wiesbaden: Harrassowitz. (*A History of Indian Literature*, J. Gonda (ed.), vol. 8, fasc. 5.)

Lotz, Barbara. 1998. 'Romantic Allegory and Progressive Criticism', in *Narrative Strategies: Essays on South Asian Literature and Film*, Vasudha Dalmia and Theo Damsteegt (eds.). Leiden: CNWS Publications. Delhi: Oxford University Press.

_____. 1999. 'Poesie, Poetik, Politik: Engagement und Experiment in Werk des Hindiautors Gajanand Madhav Muktibodh (1917–1964)', Ph.D. dissertation, Heidelberg.

Maheshwar. 1974. *Hindi-bangla natak*. Delhi: Macmillan.

Nagendra (ed.). 1976. *Bharatiya Natak Sahitya* : *Seth Govind das abhinandan granth*. Delhi: S. Chand and Company.

Pandeya, Vashishta Muni. 1987. *Prasad yugin natakom mem Samskritik chetana*. Allahabad: Academy Press.

Pant, Sumitranandan. 1957. 'Paryalochan', in *Adhunik kavi*. Prayag: Hindi Sahitya Sammelan.

Prasad, Jayshankar. 2000. *Kavya aur kala tatha anya nibandh*, N. Vajpeyi and Prasad (eds.). Allahabad: Lokbharati Prakashan.

———. 2001. *Dhruvasvamini*. Delhi: Mayur Paperbacks.

Rubin, David. 1993. *The Return of Saraswati: Translations of the Poetry of Prasad, Nirala, Pant and Mahadevi*. Philadelphia: Department of South Asia Regional Studies, University of Pennsylvania.

Schomer, Karine. 1983. *Mahadevi Varma and the Chhayavad Age of Modern Hindi Poetry*. Berkeley: University of California Press.

Sen, Priyaranjan. 1966. *Western Influence in Bengali Literature*. Calcutta: Academic Publishers, 189–202.

Sen, Sukumar. 1979. *A History of Bengali Literature*. New Delhi: Sahitya Akademi, 229–33.

Shah, Rameshchandra. [1979] 2002. *Jayshanker Prasad*. Delhi: Sahitya Akademi.

Sharma, Mahesh Prasad. 2003. *Excellent Hindi Prabha 2004*. Mathura: Excellent Publishing House.

Siddhanath Kumar. 1978. *Prasad ke natak*. Delhi.

Singh, Namvar. 1955. *Chhayavad: Aitihasik samajik vishleshan*. Banaras: Saraswati Press.

——— 1957. *Itihas aur alochna*. Delhi: Rajkamal.

Tarun, Rameshwarlal Khandelwal. 1976. 'Prasad ke natakon ka punarmulyamkan', in *Bharatiya natya sahitya*, Nagendra (ed.). Delhi: Macmillan.

Vatsyayan, S.H. 1976. *Adhunik hindi sahitya*. Delhi: Rajpal and Sons.

Neither Half nor Whole
Mohan Rakesh and the Modernist Quest

The decades between the 1930s and 1960s were witness to the kind of conceptual and formal transformations within Hindi theatre which in their speed and significance could possibly only be matched with the rapidity of change in the last decades of the preceding century, when modern drama had first begun to be written in Hindi. To appreciate the swiftness of these developments we have only to juxtapose the views of Jayshankar Prasad, theorizing in the mid-1930s, with the pronouncements and experiments of Mohan Rakesh from the 1950s onwards.

The major transformations consisted in the radical shift away from the depiction of idealized character and reality, which in their idealization were to be sources of both aesthetic pleasure—and social transformation—the position Prasad had upheld so fiercely in the last years of his writing career, as we saw in the last chapter. The emphasis in the following decades was increasingly on the evolution of the rounded personality and individuation of character, and the sharp conflict that this individuation engendered. This individuation of character, particularly as it played itself out in Rakesh's work, was a process which had two almost self-contradictory aspects. If, on the one hand, it presented the individual protagonist as attempting to attain wholeness of person, on the other hand, it portrayed the same person as also seeking completion in the partner, in 'the other half' so to speak; the underlying assumption here being that it was only in the other that, in fact, this completion could be achieved.[1] This made for, at best, a state of precarious balance. For, in trying to bring about this self-completion, the personality that sought to evolve and articulate itself could so overflow the bounds of its own person that it overwhelmed not only the self but also the other. In the final event, this twofold effort at self-evolution (of the man *and* increasingly also the woman) could lead to a breakdown in communication, to a state where the central characters talked past each other rather than *to* each other, to a disjunction in dialogue, and, finally, to a loss of face-to-face contact with the other. Since the contours of the person could only be defined in interaction, a space created in theatre primarily by means of dialogue, the loss of dialogue could lead to the dissolution of sharply etched character. As a consequence, the depiction of a reality that had been constituted by the unfolding of character receded, to give place to efforts to represent extra- or ultra-reality. This was to lead Rakesh in particular to the search for a form which was to be constituted not so much by dialogue as by an assemblage of voices that were now no more to be located in identifiable time, space, or indeed character.

In order to retrace the move, first, to establish 'reality' as a conceptual and experiential category and to then, finally, displace it, I shall, in the following, briefly recapitulate dramatic theory and practice which preceded and in part accompanied Rakesh's own efforts, to then discuss at some length Rakesh's experiments with *yatharthvadi*, realistic, plays which were to finally lead him to abandon altogether the notion of dialogue and the attempt to depict rounded character.

FROM IDEALITY TO REALITY

As we saw in the last chapter, it was, in fact, with Jayshankar Prasad (1886–1937) that Hindi drama acquired a new maturity and sophistication. The themes of most of Prasad's plays were from the Puranas and from history, but in spite of being located squarely in the past, his characters spoke the new language of subjectivity that had been the gift of the Chhayavad school of poetry to Hindi literature. Prasad sought thereby to establish an explicitly Indian point of view in literary and dramatic criticism that could do justice to what he saw as the Indian system of values, feeling free to blend Western and Eastern notions blithely all the while. He referred to the exemplary practice of the Victorian actor-director Charles Kean to stage the past with the careful attention to detail which was entirely lacking in commercial theatre production in India. While setting up his own brand of aesthetics, Prasad rejected the new realist vogue of the 1930s, which he saw as trivializing reality and as being excessively pessimistic in outlook (2000: 68).

This new realist vogue came to see itself as modernist and vehemently opposed to the traditional. It is possible to see certain parallels in the theatre of late-nineteenth-century Europe, which Raymond Williams has seen as propelled by the following influential factors: the radical admission of the contemporary as legitimate material for drama, set in contemporary indigenous (as against historically or culturally exotic) sites, an increasing emphasis on everyday speech forms as the basis for dramatic language (the formally rhetorical, choral, and monological types being steadily abandoned), emphasis on social extension—a deliberate breach of the convention that the principal personages of drama be of elevated social rank, and finally, a decisive secularism (a steady exclusion of supernatural or metaphysical agencies). Williams saw this late-nineteenth-century naturalism as the first phase of modernist theatre. 'At its centre was the humanist and secular—and in political terms, liberal and later socialist—proposition that human nature was not, or at least not decisively, unchanging and timeless, but was socially and culturally specific' (Williams 1989: 83–4). These were not quite the terms of the discussion as it unfolded in the second quarter of the twentieth century in north India, yet they serve as an important grid to measure the terrain covered since Prasad.

From the late 1920s there emerged then two dominant streams in non-commercial Hindi drama, both of which were to come together, with due modifications, in Rakesh's dramaturgy. The one stream continued to deal with historical themes, projecting nationalist aspirations into the past, yet in a language and frame shot through with contemporary concerns. Harikrishna Premi (b.1908) and Seth Govindadas (b.1896) produced a number of such plays, primarily as reading matter.

Though these playwrights made modernist moves, they did not acknowledge them as such. Rakesh was later to pass impatient and perhaps hasty judgement on these attempts: 'A vast number of historical plays have been written in Hindi, the majority of them reproduce historical episodes just as they find them; from the point of view of drama, they contain very little which is worthy of note.'[2] However, for his first two full-length plays, Rakesh himself was also to turn to historical themes and classical Sanskrit literature (rather than to the Puranas and the epics as Prasad), though he did so in order to read explicitly modern concerns and conflicts into them.

The other stream in modern Hindi drama dealt with domestic interiors, presenting psychological studies of man–woman relationships, often coupled with a desire for social reform.[3] This trend coincided with and was supported by translations from the plays of John Galsworthy, Bernard Shaw, and, most importantly, Henrik Ibsen.[4] One of the most prominent members of this group from the 1930s on was Lakshminarayan Mishra (b. 1903). Mishra reacted sharply against what he termed the unreal world presented by D.L. Ray of Bengal and by Jayshankar Prasad. In the essay '*Main buddhivadi kyon hum*' written in 1943, he held these two playwrights responsible for introducing a false and impossible world into drama and for creating characters who were either divine or demonic: 'It lies outside their power to show either the conflict or confluence of oppositional matter.'[5]

Mishra went on to advocate the use of realistic box sets, sparing use of the curtain, songs only when they suited the character, and no use of asides. He himself attempted to present the ordinary individual, rather than the exalted, and to trace the course of events as they emerged from a mundane existence, caught up in the vicissitudes of everyday, without, theoretically, attempting to impose a pattern on the course of conduct motivated by character. He translated the plays of Ibsen and considered himself indebted to Chekhov. According to Mishra, the playwright was to be merely an impartial observer of the characters of his play. For, as he specified in the preface to one of his plays:

Even if we wanted to we could not project the social and political curbs within which our souls toss into the lives of the great characters of history. Which is why, we will have to admit defeat and imagine characters grounded in our social reality.

I have brought my characters on to the street of life and then left them alone [to fend for themselves].... Like a true seeker of knowledge, I have moved behind them. I have seen them and understood them—their situations and the course of their life.[6]

Other playwrights of note who pioneered and explored various forms of realism were Bhuvaneshvar Prasad Srivastava (1912/14–57), Upendranath Ashk (1910–96), and Jagadishchandra Mathur (1917–78). Bhuvaneshvar exercised powerful influence on his generation of writers, particularly Ashk who was to edit his work and write an introduction to it. Bhuvaneshvar was also greatly admired by Mohan Rakesh, who saw in him the veritable progenitor of one-act plays in Hindi. Rakesh found that his plays were so skilfully crafted and could weather age so well that they appeared modern, even in the late 1960s. Rakesh's perceptive appraisal of Bhuvaneshvar's craft could well serve as a proclamation of his own agenda:

Bhuvaneshvar uses short, ordinary sentences in his plays, which at a superficial level can seem disconnected. But a far deeper meaning than the ostensible emerges from within the sentence, which articulates the very mind-set of the characters uttering these sentences. Bhuvaneshvar leaves more unsaid than said in his plays. In fact, this is the great specialty of his plays—what he leaves unsaid touches the heart most.... The majority of his plays deal with man–woman relationships, but with such a subtle touch that the issues at hand come to light primarily in the interaction of the characters and other slight strokes.[7]

Ashk[8] similarly wrote social-domestic drama, dropping the high-flown rhetoric of the historical play in preference for everyday speech rhythms, in order to produce credible portraits of urban family life. As he was himself to declare: 'I want to write plays which portray real life, have an analytical approach from the point of view of sociology and can also bring to focus the problems of society.'[9] Both Ashk and Mathur attempted to blend the historical and the familiar in two popularly received plays.[10]

The work of these playwrights appeared at a time when the family was reorganizing itself in accordance with the exigencies of urban life and middle-class women were beginning to participate in professional life. The efforts of women to work outside the home were sporadic, tentative, few and far between, yet they faced much hostility and suffered from much self-doubt and self-condemnation. Ashk's major plays, many of them one-act and written for radio broadcast, are largely concerned with these changes and the ensuing shift in gender relations. As many other contemporaries, Ashk sets out to emancipate women, themselves as troubled and confused as their men, only to find himself, mediated through the exigencies of the characters and plots he devises, driving them back into entrenched positions again. His work thus contains a number of strong women characters, who fight their way to the centre of the stage, only to suffer one or other kind of setback, disappointment, or humiliation.[11]

These plays, one-act plays in particular, did not suffer the fate of Prasad's dramatic production, which remained confined between book covers. They had a much wider public, for the one consistent medium for drama scripts that emerged in these decades was the radio. In 1936 All-India Radio was established and by the end of the 1930s began to regularly broadcast plays in Hindi. One-act plays were thus in great demand and a number of the playwrights earlier mentioned responded readily to this need. It was here that Mohan Rakesh's own early one-act plays were first broadcast.[12] Two of these were later to be developed into full-length plays.[13]

It was only after Independence that a yet wider forum could be set up in the capital of the new nation. In 1959 the National School of Drama was established in Delhi and for the first time there was a regular platform for plays written in Hindi. In 1962, Rakesh's *Ashadh ka ek din* was produced by Ebrahim Alkazi, the first director of the School, on an improvised open-air stage in Delhi.[14] This established Rakesh as a playwright of note and made his plays a part of the modern Indian drama canon, according to his own testimony.[15] In 1967, Rakesh's second full-length play, *Laharon ke rajhans*, was staged in Calcutta by 'Anamika', a well-known theatre group, under the direction of Shyamanand Jalan, who cooperated closely with Rakesh in shaping the final act of the play. Rakesh himself desired active participation as a playwright in the process of creating the stage interpretation of his plays. This was to lead him to experiment with dramatic structure 'as part of my creative routine' (Rakesh 1966: 16). His final full-length play, *Adhe adhure*, was performed in 1969 by 'Dishantar', an important contemporary theatre group in Delhi, once again with Om Shivpuri, the director, seeking advice and guidance from Rakesh. Rakesh also wrote one experimental play in English, *Mad Delight* (1971) in a drama workshop sponsored by Max Mueller Bhavan, as the Goethe Institute is called in India, which he later translated into Hindi himself as *Chhatriyan*.[16] Rakesh wrote his plays for public performance, in close cooperation with theatre makers and in constant dialogue and interaction with them. Though things were not to come to quite the pass Prasad had demanded—he had wanted that the stage accommodate itself to drama, rather than the other way around—the conditions for playwriting in Hindi had immensely improved. At least for the next few decades, it had become possible for playwright and theatre to create and form each other.

REALITY VERSUS IDEALITY

Rakesh's theoretical writings on drama are contained mainly in the preface of his play *Laharon ke rajhans*. His ideas on *yatharthata* or realism are to be gleaned from his essays on the *nayi kahani*,[17] the movement in the Hindi short story of the 1950s which is closely linked, conceptually and thematically, with Rakesh's plays. Further insights can be gleaned from his textbook edition of five well-known one-act plays of the period.[18]

Rakesh made no attempt to establish a link with classical Indian aesthetic theory. He thought that Prasad had neglected to develop the directions indicated by Bharatendu and had failed to himself provide any new orientation. He was very clear that he himself did not seek ideals in the past.[19] On the contrary, though his plays were set in the past, he endeavoured to endow these well-known figures with flesh and blood and to bring them to life for viewers today. In the inability of readers and audiences to come to terms with the moral failings that these figures could then display, Rakesh saw as the root cause the Indian's lack of faith in his own complex *manaviyata*, humanity, and yatharthata, reality. And he pitted this notion of the modern Indian against the traditional practice of raising generic symbols to superhuman levels (Rakesh 1963: 8).

Though he maintained that the Hindi stage would have to develop in accordance with the very special cultural expectations of the Indian audiences, and he envisaged this as being entirely different from Western theatre (Rakesh 1958), his notion of the new Indian theatre was rooted in a modernist vision that he surely shared with Alkazi. His main conceptual categories remained yatartha, reality, *sangharsh*, struggle, and *dvandva*, conflict, which Prasad had resisted as ideological importation from the West and as being incompatible with the Indian system of values. Rakesh provided some idea of his use of these new notions, within the contours of the reality that he sought to achieve, in the context of the *nayi kahani* or new short story movement that he spearheaded, along with Kamleshwar, Rajendra Yadav, Mannu Bhandari, and others.[20]

But the nayi kahani is not yet another precept of literary theory, over which there would be need to pull and push; but it provides a perspective, of seeing man within his social reality and of accepting this reality as reality, while at the same time taking count of the struggle which could take man beyond the reality of today towards the reality of tomorrow. (Rakesh 1967: 204)

In order to present reality adequately, man's mental struggle with the congestion and putrefaction of urban environment had to be depicted without losing faith in the inherent strength and gentleness of human nature. The significant conflicts of the times took place in big cities, and Rakesh clearly saw urban reality as providing the central focus of his own work.

The conflict of the forces [influencing life] can be experienced everywhere— though much more sharply in urban life, since it is towns which are the chief centres of conflict, and of these again, more so the bigger cities. If our works do not reflect the accurate pulsation of this conflict, they do not represent reality. (Rakesh 1975: 35)

In that he insisted on the city as the centre of modern writing, particularly in the nayi kahani, Rakesh was struggling against the idealizing nationalist focus on a village India.[21] In order to grasp this reality comprehensively and not narrow it to a few areas of human conflict, the writer would have to constantly widen his own field of experience (Rakesh 1975: 35–6). Thus the centrality of the concepts of reality, struggle, and conflict in Rakesh's conceptual frame, all three necessary if man were to evolve to meet the needs of the future. As he was to specify clearly in the introduction to his anthology of modern Hindi one-act plays:

Just as in the full-length play, so also in one-act plays, conflict holds immense significance. This conflict can take place between characters, between a single character and a host of other people or else between mutually hostile situations, ideals, and life-values. It is conflict which lends power and movement to drama. (2003: 7)

We have only to think of Prasad's pronouncements, to understand what Rakesh was setting out to counter. There could, however, be no universalizing depiction of reality or of conflict. According to Rakesh, each person and occasion had specificity, each contained the germ of a story, if the writer could recognize the motivating forces in these persons and events. On the face of it, *manasik vyapar*, mental transactions, could appear ordinary or even monotonous, but if the writer were to depict them in detail, registering each sound in the environment and each reaction of the person in the story, then the assemblage of these would achieve dramatic effect and generate the climax of conflict. Here there would be no need to create sudden twists in character or event, each episode would beget the next episode (Rakesh 1975: 32).

In this self-emanating series of scenes and events, there would be no scope for the expression of the personal point of view of the author or for his emotions. His scientific analysis would be contained in the *sanghatan*, assemblage, of events, so that no auctorial comment would be needed to explicate the images of the story (33). In other words, the author would not intrude with his presence. The situations in the story would not be understood as stemming from him, their causation would be made apparent in the course that events took, propelled as it was by the character of the persons implicated in them and their interaction: 'Just as in the full fledged play, so also in the one-act play, characters are a significant element, because it is they who bear the burden of the action and reveal the dramatic story through their dialogue' (Rakesh 2003: 9).

When Rakesh turned to the literary past, he unabashedly contemporized. He had been a scholar of Sanskrit and had translated plays from the Sanskrit, but his past was literary rather than historical in Prasad's sense. His realism was one of urban interiors, domestic and professional. Just as Ashk and others, he was also concerned with the working woman and the financial and social freedom that her profession could afford her. But his men often turned their backs on these women and just as often, this made for violent conflict. The politics of these riven interiors, then, revolved around the loss suffered by the men, whose weakness and inability to take strong decisions was offset by the violence with which the narratives turned on the women.

THE QUEST FOR THE WHOLE

The theme of Rakesh's three full-length plays is the conflict of individuals both within themselves and in their relationship with their partners, other family members, and, often only indirectly, with society.[22] The emphasis shifts from the importance of the development of the individual personality at the cost of a romantic relationship in the first play, to the restrictions the personality is exposed to in the marital relationship. This last is explored at length in Rakesh's second and third plays.

Ashadh ka ek din (The Last Day of Ashadh, 1958) treats of Kalidasa, the Sanskrit poet and dramatist, and his village-beloved Mallika, whom he leaves behind in the mountain village in order to receive the post of royal poet, and to whom he returns at the end of the play, having dissipated and exhausted his creativity, only to find that time has taken its toll and Mallika, in her isolation and poverty, for all her idealism, forced to seek the protection of his rival. The drama of self-realization as it plays itself out within the modern man–woman relationship is thus projected into the literary past.

Laharon ke rajhans (The Majestic Swans of the Waves, 1963), inspired by the Sanskrit epic poem *Saundarananda* by Ashvaghosha, revolves around the story of the Buddha's stepbrother Nand and his spouse Sundari. Nand seeks self-fulfilment and hovers between the ascetic renouncement preached by the Buddha and the earthly beauty of the self-willed Sundari. In the end, he rejects both and strikes off on his own, striding into an unknown future, in search of himself. Rakesh is here concerned with an idealized (non-Hindu, Buddhist) past which harbours all the tensions of the present: the self-focus which oscillates between the ascetic concentration on achieving self-fulfilment and the fulfilment that a sensual relationship offers, with all its pulls and tensions.

The final play, *Adhe adhure* (Neither Half nor Whole, 1969) has an entirely contemporary urban setting: there seems to be no more need to resort to past symbols.[23] It depicts the warring family of Savitri, wife and mother, and central figure of the play. Her relationships with the husband, the employer, the former lover, and, finally, the husband's intimate friend, embitter both her family and herself. She makes a futile effort to leave her family and entice the former lover into starting a new life with her. Her husband, who leaves her at the end of the first half of the play, returns to her in hopeless resignation at the end of the play, unable to find a centre for himself away from her.

The plays, divided into three acts, the last into two, play on a single set: Mallika's foreyard, Sundari's bedchamber, and the living room of Savitri's family respectively. The contrived effort to make the action occur naturally on a single set is not always concealed successfully.[24] The external world is excluded from these domestic foreyards and interiors.[25] The domestic world presented seems self-contained, each scene being linked to the other by the forces of psychological motivation.

The emotions of the characters cumulate gradually. Towards the end, they burst forth in a virtual paroxysm of words, long speeches in which they lay bare their inner conflicts and seek understanding. The body of all three plays is primarily concerned with the woman's experience, though there is shift to the emotional point of view of the man in the last confrontation of each play, allowing him the last long word, so to speak (cf. Sharma 1975: 57).

The audience is never addressed directly, except in the last play, where there is a narrator-like prologue speaker, who, however, does not have any further function in the play.[26] The exclusion of the audience invites passive participation in the emotional set-up of the play and identification with the characters portrayed. In this kind of character close-up, stage directions, sometimes extending over the length of a page, become an important part of the dramatic text. They detail every movement and change of expression of the character,[27] seeking subtle psychological depiction of these by the player, in fact positing the total identification of the player with the played.

Three other factors support the illusion of exclusive stage-realism: the comic scenes which interpolate the text in the first play are reduced in the second, to disappear entirely in the final play. Thus there is no ironic questioning of the pathos generated by the emotional encounters of man and woman.

Second, Rakesh's language, poetic and at the same time idiomatically close to the rhythms of everyday speech, has no need to fall back upon songs to highlight emotional moments, as prevalent in dramaturgy up to Prasad's day.

Third, Rakesh makes effective use of stage lights, isolating, blending, and fading the parts of the reality he wishes to expose or withhold.[28]

The romantic subjectivity which makes for individuation in the first play is reminiscent of the attitude of the Chhayavad poets in their euphoric delight in natural beauty.[29] Kalidasa and Mallika struggle with and defy the social and moral code that society seeks to impose on them, and this defiance often takes the form of expansive identification with nature. When her mother makes an ineffective effort to arrange a marriage for her, Mallika protests that it is her own life and if she wishes to destroy herself, no one has the right to criticize her. She proclaims the rights of the individual, of women, in a way that is new for the Hindi theatre:

What right have they to say anything at all? Mallika's life is her own property. If she wants to destroy it, what right has anyone else to criticize it? (Rakesh 1958: 20)

It is worth noting, though, that, even here, Mallika does not maintain an absolute position but craves understanding for, seconds later, she is pleading with her mother to try and understand her.

Mallika lays great emphasis on the development and nurture of *vyaktitva*, personality. When Kalidasa is asked to occupy the post of royal poet, she attributes this honour to his personality, which should now seek new grounds to enable further evolution:

The honour has been accorded to his personality. He should not deprive his personality of the right to enjoy this. (ibid.: 43)

You need new grounds now in order to make your personality more complete. (56–7)

For this completion of his personality, she sacrifices her own personal happiness, content to seek fulfilment in his creativity. When, years later, he comes back to tell her that, divested of the inspiration provided by the mountains and by her, his creativity has been quelled, her own life seems meaningless. Kalidasa sees his own unhappiness as the conflict of desire with time, rather than with Mallika herself. It is the passage of time which has prevented their union and prevented him from conveying his own inner conflicts to her, though he had come expressly to tell her of these conflicts:

So that I would be able to convince you of the conflict within me.... I did not stop to think that conflict is not restricted to one person alone. (117)

Kalidasa's mistake was not only that he saw his conflict as restricted to his own person, but that he failed to realize that his wholeness would remain incomplete without Mallika. She had already done violence to her own need for intimacy and for creativity. Now she had no further role to play, other than that of a victim of the violence perpetrated on her. However, since these realizations occur in the final encounter, in a sense they preclude the possibility of mutual understanding. Kalidasa does not engage with the needs that Mallika herself expresses; he remains content with self-mollification.

Yet, even this level of direct encounter with the partner does not come about in *Laharon ke rajhans*, for here Nand expressly seeks a self-fulfilment that is only partially dependent on the understanding that the other has of this need: 'Am I nothing, is my inner conflict nothing?' (Rakesh 1963: 129).

The emphasis here is on the conflicts within Nand and his need to find articulation and, with this, the understanding of his partner, which would form one basis for his ability to find an expression of himself and his needs. He proclaims that he has inner needs that no one is willing to accept in the closing scene of the play. He maintains that his wife Sundari has no idea of his *vastavikta*, reality. In so far, he feels defined, and ill-defined at that, by the image that she has of him; and he feels incomplete, since she is not willing to engage with the reality of his person:

Why in living here am I only as much as you want to see in me? And how far can a person go, who can acquire only so much shape, if he is seeking some point in life? (129)

Apparently, there is no wholeness away from the understanding of the other, which defines and at the same time delimits the personality. Nand and Sundari are locked thus in a dilemma, in a partnership that, ideally, should make two wholes of two halves. Unable to make Nand and Sundari reach the understanding that would bring about this sense of completion, Rakesh, according to his own account, found the following solution, thematic and structural at the same time: Nand, uttering a last helpless word was to depart, in search of his own person, leaving Sundari to address her own last words to his departing back, for as Rakesh was to note in his introduction to the play:

Is this encounter between man and woman not their actual resolution? Is this, being face to face and not being able to make their words reach out to each other, not their reality/actuality? (35).

This was to be the culminating point of the relationship between man and woman: the alienation and futility of a coexistence, where each had no access to the reality of the other and where the man at least was free to stride off into an unknown future, treating as his right the need to discover himself.

SEEKING THE OTHER HALF

Savitri in *Adhe adhure* is already beginning to speak only of incompleteness, her own and her husband's. She complains of her lonely struggle with chores and domestic crises, in addition to bearing the burden of being the family's sole breadwinner. She sees the individual as incomplete and marriage as an effort to acquire completion in the partner. However, nowhere is it implied that she and her husband seek self-fulfilment away from each other, through the development of their respective personalities. They seem to be locked in a futile struggle to find completion in an incomplete union.

There is no final confrontation between husband and wife at the end of the play. It is the husband's friend and proxy who holds a long conversation with Savitri, for communication between husband and wife has broken down entirely. The theme of mutual alienation, which runs through Rakesh's plays, remains unchanged, though now the resolution seems out of sight. As Savitri herself clarifies:

There is a human being. He sets up house. Why does he set up house? To fulfill a need. What sort of need? To fill a something—call it an incompleteness—to fill that. In this way, he has to be whole for himself, within himself. (Rakesh 1969: 100)

Savitri's words seem incoherent, but, in fact, they are an entirely adequate articulation of a paradox which remains irresolvable. The human being, man or woman, for apparently both are meant, who seeks to set up a household, sets it up since s/he is initially incomplete. But in order to enter into a partnership, s/he has to possess at the outset, a completeness of person, both for her/himself as well within her/himself, only then can s/he become further complete.[30] Savitri demands, then, a complete human being as a partner, 'vah ek pura admi chahti hai apne liye—ek pura...admi' (102), she wants a complete/whole/entire man for herself, and sees her own husband as trying to cover up his inadequacy by constantly seeking the support of his friends.

But, the husband's friend counters, Savitri does not know her husband, though she has lived with him for twenty-two years. She demands too much of a single person and she would feel the same emptiness and restlessness with any other partner she may have chosen and her partner would have lived in equal frustration with her incompletion. Here, then, the individual is presented as neither self-sufficient nor able to enter into meaningful dialogue. Savitri, working woman, sole supporter of the household, with an unemployed husband, is shown as insatiable in her sexual appetite, satisfied with neither husband, boss, nor former lover, destructive in the extreme, for she shows no understanding and has little time for her children, all of whom run wild since she is so often absent from home and, it is implied, unresponsive to their needs. There is no communication, yet the fault seems to lie with her, for she seems to have driven an already weak man to sheer despair, dejection, and resentful dependence. Yet, for all the violence of the domestic relations he focuses upon, Rakesh's brush retains its light touch and the few strokes with which he draws his characters, the economy of the speech he awards them, are masterly. His words describing Bhuvaneshvar's technique bear repetition as having so strong a bearing on his own:

Bhuvaneshvar uses short, ordinary sentences in his plays, which at a superficial level can seem disconnected. But a far deeper meaning than the ostensible comes to light from within the sentence, which allows the very mind-set of the characters uttering these sentences to find formulation. Bhuvaneshvar leaves more unsaid than said in his plays. This in fact is the great specialty of his plays—what he leaves unsaid touches the heart most.... The majority of his plays deal with man–woman relationships, but with such a subtle touch that the issues at hand come to light primarily through the interaction of the characters and other slight strokes. (Rakesh 2003)

In his three plays, then, Rakesh reached a position that corresponded closely to the dramatic structure as it had evolved and remained normative in Europe from the Renaissance to the end of the nineteenth century, the main features of which Peter Szondi (1965) put forward in the following theses in his *Theorie des modernen Dramas (1889–1950)*.[31]

- Drama since the Renaissance had Man as its theme—'Man' as a fellow human being. The tension between freedom and bondage, his will and decision were what created dramatic action. The theme, then, was the interactive sphere between men.
- Since the prologue, chorus, and epilogue were discarded after the Renaissance, the dialogue as the befitting medium of transaction between human beings, became the sole component of dramatic texture.

- Drama became absolute, recognizing nothing outside itself. The dramatist was absent in drama, he did not speak, he only caused speech, which was motivated by situations and was not to be understood as stemming from an author.
- Drama being absolute, demanded adequate motivation and discouraged chance and coincidence. The dramatic occurrence was grounded within itself.
- In that drama was not secondary to any occurrence outside it, the action was to be placed in the present, a succession of happenings becoming successively 'past', each containing within itself the seed for future germination, each scene containing the possibility of the next, thus shutting out the possibility of the manipulation of the author becoming visible and implying the superfluity of the epic-narrator.
- The onlooker was to be a passive observer of the action, and was not to be directly addressed. His total passivity was to become irrational activity, in that, in his absolute separation, he was invited to absolute identification.
- Similarly the player was to regard his relationship to the role as something which was not to be exposed to view, the player and the dramatic figure were to be united in the dramatic person. The location was also to demonstrate unity, for if the scene changed too often, the illusion that it was actually taking place in the present would be difficult to maintain. The unifying presence of the epic-narrator was not to become structurally necessary.
- The stage was to be a picture-frame stage, without any attempt at establishing a connecting link with the onlooker. It was to come into existence with the commencement of the play and be shut to view by the falling of the curtain at the termination of the play. The stage lights were to be regarded as the light that the dramatic play shed on itself.

This position, evolved in Europe in the centuries following the Renaissance, was arrived at conceptually as well as in practice, in a process of adaptation and assimilation in less than a century in Hindi drama. In the late nineteenth century, Bharatendu Harishchandra had demanded the creation of character and of suspense in drama and rejected mythical themes. In practice he had achieved these aims only preliminarily. Prasad developed the romantic subjectivity of the character, but conceptually he remained bound to Indian aesthetics and did not allow the individuality of his characters to gain the upper hand. Rakesh, a quarter of a century later, had no scruples in leaving aside values stamped as 'Indian'. Conceptually, he demanded faithfulness only to reality, which he saw reflected in conflict, internal and interpersonal. However, while developing the personalities of his characters, Rakesh encountered problems that Western drama had met with much earlier, at the turn of the nineteenth century. Within the dramatic form, which had developed around action as emanating from character and dialogue as the medium of transaction between human beings, were the seeds for its disruption that were in fact to disrupt the dramatic framework. In the effort to establish themselves as individuals, the characters of drama overflow their bounds, there is loss of communication, of dialogue and, as a consequence thereof, of definite contours, of identity, of 'character'. Without development of character, there could be no action which could evolve in the formation of it.

These developments can be traced in Rakesh's work, for in his third play *Adhe adhure*, there is neither the possibility of action nor of dialogue. Though Hindi playwrights continued to compose plays exploring these problems, in retrospect Rakesh himself came to regard his plays as faulty in construction, chalking this up both as personal failure as well as the limitations inherent in the theme and the structure.[32] He was to specify this most clearly in an interview with Mohan Maharishi. He saw his first two plays as suffering from the 'excessive literariness of my words', in the third, he had tried more directly to come to grips with 'the realities of life'. But the long speeches at the end of the play offered insights which he had somehow failed to convey dramatically in the main body of the play.

I strongly feel that those well-thought-out passages or the pieces of knowledgeable prose are literary invaders that do not really belong to theatre.

Today's reality is something that is becoming quite complex. Something is constantly happening to us and in our desperate effort to strike equilibrium with the surroundings we are making constant adjustments. Every one of us is living a life in fragments. During the course of one single day one is forced to play ten different parts and sometimes more than one version of each part. What

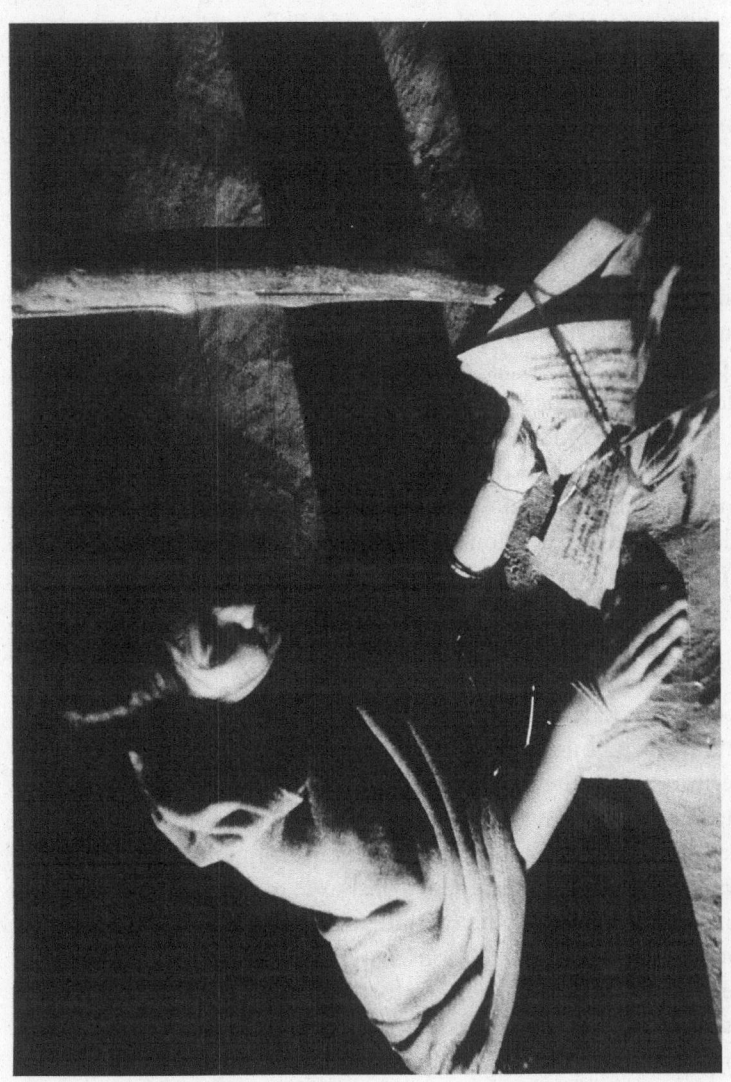

Materials of Realism. Alkazi's production of Rakesh's *Ashadh ka ek din* (early 1960s) (National School of Drama)

remains constant is one's sense of being; the idea of crisis. It is this that I call today's mood of life. And it is in this sense that one feels fragmented. Something keeps happening to one, a phenomenon quite difficult to explain; something like an atomic fission keeps taking place in the landscape of one's mind. One senses it, but cannot fully articulate the experience. I think what is occurring in man's mind must find a recurrence in the language of theatre, so as to achieve a deep and instantaneous rapport between the words and the audiences.[33]

'Straight' narrative, within a sequentially structured temporal framework, was, then, no longer possible, if one were to remain true to contemporary reality. The kind of cognition of both the self and the other that the characters of his three plays had conveyed in long passages of speech simply masqueraded as pieces of knowledge. The fragmented understanding of the self meant, for one, that Rakesh abandoned the notion of the 'rounded' character. Further, the alienation of the self from the self as well as the environment, if it were to be represented immediately rather than only expounded, meant for him as well that the levels of self-perception were themselves to be henceforth split in their theatrical representation.

THE FRAGMENTATION OF 'REALITY'

In looking for ways to present the emotional (and metaphysical) isolation of man, his inability to communicate, Rakesh embarked upon an experiment with the dramatic form itself.[34] The notes to the research he had conducted on the 'Dramatic Word' as part of a project which took him to many European theatres and brought an exchange of views with a variety of theatre persons, were to record his awareness of the need to find new modes of dramatic expression. These notes were records of immediate perceptions, barely arranged into chapters. They were yet to be organized and fully formulated when he died. However, certain trends had crystallized, as the notes published posthumously clearly articulate.[35]

Firstly, since character no longer had definite contours, the complexity of the mind and its perceptions could only find expression in the fragmentation of language itself:

Looking for simplest of words to connote the division and complexity of today's mind. The need to articulate the predicament without intellectualising it.

Discovering the language of being and finding dramatic arrangements for it. Can the image of a fragmented society be cast through a 'whole' language? Fragmenting language for dramatic purposes....

Fragmentation and Absurdism. Not seeking to discover just another dimension of absurdism. How the idea of fragmentation is linked with the reality around. The absurdities that are inherent in life reality itself. The 'seed plays' of real life.

The coherence of incoherences and meaningfulness of meaningless words. (Chap. 5)

Secondly, within this framework, there could be no meaningful attempt to communicate with the other, since mutual perception remained equally fragmentary. Dialogue as a medium of communication could then be no more than dated theatrical convention:

The orthodox role of words in theatre as dialogues.... Carrying words to the unseen and releasing them from their exclusive role as dialogues. The infinite possibilities of abstraction and fragmentation through such a use.

The importance of direction and situation of sound. Attacking the audience mind from any and every direction.... Words as part of this multidirectional use of sound. The play that may bid farewell to literature in the conventional sense and belong exclusively to theatre. (Chap. 7)

Thirdly, 'reality' was not simply reproducible. New modes were needed to represent the new awareness of its fragmentary nature. Rakesh suggested breaking up syntax, using words for their sound value, attempting new combinations of words, alternating with silence:

The idea of achieving a total acoustic constancy of words and sounds. Looking at strings of words as a series of sounds by themselves.

... The argument of silence. The intense dramatic moments when silence is far more eloquent and effective than words.

The dramatic silence is not a neutral or a negative state. It is not the same as stillness on stage before the play opens; nor is it the absence of sound as in an empty hall. The dramatic silence is a time duration that carries the charge of words spoken before and the anticipation of the words to be spoken afterwards. It is a cord between the two poles of words.... (Chap. 6)

In the last play completed before his death, *Chhatriyam* (Umbrellas), there is a single figure, *admi*, man, on the stage and there is the soundtrack off-stage. There is no interaction between these, the sound determines the movements of the man, but the man, who struggles with a cluster of mushrooms, has no influence on the sound till the end of the play, when he speaks for the first time. He asks what they (the mushrooms) are called. And the soundtrack proclaims that there is no language, no words, no emotions. Structurally and thematically, there is a close correspondence to Peter Handke's *Kaspar*, which play Rakesh had encountered on his recent research trip to Europe. The shift in Rakesh's form, however, cannot be regarded as merely derivative; it is thematically conditioned, for the loss of communication was immanent in his works as well.

Kaspar is also the sole protagonist of the play, though unlike Rakesh's *admi*, he is joined by another group of figures later. There is, however, no dialogue with them. Kaspar interacts with the furniture on the stage, just as admi struggles with mushrooms. The voices off-stage, according to Handke, 'Should, though entirely comprehensible in their meaning, speak like voices which, as also in reality, have a technical medium which is switched on in between' (Handke 1972: 7). Rakesh's voices come through a tape recorder, a gramophone needle stuck in a groove, a radio announcement, etc. Both Handke and Rakesh interpolate these voices with gibberish. Though both Kaspar and admi react to the voices, the voices themselves take no note of this, so that there is no interaction. At the end of the play, Kaspar has learnt how to speak, words which estrange him from the reality around him: 'With my very first sentence, I've fallen into the trap.... I've been made to speak. I've been transported into reality' (98–9). The suggestion is that it is this reality which is false. Rakesh's admi, as mentioned earlier, does not speak in the course of the play. At the end he just asks '*mera nam?*' (my name), and then picking up the mushrooms '*iska nam?*' (its name) (Rakesh 1998: 159). The soundtrack then sums up his situation: (What am I?

Why am I? There is no language, no words, no expression/emotion, there is nothing) (160).[36]

Chhatriyam had come a long way from the original agenda proclaimed by Rakesh. Today's reality, as Rakesh called it, was to find 'nonrealistic or ultra-realistic connotation by being juxtaposed with certain sounds and words'.[37]

Rakesh's perception of contemporary reality signalled the receding importance of one kind of 'realism'.[38] However, narrative continued to be of prime importance on the urban stage and Rakesh's experiments were not destined to be carried forth in modern Indian drama in any sustained way. The 1970s and 1980s witnessed a variety of experiments that sought to combine the most diverse regional narrative–dramatic traditions with Brecht's epic theatre. Here character and dialogue played a subordinate role, but the narrator made a reappearance.[39]

What then was Rakesh's contribution? Throughout his short but intense association with theatre—it lasted barely a decade and a half—Rakesh remained concerned with the formation of a modernist Hindi stage that catered to the needs and aspirations of urban modernity. Though he himself seldom used a nationalist vocabulary, along with Badal Sircar, Vijay Tendulkar, and Girish Karnad, he came to be recognized as one of the four 'greats' of modern Indian theatre.[40] However, unlike the other three, he reacted impatiently to the suggestion that the urban dramatist and the urban stage had any need to learn from 'traditional' theatre and he resisted the vogue for 'folk' theatre which swept through the subcontinent in the late 1960s and 1970s. He made this position clear to the enthusiasts and theatre practitioners gathered at the Sangeet Natak Akademi Round Table on Traditional Theatre convened in 1971. Badal Sircar had indicated a willingness to find out more about folk forms so that he could learn to produce cheaper theatre for larger city audiences. Rakesh conceded that there was some usefulness to this,

But I don't understand why this sort of deliberate, conscious and artificial exposure is necessary, because we are being exposed to whatever our tradition is in our daily life—if I exist in any sphere of Indian society I am exposed right from our birth to what is my tradition. Everything I have been exposed to in my daily life, I have absorbed in me, that tradition lives in me and inadvertently, whether I want it or not that tradition gets expressed in my work.... If it is unconscious, subconscious, automatic, then certainly it is most welcome, but if it is an effort because it is the fashion today, this sort of approach I would totally reject.[41]

On the one hand then, Rakesh seemed to be out of step with his times in that he resisted the moves which would help the modern stage to overcome the restraints of the 'naturalistic' stage as the urban proscenium stage was called then. It was surely a move that accorded well with his own efforts to move beyond the confines of the living room to the 'non-realistic or ultra-realistic'. However, there could be more than one way to overcome the pitfalls of the theatre of man–woman relationships. Raymond Williams has summed up the crisis that beset modernist naturalism as follows:

Its version of the environment within which human lives were formed and deformed—the domestic bourgeois household in which the social and financial insecurities and above all the sexual tensions were most immediately experienced—was at once physically convincing and intellectually insufficient. Beyond this key site there were, in opposite directions, crucial areas of experience which the language and behaviour of the living room could not articulate fully or interpret. (1989: 85).

Avant-garde theatre could then take two directions. Rakesh himself took the one direction which 'explored subjectivity more intensively'. Yet there was also the other direction, and this was indeed being explored in modern Indian drama at least from the late 1960s on, which sought to make drama 'fully public again' (Williams 1989: 86). And the use of folk forms for this end, which could open up multiple sites and avenues of representation was, in principle, as valid a move away from the living room as that which Rakesh elected to explore. However, even here, in retrospect, Rakesh can be seen as being ahead of his times in resisting the wave of traditionalism which would soon lose sight of the 'contemporary' it invoked so fervently. It is to these simultaneously emerging trends, the effort to politicize theatre, to make it more of the 'people', to which I turn in the next section of this volume.

NOTES

[1] This quest for partnership, which formed the core of Rakesh's major plays, signified a radical shift from Prasad's late plays, from the erotic fulfilment and social protection that Dhruvasvamini for instance, sought in her male partner.

[2] Rakesh made these comments with reference to a historical one-act play by Ramkumar Varma which he had included in an anthology he edited. Rakesh deplored the lack of subtlety in the handling of character, the weaker aspects of which could have been more sharply etched, and in the use of a dialogue that communicated feelings too directly. He asked that more attention be paid to stage set and lighting so that the internal conflict could be better brought out than the text alone was able to mediate (2003: 66–7).

[3] Dashrath Ojha would see the beginning of this trend with Lakshminarayan Mishra's play *Sanyasi* (1927). For an important discussion of such 'social issues' plays, see Ojha's chapter on *Samasya natakom ka udaya* in Ojha (1984: 265 ff).

[4] Premchand translated Galsworthy's *Strike, Justice, and Silver Box* as *Hartal* (1930), *Nyaya* (1931), and *Chandi ki dibiya* (1931) respectively. Ibsen's *The Doll's House* and *Pillars of Society* were translated by Lakshminarayan Mishra as *Gudiya ka ghar* (1930) and *Samaj ka sthambh* (1931) respectively.

[5] The essay was prefaced to his play *Mukti ka rahasya* (1962 [1943]). Mishra explicitly named only D.L. Ray. It was only in the note added nineteen years later that he admitted that in reality he was polemicizing against Prasad.

[6] In the essay *Apne alochak mitra se*, to my critic–friend, prefaced to his play *Sanyasi* (1930: 2, 8).

[7] Rakesh (2003: 127, 134). For a concise view of Bhuvaneshvar's extraordinary career see the monograph by Rastogi (2001).

[8] Upendranath Ashk had a long and prolific career as novelist, short-story writer, literary critic, and dramatist. His reputation in the world of Hindi letters was probably at its height in the 1950s and 1960s, to suffer a somewhat sharp decline thereafter. For a critical overview of Ashk's career, see the biography by Rockwell (2004).

[9] Cited in Birendranarayan (1981: 202). See also Mehta (1969).

[10] Cf. Peter Gaeffke on Ashk's play *Jay parajay* (1937): 'Ashk interprets Rajput history, which had before been treated of under the influence of romantic ideas, as ruled by a terrible individualism which compels heroes to self-sacrifice in mutual warfare but makes them blind to common interests' (1978: 101).

Similarly Mathur's *Konark* (1951) depicts the problems of the creative genius of an architect, set within the historical framework of the sun-temple of Orissa.

[11] The 1954 play *Alag alag raste* (Separate ways) shows the young woman protagonist accepting life as a co-wife. *Udan* (Flight, 1950) depicts the young woman choosing arbitrarily and wilfully between three suitors, without succumbing to societal pressures. However, the freedom of choice that she is able to exercise is discredited, since it is shown as wilful. *Svarg ki jhalak* (Glimpse of Heaven, 1939) shows the educated woman being rejected as a future wife by the educated young man in favour of a traditional housewife. Plays such as *Bhanvar* (Whirlpool, 1961) where educated, emancipated Pratibha finds herself unable to reconcile herself to life with any of her suitors, further confirms the suspicion that Ashk is at the least deeply ambivalent, if not outright hostile, about the power sought by these newly educated young women. His well-known play *Anjodidi* (Elder sister Anjo, 1955) depicts Anjo as obsessively clean in her housekeeping, pressuring her husband into complying with her compulsions, initially driving him away but then herself committing suicide as a final measure of revenge. The husband gives up drink and 'bad habits' in order to come to terms with the guilt with which he is now ever burdened. An earlier play *Taulie* (Towels, 1943) circles around the same themes. For detailed analyses of these plays from a perspective which views Ashk as espousing the feminist cause, see Dimitrova (2000).

[12] Rakesh also mentions the need for plays in Hindi, particularly one-act plays, felt by amateur theatre groups and schools and colleges in small towns (2003: 5). As for the support generated for dramatic composition in Hindi, we need to note that Ashk wrote regularly for the Lahore station of All India Radio from 1938 to 1943 and was employed in the Delhi station of All India Radio from 1941 to 1943.

[13] *Rat bitne tak* became *Laharon ke rajhans*, *Ashadh ka ek din* retained its title. The one-act plays are published in the collection: *Rat bitane tak tatha anya dhvaninatak* (1974). Rakesh's views on the radio-play are available in his collection of essays, *Sahityik aur sanskritik drishti* (1975: 106–10).

[14] See the Introduction to this volume for a discussion of Alkazi's impact on the fledgling national culture as it was being created in the capital of the new nation in the 1950s and 1960s.

[15] Alkazi recalled this experience many years later: 'My first production

in Delhi was Mohan Rakesh's *Asadh ka ek din*, a thing which he had not even seen, and the production of which he said had really established him. I didn't know him for six–seven years after that. And it was very much later that he told me that it had really established him. It was largely in commercial terms. Because as a result of that he said, 'My play was taken seriously and was prescribed for the BA. And as a result of that, I sold thousands of copies and I lived on the royalty for a large number of years. As result of that, my other plays were taken seriously' (Interview with Alkazi: 19 March 1981).

[16] The Hindi version was published in *Ande ke chhilke, anya ekanki tatha bij natak* (1973).

[17] There are early statements in the collection of essays entitled *Parivesh* (1967), as well as two major essays entitled *Hindi katha sahitya: navin pravrittiyan* which are available in *Sahityik aur sanskritik drishti* (1975).

[18] Rakesh's edition of five early one-act plays was put together for use in colleges, possibly in the mid- to late 1960s, to judge by internal references in the introduction. It has now been brought out in a new edition by Anita Rakesh (2003). His comments on the one-act play as genre and on the individual playwrights reveal his own concept of 'realist' drama.

[19] Introduction to *Laharon ke rajhans* (1963: 8). See also the comment by Kamaleshvar, well-known *nayi kahani* writer, '*Nayi kahani ne sanskritik punarutthan ka bida nahin uthaya*' (The *nayi kahani* has not set itself the task of cultural revival). Rakesh (1974: 61).

[20] Roadarmel (1969) remains the best introduction in English of the *nayi kahani* movement.

[21] For a discussion of this aspect of the 'official' national culture, see my forthcoming essay on Rakesh's first novel: 'Culture as a Buffer: Writers, Artistes and Patronage in Post-Partition Delhi'.

[22] In Rakesh's understanding of it, yathartha had always included mental and emotional transactions within a single person as well as the interaction with social reality (1967: 185).

[23] The play was written at the peak of Rakesh's most creative period. His thoughts on a number of issues relating to urban modernity were finding clear articulation. In reviewing Carl Weber's production of the Hindi adaptation of Brecht's *Caucasian Chalk Circle* for the National School of Drama, Rakesh took exception to the shoddy Hindi translation for one: 'Without a well-defined theatrical tradition of our own, the question of language in theatre

remains a major challenge for us. The challenge looms larger when the question is one of giving body in our own language to a work that is rooted in a different theatrical tradition.'

Regarding the timeless frame of the action, Rakesh had the following to say. He found that the experience had:

a touch of freshness. At the same time, it raised a number of questions: Are we, always complaining about an audience that stays away from theatre, really concerned with providing these spectators with a theatre of 'their own', in their own terms, in terms of their experience of and negotiations with the national mores?.... Is our quest not getting limited to seeking a new theatre form that would emerge only out of the theatrical traditions as they tend to get more and more crystallized into a single system?

A theatrical happening like this could go a long way in inspiring us to make a beginning towards subverting all traditions, to draw us out of ourselves, to start thinking about theatre in a totally new way; provided we bear in mind that such a beginning can be made only with the defiance of such a work.

Published originally in *Natrang*, 2.8 (October–December 1968) as a reaction to Carl Weber's *Kharia ka ghera*, the Hindi version of Brecht's *Caucasian Chalk Circle*, National School of Drama. Reprinted in *Rangvarta*.

[24] The characters in the play have to submit to the contrivance of the playwright to make an entrance possible and to allow a specific exchange to take place. Cf. Sharma (1975: 56–8).

[25] In his review of a performance of *Laharon ke rajhans*, Habib Tanvir (1973) pointed out that the playwright projected an inadequate concept of Buddhism, which he depicted as mere escapism. Viewed historically:

Buddhism was a dynamic philosophy of life, which sought among other things to bring about radical changes in a caste-ridden society, bedevilled by poverty, disease and death.... To begin with, Ebrahim Alkazi's set itself had done everything to shut out all environment except the domestic. The producer too, in his turn, exclusively emphasized the domestic element of the play. The external world, full of an increasing number of Buddhist monks, that surrounded Nand's house, was never made visible.

[26] This narrator wears different masks to play all the four men in Savitri's life, implying their interchangeability as well as their being only different

manifestations of the same incomplete personality, which fact Savitri also proclaims at the end of the play. The masks, however, seem more a stage device than grounded in the reality of the play, which attributes special characteristics peculiar to each of these four men.

27 As for instance in *Adhe adhure*, when the husband overhears his wife say to the daughter that she really cannot carry on like this anymore: *'stri ke shabd uske kan men parte hain, par vah jan bujh kar apne chehre se koi pratikriya vyakt nahin hone deta.*—The woman's words reach his ears but he does not allow his face to express any reaction' (23). Here the actor would have to convey that though he has a reaction, he deliberately suppresses it.

28 Rakesh's early experience with film scripts and radio plays made for an awareness of the use of lights, composition of scenes, and economy of dialogue.

29 In an interview with Rajinder Paul about his early life, Rakesh admitted to having been deeply influenced by the writings of Sumitranandan Pant and Mahadevi Varma. *Enact. Mohan Rakesh memorial issue* (January–February 1973).

30 These thoughts are anticipated in Rakesh's novel *Andhere band kamare* (1961), though it is worth noting that they stem from Harbans, the male protagonist of novel, rather than the female, making this desire to find self-fulfilling in the other a mutual, rather than a gender-specific need. Harbans has sought temporary separation from Nilima, his wife, in order to fulfil his potential as writer and thinker. However, in order to achieve the fullness of person he craves, he needs Nilima to be complete in herself also: 'I want to see some such thing in you, so beautiful, that I can acclaim it with my whole person, without having to lose a word over it. I want to see the kind of completion (*purnata*) in you which also fills my interior with it and startles me, awaking such passion that my whole being is absorbed in it' (99). As Luhman has pointed out, this self-absorbed individuation which seeks at the same time to find its complement in that of the partner, endangers the very nature of the union founded on the principle of complete merger and complete differentiation ([1982] 1998: 38).

31 The following is a summary of the opening chapter of Szondi's work ([1965] 1985: 14–19).

32 It has been maintained that Rakesh's plays deal again and again with the man–woman relationship and project only the obvious without providing any newer or deeper understanding of the changes or the conflicts in social and personal relations (*Enact. Mohan Rakesh memorial issue.* January–

February1973). However, it is not only the fate of particular individuals and their incompatibility with each other that Rakesh's work depicts. Much more, it is a social reflection of the new understanding of the individual in the urban middle classes and the crisis of communication and alienation that seems to accompany it. In fact, in depicting this adequately, the form developed to express it seems to exhaust its own potential.

[33] *Enact. Mohan Rakesh memorial issue* (January–February 1973). Alkazi's perspective on this issue bears extensive quotation:

And then I said, I know you [Rakesh] are dealing with your own problems, as a creative individual, as an artist, take Kalidasa, he's really you. Take his relationship with Mallika, it's really your own personal relations with the people around you. But then you have couched it in a language that is so remote, that it may be true to Kalidasa, but it's [*sic*] not true to our own times. In *Laharon ke rajhans* you deal with another kind of spiritual problem and again it is remote in time. At the same time, it is linked with us today in our own times by way of analogy. Why don't you deal with the problems of today in the language of today? And it seems to have struck a chord. I said, use the language of the streets, and that is the kind of language which can be hammered out into the language with all the force of literature. Literature is not literary. Ultimately, I think he [Rakesh] was so preoccupied with it that he did come out with *Adhe adhure*. And when he did, I felt very privileged. I was the first person that he read it out to and then I said again, it's a brilliant play but then you have found the normal kind of solution, which you have in a well-made play, you know the long speech in the third act. If you want to develop the modern kind of sensibility truly, then it has to be done in a much more subtle way and you have to leave the whole thing much more open, not as a kind of revelation. And as a result of that, when he did get the Homi Bhabha fellowship or the J.N. fellowship, his subject was the dramatic word, really what he meant was the language of theatre (Interview with Alkazi: 19 March 1981).

[34] This was also the theme of the play Rakesh left uncompleted, *Pair tale ki zamin* (The ground beneath the feet, completed by Kamleshwar and published posthumously) with which he had apparently struggled for many years, and which in the notes to the play, he described thus: '*kuchh sankat is*

bat ka hai ki natak ke vibhinna charitron ke bich koi sanpreshan nahin hai: unke bolne ke liye alag alag "wave lengths" ka istemal karke unki "tragedy" ko ubhara ja sakta hai' (*Natrang*, 1972: 3) (There is some concern about the issue that there is no communication between the various characters. Their tragedy can be foregrounded by using different wavelengths for their respective ways of speaking).

35 The full text of the notes was published in *Enact. Mohan Rakesh memorial issue* (January–February 1973).

36 Even optically, the printing of Rakesh's text follows Handke's *Kaspar*. Rakesh separates the sound and the description of the visual into two columns, left and right, on the page. Handke similarly separates the soundtrack off-stage and Kaspar's words and actions on-stage into two columns.

37 'Changing Role of Words in Theatre. Interview with Mohan Maharishi'. *Enact. Mohan Rakesh memorial issue* (January–February 1973).

38 But here, it seemed, East and West did go separate ways. In modern Western theatre, the rupture with 'naturalism' was more enduring: even if the words uttered on stage did not always remain indecipherable, the dramatic text, distributed between different speakers, did not attempt to resolve the tensions it threw up or recapitulate or lead to action. The resolution, if any such thing were at all possible, was left much more to the audience. Cf. Pavis (1993: 56–7).

39 I deal at length with the aesthetics of the Brechtian experiment on the Hindi stage in the following section.

40 Thus the well-known theatre historian and critic Kumud Mehta:
By the sixties this realisation [changing political and social attitudes] assumed concrete shape in the work of four different playwrights writing in four different languages. Their experience was shared to such a degree by theatre practitioners all over the country that productions of their plays came to be considered a national theatre movement. Typical of this period was the Hindi play *Adhe Adhure* by Mohan Rakesh, where the clash between a working wife and her unsuccessful husband, coupled with the frustrations of their children, pointed to the slow disintegration of the family as a viable social unit (1981: 89).

41 'Proceedings of the Round Table on Traditional Theatre'. *Sangeet Natak Special Issue* (July–September 1971: 39).

REFERENCES

Arora, Keval. 2003. 'Ebrahim Alkazi', in *Theatre India*, No. 7, 22–46.

Bardola, V.M. 1999. 'Post 1980 Plays: Hindi', in *Theatre India*, No. 2, 13–18.

Birendranarayan. 1981. *Hindi Drama and Stage*. Delhi: Bansal.

Dalmia, Vasudha. Forthcoming. 'Culture as a Buffer: Writers, Artistes and Patronage in Post-Partition Delhi.'

Dimitrova, Diana. 2000. 'Upendranath Ashk's Dramatic Work: Women and Gender in Modern Hindi Drama as Revealed in the Plays of Upendranath Ashk'. PhD. dissertation, Heidelberg University.

Enact. Mohan rakesh Memorial Number. 1973, January–February (no pagination).

Enact, National School of Drama Special Issues. 1981. Guest Editors: Reeta Sondhi and Suneeta Paul. January–March 1981, April–June 1981 (no pagination).

Gaeffke, Peter. 1978. *Hindi Literature in the Twentieth Century.* Wiesbaden: Harrassowitz.

Handke, Peter. 1972. *Kaspar*, in *Stücke I.* Frankfurt am Main: Suhrkamp.

Jayshankar Prasad. 2000. *Kavya aur kala tatha anya nibandh.* Allahabad: Lokbharati Prakashan.

Luhmann, Niklas. [1982] 1998. *Love as Passion: the Codification of Intimacy.* Translated by Jeremy Gaines and Doris L. Jones. Stanford: Stanford University Press.

Mehta, Kamalini. 1969. *Natak aur Yatharthvad.* Varanasi: Nagari Pracharini Sabha.

Mehta, Kumud. 1981. 'Indian Theatre Today—Grappling with New Realities', in *Marg*, Special Issue on Aspects of the Performing Arts.

Mishra, Lakshminarayan. 1930. *Sanyasi.* Varanasi: Hindi Pracharak Pustakalya.

———. [1943] 1962. *Mukti ka rahasya.* Allahabad: Sahitya Bhavan.

Mohan Rakesh. 1949. *Satya aur kalpana.* Reprinted Delhi: Motilal Banarsidas, 1985.

———. 1958. *Ashadh ka ek din.* Reprinted Delhi: Rajpal and Sons, 1969 [translated into English by Sarah K. Ensley: *One Day in Ashadha*, Delhi: National School of Drama, 1998]

———. 1961. *Andhere band kamare.* Delhi: Rajkamal Prakashan.

———. 1963. *Laharon ke rajhans.* Delhi: Rajkamal Prakashan, fifth ed. 1978.

———. 1966. 'Looking around as a Playwright', in *Sangeet Natak*, October.

_____. 1967. *Parivesh*. Banaras: Bharatiya Gyanpith Prakashan.

_____. 1969. *Adhe adhure*. Delhi: Radhakrishna Prakashan.

_____. 1973. *Ande ke chhilke, anya ekanki tatha bij natak*. Delhi: Radhakrishna Prakashan.

_____. 1974. *Rat bitne tak tatha anya dhvani natak*. Delhi: Radhakrishna Prakashan.

_____. 1975. *Sahityik aur sanskritik drishti*. Delhi: Radhakrishna Prakashan.

_____. 1985. *Mohan rakesh ki dayari*. Delhi: Rajpal & Sons.

_____. 1998. *Pair tale ki zamin*. Delhi: Rajpal & Sons.

_____. (ed.) 2003. *Panch parde: panch ekankiyon ka samgrah*. Delhi: Radhakrishna Prakashan.

Nagendra. (ed.) 1976. *Bharatiya natya sahitya. Seth Govinddas abhinandan granth*. Delhi: S. Chand & Co.

Ojha, Dashrath. [1954] 1984. *Hindi natak: Udbhav aur vikas*. Delhi: Rajpal & Sons.

Pavis, Patrice. 1993. 'The Classical Heritage of Modern Drama: The Case of Postmodern Theatre', in *Theatre at the Crossroads of Culture*. Translated by Loren Kruger. London and New York: Routledge.

Rangvarta: News Bulletin of the Natya Shodh Sansthan. 1994. No. 55, November.

Rastogi, Girish. 1976. *Mohan rakesh aur unke natak*. Allahabad: Lokbharati Prakashan.

_____. 2001. *Bhuvaneshvar*. Delhi: Sahitya Akademi.

Roadarmel, Gordon. 1969. 'The Theme of Alienation in the Modern Hindi Short Story'. Ph.D. dissertation, University of California, Berkeley.

_____. (trans.) [1972] 1987. *Death in Delhi: Modern Hindi Short Stories*. Delhi: Penguin.

Rockwell, Daisy. 2004. *Upendranath Ashk: A Critical Biography*. Delhi: Katha.

Sangeet Natak Quarterly. 1971. Proceedings of the Round Table on Traditional Theatre. Guest Editor: Suresh Awasthi. July–September.

Sharma, Jagdish. 1975. *Mohan rakesh ki rangdristhi*. Delhi: Radhakrishna Prakashan.

Szondi, Peter. [1965] 1985. *Theorie des modernen Dramas*. Rev. Ed. Frankfurt: Suhrkamp.

Tanvir, Habib. 1973. Review, *Enact. Mohan Rakesh Memorial Issue* (January–March).

Williams, Raymond. 1989. *The Politics of Modernism*. London, New York: Verso.

II

The Nation and its 'Folk'

Folk Theatre and the Search for an Indigenous Idiom:
Brecht in India

I t had taken almost a century to establish the idea of a modern Indian theatre which was firmly linked with a proud past enshrined in classical Sanskrit dramatic practice. Great pains had been undertaken to set up the similarities between Kalidasa and Shakespeare. This was a process which opened up multiple possibilities, for the equation made it seem both natural and desirable to borrow unhesitatingly from current Western theatrical practice as it had evolved since Shakespeare's day. Shakespeare had, so to speak, merely carried forth what Kalidasa had begun. Clearly, invoking the courtly Kalidasa and the no less exalted Shakespeare, given his standing as a British classic, could be no other than an elite enterprise, in spite of the fact that the express aim of a given play was often to address a wider public, which presumably encompassed popular audiences. However, whatever the breadth of the targeted viewership, in order to stress its moral impeccability and high social status, the self-consciously literary theatre of the fledgling Hindi literary world demarcated itself sharply from popular theatrical forms, rural and urban, which had come to be considered vulgar and uncouth.

Bharatendu Harishchandra, as we saw, distanced himself from popular traditions in the effort to establish social respectability, in principle if not in practice. He had spoken of *bhrashta*, corrupt, forms, wherein no *nataktva* or dramatic quality had survived, and as examples of these he had listed the popular *bhand, Inder Sabha, tamasha, rasa, yatra*, and *lila*.[1] Although the popular Parsi theatre and the *khela* of Maharashtrians could make some claims to belong to drama proper, he found that they could also be seen as no other than corrupt, since they lacked poetry. Jayshankar Prasad was not even to glance in the direction of rural folk forms; he reserved his ire for the irrepressible Parsis alone.

The disapproval for popular theatre forms, rural or urban, and the elite attempt to marginalize them, did not mean that they disappeared. On the contrary, they flourished through the nineteenth till well into the twentieth century, and the commercial urban Parsi or Company theatre, continued to borrow heavily from them, though without express acknowledgement. But, however vital their mode of expression and whatever their entertainment value, in the early decades of the twentieth century, it would have been difficult to convince the wider public that these rural and urban popular forms could ever come to be regarded as repositories of tradition.

In this chapter, then, I shall trace and chart the winding trajectory of folk forms, spanning a whole century of transmutations, from the first emergence and consolidation of the category 'folk' in the late nineteenth century to its transformation into the veritable storehouse of indigenous values and essences in the late twentieth. The attempt will be to trace broad patterns and shifts, and to focus on movements rather than individuals, or indeed undertake detailed analyses of plays and productions.

COLLECTION AND CONSERVATION: FOLK CULTURE AS THE NATION'S SELF-EXPRESSION

Herder in the late eighteenth century, and following him the Romantic poets through the first half of the nineteenth century, had seen the culture of the 'Volk' or people as mirroring the soul and epitomizing the spirit of the nation. This belief also inspired the work of colonial administrators in various parts of the subcontinent. James Tod's *Annals and Antiquities of Rajasthan* (1829) became a classic for all times; it was accompanied and followed by similar works that documented the annals and antiquities of other parts of the country. But documenting the lore of the people of a given locality or region was taken up in earnest, particularly by Indian Civil Servicemen, in the latter half of the nineteenth century. Perhaps not surprisingly this interest in folk culture, as well as the category 'folk' came into currency at the same time as the 'high' literature in the modern Indian print languages began to take shape and set up a canon for itself.

The word 'folklore' had first been coined coined by W.J. Thom in a letter to the *Athenaeum* in 1846: 'What we in England designate as Popular Antiquities, or Popular Literature...would be most aptly described by a good Saxon compound, Folk-Lore—the Lore of the People.' Thom was to become director of the newly founded Folklore Society in 1878. *Folk-lore*, the journal of the Society, which began to appear in the same year, carried much material on India. By the latter half of the nineteenth century, the interest in the culture of the people acquired yet another dimension and significance; it began to be seen as 'centred in the notion of "survivals", following Taylor's definition in *Primitive Culture* (1871) of elements surviving "by force of habit into a new state of society".' Thus delving into folklore meant tracing the past roots of a given culture. This had important ramifications for a fast industrializing and urbanizing society. As Raymond Williams has pointed out, '(f)olk, in this period, had the effect of backdating all elements of popular culture, and was often offered as a contrast with modern popular forms, either of a radical and working class or of a commercial kind.'[2] This backdating would remain a persistent tendency. Folklore as a field and as part and parcel of colonial anthropology, considering its dynamic connection to Indian source material, would cut a network of inroads into British India, as a cluster of enthusiastic British scholar-administrators and missionaries embarked upon extensive research into the folklore of the region in which they were posted. Many went on to found and edit journals that solicited active contributions from British and Indians alike. James Burgess established the *Indian Antiquary* in 1872, with the express intention of bridging the gap between East and West and of making Western research available in India. It was a widely read and widely quoted journal.[3] William Crooke and Richard Carnac Temple emerged as the two most powerful and prolific civil servants to engage in the field. Crooke was to be President of the Folklore

Society from 1912 to 1913, after a long career of service in the United Provinces of Agra and Oudh, with several books on folklore to his credit, the most important being the two-volume *An Introduction to the Popular Religion and Folklore of Northern India* (1894). Temple served in various military and civil capacities in India; he is best remembered for his three-volume *Legends of the Punjab* (1884–1900), wherein were contained several scripts of the popular theatrical form *svang*, the earliest to be thus documented. Crooke edited *North Indian Notes and Queries* (1891–6) and Temple *Punjab Notes and Queries*. The journals fostered interest and pride in the lore of the countryside; there were also contributions by Indians. In the following decades there was a steady trickle of publications comprising tales collected in various parts of India. The movement, if it can be seen thus, slowly but surely gathered momentum. There is no consolidated study of this period of compilation and documentation, sometimes random, at others more systematic, carried out in various parts of the subcontinent.[4] Within the frame of this chapter, it seems most meaningful to touch briefly upon the activity in Bengal, since its influence was particularly strong in the Hindi belt.[5]

There are traces of missionary or civil servant contact and influence in the lives of most folklore collectors of the day. The earliest of the Bengal folklorists, Lal Behari Day (1824–94) compiled the *Folktales of Bengal* (1881) at the request of Captain Temple, son of the more famous father. Day had been converted to Christianity by none other than Alexander Duff, whose enthusiastic missionary endeavours left behind a long trail of dispute and discussion in Bengal. Day entered the field early; he was to devote a lifetime to writing about the Bengal countryside. He is best remembered today for his *Bengal Peasant Life* (1874).

However, the towering presence in the field was none other than Rabindranath Tagore (1861–1941). He had early written an essay seeking to draw the attention of the Bengali intelligentsia to the importance of folklore (1895). Tagore's work, particularly his poetry, but also drama, is shot through with the lyrical impetus received from contact with the rural countryside, with the songs of itinerant singers, particularly the Bauls he had heard in his East Bengal estates. As a modernist who was drawn to the culture of the people as an endlessly rich resource of poetry and philosophy, Tagore inspired and drew many to work in folklore. Dineshchandra Sen (1866–1936), the best known of the cluster of thinkers and artists around Tagore, became a major presence in the field of folklore. Sen turned to 'high' and folk culture at the same time, the one seemed to emerge in sharper relief when offset against the other. Even as he searched intensively for manuscripts in various parts of the region in order to write the first history of 'high' Bengali literature,[6] he compiled the massive collection of the folk songs of his native Mymensingh district, which was to be published in four volumes as the *Mymensingh Gitika* between 1923 and 1932. *East Bengal Ballads*, the version in English, was published in 1952. Together, Tagore and Sen created a hospitable environment for the collection, documentation, and creative use of folk forms, providing much incentive for others to join the field.

In the Hindi belt, Ramnaresh Tripathi seems to have been the lone pioneer in the collection of folk songs. His first anthology of songs, *Gram gitika*, was published in 1928; he was to add considerable material to it later. Between 1925 and 1930 he managed to collect 50,000 village songs from all over the subcontinent.

But it was Gurusaday Dutt (1882–1941), a scholar–administrator turned folk enthusiast,[7] who was responsible for the significant theoretical and practical breakthroughs in creating wider public awareness about the contemporary performative potential of folk forms. Dutt grew up in an East Bengal village, surrounded by the very forms in folk art, crafts, music, and dance that he was to study and propagate later in life as an antidote to the ills of civilization. His interest in folk dance was fuelled particularly by the Folk Dance Festival in Albert Hall which he attended on a visit to London in 1929. He discovered the *raibenshe* dance during his posting to the Birbhum district in 1930. In learning this and other dance forms to teach to others, it was his aim to develop the moral and physical faculties of the youth of Bengal. He founded the Bratachari Movement in 1934, modelled on the Boy Scouts of Baden Powell. But he also undertook various other measures to realize his aims of spreading the awareness of folk forms: he organized training camps for schoolteachers on folk dances and rural sports; he founded the All-India Folk Song and Dance Society in 1932 in

Delhi; and he published widely on folk art and dance. He was to sum up his understanding of folk dance in his last work, *The Folk Dances of Bengal*, which was edited and published posthumously.

'Folk' is a relational category, as Roma Chatterjee has pointed out. It comes into use as against or in contrast with more elite formations.[8] By the 1930s, the 'classical' dances of India were beginning to be codified and integrated in the nationalist genealogy of art. 'Folk' dance could now be offset against these classical forms, not only as feeding into these but as a more vital contrast programme, since it was seen as the live expression of the people's spirit by enthusiasts. The two, the classicizing of tradition and the turn to the common 'folk', were then in a sense interdependent processes. As a keen observer of the cultural scene of his times, Dutt noted the coincidence:

In India, the classic dance, the sophisticated product of the classic stage of India as expounded in the *Natya Shastra* of Bharata, with all its intricacies and subtleties of mudra (or highly conventional gestures), has hitherto received considerable attention not only from Indian writers, both ancient and modern, but also from foreigners in recent times. (Dutt 1954: 2)

He mentioned the *nautch*, the form we know today as *kathak*, and Ananda Coomaraswamy's labours on its behalf, as also *kathakali*.[9] These had elicited much interest in art circles. But little attention had been paid to 'the simple and spontaneous folk dances'. These he saw as the 'basic forms of the nation's self-expression, evolved through the unfolding of the three great primeval impulses of ritual, war and play'. Folk dances expressed the very soul of the people, they were created by them and could on no account be seen as merely degraded forms of classical art (14). Dutt went so far as to maintain that it was only these 'spontaneously evolved folk dances' that were 'tokens of the spontaneous growth of the social and religious life of the race', rather than the 'sophisticated and laboured products of the stage or court' (1). The 'illiterate but none the less cultivated poorer classes' and the village had preserved as inseparable part of their 'ritualistic, religious and recreational activities, folk dances of great nobility, dignity and rhythm combined with rare grace, harmony and spiritual value' (3). These activities were proof of the artistic life of the Bengali race. However, folk dances not only articulated the psychic life of a people, they also shaped it (14). If raibenshe and *dhali*, the martial dances Dutt had discovered, were proof of the essentially martial character of the Bengali people, they could be used to change the future; they could be practised again in order to reinforce the martial character of the people, which needed replenishment in the meantime: 'They afford a significant and authentic reminder that Bengalis, now believed to be a non-martial race, were once renowned for their military prowess and were wedded to the profession of war' (14).

Dutt had little hesitation in equating Bengali culture with Indian culture at large, for he spoke of them in one breath (23). Thus, though his agenda began in Bengal, it was meant to set up an all-India model. His was an all-encompassing vision and pronouncedly secular; he deliberately excluded religious dance forms from his programme.

Dutt was aware that much needed to be done in order to create an archive for folk forms. He organized the Rural Heritage Preservation Society of Bengal in 1932, with the express object of undertaking research and taking steps for the conservation and furtherance of the folk dances, songs, and art of Bengal. The emphasis was on cultural regeneration and renovation.

The work of these enthusiastic hunters and gatherers of folk tales and songs, and of dance and dramatic performance, as well as of such dynamic activists as Gurusaday Dutt, was to provide the fertile ground upon which the political activism of the 1940s would sprout and grow. For Dutt had taken the important step not only of recognizing the vitality of folk forms, he had taken energetic steps to realize their performative potential for the youth of the day, seeing this as a mutually regenerative exercise.

THEATRE OF THE PEOPLE FOR THE PEOPLE

Organizationally, the people's theatre movement of the 1940s grew out of the frame established by writers and intellectuals connected to the progressive writers movement, which initially came together in England in the mid-1930s, when Mulk Raj Anand and S. Sajjad Zaheer, two of the founder-members of the Progressive Writers Association of India (PWA) called the Association's first meeting in November 1935 in London.[10] The PWA was seen as an effort to organize literary activity to meet the demands created by the new social consciousness that followed the financial crisis of 1929 and the threatening rise of fascism in Europe. The immediate forerunner for this act was the Conference of World Writers in Paris in June 1935, which led to the formation of the International Association of Writers for the Defence of Culture against Fascism.[11] Participating, amongst others, were Maxim Gorky, Bertolt Brecht, André Gide, André Malraux, and E.M. Forster. It was to this organization that the PWA of India was also affiliated. It was part, then, of an international movement that turned to local popular culture with explicitly social and political aims, and which penetrated even into the traditionally anti-communist USA.[12]

The PWA programme declared explicitly that the writer was first and foremost a socially and politically responsible member of his society. It asked the writer to take cognizance of the specific Indian situation, to participate in the struggle for political and economic emancipation, to reinterpret past culture so as to prevent narrow nationalist revival, to take culture to the 'masses', and, finally, to develop regional languages and literatures. The PWA of India opened branches in 1936 in Lahore, Delhi, Allahabad, and Aligarh and an All-India gathering of writers was organized in the same year in Lucknow.

Out of this frame grew the Indian People's Theatre Association (IPTA), which held its first meeting in Bombay in 1943. The unifying forces were, as the Draft resolution of the All India People's Theatre Conference, drawn up in May 1943, proclaimed: 'The external aggression by the fascist hordes...and internal repression by an alien Government which seeks to hold our people in subjection and prevents them from organizing an effective defence of their own home-land' (Pradhan 1979: 131).

As the First Bulletin of the Association, entitled *Historical Background* and issued in July 1943, specified, this theatre movement took up currents of renewal and reinvigoration which had already begun to manifest themselves in the arts, though it did so with a new agenda, that of social communication and commitment. Tracing the growth of this activity, the pamphlet proclaimed:

It is in this situation that the Indian People's Theatre Association has been formed to co-ordinate and strengthen all the progressive tendencies that have so far manifested themselves in the nature of drama, songs and dances. It is not a movement which is imposed from above but one which has its roots deep down in the cultural awakening of the masses of India; nor is it a movement which discards our rich cultural heritage, but one which seeks to revive the lost in that heritage by reinterpreting, adopting and integrating it with the most significant facts of our peoples' lives and aspirations in the present epoch.... It stands for justice and democratic culture. (129)

In its social commitment, the new Association set forth the agenda of the PWA. There was a new emphasis on Indianness, a new enthusiasm for the culture of the people coupled with a fervent post-1942 patriotism that condemned alien rule in its entirety. There was close cooperation with Trade Unions and Kisan Sabhas. The organizers realized the importance of traditional folk forms for the purpose of direct communication with, as well as creative participation by, the people. As a later report was to proclaim:

We have made no effort to seriously study our past classical Sanskrit drama and our folk forms of drama, so that our writers and producers could experiment in a synthesis of these forms with modern stage techniques and lighting; we shall have to make a serious study of these subjects; we shall have to compel our writers to help us to experiment in the drama and so evolve a new drama; one that will be essentially Indian, bringing forth real creative talent that will base itself on both tradition and technique.[13]

The report seemed to be echoing the sentiments Gurusaday Dutt had expressed with respect to folk dance, though in a more conciliatory tone, for it equated classical Sanskrit drama with folk forms, without privileging the one over the other. New, however, was the publicly proclaimed need to turn to folk forms if the people themselves were to be reached. Branches of IPTA sprang up all over India. If the original impulse was radiated from large metropolitan centres such as Calcutta and Bombay, it was now taken up across the country, once metropolitan groups fanned out to tour the country.[14] Bhisham Sahni, the late Hindi novelist and dramatist (1915–2004), recalls in his memoirs the emotional response of audiences in faraway Rawalpindi when a troupe from Bengal performed a play about the devastations caused by the man-made famine in Bengal in 1942–3:

They staged their play in a cinema hall in the Cantonment area. The play was about the famine in Bengal, there was no stage set worth the mention; a string bed lay at the back of the stage and some soiled clothes hung from a line. But the play sent a thrill through the viewers. The audience was spell-bound from the moment Benoy Roy entered the stage holding a hurricane lamp, and asked: 'Do you want to hear the story of Bengal?' There was so much pain in the play and the acting was so powerful that when the actors and actresses descended from the stage, extending the loose end of their garment to receive alms, the young woman sitting in front of me took off her gold earrings and dropped them into their garment. (Sahni 2003: 100–101)

The bare stage, the lack of props, the simple costumes, the act of the performers in slipping uninhibitedly from their roles on stage into that of social activists who invited the audience to participate in contemporary politics, made for 'naturalistic' theatre of a different variety. The message was transforming the medium. Rustom Bharucha has rightly maintained that 'the I. P. T. A. was responsible for changing the very structure and conception of theatre in various parts of India' (1983: 42).

IPTA's Central Cultural Squad was formed in 1943; it attracted dancers, singers, musicians, and theatre people. The cooperation of artistes from all over India made possible ventures such as the film *Dharti ke lal* (1946) in Hindustani. The Central Squad was to produce two ballets that provoked nationwide response. *The Spirit of India* (1944) and later *India Immortal* (1946) tried to synthesize classical forms with folk forms for the purpose of 'realistic portraiture of everyday life'. This was realism with a difference; it was concerned with large issues, with social and political problems, rather than the domestic travails of the urban middle class. However, on the eve of Independence, as it were, a later malaise, which would melt difference by extracting some exotic features and integrating them into a totalizing metanarrative, was in a sense already beginning to manifest itself; both productions worked with the notion of a pan-Indian cultural heritage, into which flowed the various regional forms, forming an unproblematic whole.

Given the experimental and improvisational nature of most projects, it is not surprising that IPTA produced a heterogeneous corpus of plays and performances. Three strands can be distinguished in the theatre activity and vigorous experimentation of the period; the express aspiration of reaching out to the people being the primary force that welded them together.

The first strand consisted of traditional folk-theatre forms that were remoulded for contemporary purposes. In Gujarat, Dina Gandhi, a Bombay member of IPTA worked with *bhavai*, the traditional dance-drama form of Gujarat, weaving a stronger narrative line into the music and dance that had predominated till then. She put together a collection of *veshas*, the short narrative skits that comprised the form, with a topical content which was politically oriented:

This was the time of World War II, problems like rationing, queuing for food, water, etc. were put into *vesha* form and four to six of these were strung together. All the actors were urban workers. Shows were performed all over Bombay in streets, halls and maidans. The presentation itself was in a proscenium style and the stage itself had a green room behind a curtain hung on two charpais from behind where the characters entered.[15]

This was the first creation of a scripted play in this form. To the *rangla* or narrator, Dina Gandhi added the female companion *rangli*, inaugurating thereby the participation of women in bhavai. Mulk Raj Anand recalled the effect of this kind of remoulding in Andhra Pradesh, which attempted a similar recasting of the *burrakatha*, a musical narrative enacted by three men:

I have had occasion to see how the groups of the Indian People's Theatre Association in Andhra have rescued this form from the ignorant, who practised it as a formula and how, by composing new ballads with fresh social content, they have combined with the natural vigour of the old form a new urgency of conscience, without diminishing any of the gaiety and joy which is inherent in the form itself. I shall never forget how three peasant boys held an audience of thirty thousand citizens of Guntur spell-bound up to the early hours of the morning with their recitation of the *Ballad of Venkataramani*, the bad boy who ate his mother's ears. (1951: 29)

Thus also the use of the art of the various itinerant folk performers for new purposes, such as the singing mendicant, 'dressed in strange garb, wandering through the land, fortune telling, selling medicines, diagnosing diseases and generally exhorting people to be good and charitable'. IPTA retained the old style, but changed the content: 'Instead of diagnosing bodily ills, the mendicants now diagnose social diseases' (31).

As the terms used, 'formula', 'ignorant', 'rescued', plainly betray, in spite of all the rhetoric to the contrary, the urban approach to folk theatre was inevitably patronizing. But the difference from the older folklore archivist was also evident in that the intentions of IPTA activists went beyond the conservationist and/or the merely revivalist. They were out to 'teach' not to be taught. And there was the unsentimental awareness that folk forms also needed to change with the times. Behind the sometimes heavy-handed attempt to remould the contents while leaving the form more or less intact, the patent concern was to reach and communicate with rural audiences, rather than preserve or indeed remould for urban use alone.

The second strand of IPTA's work was constituted by experiments on the urban stage, which continued to be modelled structurally on European forms; the term in vogue for Western theatre at large was 'naturalistic', used in the sense of the bourgeois well-made play. From the 1950s on it would come increasingly to be replaced by 'realistic'. But more on that anon. In the 1940s such naturalistic plays consisted mostly of short sketches that rarely attempted to rise above the level of political propaganda, for example the Marathi play *Blood and Tears*, the Bengali play *Laboratory*, and the Hindi play *Yah amrit hai* by K.A. Abbas. All three were criticized for their lack of analytical coherence.[16] A more successful attempt was *Zubeida* by K.A. Abbas, which has been described thus by Mulk Raj Anand, who extolled its 'terrific popularity among audiences both in Western and Northern India':

Zubeida is the name of a girl from the United Provinces, who is stirred by the dirges of the funeral processions and the spirited songs of the relief workers outside her house to cast away her veil and join the volunteers: she dies like many other people, through a lack of anti-cholera vaccine. Abbas made a conscious attempt in this play to unite the public life of processions with their chants and slogans with the private life of the Muslim household, and he tried to create a new form of drama very akin to the living newspaper. And I think he demonstrated one way out of the theatrical debacle, that is to say, from the present play towards the documentary theatre. (1951: 52–3)

In order to rouse social consciousness, then, the play attempted to link up the fate of one individual to the community. To this end, it combined elements of the 'peasant' play—Anand is referring here to the processional songs—with elements of the naturalistic, to create a documentary play of a new kind.

The most famous attempt to use naturalist urban theatre for new purposes was *Nabanna* (New Harvest) by Bijon Bhattacharya, which was successfully performed by members of the Bengal wing of IPTA in Calcutta, as well as in the surrounding district towns. The central character, Pradhan Samaddar, was a peasant in the devastating Bengal famine of 1942–3, a man-made catastrophe created by the British who used the harvest of these years to feed the troops fighting in Europe and Japan. Being a full-length play in four acts, it demanded a greater individuation of character, which made it more difficult 'to present the historical topicality of the dramatic situation' (Bhattacharya 1983: 9). This contradictory pull was partially resolved by maintaining the episodic character of the play and by utilizing the revolving stage to enable quick shifts of scene, facilitating thus the depiction of several aspects of social life:

The abrupt ending of the scene breaks up the single track movement of narrative, and transfers the audience with great flexibility from one aspect of social life to another, from the woes of the peasants in their village homes to the hoarder's den, from relief kitchen to charitable dispensary, from the wedding feast to the beggar's scrounging for food near the dustbin, from the child dying of malnutrition to the village wife being approached by the city tout, so that, although the main focus is on Pradhan and his family, the approach to their problems is a multi-lateral one and the sensationalism of individual scenes gives way to an analytical linking up of the different segments of social reality (9).

Rustom Bharucha has described the effect of the production on its audiences:

Enacted with fierce commitment and a burning sense of injustice by young
members of the Bengal I.P.T.A. (including six Communist Party organizers
with no theatrical experience) the first performances were revelations for
Bengali theatre audiences, who had reconciled themselves to the sensationalism
and melodrama of the professional theatre. They discovered for the first
time in *Nabanna* the extraordinary impact of realism in the dialects and the
street cries of the actors, the minutiae of their gestures, movements, and
responses, and the stark simplicity of the set and the costumes. (1983: 49)

As Malini Bhattacharya points out, this was using the naturalistic stage
for a totally new purpose, giving 'dramatic form to what was appearing
as a new political reality' (1983: 8).

The third and final form generated by IPTA could be viewed almost
as the beginning of a modern 'epic' theatre in India. In the ballet *Immortal
India*, a worker was the narrator, there was no effort to establish or
unfold the personal history of his character, strive for psychological
verisimilitude, or create suspense. And it was he, rather than the
narrative, who held together the episodes of the play, which presented
landmarks in the cultural history of India:

The latest ballad by the troupe gives a picture of India from the earliest times
to the present days, touching momentous events that form the landmarks in
the cultural history of India. It starts from the early worship of the Himalayas
and passes through past impacts of culture to modern times.

A worker sleeping in a factory through exhaustion falls asleep, but is
kicked and awakened. He grumbles but relates to his lamenting associates
the wonderful dream he had of poverty, and of exploitation and hoarding, but
also with the darker side he saw the people happy and contented. In his dream
the people finally unite together in the determination to become free, to mould
their own destiny. (Pradhan 1979: 386)

But if the structure was episodic, attempting to link the individual to
the national, the assemblage of scenes had as the principle of linkage no
analytical evaluation of historical or social conditions. This anticipated
a later approach, which would see the history and geography of India
as unproblematically unitary.

It is worth noting that the artistes associated with IPTA did not confine themselves in a given context to traditional forms alone, either 'classical' or 'folk'. They mixed freely. There was little self-consciousness about borrowing formal elements from one or the other tradition, be it rural or urban. The momentum was such that the local, regional, and pan-Indian grew out of each other, as yet in a somewhat raw, sometimes unreflected way, but with the potential for much further experiment. It was the message, the anticipation of the nation-to-be, and the resolutions of all major social problems thereafter, which propelled the movement forward. As Rustom Bharucha has put it, IPTA has become:

an indispensable point of reference for almost any discussion on cultural politics in India. But when it is being named in cultural discourse, we should qualify that what is being referred to is the movement of the early 1940s—those short-lived, euphoric years before the disintegration of the movement. The IPTA, I would suggest, is better read as a utopic movement in our cultural history, rather than as a disintegrating movement—though the lessons of its disintegration need to be absorbed in the formulation of an ongoing cultural praxis. (1998: 50)

Given their largely spontaneous regional manifestation and their utopian bent, perhaps not unsurprisingly, with the onset of Independence IPTA's activities were to disintegrate. There was one last large all-India gathering of artistes from all over the country at a three-day festival organized by IPTA in the winter of 1947. Bhisham Sahni has described with some nostalgia the boundless energy and the creative excitement of the groups that came together to perform on one stage the many kinds of folk and experimental theatre in the many languages of the country. The performance would begin at sunset and end at some point well past midnight (Sahni 2003: 142–3).

Thereafter, according to Sahni, who stayed with the Association till well into the 1950s, IPTA became the mouthpiece of the Communist Party of India. Members who did not toe the party line, who came to be seen as Nehruvian in their views, such as the prolific K.A. Abbas, were expelled. This led to a thinning of ranks and a reduction of the rich diversity of viewpoints that had made both for the diversity and the spontaneity of IPTA. Nehru and the politics of the National Congress now became the chief targets of IPTA's cultural activism. This in turn made the Association vulnerable to persecution by the state. Sahni describes the fate of *Kursi,* a lively, topical play staged by IPTA activists in Shimla. It had some politically provocative scenes and song lines, and word of this had got around. There was police presence on the first night. Sahni had anticipated this and undertaken some deletions. He had removed a line from a song that had attacked the Nehru government directly and deleted a short scene that exposed a central character as a Congress ally by having him remove his cap to expose a Gandhi *topi.* The topi had come to stand for political corruption. The play was popular, but Sahni and his friends found themselves caught between the devil and the deep blue sea. The police promptly banned the play from being shown at other places; the Party accused Sahni of a shift to the Right for having undertaken the deletions (158–9). Sudhi Pradhan has documented the concerted persecution by the state that followed.

Sahni was apparently not alone in making such conciliatory moves. Such concessions had to be made in order to find space within the new order that was emerging. The subsequent weakening of the party line in cultural activities, according to Malini Bhattacharya, became the chief cause of the decline that set in; IPTA documents of the 1950s exhibit a clear revisionist trend: 'Instead of sustained politicization of cultural workers, there is a growing tendency to neutralize the political content of cultural activities' (Bhattacharya 1983: 13).

New orientation was certainly needed now. IPTA had been a largely spontaneous movement of groups held together by a common cause, the very spontaneity of which was surely one cause for its disintegration after the passing of the British Raj (cf. Pani 1979). Fascism and colonialism, activity against which had provided the major impetus to the movement, were no longer present as visible enemies. Little wonder that the Party was able to step in with directives without facing much opposition. But the climate was increasingly determined by the Cold War, to which Nehru's government did not expressly subscribe, though, as far as the Communist Party of India was concerned, Nehru's Congress seemed almost to fall in line with the West. And clearly there was some justification for viewing matters in this light, as the episode related in the preceding paragraph illustrated: IPTA's expressly socialist agenda was obviously not viewed in a favourable light by the new government.

With the coming of Independence, the burden of organizing cultural activity became a state concern. The last All-India Conference of IPTA was held in Delhi in 1957–8. It recognized the leading organizational role that the Sangeet Natak Akademi was supposed to play in the future and offered cooperation and help so that 'the aid that is being given by the Akademi can thus be utilized most efficiently and effectively' (Pradhan 1983: 279). However, though the activity which was steered by the newly created national akademis in the new capital of the nation state gave the tone, it is important to bear in mind that, in fact, there was much that happened outside the institutional sphere, and one could almost say, in spite of it. Many a writer and theatre person was to continue to invoke IPTA as the formative influence for future work. However, the newly formed central institutions would come to exercise much directive power.

THEATRE FOR THE NATION

The Sangeet Natak Akademi was established in Delhi in 1953 as the national academy for the performing arts. The indigenization of the term 'academy', coupled with the Sanskrit compound Sangeet Natak, bespoke the hybrid character of the institution. It saw itself as taking over the patronage of the performing arts from the former princely houses; it did not even mention the British Raj, which had obviously never seen itself constrained to play this role or even project itself thus. The primary object of the Akademi, as seen initially, was to provide patronage and conserve tradition:

The idea of establishing an organization to coordinate all the activities in the sphere of dance, drama and music came to the forefront and assumed a new urgency and importance in independent India.... The necessity of such an organization was all the more compelling in view of the fact that all of a sudden the erstwhile princely patronage of the arts had ceased to function or was fast ceasing. In the void thus created, the art traditions were faced with the grave risk of breaking down in an atmosphere of general decline in our cultural and artistic values.[17]

The new propositions made for radically different dimensions in cultural activity. First, artistes came under the direct patronage of the state, exercised by the cultural bureaucracy set up exclusively for the purpose in the new capital of the nation. Second, the regional was subsumed firmly within the national. Folk forms were thus seen as rural derivations of and deviations from the all-encompassing Sanskritic tradition, from which they had emanated and into which they could, under the new dispensation, flow again. It was in this frame, as against the former IPTA aims and attitude, that 'folk' practice was now to be researched and conserved. Thus Article XII of the 'Powers and Functions of the Sangeet Natak Akademi' saw it to be the task of the institution: 'to revive and preserve folk dances and folk music of different regions of the country and to encourage the development of community music, martial music, etc.'

Theatre was specially privileged. It was extracted from within the larger frame of Music and Dance and given its own institutional base. The idea of establishing a national drama institute had long been in the air, Nehru himself being one of the instigators of it.[18] The Steering Committee of forty distinguished scholars, educationists, journalists, and theatre persons from all over the country met for a seminar in March 1958. It was V. Raghavan's paper on 'Sanskrit Drama and Performance' that called forth the most discussion. Sanskrit plays had not only to be studied but to be performed, as Ebrahim Alkazi put it 'exactly in the way they used to be done in the past'. Adya Rangacharya summed up the discussions in the observation:

i.   We ought to study Sanskrit drama
ii. We ought to make experiments with their performances
iii. We ought to gather from the Sanskrit drama anything which may help the proper evolution of modern drama.

Sanskrit Drama had become a matter of state concern, not only as the fountainhead of all past forms but also as providing orientation for all further development.

By and large, then, the preoccupation with finding an indigenous theatrical idiom showed little concern for reaching out to the 'masses'. The focus now was much more on integrating the artistic forms of the people in mainstream national culture. Mulk Raj Anand in 1951 made the proposal that was repeated again and again in the following years:

As we adapt our knowledge of the survivals of the old theatre to the needs of today, it is possible that a new indigenous tradition of the Indian theatre may be built, which is unique to our country, and which may contribute something different to the hackneyed form current in the contemporary European theatre. (1951: 60)

However, Anand's viewpoint was still determined by the IPTA objectives of reaching out to the people. He re-stressed two important points. First, that folk plays had endured because they were vital, they were high points of tradition, not mere degenerate leftovers of the once more glorious courtly Sanskrit tradition:

The Ras or Nautanki, the Ram and Krishna Lila, the enactment of the victory of the Pandus over the Kurus, the Muharram, and the Holi as well as the several harvest dance-dramas, are the apotheosis of the old drama, survivals which are an important reservoir of energy from which a new living art of the theatre can be made. (21)

Second, in that he asked that folk theatre be used to regenerate the hackneyed urban form, he did not exclude the rural. The synthesis of folk and urban was to be used to address both urban and rural audiences:

For not only do the peculiar exigencies of India require the conservation of the two main techniques which appeal to the two chief strata of the population, but the synthesis of the two will bring us to the basis of a new kind of theatrical expression. The community technique of the folk theatre, which may be impossible to re-create in its old form, could nevertheless be used to revitalize the three-act European form. (21)

A year later, in 1959, the Sangeet Natak Akademi established the National School of Drama (NSD) in Delhi, as the national institute for theatre training. Under the able directorship of Ebrahim Alkazi, who came into office in 1962, the School established a reputation for disciplined training in methods of acting, directing, and stagecraft. The

NSD was an attempt at centralization of theatre with all its advantages and drawbacks. The advantages in these early years of Independence were clear: the School provided and sustained a forum for mediation of the many regional forms and plays and it offered an institutional base for visiting directors. Though Alkazi was to remain cautious in his approach to traditional theatre, folk forms were to exercise much fascination in the decade to come. In a statement typical of the early 1960s, Mohan Upreti was to urge that an effort be made to discover and understand 'the entire heritage' of the country in the interest of creating a truly national theatre:

Against this background, the importance of folk theatre should become quite obvious to us because it embodies the creative work of countless generations who inherited and enriched it and passed it on to us.... Without a concerted move on our part to understand the entire heritage, we can neither understand the heart and mind of our people, nor can we develop the judgment to assimilate from the theatre of the West only that which is of real value to us.[19]

The first comprehensive account of the folk theatre of India in English appeared in 1966. In the Introduction to his book, Balwant Gargi used the kind of rhetoric that was fast gaining currency in official cultural circles in Delhi. Folk forms were offshoots of the classical Sanskrit tradition; they were preserved in all their colour by the multilingual and many-hued people of the subcontinent:

The wheat-complexioned bearded Sikhs in their colored turbans in the Punjab; the ebony-bodied naked Santhals in the east; the close-shaven Dravidian priests of the south, the full busted dark women of Maharashtra; the Mongolian flavored people of Assam; and the sun-baked ballad singers of Rajasthan offer a baffling variety.

He reversed the sequence of forms that folklorists such as Gurusaday Dutt and the founding fathers of IPTA such as Mulk Raj Anand believed they had divined. If Dutt, Anand, and others had seen folk traditions as the vital resource that classical traditions drew upon for their inspiration and sustenance, Gargi saw the many folk forms as offshoots of the one, the classical Sanskrit theatre:

When after the tenth century, the classical Sanskrit language splintered into vernaculars and took root in the form of regional languages, the Sanskrit drama petrified for many centuries was replaced by the growing folk theatre. Old legends, Puranic tales, mythological lore, philosophy, and stories of Sanskrit plays were popularized by the present folk theatre. In this way the tradition flowed not from the folk to the classical, but from the classical to the folk. The folk theatre inherits many of the classical conventions. (1966: 3–4)

Gargi then proceeded to enumerate these conventions, as would many others who followed him, disregarding the peculiarities of a given form, stressing instead its exemplary contribution to the composite Indian theatre that was the classical Sanskrit: the *sutradhara* (the director/narrator), the buffoon, the *purvaranga* (stage preliminaries), the benediction at the end of the play, music, dance, stylization (a diffusely used term), verse dialogue, exaggerated make-up, masks, and finally, scenes that melt into one another.[20] This attribution of absolute authority to the classical Sanskrit tradition provoked no further discussion and was henceforth accepted as a truism. The progressive views of Dutt and the early Anand receded almost entirely. The Akademi played no insignificant role in the process, adding thereby an anti-West bias to it, which anticipated the later more expressly anti-modern stance.

Suresh Awasthi, with his intense interest and involvement in the propagation of traditional theatre, became Secretary of the Sangeet Natak Akademi in 1965. Along with Nemichandra Jain, long-time scholar of theatre, traditional and modern, Awasthi propelled the move for the adaptation of folk traditions for the urban stage yet more forcefully forwards, but positioning now the traditional not as commingling with the 'realistic' or Western but rather in opposition to it. In the Introduction to the proceedings of the 'Round Table on the Contemporary Relevance of Folk Theatre', which he organized for the Sangeet Natak Akademi in 1971, Awasthi referred to the movement as identity based and as already under way, making no reference to the grounds opened up by IPTA or indeed to its political agenda:

We felt that we were passing through a very exciting phase in our contemporary theatre and that it reflects a quest for own identity. It is marked by a sense of discovery, a sense of exploration of the past and there have been very interesting experiments both in playwriting and in play production, utilising conventions, techniques from the traditional theatre. (1971: 5)

He had taken the top-down approach so uncritically adopted by IPTA, but not their politics. He asked, 'What should be our attitude; how can we assimilate, how can it become an integral part of our contemporary activity; is it going to survive only as a museum piece? How can it be adopted suitably for urban audiences? How can it be supported in its own milieu?' (1971: 7) He spoke of the traditional theatre in the singular and in his concluding words, saw it as deriving from and bound to 'Sanskrit theatre', as if the latter were also a monolithic category:

Traditional theatre represents many conventions and practices of Sanskrit theatre and it is also the inheritor of the medieval 'Variety' theatre. Thus, it provides valuable art material for reconstructing theatre tradition. Apart from its value in supplying data for reconstructing theatrical tradition, it is a living and vital theatre enjoying professional status and entertaining mass audiences. (1971: 52)

However, the search for the theatrical idioms for these new times was by no means confined to the discussions spawned by the Sangeet Natak Akademi alone. The impulses generated by IPTA had been taken up by writers and playwrights working in very different regional cultures. *Lok natak*, folk theatre, had indeed become a part of theatre vocabulary and could inspire a play such as Dharamvir Bharati's *Andha yug* (written in 1954),[21] and the 'masses' could also occupy the stage, as in Habib Tanvir's *Agra Bazar* (produced first in 1954 and published in 1979) and later in his production of Sanskrit plays, such as *Mitti ki gari*, a Hindi adaptation of Shudraka's *Mricchakatikam* (1958). In Karnataka, Adya Rangacharya had written a new kind of play in Kannada, *Suno Janmayjaya* (1964), the novelty of which he himself placed in a nationwide context. He was combining here conventions from the Sanskrit play and the folk play in Kannada, but he stressed also that the combination could not be seen as only indigenous. It was also embedded in the live contact with and knowledge of European stagecraft.[22]

The theatre of these early decades after Independence was then a mixture, of questioning but also of a belief not yet totally shattered in the idea of India, and of a groping for a culture that could be defined as Indian. It was to make of the 1960s and 1970s the most productive age in playwriting, to which Delhi in general, and the NSD and the Sangeet Natak Akademi in particular, could and did indeed provide a forum. The playwrights present at the Akademi's 1971 Round Table were not just mouthing slogans, they were already part of a process that was reconfiguring playwriting; the search for a new idiom was seen as a genuine need and the recourse to folk forms a spontaneous, unengineered act. In the decade to come, many of them would go on to become key figures in the national theatre scene. The major question at this stage was about the 'use' of folk forms for the urban stage, use in the sense of deployment as well as utility; no one seemed to be asking about the use of urban forms for the rural.

Badal Sircar stated unequivocally that he was working in an urban frame and was not really equipped to cope with rural issues, and indeed did not have any intention of going out of his way to do so. He needed new impulses to work more effectively in his own context and it was for this reason alone that he would turn to folk forms:

Now, I have to work for urban audiences and all I know is the problem of these people, it's a very narrow theatre, I admit. And I have no intention of carrying this theatre to the rural areas at all, because it is not about the problems of rural people, so I have no right to carry it to them. So I want to take it from my point; not how folk art lives, or should be preserved or recreated. I am interested in propagating my type of problems. I use theatre as I learnt it and probably everybody would agree that the concept of theatre came from the West.... But now with the complexity of the middle-class increasing, we are searching for new forms because we are finding the 'naturalistic form' and the proscenium arch inadequate to voice our problems. So we want to break this tradition inherited from the West. So while I do not want to do anything for the rural theatre, I still want to borrow from the folk form to serve my own purpose.[23]

There was a need to break out of the old moulds and to find new expression for new and complex needs. Though Sircar proclaimed the need to break from the tradition inherited from the West, he did not adopt an anti-West stance and go 'traditional'. The turn to 'folk' was thus not ideology driven as was to be the case later. Perhaps that was why it could remain creative. As Vijay Tendulkar proclaimed: 'I would like to indulge in some folk form that would suit my needs—I want to find my way out' (39). He described the exhilarating effect that the use of folk forms had already exercised:

It gave me a feeling of liberation—because I was used to the vagaries of my form of writing and consciously I was fed up with this form. And here was the technical freedom which I required at that stage. And I think that was the major thing that attracted me. Of course, the rustic quality of the form also—I mean the texture of the language. (ibid.: 40)

It was urban audiences which were being addressed—straightforwardly and unapologetically. As Girish Karnad explained: 'I mean I am attracted by the Yakshagana form. I write a play in Dharwar, using the Yakshagana form because I feel, in one particular play it helps me to give a form to what I want to say' (25). He was not committing himself to any given form as the panacea for all ills: 'One may not know what form one's next play needs' (39).

Ebrahim Alkazi, who already had several years of experience as the director of the NSD sounded a note of warning, apparently sensing even at this stage, that the means could begin to be seen as ends in themselves: 'I think the form cannot be taken for granted and merely accepted as rituals. One has to understand the significance and the validity of the form in the communication of ideas' (20–1).

Several issues remained to be resolved. In order to create 'living drama in pure form', the problems, according to Utpal Dutt, were:

a. how to adapt the myth form to modern themes....

b. how to adapt the alienated, conventional and picturesque style of acting to the needs of a credible theme wherein the audience to a degree must identify itself;

c. how to preserve the arena-style of production, with its virile rejection of sets, lights and make-believe and yet to create an atmosphere of total war that a recent play on Viet Nam demands....

d. how to create verse-drama that will preserve the tradition of old Yatra and yet capture the nuances of modern speech....

e. how to experiment but never to forget the source and inspiration of Yatra, the unsophisticated masses of the countryside,

f. how at once to be popular and elevating. (8–9)

The concern was to coin a modern urban idiom, using the vocabulary of the 'folk'.[24] Fresh input on this point could, at this stage, be no other than welcome. In 1970 J.C. Mathur, civil service officer and himself a playwright of note, in an introductory essay to a collection of medieval folk plays, expressed the hope that the song-dance mixed style of Brecht's theatre, which was proving popular on the Western stage, would point out the way to modern Indian producers and playwrights, so that they could win back the original unity of Indian theatre, folk-traditional and eminently stageworthy (Mathur and Ojha 1970: 13). In speaking of the original unity of Indian theatre, Mathur was obviously referring to the unity of song, dance, and speech in classical Sanskrit drama, which was once again being invoked in the context of folk theatre. In fact, Brecht's theatre, also invoked constantly in this context, by playwrights and directors, was to provide one way of making social and political aspects of urban theatre amenable to exposition by techniques culled from folk forms. Thus, for instance, the narrator as well as the songs which interspersed the action on stage could be used to analyse and comment on the narrative. If folk and urban could then be bridged by means which Brecht offered, then the heady invocation of the Sanskrit theatre which ever subsumed the most diverse folk forms, could indeed bring about a theatre for the nation.

DISCOVERING BRECHT: THE LINKS BETWEEN CLASSICAL, FOLK, AND EPIC

Brecht was a veritable prophet of theatre in the 1960s and 1970s, not only, though differently, in both Germanys, but in most of Europe and in many parts of Asia and Africa. His theatre arrived in India by way of the enthusiastic response it received in Britain, also a little later by the direct exposure of Indian theatre people to the work of the Berliner

Ensemble. It is worth dwelling on these moments in order to recapture the excitement of those decades, as Brecht's plays, his dramaturgy, his theories whirled through theatre in the West. It is meaningful to begin our discussion with Britain since it was there that Indian theatre people first encountered Brecht's theatre. John Willet has described the arrival of the Berliner Ensemble in London in August 1956, as a theatrical revolution:

...their season at the Palace Theatre in 1956 dumped it in our lap. That was a year when a lot happened. We invaded Egypt and changed our mind. The Russians invaded Hungary and didn't change theirs. Brecht died. And, at the Royal Court Theatre, George Devine's company performed a new play called *Look Back in Anger*. Perhaps, we were ripe for Brecht? (Willet 1977: 17)[25]

Why was Britain ripe for Brecht? An answer was provided by yet another critic in 1978, writing almost twenty years after the first encounter:

The set, particularly the box set of drawing room drama, had become an unquestioned and unquestionable embodiment of a bourgeois perception. Brecht, in denying the theatricality of the traditional set, its faded realism, draws attention to it as an encumbrance, an unacceptable political restriction of the patterns of perception of the audience. The British response to Brecht's theatre as a theatre of realism—now seen as a naive and imperceptive response—was based on the newness of the perception of the actor and the action that Brecht's sets or rather the comparative absence of them, made possible. (Holland 1978)

The box set of drawing-room drama, along with the bourgeois perception that was part and parcel of it, had never become staple fare in India. The Indian response, if one can speak in the singular of it, was differently conditioned and went different ways. It was the primacy of the fable, as emphasized by Brecht, its joints and junctures, its historicization, and at times also its expressly political orientation, which found immediate echo in the diverse regional and folk theatre traditions that had already begun to be reactivated. The search was for an idiom at once regional and national, modern and traditional, for features which in the century and half of modern Indian theatre practice, had, at times, been considered harmonious as in the theoretical considerations of Bharatendu Harishchandra, at other times as a hindrance to each other—we have only to think of Jayshankar Prasad and his polemical rejections of the 'realist' theatre of the West, which he saw as being at odds with ancient Indian theatre practice. It was less a matter, then, of struggling with the box set, with naturalistic excess, much more of casting the multiple theatre traditions of the subcontinent, some thriving, others on the wane, into new urban moulds; a complex and often contradictory process, as we have seen. Indian theatre makers were also 'ripe for Brecht', as theoretician and as playwright, but their responses were differently configured. Brecht's influence can be traced most of all in the directorial and production practice of the years. Also in playwriting, as we shall see, but in ways more intangible, since the connection to folk theatre and the politics with which IPTA had imbued them, went back a good three decades. It would be much more pertinent to see the plays of the late 1960s and the 1970s as written in a complex interaction both with the folk traditions of the given region as well as the politics of Brecht's theatre.

In retrospect, three factors seem to crystallize as creating favourable conditions for the Brecht reception in the Hindi-speaking north.[26] First, the grounds were formed by the work of IPTA in pre-Independence India with its emphasis on the need to discover and develop folk forms in order to establish communication with a widely based audience and to create theatre with contemporary relevance. Brecht's epic theatre provided a model because its open form seemed to coincide with that of traditional folk forms. The contemporaneity of the themes of his plays as well as his theoretical writings offered at the same time an ideological basis for welding together folk form and contemporary political concerns.

Second, as we have seen, the discovery of Brecht in the 1960s coincided largely with his growing popularity in the West and particularly in England. This also meant that Brecht's works were increasingly available in American and English translations, his theoretical writings in a collection translated and edited by John Willet, *Brecht on Theatre: The Development of an Aesthetic* as early as 1964 and a year later *The Messingkauf Dialogues* also translated by Willet.

Third, the interest in Brecht was fostered and encouraged by the

'Kulturpolitik' of the German Democratic Republic but also of the Federal Republic of Germany. The connection with the GDR was established in the early 1960s, when M.S. Sathyu and Shama Zaidi visited the Berliner Ensemble under the sponsorship of the Government of the GDR and produced Brecht's *Caucasian Chalk Circle* in Delhi thereafter.[27] Firm grounds for regular contact were created when Ebrahim Alkazi participated in the 'Brecht Dialog 1968' in East Berlin, organized by the International Theatre Institute and the Brecht Zentrum. In the same year, Goethe Institute, the West German Cultural Organization, sponsored the visit of Carl Weber, a former assistant director in Brecht's Berliner Ensemble, based in the meantime in the USA. Weber directed *The Caucasian Chalk Circle* for the National School of Drama Repertory Company. It was Weber's effort to present the play entirely in the style of the Berliner Ensemble and the model of the play created by Brecht. It was a great success and the Repertory toured the country with it. In 1973, Fritz Bennewitz of the Weimar theatre[28] collaborated with the Marathi director Vijaya Mehta, another major figure in the world of theatre, to produce her internationally acclaimed *The Three Penny Opera* in an adaptation that Indianized it and was based on the techniques of the Marathi folk theatre form tamasha.[29] Thereafter, Bennewitz became a regular visiting director in India from the early 1970s as part of an agreement that NSD had entered with the Government of the GDR.

Bennewitz was to go on to play a major role in the mediation of Brecht's theatre in India, not only in Delhi, but also in Calcutta, Bombay, and Bhopal. He directed the NSD Repertory Company in a widely acclaimed production of *The Three Penny Opera* in a Hindi translation in 1970. It was a great success in Delhi.[30] A year later, on a tour of India with the play, Bennewitz was to become aware of the dimensions of the country, of its masses, and to realize the inadequacy of an import from the West to meet their needs. He became aware, as he put it, of the difference between success and effect ('Erfolg und Wirkung'). When he came to direct *Puntilla and his Man Matti* for the Repertory Company in 1979, it was clear from the outset that the play would be adapted into a local setting; it was transferred to the Punjab countryside. Bennewitz managed, as he himself saw it, to retain the spirit of the original, while imparting a sense of commitment to the actors. Pankaj

Materializing social gesture: Bennewitz's production of Brecht's *Puntilla* (late 1970s) (National School of Drama)

Kapur, who played Puntilla is reported as saying, 'I tried to portray a landlord from *Punjab* but my task has to be to portray a *landlord* from Punjab.' As against character playing, then, Bennewitz was trying to communicate the importance of social 'Gestus'. *Puntilla* did indeed have more effect, on actors and audiences alike, than the previous productions by Carl Weber and Bennewitz himself.

Before we consider the views of the Indian directors who turned to Brecht and the uses to which they put his theatre, a couple of issues need to be cleared. Now that various Brecht euphorias have worn off, perhaps it is possible to view the Brecht who came to India through a broader lens and discard some misconceptions regarding Brecht's opposition to so-called 'naturalistic' theatre. Though it must be admitted that in setting down his own teachings in an almost aphoristic form, in polemicizing relentlessly against naturalistic theatre and Stanislavsky as its chief idealogue, in documenting and offering his own vibrant, vigorous theatre productions as models to be followed, Brecht helped in the process of ossification that set in inevitably after a period and that ultimately reduced his own theatre to clichés. Today it seems less meaningful to prop up Stanislavsky as the antagonist and hurl abuse at him and naturalistic theatre, a practice in which the upholders of Indian traditional theatre would indulge from the 1980s, when following their own agendas; it is more relevant to try and comprehend the fit between Brecht and the needs of the Indian theatre of the day.[31]

Several factors made for the broad-based appeal of Brecht's theatre. First, Brecht's politics exercised an immense pull, even when they seemed inconclusive and contradictory, because they offered a method, a political stance, which was considered extremely apposite, given the Indian situation and the ground created by IPTA. Darko Suvin, in reviewing Frederic Jameson's study of Brecht, has put it thus:

One of Jameson's formulations may provide a springboard: 'There existed a Brechtian "stance" [*Haltung*] which was not only doctrine, narrative or style, but all three simultaneously; and ought better to be called, with all due precautions, "method".'[32] This builds on, but considerably expands Lukac's famous assertion in *History and Class Consciousness* that 'orthodox Marxism... refers exclusively to method'—precisely because it adds the crucial factors of stance (involving the whole body) and narrative (involving a more than exclusively conceptual articulation of a possible world). (1997: 127)

This conceptual articulation of a possible world was lodged within a readily accessible system, the Marxist, it was not a privately conceived system that needed laboured decoding; Brecht thus offered something that few other moderns did, as Jameson has pointed out.[33]

Second, there was the emotional appeal of Brecht's own plays. Brecht's famous alienation effect, the estrangement from character and plot, brought about by the actor and by directorial intervention, which destroyed the illusion that they mirrored reality and foregrounded their specificity and historicity, was supposed to have done away with emotionality, an idea that Brecht himself had done much to propagate. But he had also attempted to correct the widely held view that his theatre lacked *all* emotion. He had asked, even insisted, that 'reason' be seen as coupled with emotion. With reason he meant the critical stance arrived at cumulatively through the joint activity of the director, cast, and stage hands during the rehearsal process, to be then picked up by a discerning audience trained in 'complex seeing'. Suvin has located the crucial passages in Brecht's writings which clarify this issue:

Finally, Brecht could quite consistently repudiate his 1930 'Kampfstellung' 'hie ratio—hie emotio'. Reading Gorelik's pioneering (and undeservedly slighted) chapter on his theatre, he noted on March 4, 1941:

It becomes clear to me that one must get out of the fighting position of 'emotion vs reason'. The relationship of ratio to emotio in all its contradictoriness should be exactly researched, and one should not allow our opponents to present epic theatre as simply rational and anti-emotional. The 'instincts' which automatized reactions to experiences, have become opposed to our interests. Muddied, one-track emotions, no longer controlled by reason. On the other hand the emancipated ration of the physicists with their mechanical formalism.... The epic principles guarantee a critical stance in the audience, but his stance is eminently emotional. This critique is not to be confused with a critique in an exclusively scientific sense, it is much more inclusive, not at all professionally limited (*fachbegrenzt*), much more practical and elementary. (*Arbeitsjournal* 1: 184) [Suvin 1999: 73]

The confusion regarding the aims and intentions of the famous 'alienation effect' was at least partially created by the English translation of the term. If Balwant Gargi's account of his visit to the ageing Brecht is to be taken as a verbatim report, then, according to Brecht himself, the English term 'alienation' contributed much to the misunderstanding of a concept otherwise conceived. Brecht is supposed to have told Gargi:

This man, Eric Bentley, has used the phrase 'alienation' to describe my dramatic concept of 'Verfremdung'. It is an incorrect translation of my concept. The audience must be hypnotised by action, word, colour, emotion, and then shocked out of it. Emotion is very important. I want my audience to sit back after their emotional involvement and reflect and see the historical process though reason. Look at the Kabuki actor. He delivers the lines with all the intensity, emotion and concentration he can muster. But there are other elements in the production which serve to objectify him to the audience, not alienate him. (Allana 1993: 26)

We find that most directors in India indeed did not linger unduly on speculations regarding the authenticity and feasibility of the alienation effect they had managed to create in their own productions. They accepted Brecht's politics unpedantically, at times perhaps too uncritically. This does mean that there was some short-circuiting, but it was a dynamic and productive encounter. It had its own point of departure, its own context, and its own agendas that coincided to some extent with those of Brecht. What Indian directors made of him covered a broad spectrum of needs and expectations and it varied considerably. For those working in the tradition created by IPTA, the attraction of Brecht's theatre consisted in discovering and using the most apt means of communication, so that theatre could be taken to the people—a prime example is Habib Tanvir. For those working in the urban context, Brecht provided the tools, most of all the critical stance, needed in order to interpret the social dynamics of the narrative at hand, whereas for yet others, his theatre aesthetics meant a release from the fetters of 'naturalistic' conventions.[34]

Of the directors in the Hindi-speaking north, who introduced and popularized Brecht, many were located at the centre and connected to the NSD, where the exposure to Brecht's theatre was to be the most sustained.[35] The range of responses was broad: from the IPTA-inspired folk-political, to those who saw the realism of the urban realist stage modified and brought into the purview of contemporary politics, and a younger generation that mixed freely urban and rural, pop and traditional, with little regard for provenance, while also aspiring to be politically involved and committed.

Craftsmen of folk theatre stemming from IPTA work, who were situated outside the school, such as Habib Tanvir,[36] found corroboration and stimulation in Brechtian epic theatre for their own work. Tanvir had rejected the conventions of the proscenium stage and naturalistic urban theatre. He was attempting to expand folk theatre with a view to both rural and urban audiences. At the same time, he realized that his own point of view was determined by his urban education and environment. Brecht's theatre was historically significant, in helping him to streamline folk-theatre forms, creating thereby his own particular synthesis of folk with urban.

Unlike Tanvir, though inspired by him, M.S. Sathyu,[37] today known primarily as a film director, did not use folk artistes in his productions. He was more interested in the politics of Brecht's plays and their immediate effect on audiences. In 1963, Sathyu produced with Shama Zaidi, herself just lately returned to the country from a visit to the Berliner Ensemble, the first Hindustani version of *The Caucasian Chalk Circle*. It was a pioneering effort and required directorial, acting, and staging resources that the Hindustani Theatre did not possess. The play was repeated in Kishanganj, a railway workers' colony in the suburbs of Delhi. The audience was drawn irresistibly to an overwhelmingly emotional commitment to the good characters in the play, particularly to identification with the cause of Grusha:

You can't remove human sentiment from your audience. It would be unnatural to do that. The sympathy with Gruscha must grow, must be established. I remember, that when we did it years ago...when we staged it in the Kishanganj Open Theatre, we had about eight-nine thousand people watching the show, all railway workers and some factory workers with their families, old, young. And at the end you know, when the trial of the chalk-circle takes place and the child is taken away by the real mother, not Gruscha, they screamed and yelled at Azdak 'We have to do it once again'. They screamed '*nahin, usko nahin dena chahiye*' [no, he should not be given to her]. They became so vehement about it. The audience reacts, they themselves started seeing, this child should belong to this woman who had protected. If you can get your audience by that time at that point of the play.... Gruscha should get the child. How, they don't know.[38]

Contrary to the ideological notions then current in the English-speaking world, Sathyu saw the success of his play as lying in the intense emotional reaction it provoked. It was, however, a response based on the recognition brought about by the emotional logic of the play: 'This child should belong to this woman who has protected.' Sathyu obviously did not see himself obliged to pay any lip service to the 'correct' ideological interpretations of the alienation effect current at the time, which would have all emotionality banned from a Brecht play.

However, Brecht's political stance could be seen as the single feature that made for the most enduring appeal of his theatre for the major directors of the period. Thus, it was that Ebrahim Alkazi,[39] Director of the NSD, saw Brecht's theoretical and political base as mostly closely corresponding to his own approach:

He is a great humanist poet in the deepest sense of the term; he used the Marxist view of history as a basis for all his plays. He became aware of the social responsibility of the artist... and, therefore, he went to Marxism and then exemplified the creed, as it were, more than anyone else, on a vast popular level.[40]

And it was in this context that he understood the importance that Brecht attached to social 'Gestus'. For him, Brecht's 'loose epic style' reflected the practice of the ancient theatres of Asia, the classical Indian as well as the Chinese and Japanese:

Of all Western playwrights, we believe that Brecht has the greatest relevance to the Indian theatre today, not only on account of the content of his plays, but particularly because of their form. He has broken away from the closed form of the well made 3-act play and chiefly as a result of his intensive study of the classical Indian, the Chinese and Japanese theatres; he has evolved the loose epic style. He has used such devices of our own ancient theatres as the narrator, the chorus, song, music and poetry, to bring back colour and vitality to the insipid prose theatre of today.[41]

Alkazi was, so to speak, at one end of the spectrum of the classical–folk continuum; it was the classical Indian he invoked, viewing Brecht's affinities with the classical as the grounds for the relevance of his theatre for the modern Indian stage. He did not exoticize folk theatre, which he saw as not so far removed from the city dweller, himself only recently removed from the village. Alkazi was well aware of the importance IPTA awarded to folk theatre in the 1940s. However, he would ask for a careful and sophisticated handling of folk forms for the modern stage, depending

on the kind of creative individual. If he has the rootedness in traditional culture and if he has the modern sensibility which is creative and at the same time he is able to use it, you could get a combination; it would be very powerful, it would be very strong. That is the kind of thing that Brecht tried to do.[42]

And he warned early on against the slavish imitation of a Brecht only half-understood:

It is too *simplistic* to say that Brechtian theatre is didactic, and stop at that statement. It is didactic in the sense that it is concerned with the immediate contemporary social reality. It is positive and optimistic in that it maintains that man can alter his circumstances, change his fate—that is, he is not to be regarded as a helpless victim of inscrutable, inevitable and unfathomable forces. It states that the means of scrutinising society is through dialectics in the theatre. The form of theatre Brecht evolved over a period of something like 40 years arose out of a certain political situation obtaining in the West. Merely applying the superficial stylistic aspect of Epic theatre to Indian theatre seems to me ridiculous. The Epic approach is not just a style to be indulged in or exhibited in the theatre but an attitude to one's whole way of life—to all one's relations—domestic, social, political and through that the shaping of the national consciousness.[43]

Alkazi was protesting against a too quick and facile adaptation of Brecht's theatre, which was rooted in its own political and theatrical ethos, by those who were not similarly rooted in theirs. It was not a matter of style alone, it was a question of seeking a fit between Brecht's socialist vision of the social situation in his day and urban theatre practitioners of folk theatre in India of the late 1960s and early 1970s.

The approach to Brecht was more immediate, less problem ridden for the generation that came into its own in post-Independence India. For Amal Allana,[44] distinguished graduate of the NSD and director of many plays including several of Brecht's, the importance of Brecht lay in helping to work out the dramatic structure of a play, so that the multiple social and political implications could be juxtaposed in such a way, that 'the one-short-scene-upon-another gave scope for the unfolding of large, widespread, panoramic social actions, which could encompass the showing of relevant segments consecutively. These could be juxtaposed and montaged in such a way as to reveal the existing conflicts concurrently'.[45]

This understanding of Brecht went beyond the aesthetics of production, since it had to do with the reading of the play itself. It was less concerned with the provenance of a play, whether it was eastern or western, rural or urban.[46] Brecht helped to position people and situations at particular sites on the broad social canvas that became available if a play were read through the political and aesthetic prism he provided:

Although I had studied Brecht in detail before, I only now began to understand the validity of his approach. My previous work had been contentwise non-committal towards the audience, revealing more a concern for aesthetics. In retrospect, I now regard these productions as exercises which helped me to understand the basis of dramatic structure, character development, how a production is built up.[47]

M.K. Raina,[48] another prominent graduate of the School, was also concerned primarily with the political relevance of Brecht's theatre, though he took more deliberate recourse to folk theatre. He built his productions on the fundamentals provided by Alkazi. He went on to adopt some conventions of folk theatre, but he did so with an almost deliberate eclecticism, without feeling obliged to develop a system of theatre aesthetics. He had turned to Brecht with an idea that that alone brought with it the required political relevance: 'It was Brecht. I was following him like a student with a book.' Eventually, he was to realize: 'Brecht has opened some windows. The view shall have to be my own.'[49] Thus though Brecht's 'relevance to India is definitely there', it was important to be aware that: 'Brecht was a highly elite writer. He was not a proletarian writer who wrote for the masses. In the whole design of his plays, when you think of it, he was addressing intellectuals.'[50]

The given social and political relevance of the plays produced had to be worked out in their given regional timeframe, whether it was Mughal Punjab as seen through today's eyes or industrial Kanpur in all the rough and tumble of local power politics. Thus with the production of *The Caucasian Chalk Circle* in Punjabi:

We set it in the village. Azdak was a patwari. A similar situation had occurred in Punjab. The last Moghul Emperor was killed. There was absolute turmoil after that. And we put it in old Punjab and when Gruscha flees to the hills of Chamba, the music moves into Chamba.

Raina found that Brecht's 'alienating' techniques were inherent in the text: 'It's right there in the text. For example, take that scene where Grusha's child is arrested. It reaches a climax. She says '*mera bachcha*' and runs after them. And then the chorus takes over. He is cutting it himself. Because otherwise it becomes really dramatic.'

In the loosely nautanki-style adaptation of *The Threepenny Opera* in Hindi and in a north Indian locale, Raina's primary intention was to work out the social relevance of the play in that setting. It was staged originally in industrial Kanpur, a city where 'there is organized crime, organized labour, there is labour movement. At the same time, there are criminals who are controlling it. There is a complete feudal set up on the one side and then there is labour struggle, there is nothing middle. That is the relevance of the play'.[51]

Raina's presentational methods, working with an urban pop group on the 'naturalistic' proscenium stage, were mixed and by no means restricted to nautanki in any purist sense. The leading role was played by Madhu Singh, daughter of Gulabbai, the famous nautanki actress, well known in Kanpur and the surrounding countryside. Singh was aware of the social tensions outside the theatrical performance, which coexisted with the emotional tensions within the folk play and formed its context:

I think she is remarkable, I think she is the finest Brechtian actress. She is brilliant. The only actress in my life with whom I have no problem directing. She understands everything that I tell her. Even the elements of the Brechtian type of alienation. She is quite used to that kind of a thing in her own plays. In nautanki you have a whole group of *gundas* travelling with them, to protect them. You know a thakur in one village asks you to perform. There are a lot of problems there. Another thakur says, he has asked you to perform. Once a tent was blown up.

The theme of *The Threepenny Opera* with its mixture of the sentimental and the criminal was socially coherent for the nautanki actress.

These directorial opinions and experiences cover the spectrum of traditional theatre, from classical at one end to folk at the other, as it seeks to find a place for itself in a fast-modernizing urban environment, and thus with repeated emphasis on the contemporary political relevance of the exercise. If Tanvir emphasizes folk more and Alkazi stresses the classical Indian, others such as Raina, tend to be more eclectic. 'Folk' is at all events in invigorating company, layered between the classical and the modern, between the realist and post-realist stage. It holds its grounds in any comparison with Brecht's theatre, it gains in political relevance in a mode which is much more nuanced than in the heyday of IPTA, but even in this period of enthusiasm and renewed sense of discovery, it serves urban theatre, rather than be served by it, for even in this period, there is only a sporadic attempt by those who most draw upon the resources of a given form, the playwrights and the directors who bring it to the urban stage, to study and understand it in its own context. In its own rural setting, it does not necessarily get a fresh lease of life from either urban experiments or indeed from Brecht; the theatre of Habib Tanvir is the exception that proves the rule.

Meanwhile, however, there were clear shifts in the Indian appropriation of Brecht, which moved from a first exhilarating recognition of the possibilities his theatre provided, aesthetically, politically, socially— opening thereby further approaches to the classical and folk, the traditional theatre forms already available—to a much more complacent indigenization that took for granted that a given Brecht play, once adapted into the local theatre idiom, preferably from some recognized folk form, would automatically carry its own message. The production of Brecht's plays tended then to become ever more indigenized and increasingly removed from political and social concerns.[52]

There was a marked tendency to perform the same plays in the guise of a new dialect of adaptation, a different locale and different folk music, in an effort to establish indigeneity, with the assumption that the adaptation into local dialect and costume itself ensured that it carried contemporary relevance. Brecht had become almost a cult figure, accepted uncritically as the last word on contemporaneity. By 1979, a critic could write:

I do not know of any other country where the literati have ever made one dramatist the epitome, test and symbol of progressive culture as we Indians have done with Bertolt Brecht. This cult is most evident in Calcutta where his octogenarian anniversary is being celebrated with perfervid cultural activities this year. Everywhere else in India as well the terms like alienation, epic theatre, *Mother Courage* have provided a substantial amount of carrion to the culture-vultures, as perhaps the terms surrealism, fauvism, dialectics, etc. did several decades earlier. However, there is an element of irony in this absolute affiliation to a Brechtian cult because no one has ever attempted to question whether Brechtian dramatic technique is relevant in an Indian setting. Not only that but also whether the motives of Brecht that led to his formulation could be attributed to those who are the biggest utilizers of a Brechtian legacy in our country. (Chaudhuri 1979)

The once important politics of Brecht's theatre were becoming ever more diffuse, taking what seemed to be an unavoidable folkloristic turn, which was making itself apparent in a much wider spectrum of play productions, not those of Brecht alone. What had happened to folk theatre?

FOLK FORMS FILTERED THROUGH BRECHT: PLAYS AND PLAYWRIGHTS

The 1960s and 1970s are generally considered to be the most productive decades to date in the matter of playwriting. There had been a new politicization and on many fronts, as it became increasingly clear that the benefits of Independence were restricted to a small urban and rural middle class. Unemployment, food shortage, price spiralling led to countrywide unrest. The land reforms that had never been implemented, led to armed agrarian resistance in several parts of the country. Even groups conventionally regarded as quietist, such as engineers, teachers, doctors, and civil servants, were led to protest.[53] The antagonists were not so easy to identify on the national level as in the heyday of IPTA, and it was not so easy to forge solidarity, yet there was an upsurge of theatre activity. And a great many experiments were made with folk forms, which were used in a variety of ways. They were shot through with the politics of Brecht, whom the playwrights often invoked in their prefaces. Characteristic of the early encounter with Brecht's theatre was the moment of exhilaration, the freedom that it afforded urban dramatists. As Girish Karnad was to put it,

And it must be admitted that Brecht's influence, received mainly through his writings and without the benefit of his theatrical productions, went some way in making us realize what could be done with the design of traditional theatre. The theatrical conventions Brecht was reacting against—character as a psychological construct providing a focus for emotional identification, the willing-suspension-of-disbelief syndrome, the notion of a unified spectacle—were never a part of the traditional Indian theatre. Therefore there was no question of arriving at an 'alienation' effect by using Brechtian artifice. What he did was to sensitize us to the potentials of non-naturalistic techniques available in our own theatre. (Bodden 1997: 104)

Brecht's theatre seems to have in turns sensitized, politicized, and provided further incentive for those already on a similar track. The outcome was a crop of plays, written and performed all over the country and translated into the many regional languages many were to acquire an all-India reputation. The medium of translation from one language to another was often Hindi, by virtue of its positioning at the centre.

Of those that used folk devices, and many of the best known did so, there were three broad types.

First, there were plays in which both form and narrative were taken from the folk repertoire and thematically moulded. The most typical and popular example of this would be Shanta Gandhi's version of the traditional *bhavai vesha, Jasma Odan* (1982).[54] The thematic emphasis was no longer on Jasma's heroic act of committing sati, with which the play culminated. Instead, the 'personality of Jasma as a working woman' was given importance. At the end of the play, when Jasma was asked to come back to heaven, whence she had fallen, she 'prefers to stay and struggle here on earth, rather than go back to a heaven, which is still too unchanging for her'. The other characters underwent similar changes of dimension.[55] Shanta Gandhi maintained that while 'the acting and production style endeavours to remain as close to the basic ethos of bhavai as possible', the values which the original vesha projected—'medieval values which have now become socially irrelevant and deserve to be rejected'—were sought to be radically transformed. It was an attempt to reinterpret the forces that propelled action. Retained was the presentational technique of the bhavai form and the outline of the story. This, however, could not but make for a different aesthetic experience. Further, the acrobatic skills that enlivened the bhavai of the Gujarat countryside were eliminated, since the urban performers lacked the necessary skill. The justification for using the form was found in the positive audience response that pointed to a 'common ethos, on the basis of which regional dramatic forms, if suitably recreated, can have a wider relevance and enrich the modern theatre'.

Second, there were plays that were outside the folk repertoire but were adapted into folk forms. This included Sanskrit and canonical Western plays. An example of the former was Habib Tanvir's 1958 adaptation of Shudraka's *Mricchakatikam*, The Little Clay Cart, into the Chhattisgarhi *nacha* style. There had been no attempt to add psychological details or depth to the figures in the play. Tanvir emphasized rather the political uprising in the play, which had formed one of the sub-plots in the original Sanskrit play.

B.V. Karanth's 1980 production of Shakspeare's *Macbeth* as *Barnam Vana* for the NSD Repertory in the Kannada dance-drama form *yakshagana* was the most spectacular attempt in the direction of adaptation of Western plays into traditional folk forms.[56] Karanth justified the use of this form for the urban stage, when he maintained that it was 'a part of my awareness and expression.... The tragedies of Shakespeare, especially *Macbeth*, overflow with "rasas" such as valour, wrath, terror or wonder and the characters and situations have a universality and larger than life quality which can be well expressed in the Yakshagana style'.[57]

Third, the folk form could be left more or less intact but used primarily to carry an explicitly political message. In Bengal, Utpal Dutt had used the traditional *jatra* for this purpose most consistently. In Hindi, Sarveshwardayal Saxena's *Bakri* (1974), goat, is the most characteristic and successful example of this kind of theatre. Saxena used the nautanki structure to satirize and expose political hypocrisy and corruption, its escalation before elections, centred in the play around a goat, symbol of a decrepit Gandhism. The play had a sketchy narrative line, but it was acerbic, witty, and spirited, and it raced to an agitational conclusion. The purpose of using the nautanki form was not formally driven, rather it was to reach people as immediately and directly as possible.[58]

Whereas all these three classes attempted to retain the original folk form intact, the fourth and largest group was composed of playwrights who borrowed elements from different regional folk forms in order to widen the dramatic technique and presentation of their plays. For this group of playwrights, writing for the urban middle classes, from which they themselves stemmed, there was no question of borrowing themes from the folk repertoire or being aesthetically and conceptually dependent on 'tradition'. Here a kind of spontaneous formal synthesis was attempted, whereby the playwright presented his individual compositional formula, which remained unique to his play. The best-known examples are Dharmvir Bharati's *Andha Yug*, Vijay Tendulkar's *Ghasiram Kotwal*, and Girish Karnad's *Hayavadan*. These have become classics of modern Indian theatre and a great deal of literature has sprung up around them. For our purposes here, a brief discussion of their relationship to 'folk' theatre conventions, which for Tendulkar and Karnad was possibly filtered through their awareness of Brecht's theatre aesthetics and conventions, will have to suffice.

Dharmavir Bharati's *Andha Yug* (The Blind Age) written in 1954, inspired by the post-War situation in Europe, treated the epic battle at the centre of the Mahabharata in a contemporary moral and political frame. Bharati used an epic narrator to establish links in time and space, for the narrative is partly episodic in character, as well as chorus-like characters to comment on the action: the horror and devastation of war conveyed in free-verse rhythms. The play has twofold sources for the dramatic devices used: the classical Greek play, possibly mediated through the poetic plays of T.S. Eliot, and Indian folk-theatre devices such as the narrator.[59] It was obviously addressed to sophisticated urban audiences, and was, so to speak, pre-Brechtian. It is nevertheless important to take note of this play in our context, since it provides a valuable bridge to the impetus generated by IPTA.

Tendulkar's *Ghasiram Kotwal* (1972) treated a semi-historical theme from a contemporary socio-political perspective, using the devices offered by the folk theatre of Maharashtra.[60] It is the story of Ghasiram, a Brahman, who rises to power under the ruthless Nana Phadnavis to finally become a pawn in the political strategies of the callous Nana, who does away with him once he has fulfilled his function. It was a forceful exposure of the unscrupulous and self-serving Brahmanical orthodoxy that ruled in Pune. There were those who chose to view it as a naturalistic history play and found it wanting. It was criticized for not creating 'full blooded characters'.[61] But as Jabbar Patel, the director of the Pune production pointed out in the director's note to the play, the Nana of the play was a folk character, not a historical character study; the play was in any case not dialogue oriented, there was little attempt to provide psychological motivation. Instead, there were traditional devices, such as Ghasiram addressing the public directly. The folk frame thus turned out to be more than convenient, for in spite of its historical matter and clear political line, it allowed Tendulkar to insist on the universality and agelessness of the social phenomenon presented in the play. However, Tendulkar was more of a historian than he himself laid claim to, for he recorded and thus anticipated, even if only inadvertently, the future course of Maratha history, and the passing of the feudal into the capitalist mode, by twice showing an Englishman as an observer of the scene.[62] The folk framework that was used allowed, then, for a vaster historical and political generalization than would have been possible for a more realistic mode of play composition and presentation.

Karnad's *Hayavadana* (1970) used elements of the Kannada yakshagana and a frame-story as in traditional Sanskrit narrative compendia.[63] The central narrative, itself almost like a folk tale with its focus on the solution of a dilemma posed as a riddle, also came from a Sanskrit collection of tales, via the interpretation it had received from Heinrich Zimmer and the Thomas Mann short story inspired by it. The Sanskrit tale had been given a psychological turn by both Zimmer and Mann; it was now further transformed by Karnad.[64] It became the fable of the incompleteness of the modern self, yearning for completion in the partner, reminiscent of the thematic of Mohan Rakesh's *Adhe adhure*. The frame story presents the theme symbolically, in the shape of mythologized half-horse half-man, who seeks to become whole. The actual drama of the situation, between two men and a woman, is played out in the main narrative. In addition, there is the use of such devices as the dream sequence and two talking dolls, who expose the psychological undercurrents of the story. This subtly wrought configuration, of Sanskrit tale, modern psychology, and the layering of meaning offered by masks and half curtain, the interpretations made possible by narration and song, makes for an extremely complex treatment of the story, which operates on several levels: myth, dream, fantasy, and tale within tale. Karnad was to go on to make several highly successful experiments in this direction in the next decades.

Brecht's political aesthetics, the richness of folk forms still prevailing in most parts of India, a modern urban stage seeking new means to articulate the new, made for a heady mix which produced the plays that have become staples of the modern theatrical canon and which are performed again and again, in state and national theatre festivals. However, the end of the 1970s saw the end of creative experimentation with folk forms as shot through with techniques culled from Brecht's theatre. This was a phenomenon variously registered by observers of the scene and by theatre practitioners themselves. Mudrarakshash, Hindi novelist and playwright, was to write *Ala Afsar*, an adaptation of Gogol's *Inspector-General*, in 1977. It was political satire and it used the nautanki style. The play was a success, but the playwright himself disclaimed any credit for its popularity in the preface to the printed version of the play in its second, 1983, edition. Mudrarakshash had been a reluctant comer, and a late one at that, on the folk scene, though his father belonged to the *samp-sampera* folk tradition, which was now practically extinct in Uttar Pradesh. Mudrarakshash had initially basked in the glory that the play brought for him, but, as he tells us in the preface, he soon came to realize that the play would not stand the test of time. The narrative line was thin and sketchy and its success dependent less on any creative act of compostion, more on the current enthusiasm for the folk–Brecht mix, which was becoming a formula and proving particularly attractive for young directors trained in the NSD. These young people had little understanding of the kind of drama 'which turns on the axis of a deep, inner, compassionate insight into politics. They invoke Brecht's name with extreme ease in order to claim a commitment which is shallow. And by putting some hollow sloganeering on stage, they feel assured that they are truly Brechtian' (Mudrarakshash [1977] 1983: 21).

Brecht's theatre had a catalysing effect on Indian theatre makers that lasted for a good two decades; it helped to transform production modes, made possible fresh interpretations of classics, Eastern and Western, and it supported playwrights already inspired by folk theatre in further crystallizing the structure of their plays. Yet the turn to Brecht could, on its own, hardly sustain the complex process of creation, which had drawn on several sources of inspiration and was able to maintain itself in the changing political climate of the post-Nehru political era, with its mixture of radical protest and liberal conformism. This particular process seems to have run its course as the political and with that the cultural environment changed once again, in the last years of the first spell of Indira's Gandhi's reign. The years of the internal emergency declared by her government that lasted from 1975 to 1977 put an abrupt end to freedom of expression; there was a marked change in playwriting and production. A process similar to that which set in after the Dramatic Performances Bill was passed in 1876, seems to have taken place again. A reign of terror, that while it lasted showed no signs of relaxing its grip, meant, particularly for theatre which lived from public interaction, an extreme form of muzzling. No extensive account of the effect of the emergency on cultural production has yet become available. Since it was over in less than two years, some kind of national amnesia about those years seems to have set in thereafter. Yet, even a brief run through of the process makes clear how sweeping was the change.

From the day that Emergency was declared, on 26 June 1975, there was a crackdown on all fronts, which crippled the legislature; dissenting members of Mrs Gandhi's own party found themselves in prison, several political leaders went underground, while the executive was brought to toe the line and the judiciary came under extreme pressure as wilful appointments to high positions were made summarily. The press was gagged, journals such as the English-language *Seminar* which had fostered critical discussion were closed, while national dailies such as *The Statesman* and *The Indian Express*, which refused to be muzzled, were subjected to extreme forms of harassment. Artistes, writers, and intellectuals went under cover. The performing arts, film and theatre, came under censorship control as all public utterances were subjected to close scrutiny. Draconian measures had become possible under the dreaded MISA: the Maintenance of Internal Security Act. The notorious family planning drive subjected the lowest strata of society to the kind of personal persecution and brutality unthinkable in democratic India.[65]

The Emergency alone could not bring about the changes which set in thereafter. However, the years between 1975 and 1977 were a kind of watershed. The tide, to mix a metaphor, was to turn. In the coalition government that came to power in the general election that followed, a large segment belonged to the right wing. And this in fact would increasingly be a direction taken by Indira Gandhi's Congress Party, when it came back to power. Contemporary observers noted this turn and what it meant for the politics of theatre. Folk theatre, for example, was to become decorative and conformist, losing all political sting.

Leafing through the issues of *Enact*, we come across the repeated complaint that theatre has lost its political and social bearings and that, emptied of the spark of political protest and of social unrest, playwriting and production have both become remarkably barren. Given the freedom offered by the lifting of the state of emergency, it is considered a matter of surprise that there are no new political plays. At the end of 1978, we hear:

Going through the list of plays reviewed in *Enact* this year, one finds political drama as a genre is lamentably absent... the Indian theatre today is not really dealing with live issues. There was a time of course when the proud past of the theatre personalities could be traced back to their happy association with the IPTA movement.

One would have thought, with the advent of the post-emergency era offering a passionate promise of a climate of freedom, we would have a few younger ones tearing down some of the hitherto untouched shibboleths. One would have liked to see a wild lashing out at the unreliable, impuissant, corrupt and sanctimonious edifices—a fresh attempt at understanding the myth of socialism as practised in India through the gargantuan strong arm of caste, cash and illiteracy. The real facade of this miracle of democracy certainly needs an excruciating reassessment....

So much is happening today. Pick up any newspaper—it is full of social, political and economic disasters.... And to find this aspect of theatre missing in our present plays is, to say the least, an ignoble and spineless indulgence in sweet fiddling.[66]

The creativity unleashed by the combination of urban concerns with the political restlessness of the 1960s and early 1970s, and the release afforded by the combination of Brecht's epic theatre with the freshly discovered folk forms, were a thing of the past. The best-known playwrights of this period would continue to write but the heyday of the modern folk play was over.

THE THEATRE OF ROOTS

Meanwhile there had been a crucial change in the theatre establishment in Delhi. B.V. Karanth, trained in a yakshagana troupe in his youth, had replaced Alkazi as the director of the NSD. Though he himself was universally regarded as prodigiously creative in exploring new possibilities and experimenting with new combinations, he seemed, inadvertently, to be fostering a trend, which made performances coined by folk theatre the almost exclusive direction followed by the NSD Repertory. This could be folk theatre at its most vacuous, transported to the urban stage with little reflection about its use or misuse. Thus in 1981, there were complaints:

With Karanth's background of folk and traditional theatre it seems as though he has shifted the emphasis in the training programme—i.e., if there was an emphasis which needed deliberate shifting and which would not have surfaced on its own in the process of evolution. In fact, a gradual process would have had greater stability and the present repertory theatre, which seems suddenly to be overburdened with folk, would have first assimilated and then reproduced. As of now, it appears as though it has become a messy splash of colour, comedy and caricature. Credit is to the consummate artistes who have managed to sustain interest in their new productions! (Sondhi 1981)

A year thereafter, the tenor remains unchanged. This excessive attachment to forms that were reproduced on the urban stage, more or less as exotica, had begun to be seen as a kind of inner Orientalism that corresponded to the Western theatre practitioner's incursions into traditional Indian ritual theatre, such as Grotowski's interest in kathakali, though, as we have seen, this was the kind of exoticization which also had a long tradition within India. We only need refer back to Balwant Gargi's excited discovery of folk theatre in 1962.

The theatre makers of the late 1960s and 1970s had seen their experiments with folk forms as rooted in the concerns of the urban middle class and thus in a modern sensibility. At the rate that the medium was being exploited now, folk theatre was being increasingly drained as a source of vitality for the urban stage. The international festival culture, sponsored by the Indian government and launched from the early 1980s—the first Festival of India, held in Britain, took place in 1982—cemented these very tendencies. Folk art and folk performances were being used as export items that backdated culture in a move that was as anachronistic as unscrupulous, it was as if a modern chemist was posturing as an alchemist. What could this magic be expected to bring about?[67] It was in such contexts that Brecht was once again invoked— perhaps he had not yet lost his usefulness for Indian theatre—more as a hope than as any real possibility. At this stage, the cry for help sounded almost like a cry in the wilderness: 'The content of Brecht's work is relevant ideologically and has the power to goad the Indian intelligence into thought. That is, if theatre is viewed as an instrument of change and directed towards stepping in where the press fears to tread' (Sondhi 1982).

The International cultural festivals, propagating the image of an India Immortal, had begun to draw upon the arts in a way that once again sought to bring together the classical and the folk as timeless categories, as part of a 'past that effectively dislodges the present in staking its claims over the nation's art' (Guha-Thakurta 1997: 90). What cultural impetus could these vast international shows provide?

As Arindam Dutta has noted, in the wake of Mrs Gandhi's assassination in 1984, the Congress Party under the leadership of her son Rajiv Gandhi was returned to power with monolithic majority within Parliament, which gave them 'a virtual carte-blanche in the economic politics of the nation-state'. The project of the Festivals of India to be staged in various parts of the world was then 'part of a marketing drive to introduce India to the highly industrialized G7 countries as a viable locale for investment' (1997: 122). Government officials referred publicly to the economic backdrop of these cultural shows, particularly the 1985–6 Festival of India in the USA:

S.K. Mishra, director-general of the Festival of India, and an ex-tourism top official from the state of Haryana, explained the Festivals in terms of the following: '...it's a perfect moment for India to cash in, to change existing prejudices about India in the western world and to signal a new era of Indo-American cooperation.' And Niranjan Desai, the Washington-based minister counsellor for culture, talking about economic potentials in the field of tourism, books, movies, investment and trade: 'These are things we want but cannot get until we alter our image. We are still trapped in the Heat and Dust and Indiana Jones syndrome. We have to show that India is not only exotic but contemporaneously exotic as well as modern and competent.'[68]

In our context, the term 'contemporaneously exotic' needs to be particularly noted. It was as if bits of the past were preserved intact for inner as well as outer export, frozen and perfectly packaged, with all the dirt and grime of lived reality, of poverty and exploitation, scraped off or put in soft focus. As Dutta went on to explicate, not only were Rajiv Gandhi and Nancy Reagan the official patrons of the festival,

Of the total expenses incurred, $12–15 million was paid by the Indian Government, while the expenses for hosting the events in the United States were mostly borne by various companies seeking possible markets in India, besides various grant institutions, like the Boeing company, Coca-Cola, General Foods, ITT Corporation, Armand Hammer Foundation, Ford Foundation, Andrew Mellon Foundation, etc.

Thus it came about that:

In the middle of the 1980s, no staging of the rural-as-culture in the context of a 'critical regionalism' can be understood independently of the alliance between third-world comprador capitalists, the emerging consensus on global structural adjustment and its new codings of development in the rural-as-economic scenario. By *partially* staging as fragment the spectacle of the village as a repository of culture, what gets covered over is the re-situating of the rural in the forefront of global exploitation. (Dutta 1997: 133)

The process of wilful and arbitrary fragmentation of village culture, of folk art as spectacle divorced from its context, reflected the practice within as well as without. The folk-tradition enthusiasts, active since the early 1960s, merged effortlessly with these trends, since their own perspective had been ahistorical from the start. The mechanical reproduction of rural cultures thus isolated from their moorings presented little problem. As Rustom Bharucha has put it: 'At the international level, we have projected a most cosmetic and superficial image of "Indian culture".... At home, these festivals have merely mechanised and commodified our rural and tribal cultural resources, apart from making showpieces of our "classical" art' (1992: 1676).

What, then, were the uses to which folk theatre would be put? Several schemes were under way. The Sangeet Natak Akademi stepped forward to take the lead. It instituted the Scheme of Assistance to Young Theatre Workers. It would support 'the efforts of directors engaged in exploring and developing a theatre idiom indigenous in character, inspired by the traditional folk theatres of the country'. The activity at regional or zonal level would flow into a grand show, the Natya Samaroh, in Delhi. 'Commencing with theatre festivals in the North, South, Western and Eastern Zones, Natya Samaroh culminates annually in a national festival in Delhi, featuring a selection of plays earlier staged in zonal festivals.'[69] The number of zonal centres grew to five in 1985–6, two more were to be added in 1986–7. The centres were to 'propagate a particular image of India that was essentially synthetic and homogenised. Under the guise of representing different "regional cultures" through "zones", these centres were meant to facilitate the centralisation of cultural activities at a scale which has neither been envisioned nor funded in India since independence'.[70] And yet they were to have a powerful impact on the cultural landscape of the country. The modern, as the messy, conflict-ridden, culturally hybrid, socially restless, and possibly politically unstable, would necessarily be sidelined, as far as official patronage was concerned. Key issues would simply remain unaddressed:

The question is: for whom do they exist apart from the government officials and a scattering of the cultural elite? What infrastructural facilities have they provided for communities even in their own headquarters? Where are the rehearsal spaces, open-air theatres, galleries that the report would like to see? What have they done for the 'folk' and 'tribal' peoples apart from using them as material in their spectacles? How have they initiated dialogue between communities from different states apart from hosting 'festivals' where 'experts' preside over the creative efforts of 'youth'. The point is that at every level these centres have not just failed to enrich cultural relationships and activities, they may even have jeopardized the possibilities that existed before. (Bharucha 1992: 1675)[71]

The Sangeet Natak Akademi was, as we have seen, offering attractive incentives to young theatre makers who integrated folk forms into their work. If they performed sufficiently well at the regional level to deserve recognition at the national, they could well shoot into prominence.[72] In order to propagate these ideas and surely also in a genuine attempt to thrash out the issues related to this massive new surge of official interest in traditional theatre, the Sangeet Natak Akademi organized a 'National Seminar on Perspectives of Contemporary Indian Theatre' in December 1984, once again with Suresh Awasthi taking the lead. The views presented can be broadly grouped under three heads. The first group was composed of those, and it included the organizers, who were enthusiastic and more or less uncritical proponents of indigenous theatre, which they now no longer called 'folk' theatre or even 'traditional'. The new nomenclature employed for it was 'theatre of roots' and classical Sanskrit theatre was at its unapologetic centre. Western or realist theatre, and the theatre in India which followed in its footsteps, were seen as the polar opposites of this theatre of roots. The second group, by far the smallest, consisted of those who proceeded more cautiously, who weighed the pros and cons of turning in such an uncritical manner in the direction of an unquestioned tradition. Finally, there was the group that regarded this attitude to the indigenous as unequivocally anti-modernist and as politically questionable.

The propagators of the 'theatre of roots' had the first and last word. Nemichandra Jain began with the enumeration of the factors that called for this new orientation, which he saw as already under way. These factors were:

impact of the widespread quest for an Indian identity in all aspects of life in our country, including the arts, particularly the theatre; a growing awareness of and dissatisfaction with the imitative nature of our past dramatic efforts and the desire to go to our own roots; increasing exposure to our own traditional theatre forms and their amazing vitality, aesthetic features and popularity with people; worldwide disillusionment with realistic theatre and search for alternatives, influence of the plays and performances of Bertolt Brecht, and so on.[73]

In sum, an Indian identity, our roots, and, as posited against this, the West with its bankrupt realistic theatre. However, Nemichandra Jain did not forget his own connections to the progressive writers and IPTA. He stressed the importance of 'some social and artistic vision' and he saw the need for 'expressing contemporary experience'.[74]

Suresh Awasthi in his concluding remarks was more sweeping in his pronouncements on this turn to the traditional, which he viewed as having come about, at least partly if not wholly, due to the initiative he himself had taken early in the 1960s; he owned up to the authorship of the term 'theatre of roots' ('my own guilt').[75] He also stressed the importance of classical Sanskrit theatre both as the point of origin and as the point of return: 'A return to the Sanskrit classics with some successful productions is a noteworthy feature of the new theatre movement when seen in historical perspective.'[76] The many regional forms were so many articulations of the pan-Indian theatre of roots: 'It is deeply rooted in regional culture, but cuts across linguistic barriers, and has a pan-Indian character in idiom and communicability. Never before during the last century and more was theatre practised in such diversified form, and at the same time with such unity in essential theatrical values'.[77]

Once again, there was no mention of IPTA. As Awasthi saw it, the movement now under way began *after* Independence.

As part of the great cultural renaissance generated during the post-independence period, there has occurred a most meaningful encounter with tradition in various fields of creative activity. The return to and discovery of tradition was inspired by a search for roots and a quest for identity. This was part of a whole process of decolonization of our life style, values, social institutions, creative forms and cultural modes. The modern Indian theatre, product of a colonial theatrical culture, felt the need to search for roots most intensely to match its violent dislocation from the traditional course.

Since there was no mention of IPTA, it was not surprising that decolonization, rather than colonization, was stressed. Returning to the roots would mean that the residue left behind by the West could be stripped off, as so much extra layering that had never become organically integrated. Awasthi equated proscenium theatre with 'the onslaught of realistic theatre',[78] which could now be warded off, once and for all. He maintained that henceforth, all actors would have to have been trained in some traditional form: 'With the emergence of the new theatre and its trained actors, the amateur untrained actor is fast becoming irrelevant. After AD 2000 there will be no place for an untrained actor in Indian theatre.'[79]

What was new was the polemical anti-Western tone, which was also manifestly anti-modernist. G. Sankara Pillai, director and Malayalam playwright, saw Western-inspired 'realism' as inimical to the Indian ethos. The modern Indian playwright searched instead for 'identity with the traditional idioms' because of the 'realization that we are traditionally removed from realism. Our acting dictums never recognized realism....'[80] The reasons were plain to see: 'We *are* traditional. We have a concept of time unending, and our concept of the cycle of life is absolute and complete: it is a spectrum of light with only certain transitory patches of darkness. Hence we have to find our own terminologies and definitions.'[81] Though he did not see the more codified forms of traditional theatre as seamlessly connected to the more rural, he yet believed that they were part of a continuum:

It should also be noted that it is incorrect to believe that there is nothing between the down-to-earth, local forms and the highly codified, complex forms like Kathakali, Bharatanatyam and Koodiyattam. In between, there are various levels, various systems which are to be studied with special attention. All such points of departure are important in the study of art.[82]

Why was realism being propped up as the new opponent? The use of the term 'realism' instead of the old 'naturalism' is itself instructive. 'Naturalism' had been receding as an oppositional pole from the 1970s on, to make place for 'realism'; though the two terms continued to be used interchangeably, they overlapped since both were ostensibly concerned with depicting the observable world. However, naturalism as a critical term carried echoes of nineteenth-century European usage to mean a detailed description of the social environment of the protagonists of a given literary composition, whether in the novel or in drama:

The school of *naturalisme* in France was especially affected, as in Zola, by the idea of the application of scientific method in literature: specially the study of heredity in the story of a family, but also more generally in the sense of describing and interpreting human behaviour in strictly natural terms, excluding the hypothesis of some controlling or directing force outside human nature. This naturalism was the basis of a major new kind of writing, and the philosophical position was explicitly argued: cf. Strindberg: 'the naturalist has abolished guilt by abolishing God'; 'the summary judgements on men given by authors...should be challenged by naturalists, who know the richness of the soul-complex and recognize that "vice" has a reverse side very much like virtue' (Preface to *Lady Julie*, 1888). A new importance was given to the environment of characters and actions.... Character and action were seen as determined by environment, which specially in a social and social-physical sense had then to be accurately described as an essential element of any account of life. (Williams [1976] 1983: 217).

Gradually, naturalism came to mean the accurate description of the external world. Realism had another literary trajectory; it had been counter-posed to the romantic, imaginary, or mythical world:

It is often described in terms of blame or limitation, in these senses (a) that what is described or represented is seen only superficially, in terms of its described or outward appearance rather than its inner reality; (b) in a more modern form of the same objection...that a realism 'of the surface' can quite miss important realities; (c) in a quite different objection, that the medium in which this representation occurs, whether language or stone or paint or film is radically different from the objects represented in it, so that the effect of 'lifelike representation', the 'reproduction of reality', is at best a particular artistic convention, at worst a falsification making us take the forms of representation as real. (260–1)

This was precisely the underlying tone of accusation when 'realism' was posited as the polar opposite of the Indian indigenous. However, to treat realism thus was to choose to understand it as a surface phenomenon. It could also 'be seen not as static appearance but as the movement of psychological or social or physical forces; realism is then a conscious commitment to understanding and describing these' (261). The enthusiastic votaries of the theatre of roots displayed little commitment to describing social or physical forces. They were concerned rather with timeless truths. Realism as a modernist enterprise could in this sense be considered a worthy opponent.

The second group of participants was more cautious about the direction that these excursions into the past seemed to be taking. Lokendra Arambam, Manipuri playwright and director, drew attention to the fact that 'tradition also demands in those who handle it an ability to imbibe "a historical sense to perceive, not only the pastness of the past, but of its presence". Manipuri theatre in the eighties is yet to struggle with these issues'.[83]

There was no denying that this recourse to traditional forms had once been very productive. But as Rajinder Nath, director of the Hindi stage, pointed out, 'When an idea degenerates into a slogan, the consequences can be disastrous. Something similar has happened or is happening to a very creative idea: using our folk and traditional theatre forms in contemporary theatre'.[84] The problem clearly lay in insisting that all roots were buried in the past. Indian modernity also had a history in the meantime. 'When the use of traditional and folk forms is argued, the stock phrase used is "discovery of roots" or "going to the soil". True, but are all our roots ancient? There can be modern roots too, which one has to discover to deal with contemporary reality and experience.'[85]

The third group was troubled by the facile appropriation of the rural, of which the urban theatre makers and audiences had little knowledge. The knowledge of the rural was less than scanty, making for an indigeneity that had all the trappings of the worst kind of revivalism: 'This urban exercise is usually one of short cuts, and is ambitious and exploitative in nature.'[86] Tradition was not so faint-hearted. It would survive in some meaningful way into the present. And if a given traditional form failed to do so and to 'remain relevant in our fast-changing world, it is better to let it die, and go ahead in the quest for expression with the belief that new traditions will grow and continue to enrich humanity and its culture'.[87]

The enthusiasm of some directors for folk forms was 'similar to the colonizer's enthusiasm for "ethnic" theatre or "ethnic" music'. This was internal orientalism, according to G.P. Deshpande, Marathi playwright and ever a radical presence in theatre criticism. In his contribution, entitled 'Fetish of Folk and Classic', he found that there was little understanding of the social context of folk forms, little reflection on their use today. His critique was sweeping: 'Our forms are not the playthings of the white man or the urban, alienated directors who are looking for excitement from oriental theatre comparable to the excitement an LSD trip offers. Our forms are not exotica'.[88] The problem was genuinely one not of going to the roots but of the roots that were missing.

Over the past four decades or so, the middle class in our country has grown enormously. Unlike the middle class which produced IPTA, this middle class is almost completely rootless. It does not have an ancestry. It is trying to create one for itself. The newly found love for the classic and the folk are both indications of the search for roots by an alienated middle class. This class, for the first time in India's history, has become a Trishanku, hanging in the middle air. It needs tradition but cannot relate to one. It needs classicism but does not know how to come to terms with it. It needs modernity but still does not know how to understand it.[89]

There were two issues that came up repeatedly: the unity of Indian theatre, ancient and modern, and modern Western theatre as the antithesis of Indian theatre. The one side maintained that Indian theatre was a singular entity and the recourse to roots simply meant turning to this singular entity once again; the various regional streams had always fed into it. The other side maintained that there was no such seamless continuum from the ancient to the modern and that there were multiple and heterogeneous streams that criss-crossed through the ages. As for Western theatre, the one side chose to regard Western, realist, proscenium theatre as the arch foe; in order to decolonize, the conventions of this theatre needed to be thrown off. The other side was less concerned with denying this link to Western theatre traditions, again not seen in the singular, which had also become part of the indigenous in the meantime. It sought, instead, the means for articulating the contradictions of modernity in which dramatist and viewer, director and actor, rural or urban, were alike implicated.

It was important, as G.P. Deshpande emphasized in an article written several years later—the issues were still acute—to recognize the plurality of the linguistic and theatrical idioms currently at work in the subcontinent. 'Each mode is uniquely important. There are several, equally valid and legitimate Indian theatres' (Deshpande 1999: 93). To reduce these to three—folk, Sanskrit, and modern Western—was to take unproductive short cuts, and most of all, it was to deny the very history of modern Indian theatre:

This approach dismisses nearly two hundred years of modern proscenium theatre in India. It rules out contemporary experience and therefore contemporary sensibility. All this has political meanings. Quite often they are unintended but their impact cannot be avoided. Modern Indian Theatre is a victim of a particular kind of politics—the politics of cultural nationalism which is monolithic, blind and anti-creative. (96)

However, recognizing that Western enlightenment was as much part and parcel of Indian thought as any recourse to the Indian past did not mean that in order to be modern, blind recourse could be taken to each trend in modern Western theatre: 'Our modernity has to be our own.... The tragedy is that no matter what the dominant discourse on theatre might argue, we need modern theatre. We need our *modern* theatre' (93).

Thus experiment with folk theatre, borrowings, adaptations, trans-formations of folk forms for the urban stage, would only be meaning-ful, if, as Anuradha Kapur put it, there were 'not a disenchantment with today's world but a stake in it. For if we believe that conventions of seeing are social as is art, then we must also believe that we are pro-ducing social knowledge, producing a past and producing a future in which we ourselves will function' (Kapur 1991: 12).

It would also mean creating space for the folk artistes themselves, who needed more than ever to find ways to survive in the modern world. Urban audiences could take occasional delight in performances by folk artistes. But once folk forms were considered salon-worthy, they were literally taken over by urban artistes, who then proceeded to represent folk traditions not only to each other but, most of all, on the international arena; there was little or no space left for the traditional artiste. As Deshpande pointed out:

The story of the Maharashtra Tamasha Parishad is a case in point. This Parishad was founded to help the traditional artistes survive. It has failed because the new politics of cultural nationalism does not take the traditional artist in reckoning. It would want the new high caste/high class artist to take over those activities. In the process a new semantics developed. What was once a *Tamasha* became (Sanskritized) *Loknatya*. These semantic changes mark the very anti-thesis of what undistorted cultural nationalism should be. Worse that that, this semantics suggested a cruel appropriation which involved the virtual elimination of the traditional artist. (1999: 96)

Was form to be saved at the expense of the performer? Pleading for the necessity of a truly modern theatre, could not and should not mean ignoring the folk artiste and the process of change that s/he is involved in, or indeed becoming indifferent to the traditional forms that they had once practised but which were themselves changing.[90] As Anuradha Kapur put it:

The folk performer is spontaneous, energetic, improvisational, and robust— adjectives stream forth—but once the folk performer is thus stereo-typed, the possibilities of manoeuvre are sucked away; it becomes difficult to speak about the tragic, the sinister, the problematical.... The question we must ask is how to represent the wrenching experiences of modernity—of migration into the city for example—on stage; and whether the anxieties of changing life patterns and the disruptive aspects of everyday experience can be glossed over by transcendent energy. (1991: 11)

There can then be nothing inherently good or bad about borrowing, changing, or remaking a given form. Modern urban practitioners of 'folk' theatre, who have long subsumed Brecht, can do what they do for diametrically opposed political and aesthetic purposes, as we have seen. They can question established truths, they can subvert them, they can open up new avenues and while doing so they can address both elite and popular audiences; both need to be addressed. But such folk enthusiasts can, equally, be backward looking, conformist, and serve to freeze and exclude, while *also* setting out to address elite or popular audiences.

As we have seen, there was at least a twofold use of 'folk' by urban theatre people. In the first period of its extensive usage (IPTA), the use was entirely and self-proclaimedly functional. Folk forms were used to address folks, to radicalize politics, and at the same time to reinvigorate urban theatre practice, once again, for social rather than aesthetic ends. After Independence, the term 'folk' came to be used increasingly to manipulate and integrate into the grand national master narrative. As Roma Chatterjee in her essay on the uses of the term has shown, 'folk' and 'tribe' are often used as coterminous, connoting localization and marginality; they are relational terms referring to gradation in culture. In 'nationalist' discourse the term 'folk' carried the connotation of primordial essence and was seen as the expression of an unselfconscious and timeless community life. But there were other more empowering[91] and at times radically subversive conceptions such as that presented by Bakhtin, which were articulated precisely to counter the national-chauvanist appropriation and monumentalization of diverse folk cultures. Bakhtin saw the spirit of 'folk' in

the culture of the lower orders, of the market place and the carnival. It is only in these spaces that the masses could speak using the language of parody—critiquing all that was hierarchical, authoritative and monological through laughter. This laughter that celebrated the relativity and dynamism of collective life becomes a resource against repression, allowing common people to withstand in their every day life the all-encompassing authority of a dictatorial regime.[92]

In reviewing these discussions we are left with more questions than answers. Folk-popular forms can be left to take care of their politics; they change to suit their own needs and at times merge with the urban, in a myriad as yet unrecorded ways. The questions which have been thrown up are addressed, then, more to urban theatre makers. Can folk-popular as received by urban theatre makers restore the dialogic and the subversive to urban theatre again? Can it reconnect urban to the rural and to the political, which last had been possible in the 1960s and early 1970s? And in a yet wider context, can urban theatre cease to back date and learn instead to regard folk theatre as a modern-day phenomenon? The folk performer is our contemporary, not a skirt-swishing, sword-brandishing exotic. In concluding this essay then, it may be instructive to turn once more to Brecht.

BRECHT ONCE MORE: NO HEROICS FOR THE PEOPLE

Walter Benjamin has recorded fragments of his conversation with Bertolt Brecht in 1938 in Svendborg, his Swedish exile, and it is with two quotations from this conversation that I should like to commence my conclusion. The first has to do with Brecht's lifelong distaste for officious administration of teachings that had once been radical, dynamic, creative. Benjamin reports:

June 28, 1938. Brecht speaks of his firmly entrenched hatred of clerics, a legacy inherited from his grandmother. Those who have made Marx's theoretical teachings their own and have set about using them, he implies, will always build a sanctimonious Kamirilla.

Irreverence, then, in the handling of doctrine and resistance to theories that have petrified into law in the hands of the ruling. And in this strain also the second citation from Benjamin:

June 29.... Brecht for his part cites the moment wherein the idea of epic theatre is anchored. A rehearsal of *Edward II* was in progress. The battle which takes place in the play occupies the stage for a good three quarters of an hour. Brecht was not being able to place the soldiers (nor could Asja, his directorial assistant). Karl Valentin, with whom he was very friendly in those days, was also attending the rehearsals. Finally Brecht turned to him with the desperate question, well what of it, how is it really with the soldiers. Valentin said, they're pale, they're afraid. This was the decisive remark and Brecht added: they're tired. The faces of the soldiers were smeared thick with chalk. And it was in these days that the (epic) style of production was discovered. (Benjamin 1978: 166)

Karl Valentin, the popular Munich vaudeville performer, was the reference point for both Brecht and Benjamin. His remark was cited by them as providing Brecht with the insight that made for the genesis of epic theatre. No heroics then for the soldiers, no heroics for the audience, the epic theatre was to break clichés. Viewed in this perspective, from the popular and the dialogical, Brecht still offers fresh insight:

The historicizing portrayal will have something of the sketch which preserves traces of other movements and features around the figure which has been worked out. Or, one should think of a man who holds a speech in a valley, whereby now and then he changes his opinion or simply speaks in sentences which contradict each other, so that the echo which speaks alongside him, takes over the task of confronting the sentences with each other. (Brecht [1967] 1976: vol. 16, 679)

NOTES

[1] Harishchandra sees drama in India as having three divisions: 1) Poetry-mixed or Poetical (*kavya mishra*), 2) Pure Spectacle or Curiosity (*shuddha kautuk*), and 3) Corrupt (*bhrashta*). In the second category, which he does not totally reject, he includes puppetry, mime, feats of skill, and other forms of civilized entertainment. He distances himself from the third category, in which are included the forms that possessed theatricality originally, but which have since degenerated; no recognizable dramatic quality is any longer to be found in them (*natakatva shesha nahim rah gaya hai*) and they have become devoid of poetry (*kavyahin*). Under this category he includes not only the popular forms bhand, Indar sabha, tamasha, and yatra, but also, suprisingly, given his pious bent, forms explicitly rooted in religious traditions, such as rasa, lila, and *jhanki*. Less surprisingly, he adds the theatre of the Parsis to the list of the corrupt (*Granthavali 1*: 750).

[2] This paragraph follows Williams in the annotations on 'folk' in his *Keywords* ([1976] 1983: 136–7).

[3] See Dalmia (2001) on the effect of this folkloristic activity on early Indian nationalism.

[4] See Blackburn (2003) for an account of folklore activity in what is today's Tamil Nadu, as also a more general survey of folklorists' activities through the nineteenth century (155–7).

[5] Not surprisingly, the activity which came to constitute a veritable folklore movement in Bengal is well documented and relatively easily accessible. Asok Mitra, the Registrar General of newly independent India, played a role in the publication of the two books that have become important resources for information on the movement in Bengal. He wrote the introduction for the *Folklorists of Bengal*: *Life Sketches Notes* by Sankar Sen Gupta, who had painstakingly reconstructed the genealogy of this discipline in Bengal and collated a deal of bibliographical information on each individual folklorist. Mitra writes in the introduction to the book, that under his direction, for he felt that he had inherited the mantle of folklore scholarship from his forebears in the field, one of the tasks 'that the 1961 Census of India set itself was the completion of more than 500 village surveys throughout the length and breadth of the land'. This included a separate chapter on folk tales, proverbs, myths, songs, and dances, amongst a variety of other ethnographical data (1965: xx). Mitra also edited Gurusaday Dutt's *The Folk Dances of Bengal* (1954), which had been left behind in draft form by the author. The information that follows stems largely from Sankar Sen Gupta's book.

[6] The history appeared first in Bengali (1896) and subsequently in English (1911). This last act laid the grounds for establishing Bengali literature as an academic field. It was during Sen's tenure and at his incentive that the Master's Degree in Bengali literature was introduced in Calcutta University and he was appointed the first Professor of Bengali.

[7] Dutt studied for his law examination in England, returning to India in 1905 to join the Law Department in various postings in Bihar, which was then a part of Bengal.

[8] See Chatterjee's important article on 'folk' (2003).

[9] He did not mention the form that was crystallizing under the name *Bharat Natyam* in these very decades.

[10] The following account is based on Sudhi Pradhan's compilation of chronicles and documents (1979) relating to the PWA and the Indian People's Theatre Association (IPTA). On the Urdu writing of the early 1930s that was a precursor of the PWA, see Coppola (1981) and Mahmud (1996).

[11] The International Association met again in London in 1936. India was represented by Mulk Raj Anand; Brecht was also present.

[12] As Reuss (1978) has shown, the 'Old Left' and the persons and groups who were a part of the radical milieu of the 1930s and 1940s, had a major impact on the popularization of folk songs in the US. Many of the performers of this era were to go on to achieve nationwide fame. Not all of these had

clear-cut political commitments, but many did. 'The Almanac Singers, which included Pete Seeger, Lee Hays, Millard Lampell, Woody Guthrie, and others, sang folk-songs and union and left-wing topical songs in folk style to nearly every radical group associated with the Old Left, on both American coasts, and at many points in between, during a hectic year and a half of activity immediately before and following the United States' entry into the Second World War (1941–42).' Just as in India, this heritage would become a resource for the political movements of the 1960s, surely a coincidence that needs to be further probed. Thus: 'A new and ideologically mixed generation of radicals, reformers, and social critics, led by Bob Dylan and Joan Baez, continued the movement's coupling of protest themes with rural American folk song idioms during the 1960s and 1970s in the contexts of Civil Right marches, 'Ban the Bomb' parades, anti-Vietnam War demonstrations, pollution control rallies, and other causes, rendering the once novel folk-style protest songs as common to the urban United States as the soapbox' (10–11 and 14) .

[13] General Secretary's Report, 1941–1945 (Pradhan 1979: 241).

[14] Bombay, Bengal, Punjab, Delhi, UP, Malabar, Mysore, Mangalore, Hyderabad, Andhra, Central Provinces and Berar, and Madras were represented on the All-India Committee, and there were Organising Provincial Committees in Bengal, Punjab, Delhi, UP, Malabar, Mysore, Andhra, and Madras (Pradhan 1979: 132–4).

[15] *Bhavai Mela 80*. Documentation of the National School of Drama Workshop in Sola Village, Gujarat, October–November 1980.

[16] By the writer of the Report of the programme following the first Conference of IPTA in 1943: 'The play by K.A. Abbas is of special interest as being the most popular of those presented on this occasion. It is the story of a scientist who discovers "Amrit" and all those who appear in his dream demanding immortality; Beauty, John Bull, Religion and Hitler vie with each other for this prize. This play was clever and amusing and light and everyone liked it but it had many drawbacks. In the first place, there was no central coordination between all those who came to the scientist. In the second place, it idealises the working class, and in the third place, the barrier between the worker and the scientist is not broken in the end' (Pradhan 1979: 141).

[17] *Sangeet Natak Akademi Report, 1953–1958*.

[18] The following account is indebted to the documentation entitled 'History' by Reeta Sondhi in the NSD Special Issue of *Enact* (January–March 1981).

[19] 'Foundations of a National Theatre', *Indian Express*, 6 May 1962.

[20] Gargi saw the *jatra* of Bengal; *nautanki*, *ramlila*, and *raslila* of north India; bhavai of Gujarat; tamasha of Maharashtra; *therukoothu* of Tamilnad; *yakshagana* of Kanara; and the *chhau* mask dramas of Seraikella as the 'most crystallized forms', to each of which he devoted a chapter. In spite of the manifest variety of these forms and their differences, he spoke of folk theatre in the singular: 'These forms give a glimpse of the richness of folk theatre and folk culture and the passion of the people for life and drama' (1966: 7).

[21] This was a claim that Bharati made retrospectively in the preface to the play. The more immediate source for his inspiration seems to be the conventions employed by classical Greek drama as mediated by the verse plays of T.S. Eliot.

[22] Thus his statement in the preface to the play: 'There is one thing that I can say about this play: there is an experiment here with craft (*shilpa*), which is unlikely to be seen in any other Indian language. All the same, I would not want to call it an entirely unprecedented or new craft.... It was the combination of the two—the direct knowledge and experience of western craft with the traditional stage-craft of my own country—that made it possible for this new mode of craft to occur to me' ([1960] 1964).

[23] 'Proceedings of the Round Table on the Contemporary Relevance of Traditional Theatre', *Sangeet Natak* (July–September 1971: 38).

[24] As one observer put it: 'The points that emerged were many and areas of agreement were also not few. First of all, as far as I'm concerned, folk theatre and the uses of tradition will from now on occupy pride of place in one's idea of modern theatre' (*Enact* editorial after the Round Table, March 1971).

[25] See also 'Brecht Expolosion', *Times Literary Supplement* (*TLS*), 8 August 1968; 'Brecht's Apprenticeship', *TLS*, 25 September 1970; 'At Work in the Brechtian Forest', *TLS*, 28 December 1973. For a later, more comprehensive analysis of the phenomenon, through the 1990s, see Eddershaw (1996).

[26] Bengali theatre responded much earlier and more intensively to Brecht's ideas, plays, and productions. The following data have been drawn from Samik Bandyopadhyay (1994). According to Bandyopadhyay, the early years of IPTA were not affected by Brecht in any way, though some translations published by Moscow had begun to circulate in Calcutta. Brecht only entered the theatre scene in West Bengal in the early 1960s. Translations from his plays appeared on the scene from 1961 on. In 1964 Utpal Dutt set up the Brecht Society of India, with Satyajit Ray as its first president. In 1965 Sombhu Mitra wrote for the periodical *Bohurupee* (no. 23, September) about the experience

of seeing Brecht's *Galileo* in Prague. Some Brecht plays were produced in Calcutta after that. *The Epic Theatre*, a Bengali periodical initially published by the Brecht Society of India and then by the People's Little Theatre, commenced publication in 1967, with the serialization of *Himmatbai*, Utpal Dutt's adaptation of *Mother Courage*. Brecht's reputation grew rapidly in West Bengal thereafter. A substantial body of Brecht criticism emerged from this encounter. There were intense discussions about the 'correct' reading of Brecht in the productions that followed. A landmark was Ajitesh Bannerjee's production of *Threepenny Opera* in 1969, which transported the action of the play to Calcutta in 1876. As Bandyopadhyay sums up: 'In the seventies, when left politics in West Bengal was [*sic*] undergoing both polarization and redefinition, Brecht came to represent different things to different people, leading to different attitudes and approaches to Brecht.' There were productions in a variety of modes: revolutionary politics, cultural critique, dramaturgical experiment. Noteworthy were Arun Mukerjee's *Mareech sambad* (1972), Utpal Dutt's *Suryashikhar* (1972), Badal Sirkar's *Gondi* (adaptation of *Caucasian Chalk Circle*) (1978), Fritz Bennewitz's production of *Galileo* in 1980, and Shekhar Chatterjee's *Pontu laha* (Puntila) and *Arturo Ui* in the 1970s. Dutt and Sircar were to come to appreciate the political and social possibilities of the Lehrstücke as against the 'spectacles'. 'Through all the confusion, and the greater number of failures than successes, Brecht remains a point of reference, to which the Bengali theatre worker and the Bengali theatre-goer alike come again and again, through fresh readings of Brecht's poetry, plays, prose and diaries in that order...a more depoliticized look at Brecht has started to surface only in the eighties, with signs of a Brecht withdrawal becoming evident' (Bandyopadhyay 1994: 9–10).

More extensive data is available in *Brecht in Calcutta: A Natya Shodh Sansthan Documentation* (1997). Extensive discussions on the reception and relevance of Brecht's theatre in India were carried out at the conference 'Brecht in India', held in Bombay, 13–15 March 1997, and organized by Goethe Insitut/Max Müller Bhavan, Bombay and the National Centre for the Performing Arts, on the eve of Brecht's birth centenary year.

[27] The play was accompanied by an exhibition on Brecht's theatre and a show of the film *Mutter Courage* with Helene Weigel in the star role. Helene Weigel sent a telegram on the occasion: 'Wir freuen uns gleichzeitig mit uns eine Brechtaustellung eröffnen. Ihr Berliner Ensemble Helene Weigel.' (We are glad that you are having the Brecht exhibition at the same time as us.

Your Berliner Ensemble Helene Weigel.) Published in the Brecht issue of *Hindustani Theatre*, 1.1–2 (January, February 1963).

[28] Bennewitz was drama director of the Meininger Theatre from 1954 to 1960 and from 1960 of the Deutsches National Theater, Weimar. He had vast experience in directing the German classics as well as with work in Brecht Theatre, both in the Berliner Ensemble as an associate of Helene Weigel and elsewhere in the GDR.

[29] As Vijaya Mehta specified in an interview with Vrinda Nabar, 'I needed a "vehicle" that would get the vitality and essence of folk theatre across, and I seemed to find it in Brecht' and 'I felt, and so did Bennewitz, that the potential of our folk theatre came across in this adaptation'. *Times of India*, 5 October 1982.

[30] The following account is based on the transcript of a personal interview with Bennewitz on 17 November 1981.

[31] As Benedetti has pointed out, Brecht's knowledge of Stanislavsky was initially mediated through Tretyakov, who disliked Stanislavsky, during Brecht's Moscow visit in 1931. Ironically enough, Stanislavsky had himself waged a battle against the 'dead naturalism' of the Moscow Art Theatre and used the term naturalism pejoratively. Brecht had further unhappy contact with the 'system' mistakenly associated with Stanislavsky when he visited the United States in 1935 for the New York production of his play *Die Mutter*. It was in its American form, whereby actors used Brecht's text to explore their own feelings, that he had the most sustained contact with Stanislavsky, and which he most vehemently rejected. As Benedetti points out: 'He could not know, any more than members of his cast, that Stanislavsky detested, and in his writings condemned, a narcissitic concern with what he called "actor's emotion"' (1995: 103–4).

[32] Suvin is here quoting Jameson (1998: 132).

[33] Jameson has elaborated upon this view so eloquently that it deserves extensive citation:

> Leave aside the fact that so many moderns have felt obliged to concoct just such a private philosophy for themselves, alongside their evidently equally private language: as witness Lawrence or Proust, Rilke or Wallace Stevens, Musil or Khlebnikov.... It is this, of course, that has led some to characterize the experience of modernism, or of the various modernisms, as one of a quasi-religious conversion, in which we are called upon—as our entry ticket to the unique phenomenological

'world' in question—to convert to its dominant ideology, and to learn its codes, to absorb its structure of concepts and values, in some relatively exclusive way which, in our literary enthusiasm, tends to block off an approach to other rival literary codes and languages, until at length we are deprogrammed in disabusement, and reluctantly deconverted; and pass on to similar commitments to this or that other modern writer, at which point the whole (quintessentially modernist) process repeats itself all over again. Whatever the value of this particular description, it is worth noting that Eliot himself proposes to short-circuit it and to recommend a very different framework for the poet's or the artist's work: 'A framework of accepted and traditional ideas which would have prevented him from indulging in a philosophy of his own'—which is to say, in his own case, the Roman Catholic tradition as preserved in the rituals of the established Church of England (1998: 23).

[34] This was true of most Asian encounters with Brecht, as a recent critic has pointed out:

The connection between Brecht's work and contemporary [Asian] theatre is, in fact, better described as one of 'cross-cultural appropriation' rather than 'influence'. This appropriation is a creative, dynamic process of reinterpreting and retooling certain of Brecht's ideas or techniques rather than a stiff imitation of a transparent model by groups that 'lag behind' the times aesthetically due to a 'backward' state of social and cultural development.... Certainly, throughout Asia, many dramatists and groups are attracted to Brecht's work because he developed plays and techniques that they have found useful in articulating a critique of existing power structures on behalf of the disenfranchized and marginalized. Critiques of this nature by Asian theatre practitioners are, however, never undertaken from the same ideological position as that occupied by Brecht during his life (Bodden: 1997: 380).

[35] A cross-section of the plays offered for public viewing by the School from 1962 to 1978 as documented in the NSD Issue of *Enact* (January–February 1981) shows that Brecht with his 4 plays was ahead even of Shakespeare: Albee, Anouilh, Beckett (2 plays), Brecht (4 plays), Büchner (2 plays), Camus, Chekhov, Euripides, Ibsen (2 plays),Ionesco, Sartre, Seami, Shakespeare (2 plays), Sophocles, Stindberg (2 plays).

[36] Tanvir will be discussed at length in Ch. 6. Some brief facts and figures about his life and work will suffice here. He was born in 1929 in Raipur, Madhya Pradesh. He joined IPTA in Bombay, an active centre of IPTA in this period, in the mid-1940s as actor, director, and playwright. The work with IPTA remained a guiding and motivating force in all Tanvir's later work and also defined his political attitudes. In 1954 Tanvir came to Delhi where he founded the Hindustani Theatre with Begum Qudsia Zaidi. Here he produced his first play in Delhi, *Agra bazar*. In 1955 he left for training in acting at the Royal Academy of Dramatic Arts and production at the Bristol Old Vic School. Tanvir's two-year stay in Britain coincided with the years when British theatre-makers were increasingly responding to Brecht's plays. Tanvir read his first Brecht plays there. He returned to India after a period of observation in Europe. In Delhi in 1958 he produced a Hindi translation of Shudraka's fifth-century Sanskrit play *Mricchakatikam* in a predominantly folk style. In 1959 he established his own group, Naya Theatre, with members from the tribal Chattisgarh area in Madhya Pradesh. By 1970 the group was composed entirely of these tribal folk players and was registered as a professional theatre company. In this period Tanvir produced among other plays *Charandas Chor*, a folk play, and in 1978 Brecht's *The Good Woman of Sezuan* in a Chattisgarhi adaptation.

[37] M.S. Sathyu, successful and well-known Hindi film director in Bombay, had been associated with the Hindustani Theatre in Delhi in the late 1950s and early 1960s. He had designed the costumes and masks Habib Tanvir had used in 1958 in his production of the *Mricchakatikam*. Tanvir's use of a mixture of folk and Brechtian techniques was Sathyu's first introduction to this kind of theatre. Later, on invitation from the Government of the German Democratic Republic, Sathyu spent four and a half months as a visitor to the Berliner Ensemble. He saw Ekkehard Schall play Arturo Ui and studied the 'Modellbücher'. He was acquainted with Brecht's own staging of *Der kaukasische Kreidekreis* with Ernst Busch in the role of the narrator and of Azdak.

Back in India, in 1963, he produced with Shama Zaidi the first Hindustani version of *Der kaukasische Kreidekreis*.

Seventeen years later, in 1980, as a successful film director, Sathyu repeated the play in Bombay in a revival of the Hindustani Theatre version. He directed the play for the Bombay IPTA, with Shabana Azmi, the well-known film actress, in the leading role as Grusha. This alone was enough to ensure the play great success. It was brought to Delhi in the same year, along with Sarveshwardayal Saxena's agitprop style nautanki play *Bakri*.

[38] From my interview with Sathyu on 31 October 1981.

[39] Alkazi's immense influence in the world of Indian theatre has been discussed at length in the Introduction and in Ch. 3.

[40] From my interview with Alkazi on 19 March 1981.

[41] In an interview with Nissim Ezekiel, *Indian Express*, 17 January 1971.

[42] From my interview with Alkazi on 19 March 1981.

[43] In an interview with Avik Ghosh, *Enact* (November 1969).

[44] Born in Bomaby in 1946, Amal Allana directed a Brecht play *The Elephant Calf* in a Hindi translation in 1967 while still a student of the NSD. After her graduation from the School in 1968, she spent two years at the Berliner Ensemble as an observer. Back in Delhi in 1970, she assisted Fritz Bennewitz in the direction of *The Threepenny Opera* for the Repertory Company of the NSD. In Bombay, in 1971, she staged two Brecht plays in English *Man is Man* and *The Good Woman of Sezuan*. Here she had her own theatre group 'The Workshop'. She visited Japan to study the Noh and Kabuki theatres and was Head of the Department of Indian Theatre at Punjab University from 1977 to 1978, where she staged *The Threepenny Opera* and *The Exception and the Rule* in Hindi. She formed her own group, Studio 1, in Delhi in 1978. Here she repeated her production of *The Exception and the Rule*. By the mid-1980s, Allana had directed well over thirty plays, adaptations from Western, as well as modern Indian plays. She was invited to direct *Mahabhoj* in 1982 for the NSD Reportory and in 1984, to hold a workshop and to direct *The Good Woman of Sezuan* in a Hindi adaptation for the Second Year students of the NSD. Allana went on to direct many landmark productions, particularly of Shakespeare and Brecht plays, including a memorable *Mother Courage* with the late Manohar Singh in the title role.

[45] Allana in her note 'Brecht—A Man of his Times', in the brochure of the play *Chopra kamaal, naukar jamaal*, an adaptation of Brecht's *Herr Puntilla und sein Mann Matti*, directed for the NSD by Fritz Bennewitz in 1978.

[46] Thus: 'His [Brecht's] style at once resembles the magnitude of Shakespeare in panoramic sweep, the infinite attention to detail as in a Breughel painting, and the brevity and austerity of expression as found in the work of the cartoonist, George Grosz. Like a cartoonist, Brecht possesses biting humour and the ability to relate the individual to the larger canvas of his times.' (Ibid.)

[47] Allana in 'Director's Notebook: The Making of Mahabhoj', *Enact* (May–June 1982).

[48] While a student of the NSD, Raina participated in both the grand Brecht productions of the School. He graduated in 1970 and for a year worked in the Repertory Company of the School. Since 1972, he has been freelancing, directing a variety of plays, and has also been involved with the experimental film as an actor. Besides these, he has conducted theatre-workshops in different Indian states. In 1977, he formed his own group Prayog in Delhi with the programme of 'doing relevant, socially committed and experimental theatre in Delhi'. In 1978, he participated in the 'Brecht 80' festival, organized in Calcutta by Max Mueller Bhawan, where Prayog presented Brecht's *Mother*. The group has a wide repertoire of plays, classical and modern, Western and Eastern. In 1982, Raina directed a Hindi adaptation of Brecht's *Die Dreigroschenoper* with a Kapur group, The Hellions. It was performed in Kanpur, Lucknow, and Delhi. In Calcutta, he repeated *Mother* in 1983, with the theatre group Rangkarmi.

[49] From the interview with M.K. Raina in *Enact*, NSD Issue 2 (April–June 1971).

[50] From my interview with Raina on 28 September 1984. All subsequent quotations are from this interview.

[51] Raina elaborted further: 'I wish you'd come to Kanpur with us and see it there. In UP, anywhere in UP, the moment you open your mouth and say in the third scene, "*bhag jaega to encounter men mara jaega*" [if he tries to run, he'll be killed in an encounter], there was two minutes laughter and all the time, people knew it. On the third night of the performance, we had an "encounter" right where we rehearsed. They said it was Matthew who was killed, not Mack. The actors said, "*Munna mara gaya!*" There is a market called Arya Nagar. Openly the police said, "At eight o'clock in the evening, close your doors, close shop." The moment you lose political patronage, any criminal in UP particularly nowadays, there is an "encounter": he is to be killed. And people know who is on the "encounter list" and who is not. And I was surprised. Eight o'clock they said and two in the morning they shot him. And till three o'clock in the afternoon, next day, they exhibited him, right there in the street.'

[52] The influential Anamika Kala Sangam of Calcutta joined in the rising tide of Brecht productions in Hindi with *The Good Woman of Sezuan* in 1977. Pop music was used, as also masks, the use of which was generally equated

both with Brecht's 'alienating' technique and traditional folk theatre. Brecht in Indian attire, adapted into local or near-local dialects often with folk music and with devices common to both Brecht and folk theatre, became increasingly the trend in the 1970s.

The trend continues unabated into the next decade. In 1982, Fritz Bennewitz directed *The Caucasian Chalk Circle* for the NSD in a Hindi coloured by Bihari dialect; it was also located in Bihar. In the same year M.K. Raina produced *The Threepenny Opera* with elements of the folk form nautanki. In 1983 Kartik Awasthi, an NSD graduate, produced *The Exception and the Rule* and *Puntilla und his Man Matti* in the dialect version used by the School, with his own group 'Awadh Theatre Group'.

In 1983 Fritz Bennewitz directed an adaptation into the local Bundelkhandi dialect of *The Caucasian Chalk Circle* for Rangmandal, Bhopal. Here again there was an attempt to establish an equation with folk theatre, in costumes, music, and presentation.

Meanwhile M.S. Sathyu, formerly of the Hindustani Theatre, Delhi, produced *The Caucasian Chalk Circle* with IPTA, Bombay in 1980. Though it was unavoidably influenced by the Hindi commercial film in acting style and music, Sathyu adopted the techniques of folk theatre. A production on the same lines, more self-consciously 'folksy' but technically less well coordinated was Ekjut's (Bombay) *The Good Woman of Sezuan* in 1984 under the direction of Nadira Babbar, an NSD graduate.

[53] The most readily accessible account of these years is to be found in Tharu and Lalita (1993: 97ff).

[54] Shanta Gandhi was a member of IPTA in its heyday and had vast experience with bhavai veshas. She wrote her version of the play first in Gujarati for the occasion of the Gujarati Sahitya Parishad held in Delhi in 1967. It was translated into Malvi Hindi with the help of Shyam Parvar, and published in 1984, with extensive notes on bhavai staging conventions added to the text. Shanta Gandhi directed the play for the NSD Repertory Company in 1982. The following quotations are taken from the 'Note on the Play' that she wrote for the NSD production brochure.

[55] The figures in the frame story and the main story of the play become interdependent. 'Siddharaj–Indra, Rudio(Rupali)–Nala Rishi, Jasma–Kamakundala, Nayak–Kaldev and Rangla–Laldev become extensions of each other and thus alter the basic pattern of interpretation. In the traditional version, Kamakundala is simply the sensual temptress; here she becomes a

creative artist working in a celestial troupe. She shares with Jasma her pride and dignity in her vocation. The traditionally hypocritical Nala Rishi becomes a fearless seeker of truth and the physically and mentally disgusting, foolish husband of Jasma retains the philosophic temperament of Nala Rishi in my version. He acquires knowledge and wisdom from wandering minstrels, sufis and sadhus.' Shanta Gandhi in 'Notes on the Play' (1984).

[56] The play was translated into Hindi by Raghuvir Sahay and produced for the NSD Repertory in 1980.

[57] A similar attempt was Bansi Kaul's adaptation of Ben Jonson's *Volpone* in the bhavai form for a student production of the NSD in 1980. Kaul made a programmatic statement regarding his play; the frame of reference seems very Brechtian: 'We don't want illusionistic theatre as it has been imposed on us by the West. We want to maintain a distance between our actions and emotions so that we can think. This has always been present in our folk forms and elements of it always strike a chord in us no matter how conditioned we are by the Western theatre of the cities.' In an interview with Yashodhara Dalmia in the *Times of India*, 1 March 1981.

[58] The play was produced most often by the street theatre group Jan Natya Manch, an active participant in the Delhi theatre scene, though only to be met with on the street. Though I interviewed Safdar Hashmi in the course of my research in the 1980s, since Jan Natya Manch did not at any time subscribe to the 'folk' theatre, which is the focus of my discussion of Brecht, neither Hashmi nor Jan Natya Manch have been discussed in the context of the Brecht reception in the 1970s and 1980s.

[59] Bharati has himself spoken of the affiliations of the play to Greek theatre and Indian folk theatre in the preface to the play. His concerns were existential. If action was preordained, what moral compunctions dictated the choices that individuals made at critical junctures in life? The dilemma was no smaller, if the individual had free choice, for morally 'right' choices did not always receive social sanction and recognition. Bharati discusses this existential dilemma and the resolution that he found at some point in the course of writing the play at some length in his (1987) article.

[60] The original Marathi play was produced and directed by Jabbar Patel for the Progressive Dramatic Association of Poona in 1972. It was produced in Delhi in 1973 in Vasant Dev's translation and directed by Rajinder Nath for 'Abhiyan'. The Hindi translation was published as early as 1974. The folk devices used have been borrowed from the multiple traditions popular in the

region. Kumud Mehta has a particularly colourful description of one such. According to her, the 'full fabric of the play was revealed through the brilliant device of a human wall, a convention used in the folk "khela" of the Konkan. The choreographed movements of the members of this wall (who would freeze at one moment to become plants in a garden or turn into a wedding procession, or transform themselves into a frenzied mob or simply cease to exist through the expedient of turning their backs to the audience) lent rhythm and pace to the presentation' (Mehta 1981: 91).

[61] Dhyaneshwar Nadkarni in a review of the initial staging in Pune, brought up what he considered 'serious flaws in the mainstream of the play': 'One of the flaws is the lack of full-bloodedness in the characterisation of the Nana and Ghasiram with the result that they are not projected as contenders worth all their ghastly struggle. Tendulkar should have given the Nana a touch of the skilled diplomat he was, instead of making him out to be a cowardly old lecher. Similarly, he should have portrayed Ghasiram consistently, as a man who plays his cards shrewdly' (*Enact*, January–February 1973).

[62] In the introductory preface to the Hindi edition of the play, Tendulkar clearly states that the theme of the play is not bound by historical time and geographical place and that it depicts a situation that will always recur, generated by social conditions which are neither new, nor old, and which thus transcend time and space. Jabbar Patel pointed out the importance of the Englishman in his note and G.P. Deshpande made the point about the feudal passing into the capitalist mode, in a personal conversation in the early 1980s.

[63] Written in 1970, the play was translated a year later into Hindi by B.V. Karanth, who directed it for the Delhi group Dishantar in the same year. The Hindi version was published in 1975.

[64] The Sanskrit compendium of tales is the popular *Vetalapanchavimshati* which was translated early into the modern print languages. See Brückner (1999) for details of the European route taken before the tale wound its way to Karnad's work.

[65] A recent exception is the account of slum displacement and the forcible sterilization campaign that accompanied it in Delhi by Emma Tarlo (2003), wherein is contained an extensive bibliography of the publications documenting and discussing the Emergency years, all of which stem from the late 1970s; most appeared immediately after the state of emergency was lifted, that is, in 1978 and 1979. A first collection of documents and of the pamphlets of protest which circulated publicly and in the underground is available in Basu

(1976), from whence the following protest statement by writer Annada Sankar Roy, circulated from the underground, which speaks for a whole generation of writers and artistes:

> On the pretence of exercising control over the writing of persons who are, in officialese, described as irresponsible journalists, censorship has been imposed upon all writers. Minor government officials who are both young and inexperienced have been given the responsibility of doing this task. These censors do not consider it necessary to inform themselves what writers of repute and conscience are actually saying nor have they considered it necessary to understand what is meant by literature. They use the scissors with lighthearted abandon, without inhibition of any kind apparently. How are they going to explain what they are doing or excuse themselves to the public of the future? (28)

[66] *Enact*, editorial (November–December 1978).

[67] As the *Enact* editorial of May 1982 noted with some bitterness:
At about the time the West's interest grew in ancient Indian theatre, Grotowski and all—its audible echo was heard in the Indian theatre's need to search for its own roots. Fortunately, the urban Indian theatre had a more or less thematic validity to offer its middle class audiences.... Karnad had written *Hayavadana*, and Tendulkar *Ghasiram Kotwal*, which became the rallying point of folk form protagonists. A lot of what has followed these successful plays, along with Shanta Gandhi's production of *Jasma Odan*, is the recent history of a vice-like grip on Indian theatre...unless there are powerful alternatives to folk-oriented theatre, the forever contemporary medium will only become venerably toothless....

Theatre in India is in dire need of facing reality. Indulgence in folk tales—ancient and modern, garbs rich and colourful, themes elemental and transcendental—can wait for other media or times. With so much activity and restlessness in theatre people today, the search for usable or unusable folk forms is like a modern chemist's indulgence in alchemy.

[68] Dutta (1997: 122) has culled these official statements and the information which follows from the report published in *India Today* (15 June 1985).

[69] From the tabular information appended to the special issue of *Sangeet Natak*, on the 'Traditional Idiom in Contemporary Theatre' (1985).

[70] Bharucha (1992: 1675). The essay from which this citation stems is

an important discussion and analysis of the Haksar Committee Report, 24 March 1988 which was submitted to the Department of Culture, Ministry of Human Resource Development. The Committee had been appointed to review the activities of the National Akademis and other major cultural institutions in the country.

[71] There are the instructive parallels with the cultural practice of the Soviet Union in its Stalinist heyday, as documented and analysed by Oinas (1978). The various folk forms, with their emotively and socially familiar vocabulary, came to be seen as useful because they provided access to 'the people'. Folk forms could be subversive, but they could, equally, be socially regressive in outlook. In the Soviet Union, the first decade after the October Revolution was considered the golden era of folklore research. 'As a result, significant studies, perhaps the most significant folklore studies ever made in the Soviet Union (such as those by Propp, Zirmunskij, and others) were completed.' However, literary circles in the 1920s came to regard it with suspicion; there was widespread belief that folklore reflected feudal values. But then came the opportunistic turn. The leading Soviet writer of the 1930s, Maxim Gorky, made a passionate appeal for the preservation and use of folklore. Gorky stressed the connection between folklore and labour; his arguments in its support, that there was a close connection between folklore and people's concrete life and working conditions, that it reflected the life optimism of the people, and that it had high artistic value, swung the official policy in its favour. 'As if by magic, it opened the eyes of the party leaders to the possibilities that folklore would have for the advance of communism. And from that time on, we can follow the conscious use of folklore for social and political purposes.' Large-scale folklore collecting projects followed, initiated and supported by the party functionaries. 'The expedition had to collect both old and new folklore and had to establish which forms of folklore should be cultivated in the village for healthy Soviet esthetics. The collected material had to be polished and returned en masse to the people, so as to force out "various disgusting phenomena of thieves" and bourgeois poetry which had become grafted in various ways to the kolkoz and worker's milieu.... The collection activity became so all-encompassing and vigorous, extending over the whole country, that it was possible to speak of an all-Union folkloric movement. Local centers of folklore were founded in numerous districts and the collection of folklore was made obligatory for ethnographic organizations.... On their collection trips folklorists were required to keep a critical attitude towards folklore material

they encountered, since not all of it by any means warranted recording. They must not only reject songs and tales which were ideologically unacceptable, "reflecting the survivals of class-hostile ideology, by launching an active fight against them"' (79). Folklore scholarship in the Soviet Union was aware of the 'tremendously effective role of folklore, which in one way or another shapes the consciousness of the people and either contributes to the growth of socialist construction or hinders it. Therefore, folklore scholarship could no longer be only an observer and recorder of facts, but had to combine the tasks of scholarly understanding with the urgent task of social education' (80). Thus was folklore manipulated for official propaganda purposes.

[72] This intervention was variously resisted and resented. Thus an editorial of the Calcutta-based journal *Rangvarta* entitled 'The Indian theatre situation': 'For any singular, synoptic view, especially one taken from within the over-centralized, generally short-sighted, "administrative" culture of Delhi, tends to impose a straitjacket on the adventurous swings and creative violence of the regional cultures and traditions. More often than not, decisions and positions taken in Delhi at different levels have served either to curb the regional cultural particularities and lay down readymade national (or export-oriented) models; or to celebrate and institutionalize particular regional "expressions" brutally torn from their cultural roots, and thus allowed to stultify into exhibits in a showcase (more like the horror gallery of foetuses immersed in chemicals in glass jars I saw at the anatomy museum at Manipal), incapable of further growth or even natural life (the fate of so many of the dance forms given institutional locations in the capital!).'

[73] In 'Traditional Idiom in Contemporary Theatre'. *Sangeet Natak* Special Issue (July–December 1985: 9).

[74] Ibid.: 12.

[75] He reminded his listeners of his own agency in propelling this movement forward, an activity he had tirelessly sustained over three decades. Beginning with the seminar 'Contemporary Playwriting and Play Production' that he had organized for the Bharatiya Natya Sangh in 1961 as its General Secretaty, he had gone on to convene the 'National Round Table on Contemporary Relevance of Traditional Theatre' for the Sangeet Natak Akademi in 1971. 'It will always remain a point of reference for students and historians of contemporary Indian theatre.'

[76] Suresh Awasthi (Ibid.: 93).

[77] Ibid.: 85.

[78] Ibid.: 89.

[79] Ibid.: 91.

[80] Ibid.: 45.

[81] Ibid.: 44.

[82] Ibid.: 44.

[83] In 'Traditional Idiom'. *Sangeet Natak* Special Issue (July–December 1985), 77.

[84] Ibid.: 26.

[85] Ibid.: 28.

[86] Ibid.: 31.

[87] Ibid.: 31–2.

[88] Ibid.: 48.

[89] Ibid.: 49.

[90] As Komal Kothari put it: 'Everybody tends to assume that folk songs are anonymous, and therefore, no one has any rights over a particular song...there is some truth in the anonymity of many folk compositions, but it is equally true that folk musicians go on composing new things, both at textual and musical levels. And the people who belong to a particular region are in a position to recognize a contemporary composition' (Bharucha 2003: 278). The most notorious case was that of Gazi Khan of Harwa village. He composed the Nimbuda song, which became wildly popular through Rajasthan. It was taken up by the Hindi film *Hum dil de chuke sanam*. The pertinent question was never asked: who gets the royalties? 'Today the film song is copyrighted, so ironically, if Gazi had to sing his own song, he could be infringing this copyright' (286). There are other well-known singers like Bhungar Khan and Ramzan Khan, they are composers who have 'a right to their particular composition' (279).

[91] Roma Chatterjee (2003) traces the use of the term 'folk' in three kinds of discourses, in nationalism, religion, and art.

[92] Quoted in ibid.: 574.

REFERENCES

Adya Rangacharya. [1960] 1964. *Suno Janmeyjaya*. Translated from the Kannada into Hindi by Nemichandra Jain and B.V. Karanth. Delhi: National Publishing House.

Allana, Nissar. (ed.) 1993. *A Tribute to Bertolt Brecht 1993*. Delhi: Theatre and Television Associates.

Anand, Mulk Raj. 1951. *The Indian Theatre*. London: Dobson.

Awasthi, Suresh. 1971. Introduction, 'Proceedings of the Round Table on the Contemporary Relevance of Traditional Theatre'. *Sangeet Natak* Special Issue (July–September). Guest editor, Suresh Awasthi.

Bandyopadhyay, Samik. 1994. 'Theatre History: Brecht in Bengali/West Bengal', *Rangvarta*: *News Bulletin of the Natya Shodh Sansthan*, 55, November.

Basu, Sajal. (ed.) 1978. *Underground Literature During the Indian Emergency*. Calcutta: Minerva.

Benedetti, Jean. 1995. 'Brecht, Stanislavsky, and the Art of Acting', in *Brecht, Then and Now. The Brecht Yearbook,* Guest Editor: John Willet. 101–10.

Benjamin, Walter. 1978. *Versuche über Brecht*. Edited with an afterword by Rolf Tiedeman. Frankfurt am Main: Suhrkamp.

Bharati, Dharmvir. [1954] 1980. *Andha Yug*. Allahabad: Kitab Mahal.

———. 1987. 'Andhayug kab kaise likha gaya', *Dharmyug*, 27 December.

Bharucha, Rustom. 1983. *Rehearsals of Revolution*: *The Political Theatre of Bengal*. Calcutta: Seagull Books.

———. 1992. 'Anatomy of Official Discourse: A Non-Government Perspective', *Economic and Political Weekly*, 1–8 August: 1667–76.

———. 1998. *In the Name of the Secular*: *Contemporary Cultural Activism in India*. Delhi: Oxford University Press.

———. 2003. *Rajasthan*: *An Oral History. Conversations with Komal Kothari*. Delhi: Penguin Books.

Bhattacharya, Mrinalini. 1983. 'The IPTA in Bengal', *Journal of Arts and Ideas*, January–March.

Bhavai Mela 80. Documentation of the Workshop held in Sola Village, Gujarat. Organized by the National School of Drama et al. Typescript. October–November, 1980.

Blackburn, Stuart. 2003. *Print, Folklore, and Nationalism in Colonial South India*. Delhi: Permanent Black.

Bodden, Michael. 1997. 'Brecht in Asia: New Agendas, National Traditions, and Critical Consciousness', in *A Bertolt Brecht Companion*, Siegfried Mews (ed.). Westport/Connecticut, London: Greenwood Press.

Brecht, Bertolt. [1967] 1976. *Gesammelte Werke* [Collected Works] in 20 volumes. Frankfurt am Main: Suhrkamp.

Brecht in Calcutta: A Natya Shodh Sansthan Documentation. 1997. Calcutta: Natya Shodh Sansthan.

Brückner, Heidrun. 1999. 'Thomas Mann's *Transposed Heads* and Girish Karnad's *Hayavadan*: An Indian Motif Re-imported', in *Of Clowns and Gods, Brahmans and Babus: Humour in South Asian Literatures*, Christina Oesterheld and Claus Peter Zoller (eds.). Delhi: Manohar, 118–45.

Chatterjee, Roma. 2003. 'The Category of Folk', in *The Oxford Companion to Sociology and Social Anthropology*, Veena Das (ed.). Delhi: Oxford University Press, 567–97.

Chaudhuri, Satyabrata. 1979. 'Brecht in Strained Sense'. *Enact* (November–December).

Coppola, Carlo. 1981. 'The *angare* Group: The *enfants terribles* of Urdu Literature', *Annual of Urdu Studies*, 1: 57–69.

Dalmia, Vasudha. 2001. 'Vernacular Histories in Late Nineteenth Century Banaras: Folklore, Puranas and the New Antiquarianism', *The Indian Economic and Social History Review*, 31/1, 59–79.

Deshpande, G.P.D. 1999. 'History, Politics and the Modern Playwright', *Theatre India*, May, 91–7.

Dutt, Gurusaday. 1954. *The Folk Dances of Bengal*, Asok Mitra (ed.). Calcutta: Birendra Sahay Dutt.

Dutta, Arindam. 1997. 'The Politics of Display: India 1886 and 1986', *Journal of Arts and Ideas*. Special Issue on 'Sites of Art History: Canons and Expositions'. Guest Editor: Tapati Guha-Thakurta. 30/31, December.

Eddershaw, Margaret. 1996. *Performing Brecht: Forty Years of British Performances*. London and New York: Routledge.

Enact. The Theatre Magazine. All volumes from 1967–1982.

Gandhi, Shanta. 1984. *Jasma Odan*. Delhi: Radhakrishna Prakashan.

Gargi, Balwant. 1966. *Folk Theatre of India*. Seattle and London: University of Washington Press.

Guha-Thakurta, Tapati. 1997. 'Marking Independence: The Ritual of a National Art Exhibition', *Journal of Arts and Ideas*. Special Issue on 'Sites of Art History: Canons and Expositions'. Guest Editor: Tapati Guha-Thakurta. 30/31, December.

Harishchandra. 1975. *Bharatendu Granthavali*. [Collected works in 3 Volumes] *Volume 1: Natak* (cited as *Granthavali I*) Shivaprasad Mishra (ed.). Varanasi: Nagaripracarini Sabha.

Holland, Peter. 1978. 'Brecht, Bond, Gaskill and the Practice of Political Theatre', *Theatre Quarterly*, 8/30.

Jacobs, Nicholas, Prudence Ohlsen, and J. Willet. 1977. *Bertolt Brecht in Britain*. London: Irat Services Ltd.

Jameson, Fredric. 1998. *Brecht and Method*. London: Verso.

Kapur, Anuradha. 1991. 'Notions of the Authentic', *Journal of Arts and Ideas*, 20/21, March.

Karnad, Girish. [1975] 1977. *Hayavadan*. Translated into Hindi by B.V. Karanth. Delhi: Radhakrishna Prakashan.

———. 1989. 'In Search for a New Theatre', in *Contemporary India. Essays on the Uses of Tradition*, Carla M. Borden (ed.). Delhi: Oxford University Press.

Mahmud, Shabana. 1996. '*Angare* and the Founding of the Progressive Writers Association', in *Modern Asian Studies*, 30/2: 447–67.

Mathur, J.C. and Dashrath Ojha. 1970. *Prachin Bhasha Natak Sangrah*. Agra.

Mehta, Kumud. 1981. 'Indian Theatre today—grappling with new realities', in *Marg*, special issue on *Aspects of the Performing Arts of India*, 34/3, 84–95.

Mudrarakshash. [1977] 1983. *Ala Afsar (nautanki shaili mem prayog natak)*. Delhi: Akshar Prakashan.

Oinas, Felix J. (ed.) 1978. *Folklore, Nationalism, and Politics*. Columbus, Ohio: Slavica Publishers.

Pani, Narendar. 1979. *Staging a Change*. Bangalore: Samudaya Prakashan.

Pradhan, Sudhi (ed.) 1979. *Marxist Cultural Movement in India: Chronicles and Documents (1936–47)*. Calcutta: Mrs Santi Pradhan.

——— (ed.) 1983. *Marxist Cultural Movement in India. Vol. II. 1947–1958*. Calcutta: Mrs Santi Pradhan.

Rangvarta. News Bulletin of the Natya Shodh Sansthan. 1994. No. 55, November.

Reuss, Richard A. 1978. 'American Folksongs and Left-Wing Politics: 1935–56', in *Oinas*, 1978: 9–32.

Sahni, Bhisham. 2003. *Aj ke Atit*. Delhi: Rajkamal.

Sangeet Natak. 1971. Special Issue: 'Round Table on the Contemporary Relevance of Traditional Theatre'. Guest Editor: Suresh Awasthi. July–September.

———. 1985. Special Issue: 'Traditional Idiom in Contemporary Theatre.' Guest Editor: N.C. Jain. 77/78. July–December.

Sangeet Natak Akademi Report, 1953–1958.

Saxena, Sarveshwar Dayal. [1974] 1980. *Bakri*. Delhi: Lipi Prakashan.

Sen Gupta, Sankar. 1965. *Folklorists of Bengal: Life Sketches and Biographical Notes.* Volume 1. Calcutta: Indian Publications.

Sharma, Biren Das. 1995. 'How Apolitical is Cultural Policy? The NSD Example', in *Seagull Theatre Quarterly*, August: 8–12.

Sondhi, Reeta. 1981a. 'History'. *Enact* NSD Special Issue I (January–March).

———. 1981b. 'Impression: National School of Drama'. *Enact* NSD Special Issue II (April–June).

———. 1982. Delhi Report. *Enact* (March–April).

Sundaram, Vivan. 1991. 'A Tradition of the Modern', *Journal of Arts and Ideas*, 20/21, March.

Suvin, Darko. 1995. '"On Haltung", Agency, and Emotions in Brecht: Prologemena'. *Communications from the International Brecht Society.* 24/1, May. 65–77.

———. 1997. 'Centennial Politics: On Jameson on Brecht and Method', *New Left Review*, 234. 127–140.

Tanvir, Habib. 1979. *Agra Bazar*. Delhi: Radhakrishna Prakashan.

Tarlo, Emma. 2003. *Unsettling Memories: Narratives of India's Emergency.* Delhi: Permanent Black.

Temple, Richard Carnac. [1884–1901] 1977. *The Legends of the Panjab.* Reprint, New York: Arno Press.

Tendulkar, Vijay. [1974] 1978. *Ghasiram Kotwal.* Hindi translation by Vasant Dev. Delhi: Radhakrishna Prakashan.

Tharu, Susie and K. Lalitha. 1993. *Women Writing in India: 600 BC to the Present.* Volume 2: *The 20th Century.* Delhi: Oxford University Press.

Times Literary Supplement (TLS), 'Brecht Explosion', 8 August 1968, 'Brecht's Apprenticeship', 25 September 1970, 'At Work in the Brechtian Forest', 28 December 1973.

Tripathi, Ram Naresh. [1928] 1955. *Kavita Kaumudi.* Bombay: Navnit Prakashan.

Upreti, Mohan. 1962. 'Foundations of a National Theatre', *Indian Express*, 6 May.

Willet, John. 1977. *Bertolt Brecht in Britain.* London: TQ Publications.

Williams, Raymond. [1976] 1983. 'Folk', 'Naturalism', and 'Realism', in *Keywords.* London: Flamingo.

Brecht in Hindi
The Poetics of Response

M uch was said and written within India about the importance of Brecht for modern Indian theatre through the 1970s; it reached a peak in the mid-1980s. But it was part of larger East–West discourse, as it was carried out in the West, particularly in Germany, which conceded readily enough that Brecht's theatre, overplayed in the West and almost a spent force, was gaining new lease of life in the countries of the so-called Third World. It was even suggested that the two-dimensional dance-theatre of Asia, with no experience of realistic or realistic–naturalistic depiction could approach Brecht straight as it were.[1] The widespread belief that traditional theatre forms were particularly suited for adaptation of Brecht, that Brecht offered incentive to revive and meaningfully use these very forms, persisted and was voiced again and again. Certainly there was no denying the reality of Brecht's presence in the form of repeated productions and adaptations of his own plays. There were constant, almost insistent, comparisons between various folk/traditional forms and Brecht's theatre, thus in some ways legitimating the appropriation and urbanization of the former. Possibly the parallels with Brecht's theatre went beyond the more facile similarities pre-proscenium theatre conventions, West or East, exhibited with

Brecht's theatre. For pre-proscenium folk theatre also had subversive moments—however harmonious the final resolution of social conflicts and tensions—which had political affinities with Brecht. However, these subversive moments seldom found mention. The similarities and differences, what could genuinely be learnt and what discarded in a given case, were glossed over, by speaking in one breath of the aesthetics of Brecht's epic theatre, of classical Sanskrit theatre, and of the diverse folk/traditional forms that could at any given moment span a vast range, from the highly codified *kathakali* of Kerala to the virtually uncodified *nacha* from Madhya Pradesh. This is a practice that still finds adherents.[2] In the heyday of the Brecht euphoria, it was as if, merely by citing Brecht, a playwright or a director could claim to have contemporary relevance, just as by invoking the Sanskritic past, the claim to pan-Indian dimensions, past and present, could then without further ado also be staked.

There was also the widespread assumption that Brecht had borrowed and learnt from Indian theatre, so that the affinities were given, so to speak, and needed no further justification. Brecht himself had done much to promote this belief. In an oft-cited poem, he had proclaimed that he borrowed from where he could in order to serve his needs. He had learnt from the feudal English, from the moralizing Spaniards, from the Indians, masters of fine feelings ('*Meister der schönen Empfindungen*'), and from the Chinese who depicted families and the colourful life in cities (Brecht [1967] 1976: vol. 9, 790). Brecht was here listing the general sources of his inspiration, with little specific information about concrete sources. If it is possible to deduce Brecht's knowledge of Indian literature from the mention he makes of it, then we have the sole reference in a diary entry dated 26 September 1920 to Tagore's *Home and the World*, which he found to be a wonderful book, strong and mild ('stark und mild').[3] He had much more extensive knowledge of the Chinese and the Japanese, as Antony Tatlow (1977) has so finely documented and analysed.

Brecht himself had clearly specified the function of the 'epic' devices he used; he had borrowed for a reason. And by the mid-1980s, particularly through the decades of radical politicization of student and labour unrest, of protest against Vietnam in the late 1960s and 1970s, a great deal of critical literature had grown around Brecht, an exegesis of his work that supported his political stance. In the following, I undertake a comparison between Brecht's epic theatre and a specific north Indian folk form, *svang* or *nautanki*,[4] rather than folk theatre at large, marking at the same time, those of its devices that could be loosely covered by Sanskritic categories. This last in order to stress that the connection between folk- and Sanskrit-theatre aesthetics is also not one that can be made automatically, for, in most discussions of folk theatre, as we saw in the last chapter, the aesthetics of 'classical' Indian drama were uncritically accepted as the fountainhead of the most diverse traditional forms that were set forth without break, as it were, in the centuries that followed their first formulations. If in rehearsing these classical aesthetics here I recount the well known, it is primarily in order to recall the gaps that are skimmed over, when slick continuums are posited.

CLASSICAL SANSKRIT POETICS AND DRAMA

The principle of *rasa* around which a whole system of aesthetics was to evolve, appears for the first time in the *Natya Shastra,* a treatise on drama, in its present form from about the sixth century AD, in its oldest parts going back to the second or third century BC.[5]

Rasa is 'sap', 'essence', 'taste', and it is the principle which holds together the disparate parts that go into the making of drama.[6] The *Natya Shastra* maintains that the eight generally existing dominant states, *sthayibhava*, correspond to the eight rasas. These states are complex and appear in association with causes, effects, and concomitant states. When these last three appear as elements of poetic expression, as *vibhava*, determinants, i.e. persons and situations forming constellations that determine the course of action, *anubhava*, consequents, i.e. the corresponding theatrical expression, and finally, *vyabhicaribhava*, accompanying transitory states, they bring about the aesthetic experience corresponding to the respective dominant state and known as rasa.[7] The rasa and bhava concepts were closely interlinked with *itivrtta*,[8] the structural scheme or plot of drama on the one level, on the other with *abhinaya*, the language of gesture, of interpretation.[9] In the *Natya Shastra*, therefore, rasa was contained within an elaborate structure, linking dramatic composition with actual performance techniques in theatre.

The bhava and rasa principles were further developed to become universally applicable to most forms of artistic creation in the ninth and tenth centuries. Central categories of these new interpretations were *sadharanikarana*, generalization, the aesthetic state of consciousness that is distinct from the experience of everyday life and thus completely independent of any individual interest, and *chamatkara*, wonder, astonishment, as the quality of the moment when the viewer perceives the latent impressions of the mind (*vasana*) in a density not experienced in everyday life. Further, the concept of *sahrdaya*,[10] the partaker of aesthetic experience, as one whose sensibility and perception had been trained and prepared for reception, circumscribed aesthetic experience as limited to those thus privileged.

Hereafter, theatre aesthetics were absorbed into general poetics with distinctly spiritual affiliations.[11] By the eleventh century what has come down to us as classical Sanskrit drama had in all probability ceased to be performed, both through lack of patronage and through the emergence of modern languages, though popular drama and lyric are likely to have flourished.

In the sixteenth and seventeenth centuries, rasa aesthetic became explicitly linked with religious and personal devotion. *Shringara*, the erotic rasa, was accorded the highest status amongst the rasas and was identified as the state of being, as well as the response of the devotee to Krishna sporting with the milkmaids on the bank of the river Yamuna. Rasa aesthetics, then, were handed down and have survived up to the present day, 1) as part of the theology of the religious movements that came into existence then (see De 1961 and Dimcock 1966), 2) in the traditions that have grown up around what has come to be known as 'classical' Indian music and dance; particularly in south India, where there were much more plausible continuities, and 3) but also as analytic tools in the exegesis of Sanskrit and Sanskritic literary composition in continuation of the traditional scholarly exposition of poetics, also applied somewhat indiscriminately to all manner of art practice.

THE GENESIS OF 'SVANG'

While rasa was becoming increasingly theological on the one hand and 'secularized' in music and erotic court poetry on the other (see Schokker 1983), theatre itself had little presence in north India. We find some evidence of the existence of folk-religious theatre, in the court chronicles of the Mughal emperor Akbar, who reigned from 1556 to 1605. Towards the end of Mughal rule, whether as a consequence of official policies of suppression or of political upheaval, drama in north India seems to have receded, surviving as performance on the outskirts and borders of the Mughal empire, in Nepal, Mithila, and Assam. A rudimentary form of drama surfaced again in the early nineteenth century in the north Indian plains. Its emergence in the oral-narrative tradition can be reconstructed on the basis of the tales collected by Sir Richard Temple in the Punjab. It is supposed to have spread eastwards from the Punjab.[12]

The play, svang, as it developed in the heartland of rural north India through the nineteenth and twentieth centuries was of inordinate length, the performance lasting from ten to twelve hours or for several consecutive nights. Composed in traditional verse forms, it was recited or sung by a company of male actors. These could be professional or amateur, the practice developed according to different local traditions. In its organizational and cognitive principles it was firmly rooted in the feudal countryside in spite of the subversive elements it also contained, particularly in the role played by the 'clown'. Till well into the middle of the twentieth century, the svang troupe comprised a cross-section of the village community, both Hindu and Muslim. The audience similarly consisted of the 'people', however, the troupe itself was patronized and supported by landowners and the village as a community.[13] Though it was later to become popular in industrial Kanpur, it was a primarily rural form.

In the 1960s, svang or nautanki, along with other such folk forms, began to attract urban theatre makers.[14] There was renewed awareness that there was a need to evolve critical and evaluative terminology that not only linked folk forms with the Sanskritic past, but also modernized and even politicized. It was here that Brecht bridged the gap, both as theorist and playwright, by providing an apparently firm political-aesthetic basis for utilizing folk-theatre forms in an urban context, thereby for all apparent purposes endowing them with contemporary relevance. However, there was a clear tendency to skim over the inconveniently radical politics of Brecht, who, and this cannot be emphasized enough, 'never had an idea or an experience which was not at once filtered through the political' (Jameson 1998: 7).

CONVENTIONS COMPARED: FOLK THEATRE AND BRECHT

In respect, then, of the repeated claims that Brecht's theatre bears similarities to the folk traditions in India, a typological comparison between the two will be attempted here. In the nature of 'elementary juxtaposition', some features of the Indian folk play as represented by svang and considered to correspond with classical Indian aesthetic norms[15] are set beside similar formal–aesthetic features of Brechtian epic theatre and contrasted with their functions. This is necessarily schematic and with regard to Brecht restricted to the express *intentions* for his theatre. This needs to be emphasized: only the intentions of Brecht's theatre are treated here, since in practice diverse functions can combine, coexist but of course also remain at odds with each other.

1. The Narrator

The svang is held together by the narrator, *ranga*, who is the representative of both the poet—his lines are inscribed *kavi ka*—and the director. He is the storyteller, responsible for carrying the action forward, such as it is. Apart from this, he also participates in the fate of the chief characters. The most important function of the narrator is that he invites the onlookers to emotional identification with the good characters. He himself laments their misfortunes and participates in their triumphs. Thus, though the figure of the narrator mediates between the players and the onlookers, he is in fact there to bridge the distance and invite empathy with his own emotional and ethical standpoints. He is not a distant observer; he asks the listener to approve the good and condemn the evil in the play.

Svang does not distance by comment from 'outside' the story, it invites empathy instead of inviting critical judgement, and finally it does not convey unspoken thoughts, since the figures of the svang react directly to the situations in the play.

Brecht's narrator or the chorus or title-projection, combined with the expository narratives of the figures of the play seek less to bridge the gap between episodes or that between player and onlooker, their function is rather 'to clarify the determining relationships in historical processes' (*die bestimmenden Zusammenhänge der geschichtlichen Verläufe aufzuhellen*) (Brecht [1967] 1976: vol. 15, 466).

2. The Figures of the Play

The figures of svang are more 'types' than rounded character studies; there is no marked development or unfolding of character and no modification that is not explicitly indicated.[16] Their meetings with each other are ruled by convention. They are not conceived as an exploration of possible relationships between sharply differentiated individuals. The figures themselves evince no desire to be understood as different from others of their kind. They speak in set metrical conventions and this itself provides a formal framework for the exchange of dialogue; they fulfil mutually the functions and the expectations aroused by their position in the story. They are not lifelike, they are larger than life.

Here the classical Indian aesthetic conception of *sadharanikarana* or generalization could be pressed into service, 'freed from all distinctions in time and space and therefore from individual relationships and practical interests' (Gnoli 1968: preface). Yet the figures have a clearly local character also; they belong to the world of the audience and their asides and comments indicate and even proclaim this relationship.

According to Brecht, plays were to be regarded as raw material and the interpretation of character was to go beyond the information contained in the text roles, for the features that helped compose an individual character were to be derived not only from the information available in the play and in the world of the poet but from their correlation with the real world known to the actor. The figures thus composed have a concrete, unique position: concrete enough for the character to act differently, given other societal boundaries. The figure was thus to forfeit his self-evident character and to be depicted as a social phenomenon, historically explicable. The player, in his interpretation of character, was not to leave out those clearly discernible features which seemed contradictory and did not coalesce easily with the conception that seemed central to the player. It was precisely these contradictory features, which were to be used to build the figure. This was to take place in cooperation with the critical evaluation of the 'utterances' (*Aüsserungen*) of the play's other characters. Most important of all: the relationships of the characters to each other were to be determined by the social *Gestus* ([1967] 1976: vol. 16, 688–90).

3. Conflict

Svang presents conflict, but the established order is not, in the last event, questioned, ethically or socially. The conflict is not that of an individual pitted against social or metaphysical odds. Rather, it consists of a situation, often created by the machinations of a villain. The characters act and react within a given situation. The individual 'I' is not presented in conflict with a group 'We'. The 'I' and 'We' together form a unity or coexist in plurality.[17]

In Brecht's theatre the intention is similarly not to present individual conflict or for that matter individuals in their individuality, 'for the smallest social unit is not man but two people' (*denn die kleinste gesellschaftliche Einheit ist nicht der Mensch, sondern zwei Menschen*) ([1967] 1976: vol. 16, 688). But the attitude of the two figures to each other is not to be determined so much by individual, personal, domestic conflict as by the social *Gestus*—thus, for instance, master/slave.

4. Identification, Illusion

The player in the svang makes no attempt to identify totally with the figure in the play and in costume and manner preserves the characteristics of his own person. He accepts the role of the figure he is playing and attempts to fit the role.

This could be said to conform with the concept of the player as a *patra*, a vessel, merely conveying the role to the spectator, and once again to the notion of sadharanikarana, whereby the player is expected to play a part that is to transcend individual existence and represent an aspect of character common to all men. These are high-flown sentiments, and could be as true as untrue of the lively and often raucous svang performance.

Brecht's expectations of the player are complex. In his well-known description of the Chinese player he had pointed out that the player not only demonstrates the behaviour of human beings but also that of the actor—the played and the playing, and he does this in such a way that the situation becomes an object of criticism for the onlooker ([1967] 1976: vol. 15, 427–8). Imitation reproduces the observed alone, 'epic' playing is to be accompanied by opinions and intentions. These can only be acquired outside the theatre, by obtaining the knowledge of the times about 'daily social relations' (*menschliches Zusammenleben*) and by participating in the struggle of the classes.

5. Scenic Structure

The body of the svang play consists of a series of dialogues of uneven length, having as their kernel an emotional moment; the information received or exchanged is secondary. The emotional occasion can be repeated a number of times, each time with some variation. Together these dialogues or scenes (so-called because they take place at one scene of action and not because they are a division thus foreseen) cumulate to build up an emotional moment, which could be said to correspond to the theory of dominant states. However, once again, this is a diffusely applied notion. The origin of svang in a narrative form with high emotional content would provide as plausible an explanation as any other for the emotional build-up of the play.

The structure of Brecht's epic theatre is also episodic. Each episode, however, has a *Grundgestus*. The story or the fable as the centre of the theatrical performance is 'the ensemble of all gestic events, including communications and impulses, and which now should be the source of the audience's enjoyment' (*die Gesamtkomposition aller gestischen Vorgänge, enthaltend die Mitteilungen und Impulse, die das Vergnügen des Publikums nunmehr ausmachen sollen*) (Brecht [1967] 1976: vol. 16, 693).

As Walter Hinck showed years ago, Brecht's late plays do not have a definitive ending enforced by the structure of the play (1977). They demonstrate the possibility of, even the necessity of, 'continuability' (*Fortsetzbarkeit*) after the play is over, as in the epilogue of *The Good Woman of Sezuan*.

6. The Songs

The songs in the svang have a clearly emotional function. They serve to highlight a moment already apparent in the play. They do not exist independently but as part of the overall tone of the play. Considered from the rasa aspect, they can of course be regarded as contributing to the creation of a dominant state.

The songs of the Brechtian epic play, according to Walter Benjamin expressly '*gestische Konvention*', were to be regarded as an independent element of theatre art and to be structured into the play so as to retain their distinctive function (1978: 37–8).

7. Rasa

The efforts made in the 1960s and 1970s to reclaim rasa to explicate the folk play were part of a strategy to relocate the folk play in an urban setting and integrate it into an all-encompassing, unitary national tradition.

Together, the generalization of character and situation and the exemplary nature of the plot, the comments of the narrator that in the main invited empathy, the scenes which repeated themselves with slight variations and which together could be said to form a cumulative climax all combined to create an aesthetic experience, which was and still is generally compared to the classical concept of rasa so that in having recourse to the folk form it seems entirely legitimate to hope that lost ground might yet be recovered and Sanskrit theatre relived in the present. Yet, as we saw, the aspects of folk theatre explicated by rasa could as well be accounted for in other ways, even at the risk of letting go the eternal and the unchanging which is attributed unreflexively to the Sanskritic tradition. The equation folk–rasa–aesthetics–Brecht is then, each time it is made, nothing short of a renewed affirmation of a grand national heritage. It can do no other than overlook the peculiarities of specific folk forms as well as of Brecht's theatre, effectively denying thereby the poetics of rasa any historicity.

In the early twenty-first century, as much as in the period of enthusiasm for folk forms in the 1970s and 1980s, it remains necessary to recontextualize rasa—if it is to serve any practical evaluative and analytic function—rather than use it so indiscriminately and diffusely.

THE UNEASY TRUCE

For all their aesthetic–formal similarity, the devices of folk theatre and Brecht's epic theatre in their intentions often contradict each other.

Indian folk-theatre forms were rooted in a largely feudal countryside; in spite of subversive aspects and social satire, ideologically, they remained socially conservative. And for the forms to be changed in order to meet the needs of urban theatre makers, much more would be required than the fragmentary formal appropriation by the latter, which was what fell to their lot.

In 1936 Brecht had written that he did not believe that his theatre could be practised everywhere: 'Apart from a certain technical standard, it assumes a powerful impulse in social life which is interested in the free discussion of vital questions with a view to solving them and can defend this interest against all forms of opposition' (*Es setzt ausser einem bestimmten technischen Standard eine mächtige Bewegung im sozialen Leben voraus, die ein Interesse an der freien Eröterung der Lebensfragen zum Zwecke ihrer Lösung hat und dieses Interesse gegen alle gegensätzlichen Tendenzen verteidigen kann*) ([1967] 1976: vol. 15, 272).

Of his own attempts to realize the intentions of his theatre in post-War Europe, he is quoted as saying in 1954: 'I must admit that I did not succeed in making it clear that the "epic" in my epic theatre is a social and not a formal aesthetic category' (*Ich muss zugeben, dass es mir nicht gelungen ist, klar zu machen, dass das Epische meines Theaters Kategorie des Gesellschaftlichen und nicht des Ästhetisch-Formalen ist.*)[18] Thus the two-dimensional dance theatre of Asia is not necessarily a shortcut to Brecht. The case becomes further entangled once folk theatre is moved to the urban stage and 'expanded' where the expansion cannot be registered as such, since the awareness of traditional performance modes, heritage of theatrical history, will be lacking as well as the expectations deriving from knowledge of other performances (see Elam 1980: 57–62). Moved to a domain where the folk-play is at all levels a pleasing curiosity, and there 'psychologized' or 'politicized', folk theatre tends to be little more than popular middle-class entertainment, where a few social evils can be exposed in a way already familiar through the other media.

In this context to speak of the expansion of rasa serves no useful purpose, apart from invoking 'eternal' categories that cover up, rather than uncover, the intricacies of reception. Theoretically it should be possible for rasa to be 'progressive', to absorb and encapsulate newer modes of aesthetic experience rather than become a tool for interpreting the latter in traditional terms alone.[19] But for this a collective reassessment is called for.

At this point, however, certain qualifications need to be made with regard to the fructification brought about by the encounter with Brecht. The conventions that link folk theatre with Brecht were not only a trap for the unwary theatre practitioner. However tenuously, they provided a certain access to Brecht's theatre and through this to his theatre aesthetics, for the 'folk' forms had to bend and stretch in order to accommodate Brecht, even a Brecht partially understood. And, willy-nilly, something novel did take place; however imperfect the synthesis on the reflexive plane (for a certain amount of eclecticism is inevitable), new patterns did emerge and new horizons of expectations were created. For Brecht's theatre could also be transformed in performance, it too could emancipate itself from orthodox interpretation, Marxist or otherwise. And traditional folk theatre could grow to meet urban needs as it has indeed on its own initiative in urban industrialized centres like Bombay.[20] It could also be transformed in the much more complex way which sought to accommodate rural as well as urban audiences, as in the work of Habib Tanvir, to whom we turn in the next chapter.

NOTES

[1] Thus, for instance, Peter von Becker (1985: 17): 'Wo Märchen wieder wahr werden. Beobachtungen zwischen Kalkutta und Peking. Der freie Brecht in Asia, da sieht man ihn,' (Where fairytales come true. Observations between Calcutta and Peking. The Free Brecht: In Asia, it's there one sees him).

[2] Thus, for example, Maharishi (2000).

[3] That Brecht knew some of Tagore's work is corroborated by Werner Frisch and K.W. Obermeier in their documentation of Brecht's youth in Augsburg (1975: 56). They quote his school friend Stephan Buerzle, who recalled that Brecht was reading Verlaine, Rimbaud, Villon, and Tagore in 1913/1914. Besides this, in his library, conserved in the Brecht Archive in Berlin, there are three Indian books; two slim Reclam paperbacks of the two best-known Sanskrit plays in German translation: *Shakuntala* and

Mricchakatikam, as also Damodargupta's *Kuttanimatam*, a manual of erotics. On the last, there are Brecht's characteristic pencil marks, proof that he had actually gone through the work.

[4] I refer to the form here as svang, since most Hindi-language texts and studies use this term. Ramnarayan Agrawal (1976) in his seminal study has used the generic term '*sangit*' for the form as prevalent in present day UP. The term 'nautanki' has become more current in English; it is also part of the title of Kathryn Hansen's densely scholarly study (1993).

[5] In the following brief summary, only the barest possible outline of the complex philosophical and theological systems that developed during the course of two thousand years can be suggested.

[6] Gerow (1977: 245–50) offers a brief, lucid account of this early stage.

[7] The translation of the Sanskrit terms, which stem from Gnoli ([1956] 1968), can only be approximate. The eight dominant states are: Delight (*rati*), Laughter (*hasa*), Sorrow (*shoka*), Anger (*krodha*), Heroism (*utsaha*), Fear (*bhaya*), Disgust (*jugupsa*), and Wonder (*vismaya*). The eight corresponding rasas are: the Erotic (*shringara*), the Comic (*hasya*), the Pathetic (*karuna*), the Furious (*raudra*), the Heroic (*vira*), the Terrible (*bhayanaka*), the Odious (*bibhatsa*), and the Marvellous (*adbhuta*). Later a ninth dominant state and rasa were added, Serenity (*shama*) and the Quietistic (*shanta*) respectively.

[8] See Byrski (1974), especially pp. 101–161 for the intricate linkages of plot with rasa.

[9] The relationship between rasa and abhinaya is explored by Heckel (1987), which also contains a fine discussion of the bhava concepts as part of the communication model of theatre.

[10] All three concepts are depicted in their context in Gnoli ([1956] 1968).

[11] The tenth-century philosopher Abhinavagupta likened the tasting of rasa (*rasasvada*) to the experience of the absolute (*brahmasvada*). The difference lay primarily in the impermanence of the former. See Gnoli ([1956] 1968: preface) and Gerow (1977: 268).

[12] Temple [1884–1901] 1977. Temple's collection contains at least two tales, *qissa*, and three plays, svang, which could be regarded as predecessors of the present form of svang. They are all composed in verse and the tales, qissas, are embryo plays, for within the narrative portions there are large stretches of dialogue, lively and well-developed, which are, however, not played but spoken by the storyteller. Conversely, the play, svang, dispenses with the storyteller, though it contains narrative portions. These are incorporated

by the players into their speeches. In short, the narrative and the play-acting are initially treated as mutually exclusive activities, to fuse again in a later form, where the narrator wins an independent role as one of the players and is present on stage to sing and recite the narrative portions. I have relied on Ramnarayan's Agrawal's (1976) study in the reconstruction of this data.

[13] The social organization of the troupe is documented by Vatuk and Vatuk (1967: 29–51).

[14] Such as Sarveshwar Dayal Saxena's *Bakri* (1974) and *Ala Afsar* (1977) by Mudhrarakshash, discussed in Ch. 4 in this volume.

[15] In the framework of this chapter it is not possible to offer a more extensive account of the svang. A general account of this and other forms of Indian folk theatre is available in Gargi (1966). For a detailed study of nautanki, in Hindi see Agrawal (1776) and in English Hansen (1993). The following account is based on the survey I undertook of a number of svangs and the detailed analysis of one particular play by the prolific Natharam Sharma Gaur (1874–1947) of Hathras, credited with having composed 146 plays. *Amarsingh Rathor*, the play chosen as prototype, has been especially popular; it was selected for revival on the urban stage and made into a Hindi film. Natharam Sharma Gaur's plays, as well as many others, are still available as cheap reading matter on the pavements of most north Indian cities.

[16] Useful in this context are the distinctions Suvin makes between 'type' and 'character'. He defines 'types' 'as classified by sex-cum-age, by nationality, by profession, by social estate or class, by physiology and moral philosophy... often by what we could feel are combinations of the above categories (Diderot's *coditions*, e.g. father or judge, seem to contaminate profession, class, and social role), etc' (1986: 120). Further: 'What seems to me constitutive of any type is that it possesses a relatively small number of traits (I have not found more than half a dozen in any so far examined, but this remains a field to be investigated), which are all culturally congruent or compatible. This compatibility should in every particular historical case be explainable as the result of a feedback interaction between the social reality from which the traits are taken and the criteria of verisimilitude of the social addressees for whom the text is intended' (122).

[17] See Vatsyayan (1964: 49–65).

[18] Cited by Voigts (1977: 178).

[19] Norvin Hein in his extensive study of the cycle of religious Krishna plays thus justifies the use of aesthetic categories long out of use:

The rasdharis themselves do not classify these dramas in any explicit and widely accepted manner. They are not familiar with the ancient science of dramaturgy and its theory of dominant *rasa*. However, the ancient Indian way of cultivating traditional types of feeling lives on in their work, even in the absence of the ancient self-consciousness about the matter. The recognizing of these dominant emotions is the natural method of classifying the plays. In naming the categories, we can do no better than to bring into use some of the terminology of traditional Indian dramaturgy (1972: 164).

Edwin Gerow is similarly averse to acknowledging any break or change in tradition:

Can we identify a vehicle that will bring the *rasa* from the seventeenth century to our own day?... The answer is to be sought in the relation between rasa and character, both literary and psychological. The *rasa* has always been determined as a way of experiencing. Therefore it would not seem difficult to postulate its perpetuation as a habit— a form of perception that structures reality and life.

Indeed the classical psychology proposes such a vehicle to account for the transmigratory soul: *vasana*. This disposition or propensity to experience, brought slightly up to date, would also serve to characterize the *rasa* and account for its psychological potentiality, as well as its crystallization in certain works of contemporary fiction (1981: 248–9).

In contemporary Indian scholarship this traditional, reductivist trend is, if anything, even more pronounced at times and does not seek to justify itself.

[20]Deshpande (1982: 47–57) discusses the cleavage between the 'elite' and the 'rebel' theatre in Bombay.

References

Agrawal, Ramnarayan. 1976. *Sangit, ek loknatya parampara*. Delhi: Rajpal and Sons.

Becker, Pater von. 1985. 'Wo Märchen wahr werden', *Theatre heute*. 2.87.

Benjamin, Walter. 1978. *Versuche über Brecht*. Frankfurt: Suhrkamp.

Birkenhauer, Klaus. 1971. *Die eigenrhythmische Lyrik Bertolt Brechts: Theorie eines kommunikativen Sprachstils*. Tübingen: Max Niemeyer.

Brecht, Bertolt. [1967] 1976. *Gesammelte Werke* [Collected works] in 20 volumes. Frankfurt am Main: Suhrkamp.

———. 1975. *Tagebücher 1920–1922. Autobiographische Aufzeichnungen 1920– 1954* [Diaries and Autobiographical Sketches], Herta Ramthun (ed.). Frankfurt am Main: Suhrkamp.

Byrski, M. Christopher. 1974. *Concept of Ancient Indian Theatre*. Delhi: Munshiram Manoharlal.

De, S.K. 1961. *Early History of Vaishnava Faith and Movement in Bengal*. Calcutta: Firma KLM Pvt. Ltd.

Deshpande, G.P. 1982. 'Some Perspectives on the Theatre of Tomorrow', in *Journal of Arts and Ideas*, October–December.

Dimock Jr., Edward C. 1966. *The Place of the Hidden Moon*. Chicago: University of Chicago Press.

Elam, Keir. 1980. *The Semiotics of Theatre and Drama*. London, New York: Methuen.

Frisch, Werner and K.W. Obermeier. 1975. *Brecht in Augsburg: Erinnerungen, Dokumente, Texte, Fotos*. Berlin: Aufbau Verlag.

Gargi, Balwant. 1966. *Folk Theatre of India*. Seattle, London: University of Washington Press.

Gerow, Edwin. 1977. *Indian Poetics*. Volume 5, Facsimile 3 of Jan Gonda (ed.), *A History of Indian Literature*. Wiesbaden: Harrasowitz.

———. 1981. 'Rasa as a Category of Literary Criticism: What are the Limits of its Application', in *Sanskrit Drama in Performance*, R. van Baumer and James R. Brandon (eds.). Honolulu: University of Hawaii Press.

Gnoli, Raniero. [1956] 1968. *The Aesthetic Experience According to Abhinavagupta*. Varanasi: Chowkhamba.

Hansen, Kathryn G. 1993. *Grounds for Play: The Nautanki Theatre of North India*. New Delhi: Manohar.

Heckel, Angelika. 1987. 'Untersuchungen zur Rasa-Lehre in Natya Sastra und in Abhinavaguptas Abhinavabharati'. Master's thesis, University of Tübingen.

Hein, Norvin. 1972. *The Miracle Plays of Mathura*. New Haven, London: Yale University Press.

Hinck, Walter. 1977. *Die Dramaturgie des späten Brecht*. Göttingen: Vandenhöck und Ruprecht.

Jameson, Fredric. 1998. *Brecht and Method*. London: Verso.

Maharishi, Anjali. 2000. *A Contemporary Study of Brechtian and Classical Indian Theatre*. Delhi: National School of Drama.

Schokker, G.H. 1983. 'Keshavadas's Method of Basing Braj-Krsna Lyrics on the Tradition of Literary Aesthetics', in *Bhakti in Current Research 1979–1982*, M. Thiel-Horstmann (ed.). Berlin: Dietrich Reimer.

Suvin, Darko. 1986. 'On Fiction as Anthropology: Agential Analysis, Types, and the Classical Chinese Novel', in *Literature and Anthropology*, J. Hall and A. Abbas (eds.). Munich: Wilhelm Fink.

Tatlow, Antony. 1977. *The Mask of Evil: Brecht's Response to the Poetry, Theatre and Thought of China and Japan. A Comparative and Critical Evaluation*. Bern, Frankfurt a. M., Las Vegas: Lang.

Temple, Richard Carnac. [1884–1901] 1977. *The Legends of the Punjab*. New York: Arno Press.

Vatsyayan, S.H. 1964. 'Conflict as a Bridge', in *Diogenes*, 45.

Vatuk, Ved Prakash and Sylvia Vatuk. 1967. 'The Ethnography of Sang: A North Indian Folk Opera', *Asian Folklore Studies*, 26/1.

Voigts, Manfred. 1977. *Brechts Theatrekonzeptionen: Entstehung und Entwicklung bis 1931*. Munich.

'To be More Brechtian is to be More Indian'
On the Theatre of Habib Tanvir

In following the itinerary of Habib Tanvir across a career of intense theatrical commitment and activity, spanning the period of nationalistic fervour immediately before Independence in the 1940s through the resistance to the violence of power politics in the 1990s, I hope to outline the process whereby Brecht's theatre was creatively appropriated by a theatre practitioner involved in, but at the same time acutely aware of, the pitfalls of mindlessly transporting folk theatre to the urban stage.

WITH IPTA IN BOMBAY

Tanvir was born in 1923 in Raipur, Madhya Pradesh, where the most immediate theatre experience was the Parsi theatre, the vital hybrid form which had come into existence in the nineteenth century as a result of the contact with the melodrama produced by amateur British troupes for the entertainment of the local British population (Tanvir 1969). He became acquainted with members of the Progressive Writers' Association (PWA) while he was doing his MA at the Aligarh Muslim University. He moved to Bombay where he explored several avenues as career options, the new media—radio and film but also theatre. He joined the Indian People's Theatre Association (IPTA) in Bombay in the mid-1940s as actor, director, and playwright. Bombay was one of the most active centres of IPTA in this period; the Association had been founded here in 1943. The work with IPTA was to remain a guiding and motivating force in all of Tanvir's later work as also to ground his theatre in political activism.[1]

Tanvir was introduced to the group of artistes and thinkers who worked for IPTA by K.A. Abbas; he came into close contact with the leading members of the group, with Balraj Sahni and Dina Gandhi (later Pathak), and he acted in his first play under the direction of Balraj Sahni.[2] He was to go on to become secretary of IPTA; he organized its activity, wrote plays, and acted in them; eventually he also directed. Things were to change radically after Independence, as the political scene itself changed. IPTA now directed its protests against the party in power; the Congress Party had been an ally, now it had come to represent oppression. A protest march drew police action. There was a death, and Balraj Sahni and Dina Gandhi found themselves behind bars (in Agrawal n.d.: 12). Tanvir promptly went underground, to surface again, once he realized that he was not important enough to interest the police; he came 'upper ground', as he calls it. He was to recall IPTA's mode of collective creation, which brought together well-known artistes with people from ordinary walks of life, some were straight from the village. They were housed in Damodar Hall in those days, just opposite the Opera House, and they worked in the multiple languages of the teeming city. There was a Marathi Wing, a Hindi Wing, a Telugu Wing, and a Gujarati Wing; they sat in different rooms, but they came together for what Tanvir called 'collective functioning'. An idea, in itself often banal, was taken up by others and worked upon until a narrative line emerged; the dialogue was improvised by the actors. Thus for instance, when someone came up with a skit on the theme of unemployment, Balraj Sahni went on to further improvise it and make a comedy out of it. In a short space of time, a ten-to-fifteen-minute skit became a play of an hour and a half. A bitter but entertaining satire, it depicted how a director who worked with his actors as one of them, changed the moment a chair was brought for him. It was called *Jadu ki Kursi* (The Magic Chair) and was directed by Mohan Sehgal, with Balraj Sahni in an exquisitely comic performance in the leading role.

Tanvir remained connected to IPTA from 1944–5 till 1950–2. It was a period of very diverse activity, connected to people at the most diverse sites and interacting with them. There were street-theatre performances at the gates of mills in Bombay. Workers leaving the mill in the evening would see a happening, which did not announce itself as a play; the idea was to provoke discussion and the play would conclude with that. They played in *chawls* with skits improvised on the problems of the chawl-dwellers, throwing up issues, looking for resolutions. This could also happen in a restaurant. The actors would start a quarrel, in order to draw people's interest and involve them in dialogue. A play thus improvised *Shantidut Kamgar*, was performed under Tanvir's direction.

IPTA had begun to subside as a popular movement by 1948; it was to last for less than fourteen years, from 1943–4 to 1956. The official persecution that followed became one cause for its dispersal, for imperialism had not gone away with Independence, the enemy had just become more elusive. The more pointed was the resistance directed at the Congress Party. But there was also the split in the Communist Party line. IPTA had no policy of its own; it was the cultural wing of the Communist Party of India and followed its line. P.C. Joshi and B.T. Ranadive had major differences of opinion, which became apparent in the Party conference. With the split came a loss of direction. After eight years, Niranjan Sen organized a large IPTA conference in Delhi, to which came people from all over the country. They reminisced and went their way; it was a funeral party. IPTA left behind a legacy but also an immense sense of loss, of an opportunity lost. For Tanvir it had been a natural consequence of the national movement led by Gandhi, which also had a large peasant base. The recourse to folk theatre had emerged from that base: 'It was only natural that theatre should have looked for indigenous material, for innovative method and peasant resources. So the folk theatre techniques that one fell back upon was a most natural thing'.[3]

The model for the use of folk forms came from Bengal:

Actually, in those days we looked to Calcutta for leadership. We used to be impressed by whatever happened in Calcutta. The people there used folk poetry and melodies in great quantity, they were peerless in their way, and they had great influence on us, but everything came to an end very quickly. The opportunity for artists from different parts of the country to come together under the label of art, for people to become acquainted with art from other parts of the country, came to an end, and people went back to their own nooks. Such a major event in the art world of India, such a major movement came to an end; it just became a chapter in our history. (in Agrawal n.d.: 20)

Tanvir's later involvement with folk forms was based on this understanding of its function as a mode of communication with audiences, of addressing social issues directly and pertinently.[4] The lesson learnt from the work with IPTA was to remain with him through life. Tanvir later performed plays on issues such as family planning, but two things remained important for him. For one, the answers to problems were not to be served to people, they could only be resolved together. And second, in impromptu performances, due regard was also to be paid to the aesthetic quality of performance, for beauty and wealth of expression were be found in folk theatre.[5] The stress on 'Indianness' in this period was the expression of resistance to modes of thinking that were an obvious result of decades of colonization.

Once IPTA began to disperse, Tanvir left for Delhi. He founded the Hindustani Theatre along with Begum Qudsia Zaidi in 1954. It was one of the earliest attempts in post-Independence India to establish theatre not directly sponsored by the state. The dominant dramatic activity up to then had been centred primarily upon historical and pseudo-historical themes concerned with evoking the national past or on domestic interiors as the locus of psychological studies and as pointing to the need for social reform. It was as a counterpoint to this and as setting forth the work of IPTA, that Tanvir wrote and produced his first play *Agra bazar*, set in the market place and teeming with bazar life, which was to go on to become a classic of its kind. 'Produced by the Okhla Theatre, the play was performed open air in Jamia University. Tanvir involved street artists and even curious Okhla villagers to act on stage' (Malick 2004: 30). Soon thereafter came the opportunity to study in England.

EUROPE AND BRECHT

Tanvir left for training in acting at the Royal Academy of Dramatic Arts (RADA) in London. Dissatisfied by what he was learning there and finding that it had little use for the kind of theatre he envisioned, he moved on to study production at the Bristol Old Vic School in 1955. In autumn and winter 1956 he toured Europe, financing his trip by singing Chhattisgarhi songs in nightclubs and pubs (cf. Malick 2004: 31). He found the eight months that he spent in Germany to be the most productive. Brecht himself had just passed away but his legacy was very much alive. Berliner Ensemble was still at the height of its creativity and exuberance and Tanvir saw several plays there. He was impressed most by Brecht's work;[6] he found that the theatre he had known in India had several affinities with Brecht's theatre practice:

I find him very contemporary, full of humour,...poetry, and meaning. So it was natural to take Brecht, especially because he's so open in his form, he's imbibed so much from the East, Eastern techniques, that for any Eastern man to take to Brecht to try out his own Eastern techniques is a natural thing.[7]

Brecht's theatre was from the beginning an ally in the evolution of a resistant theatre, providing vital support in the re-use of techniques, modes of presentation, which in the efforts to create 'modern' theatre as part of a process set in motion under the British in the nineteenth century, had been relegated to the past, as rural, outdated. Tanvir found that Westernized urban theatre in India was ill-equipped for projecting the problems of the country. Urban education not only cut off young people from their cultural roots and widened the gap between city and village, it also inhibited and prevented young actors from being spontaneous and expressive.[8] He decided, however, to explore and exploit techniques already available in Indian traditional forms, for '*to be more Brechtian meant for him to be more Indian*' (Rea 1979: 60).

BACK TO INDIA AND 'FOLK'

Tanvir was not interested in preserving any given traditional form intact; he did not insist on the purity, on the 'authenticity', of any specific folk form. With change inevitable in village life, folk forms were ultimately destined to die, but they could, while still available, while still signifying continuity, through the interpenetration of contemporary values, through catalytic, sensitive intervention, enrich urban theatre, 'tranform the body politic of theatre'.[9] By evoking enough interest in the urban younger generation, it would be possible to help in the survival of folk arts by assimilation.

The absorption of folk forms could take place according to the needs of individual urban people with a particular inclination and aptitude. 'These mergings should be allowed to take place in the manner so that your urban culture emerges transformed, having absorbed and assimilated all these forms.'[10]

Back in Delhi in 1958, he undertook the production of what was later to acquire model character: Shudraka's fifth-century Sanskrit play *Mricchakatikam* (The Little Clay Cart) in a Hindi version and in a style adopting certain features of folk theatre. For some of the scenes, he used players from Chhattisgarh. He went on to establish his own group, Naya Theatre, in 1959, with members also drawn from Chhattisgarh in Madhya Pradesh.

The idea was not to establish urban hegemony over rural art forms; it was rather to expand the urban to meet the rural and transcend thus the dichotomy that had evolved and the estrangement that had set in as a result of colonial cultural and social policies. This entailed extreme caution, so that urban patterns of experience were not imposed on the rural. In his own practice and as an urban playwright working with folk forms, Tanvir was aware that he was bound by the limitations of the urban imagination.[11] He sought to overcome these limitations by evolving various strategies. For one, he contributed the stories, taken either from the folk reservoir or the traditional classical stock, cautiously questioning the feudal values inherent in these. But the dialogues and scenes were improvised in interaction with the players.[12] The possibility of striking a false 'folksy' note could thus be ruled out, since the play eventually reflected the player's reception of Tanvir's story ideas. If Tanvir was responsible for the final assemblage, the composition of the play was collective.

Though Tanvir worked with a number of folk forms, the theatre that his players are familiar with is *nacha*, which has a relatively simple performance code. It is an all-night performance, consisting of music and dance, interspersed with four or five skits, each of forty to fifty minutes duration, held together by a loose narrative. Comic and satiric, dealing with village matters, the skits consist of improvised dialogue between the two main characters, with a third performing odd functions when necessary. In all, a nacha troupe can consist of ten to twelve players. Though it has its own characteristic music and instrumentation, since the whole performance is loosely strung together, Tanvir worked out a clearer narrative line. He held several workshops with nacha groups, the first one being in 1973 in Raipur, whereby he worked with around one hundred performers for two to three months. He was learning from them as much as guiding them, as also conducting research in their methods of presentation, make-up, costumes, jewellery; these were aspects to which the nacha troupes themselves did not pay any special attention. The workshop resulted in the production of an improvised play. He was to hold another important workshop on *Pandvani*, a form that consists of dramatizing monologues from particularly climactic moments in the Mahabharata. The film director Shyam Benegal became interested in Tanvir's work and accompanied him for the next year, making short documentaries on the rich folklore of Chhattisgarh (cf. Agarwal n.d.: 52).

Tanvir went on to evolve his own particular blend of forms. Much had gone into the making of the synthesis that emerged, which could only be loosely connected to nacha pure:

The fallacy is that I have been reproducing the nacha form. The nacha is a primitive form with only two actors. The third comes and goes like a messenger or something. The fact that I'm fond of crowds itself means that I have nothing to do with the nacha form.[13]

When necessary, the troupe incorporated song, dance, and ritual, not normally used in nacha, which brought their own ritual associations. Religion could not be blended out entirely; for Tanvir it was a question of according due respect to the religious beliefs of his players while trying to expand the social perspective. Here only compromise with the sense of form and the sensibilities of the players was possible (Rea 1979: 63–5). The compromise was partly achieved by a shift of emphasis to social awareness and satire, with which his players were in any case familiar. In the matter of interpretation and coordination of all these elements, Brecht's theatre acquired great significance, for by means of narrative comment and analysis, episodes that seemed disparate could be linked, and those where the links seemed obvious, could be taken apart and subsequently so interlinked that the joints appear visible. With experience in the coordination and organization of these elements, Tanvir considered the Chhattisgarhi actors equipped to perform the most diverse plays: 'And I felt that through them I could interpret many things—an Indian classic or even a modern playwright, Brecht.'[14]

By 1970, the group was composed entirely of Chhattisgarhi players and in 1972 was registered as a professional theatre company. Tanvir gained increasing official recognition for his pioneering work—in 1969 he received the Sangeet Natak Akademi award for drama and from 1972–8 he was nominated member of the Rajya Sabha, the Upper House of Parliament. This was the decade when Tanvir developed his 'counter' theatre, the use of traditional forms for the most diverse purposes. It was in this period that he produced among other plays *Charandas Chor*, a vastly, popular folk play, and in 1978 Brecht's *The Good Woman of Sezuan* in a Chhattisgarhi adaptation. Working and experimenting in folk forms, he held several theatre workshops in Raipur, Borunda in Rajasthan, Rai in Haryana, as well as in Orissa and Mysore.

Though *Charandas Chor* was an immensely popular item at the Festival of India staged in Britain in 1982, Tanvir managed to resist co-option into the culture industry. Two factors came to distinguish him from most folk enthusiasts. First, he has exercised caution in his mode of adaptation for urban theatre, in itself a legitimate enough exercise, though open to abuse.

It is people who matter to me. There are urban traditions created over 200 years if not more. Cash in on them, get them out, do something with them in your own way. But don't go to the *bhavaiyas* for a month and produce a feeble version of a strong *bhavai* while not doing anything for the *bhavaiyas* themselves and their art which is dying out. I was strongly against it. It's aping of the worst order, sucking their blood in double exploitation using the form and doing nothing about them.'[15]

Second, in the course of interaction with village communities, he has managed to inject new life into their repertoire of plays:

Parts of plays I've done have found their way into local performances. We heard a nacha version of the second act of my *Mitti ki Gadi*. I've seen a vibrant Chhatisgarhi version by a young party of another play of mine. I asked them this: 'Had you seen my production?' They hadn't. They sit around in tea shops. Some one tells a story. They make their own play from it. It adds to their repertoire.[16]

The play then proceeds to evolve in its own way, improvised to suit the needs of its audiences. Taking an interest in forms still practised has also provided encouragement and an incentive to go on:

I noticed an old man with a lantern performing. I asked him, what are you performing? He said, *Chandaini*. It takes 18 evenings of three or four hours each day to complete the story of *Lorik and Chanda,* an ancient folk tale.... I hunted for other performers of *Chandaini,* assembled them and now there are several *Chandaini* parties.[17]

Tanvir was not a conservationist, he was interested in mutual fructification of the rural and the urban, where he continued to play a major role. His most noteworthy ventures in the late 1980s were *Moteram ka Satyagrah* (1988), a play co-written with Safdar Hashmi and directed by Tanvir for the Jan Natya Manch, one of the most prominent and politically radical street-theatre groups in the country, and the performance under his direction and script modification of Asghar Wajahat's *Jis Lahore nahi vekhya* (1990).[18]

In forty years of theatre practice, Tanvir had evolved a style that moved effortlessly from urban to rural and back again to urban, which did not backdate folk but instead merged folk with the urban popular. His plays could be performed on the proscenium stage before urban audiences, they could as easily be presented to the rural, more interactive, audiences on a makeshift stage. He had perfected the art of presenting a tale punctuated by comment and song, though the peculiarity and attraction of *Agra bazar*, his first major play, was precisely that it lacked narrative in any linear sense. In the discussion which follows, I retrace Tanvir's trajectory from his early experimental days in Delhi to the synthesis between rural and urban, classical and popular, that he evolved upon his return from Europe. My focus will be upon the major, formative plays of the 1950s into the 1980s.

THE ORGANIZATION OF NARRATIVE IN THEATRE

Agra Bazar (1955) was based on the life of the eighteenth-century Urdu poet, Nazir Akbarabadi, who himself was something of a rebel; he broke away from the ornate diction of Persian court poetry and wrote lyrics dealing with mundane experience and the market place. Though he could write melancholy haunting poems that linger in the memory, he could as easily write popular jingles for hawkers and vendors advertising the attraction of their wares. The poems of Akbarabadi formed the body of Tanvir's play, not the person; for though he figured constantly in the conversation in the bazaar, the figure of the poet did not enter the play. Since no biography of the poet had been preserved, the details of his life were in any case accessible largely through such poems and songs as were preserved in the memory of the people for whom he wrote his verse. It was the values of this poetry of the people, for the people that formed the theme of the play.[19]

I didn't bring Nazir on stage because I felt—this became my inspiration— that there wasn't very much known about his life, except some anecdotes, but his poetry pervades the country, so let it pervade the stage. Poetry everywhere, which has his presence, but not the man. So I went about producing a bazaar in which I created two poles, the kite-seller's shop with conversations about kites in colloquial, spoken languages, and the book-seller's shop where poets and critics and historians gather and speak an ornate literary language, spurn Nazir and uphold Ghalib and others; and the vendors who sing his poetry because they obtain it from him and their wares, which were not selling, immediately get sold when they begin to sing the songs of Nazir.[20]

The play has practically no storyline; the action, such as it is, punctuated with Akbarabadi's songs, takes place as vendors, prostitutes, beggars jostle each other, commenting on the powerful and the politics of the day. *Agra Bazar* reflects the reality of bazaar life and the rhythms of bazaar speech:

As part of my research into the language, I looked up Mirza Farhatullah Beg, a writer of Delhi writing in Delhi language; or Ahmed Shah Bokhari, who wrote *Dilli ki Galliyan*—beautiful language. And the sounds of Old Delhi, the sellers, the vendors, they all have musical calls; there's a book called *Dilli ki Awzan*, it has all these things, *kaun kaise bolta hai, kaise pukarta hai* (who speaks in what way, who calles out in what manner). And then you go to Old Delhi and hear this language. And a lot that I heard then, of the people's language, has gone into *Agra bazar*. Therefore it has that vigour.[21]

Street performance had been raised to form the very narrative of the play. *Agra bazar* initially astounded and unnerved Delhi audiences, unused to this freedom with form.[22] It was later to become an all-time favourite with theatre-goers, even after it had lost some of its original urban character once it had begun to be performed by actors from Chhattisgarh. With its intense awareness of the multiplicity of social forces that were at work, the play could be seen as continuation of the work done by IPTA and formed fertile ground for the encounter with Brecht's theatre.

Mitti ki gari (1958), the Hindi adaptation of *Mricchakatikam* was produced as a blend of folk forms with Brechtian modes of narrative interpretation, using folk artistes from Chhattisgarh for the proletarian character roles such as the 'gambler' and the 'thief'.[23] The influence of Brecht made itself most apparent in the handling of the fable, whereby the main love story, though left untouched, was interpreted in the light of the sub-plot: the figure of Sharvalika, the thief in love with the courtesan's maidservant and party to the political uprising with which the original play culminates, became the dominant focus. Sharvalika was a rogue, like Brecht's Azdak and like Azdak he cunningly agitated for a better world. By the end of the play, the increasingly hostile masses hovered menacingly in the background of the love scenes. The concentric circles of the revolution finally engulfed all the characters in the play and the threads of the various plots merged into the climactic political upheaval, which became thus the focal point of the fable.

In order to 'distance', Tanvir used masks for some characters and song and dance for interpreting the fable as well as to comment on the action or on a figure. The songs, using the folk melodies of Chhattisgarh, were sung both by the narrator and the figures in the play.[24] It was clearly possible to blend Sanskrit play with techniques culled from folk plays as also Brecht, the formula that would be invoked so fervently by theatre people in the 1970s, but the point was precisely that it could not be reduced to a formula. It was a political act which demanded reflection and asked for social choices. The merging of folk with urban was then to take place in a manner 'so that your urban culture emerges transformed, having absorbed and assimilated all these forms.' At this stage, Tanvir called this blend of folk and urban, classic and contemporary, *nai nautanki*, the new nautanki.[25]

Though Tanvir produced short political sketches in 1971, the year of the Bangladesh war, he increasingly concentrated on social satire. The troupe's most popular play, *Charandas Chor* (1974–5), was based on a folk story which circulated in Rajasthan, retold by the writer and folklorist, Vijaydan Detha.[26] The story concerns a professional thief, who when obliged to seek shelter with the guru of a religious sect, takes four hasty and unlikely vows in order to gain admission to the sect, amongst these that he would never marry a queen or occupy the throne. At the guru's behest, Charan is obliged to take the most important of the four vows, that he would never tell a lie, and it is this, paradoxically, the frequent admission, in the most diverse circumstances, that he is a thief, which ensures his phenomenal success and rise in social status. In fact, the class of merchants and nobles to which the thief now has access, is itself composed of thieves and liars who live by mutual conspiracy and acceptance of make-believe moral standards.[27] By an ironic turn of events when the thief does have the chance to wed the queen and claim the throne, it is his persistent refusal to lie, to behave in fact like a thief, that finally costs him his life.

Tanvir first heard the story from Detha in 1973. He produced a short play based on it in the local *khyal* form in Rajasthan. The first trial of the play was followed by another workshop with a nacha group in Bhilai. The ironic comment in the story had already been stressed by Detha. The dialogue and the scenes were improvised by the players under Tanvir's guidance. The still rather sketchily worked out play was presented at an all-night open-air function of the regionally important Satnami sect, which drew its membership from subaltern classes and laid great emphasis on moral purity. The performance was open in more ways than one; it incorporated several songs of the Satnamis and improvised upon others, so that the sect itself came to be figured centrally in the play. In Tanvir's own words:

There were some 18,000 people sitting there all night and they all seemed so receptive. The crowd was full of Satnamis. Listening to them and looking at them, I thought that this play about a thief who does not abandon truth as he clings to his profession of thievery, was very much up their street. I was inspired by these people, the central article of whose faith is 'god is truth'. So, at about 6 p.m., I announced that we had a little green room show—not at all stage-worthy at the moment but, considering that there were so many Satnamis present and the fact that the play's theme was also truth, I felt inspired to present it, no matter how raw it was. They welcomed it, I also told them that they should not mind if I intervened in the middle to correct something or to sing something or to improvise something. I had a book of *panthi* [sectarian] songs. We improvised the melodies from that. I also sang together with the others and they caught on. We even managed some songs sitting there.[28]

It would be an exercise in pedantry to attempt to isolate the strands of Brechtian theatre that Tanvir had once incorporated into the composition of narrative and its presentation. The bare stage, the spare use of props, and the disinterest in working out the finer psychological details of character and plot could be interpreted as Brechtian, were there any need to do so, but they were also common practice in most traditional plays. The scenic sequence of Charan's 'picaresque encounters'[29] exhibited some resemblance to the episodic construction of Brecht's plays and the characters in Tanvir's play would not be out of place in one of Brecht's own plays. It was in its intention and assemblage that Tanvir's play most resembled the social comedy, the *Gesellschaftlich–Komische* (cf. Koller 1982: 224–5) of Brecht's theatre, a laying bare of the barter contained in bourgeois institutions. The explicit social and political comment of the songs could be seen as an expressly Brechtian device, the twist of expression in the *panthi* songs, which made of them something other than a devotional exercise; however this went beyond Brecht, to reflect the stance of Tanvir who was also a lover of Urdu poetry:

However, in a style reminiscent of Brecht, Tanvir also uses them to comment on an action and to elucidate and underline its larger moral and social significance. In some cases, they reflect a certain complexity of articulation and consciousness which is obviously Tanvir's contribution. For example, the refrain in the panthi song in the second act, 'Oh, Charandas, don't try to rob Death of his due,' was added because Tanvir wanted it to work on the audience's mind subliminally, preparing them for the death that comes at the end of the play. Similarly, the last chorus, 'An ordinary thief is now a famous man,' which comments on Charandas's fate and articulates its significance, was almost half-written by him, using 'the simplicity of Nazir Akbarabadi's poetry.'[30]

Tanvir modified the ending of the story as originally retold by Detha by the time he had worked out the final full-fledged version:

In Detha's version, the thief is killed for his vows and the queen's offer is accepted by the guru who becomes the king. Tanvir's plays departs from this. While he ends the story itself with the dramatic high point of the thief's execution (leaving out the guru's opportunism), he prolongs the play itself by adding a sequence which, accompanied by a chorus in praise of truth, shows the thief's posthumous deification by the people. Through this and the last chorus, he brings the performance to an anti-climactic conclusion.[31]

By emphasizing Charan's act of asceticism rather than the greed displayed by the gurus, he avoided the trap of easy cynicism. Even if posthumous fame could not revive a dead man, even if truth did not finally win, the regard for truth found at least some space in men's memory. Charan gained in stature, and in doing so, the social order was put into question and hierarchies disrupted:

The promise to his guru, then really causes him to abandon his nature as a man, and unleash the fury of the woman he has scorned. Like Basanna, Charandas is a sacrificial victim, but he dies not because he is sexually transgressive male, but because he wants to retain his chastity in the face of female desire. In this contest between a fellowship of ascetic males and the sovereign authority of women, patriarchy becomes increasingly irrelevant. (Dharwadker 2001: 20)

With the vivacious and imposing Fida Bai in the role of the queen, Tanvir had created a play that transgressed several boundaries, but would itself acquire canonical status in modern Indian theatre.

The urban–rural continuum:
Habib Tanvir's *Charandas Chor* (1970s)
(Sangeet Natak Akademi)

Brecht Filtered through 'Folk'

By the time Tanvir adapted Brecht's *The Good Woman of Sezuan* into Chhattisgarhi in 1978, the Brechtian elements in his theatre had merged totally with the rest. The theme of this play Tanvir found to be especially applicable to the Indian situation. The characters represented familiar figures in Indian village life:

One of the themes of the play is poverty and poverty is a theme they know very well. They have no trouble in understanding it and the figures are familiar to them, the moneylender, the barber, the prostitute.... The three gods—we know gods very well, they are also human beings, they have all the imperfection of human beings, their weaknesses. There is singing and dancing and the troupe are natural singers and dancers.[32]

Most of all, it was the vulnerability brought about by extreme poverty which his players could effortlessly recreate; they needed little training to catch the minute details of its many frustrations, anxieties and acts of mutual betrayal:

Brecht does not romanticize poverty. The poor man is a human being and he also has the tendency to suck another's blood, to become the parasite of another, to stretch out his legs and remain jobless, To be poor does not mean that everything that you do is only good: envy, ill-will, greed, deceit and cunning, all of this exists in the poor man, it is engendered by poverty. They don't have to do much to portray the poor man, they don't have to be taught, their gestures and mannerisms come on their own.[33]

Tanvir saw no reason to be apologetic about the anomalies that the rural adaptation of a suburban play entailed, or indeed for the lack of any kind of deliberately effected 'alienation' effect in his production. The suburban misery of Brecht's industrialized Chinese city in being transferred to a Chhattisgarh village was necessarily bound by the horizon of the village and the Chhattisgarh dialect into which Tanvir adapted the play:

The players played it their way, there can be no imitation of Brecht's models. They are good and powerful actors. They understand their roles spontaneously.

No concept of alienation. Brecht looked towards the Orient as one of the inspirers of his kind of theatre which he used—the narrator, song and dance. It would be silly to go to him for that, when we have our own living tradition to draw upon. Our folk theatre has a lot in common with our classical theatre.

In invoking the classical in the same breath as folk theatre, Tanvir was not indulging in the usual clichéd comparisons between the folk and the classical. He had shown that it could be a meaningful exercise to interpret the classical through the prism of the present, using the liveliness and irreverence of folk theatre practice and players to provide one frame. But his other frame was, as always, modern, contemporary, and political. He also avoided the trap of seeing folk theatre as deriving from the classical, as some kind of unproblematic continuum. Classical and folk had always interacted, fed into each other, as he stated clearly in the late 1970s, when the folk–classical–Brecht excitement was at its peak:

It is no use turning to the dead book of the classical theatre in India and trying to revive the archaic theatre forms of yesterday without relating them to the living traditions of today. There are some people who tend to do this. These are revivalists, who have failed to perceive the complex but obvious interrelationship between the classical and the folk performing arts. They do not realize that the folk traditions in art are not only the progenitors of the ultimate classical structure but also the carriers of classical traditions when the latter came to a dead end in their own habitat.[34]

The final folk–classical–contemporary synthesis was uniquely Tanvir's own. He could then also afford to admit the shortcomings of putting a suburban play from industrialized Europe into the Indian countryside:

The Pilot, the German love of machinery, of flying. Even in the English production of 1962 when Deepak Majumdar played the pilot, an educated person, it remained a difficulty. For the illiterate Chhattisgarh player it is difficult to play this role and it is a difficulty we have to accept.

The play may not have become an all-time classic, in the style of *Charandas Chor*, but it was an important milestone in the career of the troupe. The lexical poverty of the English translation was more than compensated by the vivacity and the forceful use of a dialect, which had preserved the rhythms of spoken language. The songs were recast in the idiom and metaphor of life in the village, melancholy alternating with mocking gaiety, riddles with harsh comment.

THE MERGING OF FOLK WITH POPULAR

The genesis of one of Tanvir's popular 1980s plays, *Moteram ka satyagrah* (Moteram's Satyagrah, 1988) remains the most clear indication of the social and political direction of his theatre, confined neither to the rural nor the urban, but seeking an amalgamation of both. The Jan Natya Manch, a street-theatre organization, affiliated with the Communist Party of India (Marxist), which came into being in 1974 and saw itself as the direct heir of IPTA in its political heyday, asked Tanvir in cooperation with Safdar Hashmi, one of its founders, to adapt a story by Premchand (1880–1936) for one of its rare proscenium productions. Premchand is the acknowledged master narrator of rural life and the exploitation of peasant labour in the villages of colonial India, but he is almost equally at home in the politics of the urban street. His 'Satyagrah' is the story of an ironic inversion of the political–ethical concept, developed by Gandhi as a tool of resistance. Set in pre-Independence Banaras, the story highlights the spontaneous alliance between the local British magistrate, native magnates, and the Brahman pandit they co-opt, in an effort to jeopardize the attempts of the National Congress Party workers to organize a *hartal*, a total halt in the business life of the city, during the visit of the British viceroy. The Brahman pandit, Moteram, offers to fast unto death, should the city decide to commence with the hartal. After a series of encounters, scenes depicting the confusion of the local leaders of opinion and the attempts by the British magistrate and his allies to manipulate religious emotion, Moteram, a notorious gourmand, gives into the temptation to partake of the choice delicacies, picked for him by the Congress leader. The fast is thus abruptly terminated, the final confrontation avoided, but not before the machinations of the allies have been effectively exposed. Though hilarious, the play lingers on the verge of the kind of violence so familiar in the contemporary political landscape of the country.

Linked by narrative verse recited by a lively chorus, which was a 'Brechtian' addition deliberately introduced by Tanvir, the play improvises freely on Premchand's story. The city magnates, Hindu and Muslim, anxious in the face of business losses and united in their desire to appease the British, develop into dynamic characters, with just a touch of caricature. Several additional figures, the lackeys of the magistrate, the ravishing young local courtesan, provide further density to the narrative. If there are links here with *Agra bazar,* the organization of the narrative leaves no doubt as to the social configuration: the colonial setting, which has obvious continuities with the neo-colonial regimes of the day, serves as an ironic point of reference, the *satyagraha* further highlighting the misuse of Gandhi's legacy by the Congress, the very political party that had once been the emblem of resistance to imperial exploitation. In the post-1980s political climate such political alignments with religious forces, which easily erupt into communal violence, had become the reigning order of the day.

Particular poignance linked the play with the political life of the capital of the country. Safdar Hashmi as co-writer and charismatic performer had contributed centrally to the success of the play. On 1 January 1989, Hashmi and his Street Theatre Group, while performing a street play before factory gates in a suburb of Delhi, were attacked by armed supporters of a candidate of the ruling party to the local municipal elections. Hashmi was dragged through the streets, his head beaten to a pulp. He was to succumb to his injuries the following day. His death made theatre workers, writers, artists, and intellectuals from the most divergent political camps aware of the potency of theatre and the need to establish and retain alternate channels of communication and interaction.

In 1990, at the peak of the politically manipulated communal tensions that would lead to the destruction of the Babri Masjid, Asghar Wajahat's historical–topical play *Jis Lahore nahi vekhya*, was performed in Shri Ram Centre in Delhi under Tanvir's direction. A politically charged play, the theme was the partition of the subcontinent and the havoc wrought in people's lives by the radical hardening of the Hindu-Muslim front. Ghazals and poems by Firaq Gorakhpuri, Amrita Pritam, Rahi Masoom Raza, and Pakistan's famous poet, Nazir Qazimi were woven in. This did not lead to lyrical excess; on the contrary, the script was tightened and given further focus. As Tanvir himself reported: 'I edited Asghar Wajahat's play *Jis Lahore nahi vekhya* from nineteen scenes to nine. I wanted to connect the lure of money with vandalism.

The economic dimension of communalism has not been highlighted enough.'[35] This exposed the machinations of both Hindu and Muslim religious leadership. The original script had itself been considered too radical to receive official support:

Asghar first submitted the script to Doordarshan, which found it too hot to handle because of Asghar's acidic comments on the clergy in Pakistan. Asghar submitted the script to a workshop conducted by Shri Ram Centre where Habib Tanvir, one of the participating directors, liked it and agreed to produce it. Since the play was written in a realistic format, Habib Tanvir, despite vehement protest from Asghar, gave it a Brechtian format and introduced the chorus, which he himself wrote. Besides, he added a few more scenes to it. The production was a success and one believes Asghar, too, came around to the director's viewpoint finally. (Bardola 1999: 17)

Brecht's political theatre was present at its most inspiring in Tanvir's work when it turned to the urban and the popular, a reflection perhaps of Brecht's own urbanism.

ON THE USES OF BRECHT

Brecht himself had been part of the widespread modernist movement around the turn of the century, which appropriated popular presentational forms, in an effort to reform elite culture and forge new models of community. Bourgeois culture in the nineteenth century was 'itself a bricolage of earlier elite and popular forms', which had 'tended toward non-critical, nonparticipatory, and nonregenerative banality' (Jelavich 1982: 225). The use of popular forms, in resisting this bourgeois culture, could proceed along two routes: 1) withdrawal—new varieties of elitism, or 2) social, political, cultural criticism. Brecht utilized the critical and adversary spirit in popular culture, the grotesque realism of circus and vaudeville, epitomized in the art of Karl Valentin, but also the didacticism inherent in the comments which interspersed the narratives of fairground actors and moritat singers. If these were all devices which were to create the estrangement, for which Brecht's theatre is so well known, they were also always supposed to enable participation, the forging of community, encouraging community values—

an alternate tradition, antagonistic to bourgeois values, resisting the all too apparent gravitation of spectators to a mass culture, atomistic and amenable to social control (cf. Jelavich 1982: 247–50). By suggesting the kind of relevance that popular forms could convincingly contain, Brecht could indeed be used as an impetus for the synthesis of folk and urban theatre. It was to this Brecht who provided a resistant, alternate tradition that the theatre of Habib Tanvir was initially indebted, not to the Brecht, who by the mid-1970s was himself to be absorbed into the culture industry in the West.

In the decades after Independence, Tanvir has been one of the directors who has worked most consistently with social and political narrative in theatre. It becomes formally irrelevant whether Sanskrit drama is being performed, or a play by Brecht, since the details are worked out in constant interaction with the players and their rootedness in and awareness of their own referential experience. The factor then, which has most contributed to the success of Tanvir's experiments, has been his determination to remain rooted in the context and environment of his players, and not to extract and isolate them from this. His troupe continues to perform in Chhattisgarh and has never been put at the total service of the urban stage.

After the successful European tour of *Charandas Chor* in the early 1980s, Peter Brook had commented on the social perspective of this theatre:

Tanvir's work comes from the village viewpoint. It's comic and it doesn't attack big social problems. It sticks to day-to-day questions of greed, hypocisy and exploitation. Its line is to prick bubbles. The motivation behind it is social–political in the old sense: not exactly communist in the orthodox Soviet–Marxist terms of the urban street theatre groups, which are very strong in India. The Naya's position is closer to the socialism of Satyajit Ray's film, a clear-cut political line based on the simple facts of injustice. There is no ambiguity on the Indian scene; you can simplify.[36]

Possibly it is also easy to simplify the Indian scene. As stemming from Brook, the comments acquired wide circulation and were duly cited by a number of critics.[37] To simplify thus is also one way of marginalizing the rigour and political potency of this theatre. Since it is performed by villagers, to relegate it once again to the village, and there to further dilute it by speaking of common human failings—greed, hypocrisy, and exploitation—is to indulge in a process that paradoxically raises the whole to a 'universal' level, since it refuses to take cognizance of the social configurations, the links between village and the politics of the city, which Tanvir locates explicitly. It is not 'village' being offered for the delectation of 'town' in an amorphous universal way. Though, as we have seen, it is one of the pitfalls of the ideology associated with 'folk', that it can indeed be thus explicated. In the late nineteenth century, the term 'folk', signifying pre-industrial, pre-urban, pre-literate, 'had the effect' as Raymond Williams has noted and as we have discussed in the last chapter, 'of backdating all elements of popular culture, and was often offered as a contrast with modern popular forms, either of a radical and working class or of a commercial kind' ([1976] 1983: 137). The backdating made possible projections of uniformist, nationalist readings into the past (Burke 1983: 30). Folk art, as Tanvir practised it, was contemporary, not an exoticized ethnic item. And it was part of a continuum with the urban popular; it took a stance on current political issues. 'For art to be impartial, means', as Brecht had noted, 'to belong to the ruling party' (Brecht [1967] 1976: vol. 16, 687).

Tanvir has always been wary of the nomenclature 'folk' for the theatre he has evolved, since he has emphasized that traditional forms are neither items for conservation, nor for revival for 'compromised theatre' as he calls it. To release an army of cultural workers into the villages, in order to cash in on this vogue, would destroy rather than create theatre. Correspondingly, for theatre practitioners who resisted co-option into the state culture industry, there was refusal to accept to the 'folk fungus' in the awareness that it had acquired official status, and a shift in emphasis from 'folk' to 'popular' which has urban connotations also and is thus more inclusive. But no form is in and of itself ideologically fixed, the notion of political theatre, whatever its locale, presumes an interested audience, and as Tanvir's production of *Moteram* and later *Jis Lahore nahim vekhya* adequately demonstrated, these can be mobilized, in spite of television and gripping family serials, when a chilling political moment generates this need, as the massacre in Gujarat in March 2002 did once again.

At a time when he was himself under attack because he was Muslim, Tanvir restaged his version of a popular Chhattisgarhi satire, *Ponga Pandit* or *Jamadarin*. Composed originally by two Chhattisgarhi playwrights, Sukhram and Sitaram, it dealt with the comic dilemma of a caste conscious Brahman who maintained a relationship with a Dalit woman. What could a Dalit woman touch and not defile? The body, the gods, or indeed money? It was seen as anti-Hindu by the Right Wing Hindu ruling coalition and, once again, Tanvir found himself under attack.[38]

I do feel very angry but what matters is the tenacity to resist. I also try to see other aspects of it. *Ponga Pandit* is a folk tale. It has been accepted by Hindu society for years and years. But now the play is so much in demand that I can only thank the Bharatiya Janata Party (BJP). For the first time I've had the play translated into *khadi boli* with a tape of music and a note on how we have done it. It is to be published in a literary magazine in Bhopal. There has also been a video recording so that they can see how we do it.[39]

In the effort to forge an alternate resistant tradition, to create and retain channels of communication and analysis in theatre, Brecht has remained an ally. In more than half a century of theatre making, from the heady days of working with the IPTA team in Bombay in the late 1940s, through the many experiments with classic, folk-popular and the urban-proscenium, in rural and in urban settings, Tanvir has blazed a trail in which the stimulus received from Brecht has been so smoothly integrated that is it not difficult to see what he meant, when almost three decades ago, he declared that 'to be more Brechtian is to be more Indian'. With 'Indian' he has always meant the cultural attitudes of people in their historically specific situation, as human beings who react in everyday ways to big events, as Brecht had realized, when Karl Valentin had reminded him, that the soldiers were pale and that they were afraid. No heroics for the people.

NOTES

[1] 'My social background and political affiliations, which are left-wing, also pushed me towards folk theatre,' in interview with Rea (1979: 64).

[2] Based on the long interviews conducted by Pratibha Agrawal (n.d.) reported on pp. 10–21 of her book.

[3] In a personal interview, 7 March 1981.

[4] 'My first attachment and love for Indian folk theatre, epics and folk artists I got from my association with IPTA' (personal interview, 7 March 1981).

[5] Personal interview, 14 August 1989.

[6] 'Brecht in particular had impressed him, but mainly because Brecht was, like himself, using folk techniques, some of which were based on Eastern styles' (Rea 1979: 60).

[7] Personal interview, 7 March 1981.

[8] 'Borrowing of necessity from the British, it hardly ensured an identification of the young with their cultural roots. On the contrary, it tended to widen the cultural gulf that already existed between the city and the village.' Tanvir cited by Rea (1979: 62).

[9] Personal interview, 14 August 1989.

[10] In 'Round Table on the Contemporary Relevance of Traditional Theatre'. *Sangeet Natak* Special Issue (July–September 1971): 31.

[11] Ibid.: 30.

[12] 'There was no dialogue to it and we talked about how we might turn it into a play. I suggested we relate it to our times.... They came up with ideas to stimulate further ideas from me. I would build on that and they in turn were further stimulated.... When there were several characters speaking at once and cues were very important, I gave them written dialogue. But most of it we left as improvisation' (Tanvir cited in Rea (1979: 65)).

[13] In an interview with Gokhale (2004).

[14] Personal interview, 7 March 1981.

[15] From Gokhale interview (2004).

[16] From ibid.

[17] From ibid.

[18] For an account of his later work as also for a complete list of productions, see Mallick (2000).

[19] Personal interview, 14 August 1989.

[20] In conversation with Anjum Katyal, in Tanvir (1996: xxi–xxii).

[21] Ibid.: xxi.

[22] Tanvir reports that the *Hindustan Times* reviewer reacted summarily with 'no plot, no theme'. See Agarwal (n.d.: 8).

[23] The play has not been published. Tanvir however has described the experience of producing the play (1965) and the following account is based on this article.

[24] Tanvir considered these devices explicitly 'Brechtian' (1965: 11–13).

[25] In order to distinguish it from the original folk form. Interview, 14 August 1989.

[26] Published first in Marwari (1972), it was to appear in Hindi in 1982.

[27] Cf. Detha's comments in the Hindi version of the story (1982: 85–6).

[28] Cited by Javed Mallick in his introductory essay, in Tanvir (1996: xiii-xiv).

[29] 'Punctuated with folk dances and songs that unite the Sanskrit tradition with Brecht, the show develops in a series of picaresque encounters between Charan and his clients' (Irving Wardle in *The Times*, 25 August 1982). Though 'picaresque encounters' is an apt phrase, the link between Sanskrit drama and Brecht through folk dances and songs is as arbitrary as it is symptomatic of the tendency to collapse disparate traditions by means of extreme simplification.

[30] Mallick in Tanvir (1996: xv).

[31] Ibid.: xiii.

[32] Personal interview, 7 March 1981.

[33] Interview woven into Agarwal's text (n.d.: 93).

[34] From 'The Indian Experiment', essay in *Enact* (March–April 1977), reprinted in Agrawal (n.d.: 205). As Tanvir further expostulated: 'The *interrelationship* between the classical and the folk is no less evident in the sphere of drama. Those who refuse to see the *mutual* interflow of influences between the two categories of art allow themselves to be misled by the fact that the classical Sanskrit drama of India has ceased to exist as a living force for a thousand years' (206, emphasis mine).

[35] From Gokhale interview (2004).

[36] In an interview with Wardle (*The Times*, 5 May 1982).

[37] In *India Today*, 31 October 1982, and in *Times of India*, 1 July 1982.

[38] Tanvir continued to draw the support of radical youth. In September 2003, an email message circulated in the alternative mailing lists which keep track of acts of communalism acts in the country:

Hi, have you heard about the new attacks on Habib Tanvir's 70 year-old play *Ponga Pandit*, also known as *Jamadarin*, recently during his MP tour? The play is about a pandit who falls in lust with a jamadarin, and is now caught in the dilemma of touching the untouchable—

'*chhooye to museebat, na chhooye to museebat*'! [Trouble if you touch her, trouble if you don't touch her!] How the shrewd little jamadarin teaches the old ponga pandit a lesson is the climax of the play.

In August during his MP tour, the Hinduwadis (read RSS and BJP goons, also known as the upholders of the true Indian nationalism) of our secular nation decided to protest against the anti-Hindu strands in the play...by attacking the artists with stones, *tamatars* and other assorted pelting devices. They systematically followed Naya Theatre from city-to-city, town-to-town strategically attacking each and every performance. The other play in performance along with *Ponga Pandit*, Asghar Wajahat's *Jis Lahore nahi vekhya vo janmyayi nahi* also fell under attack of course.

I am grateful to Shayoni Mitra for drawing my own attention to this circular.
[39] From the interview with Gokhale (2004).

REFERENCES

Agrawal, Pratibha. (ed.) No date. *Habib Tanvir: ek rangvyaktitva*. Calcutta: Natya Shodh Samsthan.

Bardola, V.M. 1999. 'Post 1980 Plays: Hindi', *Theatre India*, November, 13–18.

Brecht, Bertolt. 1976. 'Kleines Organon für das Theater', in *Gesammelte Werke 16* [Collected Works] Frankfurt am Main; Suhrkamp.

Burke, Peter. [1978] 1983. *Popular Culture in Early Modern Europe*. Aldershot: Wildwood House.

Detha, Vijaydan. 1982. 'Phitarti Chor', in *Uljhan*. Selected and trans. from the Rajasthani into Hindi by Kailash Kabir. Delhi, Patna: Rajkamal Prakashan.

Dharwadker, Aparna. 2001. 'Male Playwrights, Female Folk: *Hayavadana, Jokumaraswami, Charandas Chor*', in *Theatre India*, November, 16–21.

Gokhale, Shanta. 2004. '"Art is always anti-establishment": Interview with Habib Tanvir', *The Hindu*, September 26.

Jelavich, Peter. 1982. 'Popular Dimensions of Modernist Elite Culture: The Case of Theatre in Fin-de-Siècle Munich', in *Modern European Intellectual History*, Dominick La Capra and Steven L. Caplan (eds.). Ithaca and London: Cornell University Press.

Koller, Gerold. 1982. 'Parabolischer Realismus', in *Der Gute Mensch von Sezuan*, by Bertolt Brecht, Jan Knopf (ed.). Frankfurt am Main: Suhrkamp.

Malick, Javed. 2000. 'Habib Tanvir: The Making of a Legend', *Theatre India*, November, 93–102.

———. 2004. 'Habib Tanvir: Artist of the Impossible', *Tehelka, The People's Theatre*. November 6.

Premchand. 1968. 'Satyagrah', in *Mansarovar* [Collected Short Stories] Vol. 3. Allahabad: Hams Prakashan.

Rea, Kenneth. 1979. 'Theatre in India: The New and the Old, three approaches to blending folk traditions with contemporary needs', Part III, in *Theatre Quarterly*, 18/32, 47–66.

Sangeet Natak. 1971. 'Round Table on the Contemporary Relevance of Traditional Theatre,' Sp. Issue, *Sangeet Natak*, July–September.

Tanvir, Habib. 1965. '*Mera mricchkatika ka prayog, ek adhuri kahani*', in *Natrang*, January.

———. 1968. '*Brecht aur bhartiya rangmancha*', in *Natrang*, October.

———. 1969. '*Parsi thieter ke natak, aj ke vatavaran mem*', in *Natrang*, January–March.

———. 1972. Interview given to Vibhukumar, *Natrang*, October–December.

———. 1979. *Agra bazar*. Delhi: Radhakrishna Prakashan.

———. 1986. *Charandas Chor*. Delhi: Pustakayan.

———. 1996. *Charandas Chor*. Translated into English by Anjum Katyal. With an introductory essay by Javed Malick and an interview with Anjum Katyal. Calcutta: Seagull.

Wardle, Irving. 1982. 'The Indian Pilgrimage of Peter Brook', *The Times*, 5 May.

———. 1982. Review of Charan the Thief, *The Times*, 25 August.

Williams, Raymond. [1976] 1983. *Keywords: A Vocabulary of Culture and Society*. London: Fontana Paperbacks.

III

What is Indian?

Encountering the Other, Accosting
the Self

Two deeply entrenched views meet and reinforce one another, when a sage with a floating white beard speaks to a wide-eyed stripling of having composed a poem, which is 'the story of your race, how your ancestors were born, how they grew up, how a vast war arose. It's the poetical history of mankind. If you listen carefully, at the end you'll be someone else' (Carrière 1988: 3).

The speaker is Vyasa, the poet–seer, who is also the legendary ancestor of the warring clans of that vast epic, the Mahabharata, and he is seeking a scribe who will hold fast his words, for the benefit of all those who come after. In their dramatization of the epic, Peter Brook and Jean-Claude Carrière have carried Vyasa's message to Western audiences. Two well-established self-views have here accosted and reconfirmed the modality of each other's existence. The 'East' has often been convinced that it is the bearer of spiritual traditions no longer accessible in the 'West', and the 'West', tiring of the breakneck speed of the business of living in industrial and post-industrial society, has often looked for succour to the 'East'. In Vyasa's words, the 'West' and the 'East' seem at last to have met to become all of mankind, the 'East' in some ways to have even ancestored mankind. But where does this encounter take place and where, all said and done, is the 'East' located?

East and West were meeting in the kind of performative situation for which the expression current in the 1980s was 'inter-cultural encounters'; the term is less current now, and people tend much more to speak of globalization, of 'diffusion'. There have been few sustained efforts to gauge the phenomenon, which excited much critical comment at one time. However, the symposia and conferences organized to throw light on the matter largely left the basic issues untouched; they tended rather to spend time elaborating and illustrating the many possible varieties of inter-culturalism. Erika Fischer-Lichte in her edition of the proceedings of a symposium on the theme (Bad Homburg, Germany 1988) defined inter-culturalism in the all-encompassing fashion needed to cover the very different phenomena that were being subsumed under this head:

In Europe, North America, Asia, and Africa, the aesthetically most advanced contemporary theatres are significantly different from the traditional theatres of their respective cultures in that they deliberately adopt theatrical elements from foreign cultures. In each case, this results in an 'inter-cultural performance' which is constituted by the relationship between the continuation of the own traditions and the productive reception of elements of foreign theatre traditions.[1]

Rustom Bharucha, dramaturge and theatre historian, was one of the few who have followed the unfolding of this phenomenon over the past decades. With his knowledge of Indian theatre, especially of the vigorous Bengali theatre movements of the 1960s and 1970s,[2] as well as of American and European theatre, Bharucha was ideally suited to take stock of both sides of the encounter. His thought-provoking, witty, elegant, informative, polemical essays collected under the title *Theatre and the World: Essays on Performance and Politics of Culture* (1990) offered a series of reflections on the issue of inter-culturalism, while, unavoidably, throwing up a number of questions, which continue to remain open, decades later. Bharucha sought to disentangle Indian theatre from the more diffuse 'Eastern' components in the much vaunted Euro-American inter-cultural encounters of the 1980s. The essays covered a theatrical journey across spatial and temporal territory, which was divided into three stages as also representing three phases in a self-encounter. The book was correspondingly divided into three sections: 1) 'Points of Departure' observed and analysed the Euro-American uses and constructions of Indian theatre, tracing thereby the history of the modern European encounter with Indian theatre. 2) 'Transition' returned to India with a German play, Franz Xaver Krötz's *Wunschkonzert* (1971), a wordless play, which was adapted under the co-direction of the author, to accommodate the urban context of three cities—Calcutta, Bombay, and Madras. 3) 'Returning' then finally considered indigenous traditions and innovations, urban, rural, and ritual in the search for, in his own words, 'specifically Indian theatre cultures, both traditional and contemporary, where I attempt to search for alternatives that go beyond the limits of inter-culturalism' (212).

I took up these themes in a long review essay of Bharucha's brilliant book for the *Journal of Arts and Ideas* in 1992, which, in a slightly modified version, I present here again. The dialogue, of which the essay consisted, retains its urgency. In the first part of this essay, I recapitulate and comment upon Bharucha's observations as far as they relate to the inter-cultural encounter; in the second part I question some of the assumptions and premises of the inter-cultural debate. In a third and final section I look at the two models that Bharucha himself offers as a possible alternative to the politics of unreflected inter-culturalism. Though I shall be summarizing Bharucha's argumentation in the first section, I shall indicate where my own comments complement or part ways with his.

The Modalities and Pitfalls of Inter-culturalism

The essays in the first section of *Theatre and the World* deal with three distinct though interrelated issues. Firstly, Bharucha pinpoints the modes, often reductivist, of the borrowing, adaptation, and transformation of Indian theatre. Second, he questions the authority with which Indian theatre is represented in the West and the claims to authenticity which accompany it, and, finally, he counters by reclaiming the theatrical and cultural territory thus 'ceded' to Western authority. The categories under which I present his arguments are part of the ongoing 'orientalist' debate of the 1980s.

1. Reductivist Tendencies

Western theatre practitioners have with remarkable consistency restricted their interest in Indian theatre to what they have regarded as classical theatre, or at the most extended it to the kind of theatre that can be considered to have been sanctified by tradition. Traditional sources, then, have inevitably been seen as repositories of ancient wisdom. Whereas in itself taking resort to these sources seems a legitimate enough undertaking, it has seldom been accompanied by any serious attempt to understand the historical, social, aesthetic, and most of all religious context of the performance tradition thus abstracted. Once extracted from its respective setting, however it is easy enough to see any given aspect of the performing arts as exemplifying and representing the essence of Indian culture. For all its essentializing, the engagement with traditional Indian theatre has inevitably been partial, eclectic, restricted often to a preoccupation with technique. Of late there has been increasing fascination with ritual theatre, which when transplanted can only lead to a deliberate desacralization of context. To this I would add that the essentialist perspective, in its almost consistent disregard of the recent developments in the country, has often been accompanied by an underlying disparagement of current cultural and political processes.

Bharucha considers a series of theatre practitioners as participating in this inter-cultural encounter, whereby he seeks to view them in their context. Earlier theatre practitioners had limited access to Indian theatre aesthetics and tradition and for all their essentialist categorization had approached it with some caution. Edward Gordon Craig, actor, director-designer, as well as dramatic theorist (1872–1966) devoted most of his life's work to a visualization of theatre, which in its early phase seemed entirely futuristic. Both attracted and repulsed by what he knew of Indian theatre, mediated as it was through Coomaraswamy, he could write in 1918: 'Whenever you see an Indian work of art, tighten up the strings of your helmet. Admire it...venerate it...but for your own sake don't absorb it.'[3] He tended to regard Asiatic traditions as static and monolithic, he did not seek to imitate. He maintained a distance and seems rather to have sought analogies in European tradition. He remained faithful to what he considered as setting forth European practice, breaking thereby new grounds in stage design and the art of the actor.

Yet limitation of access can lead both to a decontextualization as also a resultant eclecticism in the borrowing, for once relationships with other factors have been severed, it is possible to select and combine according to any given criteria. Antonin Artaud (1896–1948) is a well-known instance of this kind of eclecticism. He allowed himself to be inspired in his theatrical vision by Balinese and Cambodian theatre, but also by yoga, *The Tibetan Book of the Dead*, mysticism, acupuncture, astrology. Counterposed to the vision of Eastern theatre that he created was his view of the European situation: 'Our spirits suffer from other needs than those inherent in life. We suffer from a rottenness, the rottenness of Reason.'[4] Yet, while Artaud made no attempt to situate his vision within the performative context of the respective cultural tradition, he also did not himself propagate it as a technique for acting. As Bharucha points out, it was Artaud's followers who tended to accept his vision at face value, to mistake it as truly capturing the essence of Eastern theatre practice.

A part of the fascination traditional theatre exercises on contemporary theatre practitioners is expressed by the preoccupation with technique. Polish director Jerzy Grotowski's experiments in the Theatre Laboratory began with a production of *Shakuntala* (1960)—an irreverent, bold production, innovative in its use of a ruthlessly edited text, interpolated with Manu and the *Kamasutra*. The play marked also the beginning of Grotowski's interest in Indian theatre. Yet this interest was dictated by pragmatic considerations: the use of the techniques of kathakali and yoga for the psycho-physical training of his actors. Mere virtuosity of technique was not to be mistaken for the innate understanding and control of these forms. It is to Grotowski's credit that he remained wary of virtuosity; he altered the training programme of the actor, once he saw him approaching virtuosity. He was aware of the absence of ritual framework in Western theatre; later, he was to move away from such experimentation to paratheatrical work.

Eugenio Barba, who visited Kalamandalam and discovered kathakali for Grotowski in the 1960s, has continued to work on the psycho-physical art of the actor. It has been his contribution to cut across and through traditional 'oriental' theatre forms such as *odissi*, *noh*, *kabuki* and some non-naturalistic, non-psychological Western forms like the Decroux school of mime and Dario Fo, in order to try and reach a 'common technical substratum', the 'domain of pre-expressivity'.

Though Barba is aware of the cultural, social, and historical differences between these forms, he believes that the principles underlying the varied developments operate on an analogical basis 'born of similar physical conditions in a different context'.[5] As Bharucha points out, in this transcultural creation of the fictional body, the details of social life go missing. Correspondingly, there is no attempt to examine the individual histories underlying terms like *tri-bhangi*. Barba's kind of transculturalism means subsuming the differences of history. And as far as the traditional theatres are concerned, for all its expansiveness, it necessarily involves a reduction of the specificity of individual forms. It is a theatre that addresses itself to an initiated and therefore limited body of spectators.[6]

It is the transportation of ritual theatre however, which is the most hazardous of the projects of inter-culturalism and, in this respect, it is the work of the inter-culturalist Richard Schechner, which provokes, as Bharucha himself admits, the oppositional energy of his book. The hazard consists in the arbitrary mode of transportation of the ritual concerned and the subsequent lack of reflection concerning the creation of new meaning, for Schechner has no qualms about, on the contrary he seems verily to celebrate with post-modern felicity, the fragmentation and transportation of ritual processes from their own context into other, disparate ones.[7] For Schechner, the meaning of ritual can, without further ado, be 'metabolized' in its new context, since the various cultures in question seem themselves to be at once free-floating and inter-connectable. They are placed on what Bharucha calls 'his own map of post-modern performance...through links like sociobiology, computer languages and multinational corporations'. Schechner can ultimately absorb all cultures into post-modern performance by means of a relatively diffuse use of philosophical-theological concepts that have, in fact, a variety of different but precise meanings in the long and multifarious history of what is today known as the Indian tradition. He maintains:

These apparently different systems view experience as what the Hindus call *maya* and *lila*—illusion and play—a construction of consciousness. The 'ultimate reality' lies somewhere else—in the genes say the sociobiologists; in the flow of goods say the economists; in the exchange of information say multinationals.

What about post-modern performance?... Post-modern means something close to what postwar means: the organizing of experience in a period when experience is *maya–lila*. (Bharucha 1990: 34–5)

His willingness to equate one ritual process with another, his astonishing versatility in establishing analogies, is made possible by his belief in universals. The universals are constituted by Victor Turner's 'western pattern of beach, crisis, redressive action and reintegration...the theatre of every culture I know about also conforms (to this dramatic paradigm)'.[8] It is with the smoothest of gestures, then, that Schechner is able to establish the link between the spatial explorations in American experimental theatre and the use of the environment in the *Ramlila* of Ramnagar. Although Schechner himself remarks on the juxtaposition of the sacred and the secular during the period of the *lila*, he is not interested in, or is unable to, grasp and articulate the interpenetration of the two, which makes for the ritual complexity of the performance.

It is Schechner's fragmentation of and at the same time reduction of the whole ritual process to a single universal pattern that makes the enterprise questionable and in part contradicts his own observations regarding the interpenetration of what he views as the sacred and the secular. What he views as the secular is the very context within which the performance is ensconced and with which it is at the same time interwoven, to form a complex whole. To fragment is to destroy links, to deliberately sever interconnections; to speak of universals is to impose a uniform pattern without making the effort to reflect on the change of meaning involved in the change of context. 'The responsibility of any director, then,' as Bharucha points out, 'is first to learn what the ritual means within its own culture, and then to reflect on what it could mean in his own' (Bharucha 1990: 41).

2. Global Authority, Terms of Exchange

Theatre and ritual could continue to be performed and to evolve in the Indian subcontinent and the use or misuse of borrowed forms could remain irrelevant to actual events and developments in India, were it not for the fact that Indian practitioners tend, in their turn, to be affected by the representation of which they become objects. Western understanding and exposition of classical and traditional forms from the non-West tend to become authoritative; they claim to represent the authentic and these in turn alter modes of self-perception in the non-West.

This brings us back to the modalities of inter-culturalism. The very term implies that some kind of interaction, exchange, takes place. Who determines what is exchanged and when? What is the basis of exchange and what are the various modes of representation and authority? The practice of Western inter-culturalists demonstrates a remarkable correspondence to some of the operations Edward Said sees as being constitutive of 'Orientalism': 'as the corporate institution for dealing with the Orient—dealing with it by making statements about it, authorizing views of it, describing it, by teaching it, settling it, ruling over it: in short, Orientalism as a Western style for dominating, restructuring, and having authority over it' (Said [1978] 1985: 3). Even Said admits, however, that Orientalist discourse is not produced unilaterally. I would say that it is produced with the collusion of post-colonial elites in the countries of the East.[9] These are issues that Bharucha addresses vigorously. He would go so far as to see the whole encounter as determined by the interests of the West alone, as one sided, as a 'dead end street' in fact.

The mode of selection and the authoritative use of aspects of other cultures as exemplified for instance by Schechner's concept of the choice of cultures, of being able to choose from a vast palette of possibilities, the Indian, the Japanese, the Asian and so on in the construction of 'pan-human, even supra-human communication net-works', is a privilege that only a few can practise, and these few stem largely from the Western hemisphere. As a notion, it is especially bizarre when regarded in its absolute impractability for most of mankind. Schechner, as Bharucha points out, would subsume without any qualms, the manifold traditions, 'Indian, Japanese, Southeast Asian, native American, and perhaps Euro-American performance', under a single performance theory (Bharucha 1990: 49). The practice contradicts itself in its very constitution: on the one hand it draws upon single, homogeneous (essentialized) cultures to construct the inter-culturalist, cultures that are contained within national boundaries; on the other hand, it dissolves these nationalist boundaries as irrelevant and outmoded, asking for the eradication of cultural borders in the interest of global culture. Such euphoria bypasses the struggle of most nation states to come to terms with the pluralities that have to be contained, while presenting, in the interests of self-protection and self-definition, some unitary front to the world at large.[10]

Further, the inter-culturalists, in transporting aspects of Indian theatre, seldom pause to admit that the representation of these in another context can only be partial, tentative. They claim at the same time, as the initial citation so unself-consciously maintains, to represent the Indian and through the Indian, in fact, the universal. As I see the problem, when Shakespeare is played in India, the effort is to assimilate his plays to known traditions. Thereby there is some rhetoric about the universality of Shakespeare. Yet it would not occur to any Indian theatre practitioner to maintain that any given presentation is the authentic representation or even the essence of Shakespearan or even Western tradition. The question is all too apparently one of power and authority and therein lies the difference. The same rhetoric when used in the inter-culturalist context in the West acquires a completely different hue. For me the following proclamation epitomizes the problem involved: the Mahabharata, in the words of Peter Brook, is:

Shakespearean in the true sense of the word. Its form is essentially Indian but based on universal conflicts and ideals.... We tell a story that is universal but which would never have come into being without India. To tell this story we had to avoid evoking India too strongly so as not lead us away from human identification, but also we had to nevertheless tell it as a story rooted in Indian earth. (In Schechner et al. 1986: 68)

There are some staggering assumptions here. To take from the Indian, but to retain this at the merely evocative level, to recast it in a universal—Shakespearean—garb, so as not to distract from the truly human. Yet who is to decide what is essentially Indian and what, finally, universal? The final interpretation of Indianness lies in the hands of Brook and Carrière. And it is they who can authoritatively pronounce as to what the epic has finally to say to contemporary audiences. 'The Mahabharata', says Brook, 'tells a history that is as sombre, tragic and terrible as our contemporary situation' (ibid.: 71). And this in fact provides the cue to his understanding of the epic, for in his interpretation it depicts the situation of post-War and post-industrial Europe. The Mahabharata alienated from its original context, has a message, ostensibly still Eastern, for the West. Centuries of Indian tradition are subsumed within a reading which makes a global claim to representational authenticity.[11]

3. Representational Authenticity

It is a crucial counter measure which, in resisting this tendency to reduce, seeks to reappropriate lost ground by focusing once again on the lost referentiality of the theatrical forms thus transferred. Since even in their original context, dramatic worlds are never completely stipulated, and no form in itself completely specifies all that it *means*, it is necessary to recall attention to the semantic and cultural rules that enable the spectator of the original event—and we must necessarily practise some abstraction here and posit an 'original event'—to read a performance (cf. Elam 1980: 102). It is not a question then of mere quibbling as to the right and wrong interpretation of a given symbol, ritual sequence, or character, much more of providing information about the given performance traditions in their own referentiality, of restoring the context.

As far as the dramatization of the Mahabharata is concerned, it is well worth the effort to follow Bharucha and question the details of the narrative, the characters, and their setting. For though, according to Brook, the narrative is to speak for itself and reproduce the original meaning by its very presentation (in Schechner et al. 1986: 66–7)—the space, the visuals, the plot, the events as they are connected to each other, and the characters—are there primarily to *evoke* India. All these have at the same time claims to be authentic, specific, though they have been created or rather recreated, without previous or retrospective analysis, in fact intuitively, and they are similarly to be grasped intuitively by Western audiences. Yet in order to be thus accessible to these audiences, they have, in fact, been assembled anew. Carrière himself is specific enough in his introduction to the printed version:

In order to adapt the *Mahabharata*, to transform an immense epic poem into a play, or three plays, we had to draw new scenes from our imagination, bring together characters who never meet in the poem itself. All this within the context of deep respect for the shape and sense of the story. Each of these characters has a total commitment, each probes in depth the nature of his actions, each considers his dharma, and each confronts his idea of fate. So we had to make it possible for each of the characters to go into his own deepest places without interposing our concepts, our judgements or our twentieth century analysis, insofar as that is possible. (1988: xi)

Is it possible to edit, extend, amend the narrative without altering the basic concepts underlying the complexities and contradictions of the original? Obviously also, the process of thus restructuring the narrative implies both interpretation and selection on the basis of some criteria, which remain unspecified, apart from their professed relevance for posterity. What is the understanding that informs the recreation of the sixteen major characters whom Carrière selects as protagonists for his story and the dynamism of, the impact of, these characters on each other in this new constellation, in the new situations that he creates when he lets them accost each other?[12] To create is the prerogative of a playwright, to philosophize as if he were summing up some essential philosophical kernel of Hindu thought on the basis of his newly created narrative is a risky venture, to say the least. What is Brook's and Carrière's understanding of the *dharma* of each character, and does it have any relationship to the original, as far as it is possible to deduce this? For, the question of authenticity is coupled with that of authority. To answer these questions at any length would mean writing a new book, and imply the kind of knowledge of the epic which few of us possess. Bharucha undertakes to examine some of these assumptions, and in the following I bring a few examples.

According to Bharucha, since the Bhagavadgita is reduced to a five-minute encapsulation, it can possess little of the function it could have as a possible part of the referential framework. In fact, the play lacks such a frame altogether. The New York audiences laughed when they heard Krishna advise Arjuna: 'Act, but don't reflect on the fruits of action.' At such moments the overall banality and triteness of the Carrière–Brook text becomes particularly apparent. Such is also the case when it comes to the general references to dharma. The framework continues to be, not unexpectedly, determined by the Western context. In fact, as Bharucha rightly points out:

In the absence of any defined religious framework, it is only inevitable that the characters seem to share the Christian universe of their audience—a lapsed Christianity, perhaps, neither fervent nor cynical, but one which nevertheless continues to assume that there is a definite beginning and end to life, a Heaven and a Hell. When the fire burns on the stage and there is an aura of incense and marigolds, these are merely oriental touches. (1999: 100)

The scheme of rebirth, which pervades the universe of the Mahabharata and which puts beginnings and ends in quite another context, obviously plays no role here. Inevitably, the interpretation becomes a mixture of a perhaps 'lapsed Christianity' and a view much shaped and determined by modern European interpretations of Greek tragedy. As Pradip Bhattacharya pointed out in response to a review of the film (the play was never performed in India) by the Sanskritist John D. Smith:

Smith's [John D.] comment that the central narrative conveys a 'clearly readable' message, namely that the epic 'is a highly fatalistic account of destruction visited on men by gods', shows a typical occidental make-up at work, incapable of apprehending the Indian situation. Whatever else it might be, the Mahabharata certainly does not depict the Pandavas as 'pressed by the will of the gods into ever worsening moral and physical conflicts, culminating in a cataclysmic war of annihilation.'... Smith's idea, 'But whatever he does, he will not avert the destruction the gods have called for,' belongs wholly to the realm of Greek tragedy and is not part of the ethos of Vyasa's epic. Here it is the individual who shapes his destiny.[13]

Clearly, there were stereotypes of the Orient at work, which, in fact, imposed Occidental readings on an epic teeming with individualistic personalities, at odds with each other and determining their own fates as much as suffering it.

Of the social context and constraints of the individual characters, important aspects are left untouched, since the entire *varna* issue is simply passed over. There is no thematization of the code of honour of the Kshatriyas, so essential, when it comes to the relationship of Krishna and Arjuna to each other, when it comes to the unacceptability and rigorous exclusion of Karna from the ranks of Kshatriyas. That no pedantic footnotes are necessary to dramatize such situations is demonstrated in an episode that is handled skilfully by Brook. Ekalavya as a Shudra pupil of Drona is counterposed to the relationship the teacher has to Arjuna. Drona allows no rivalry to come up between two of such unequal status, for he simply demands Ekalavya's thumb as his fee. The tensions of the situation are deftly exposed by juxtaposition and contrasts.

The figure of Krishna is the one that is most severely reduced. His misdeeds are summarized and there is little or no information on this most elusive and most central of characters. The problem of his divine status is a real one, and this is corroborated, I feel, by Carrière's own statement:

Man or god? It is obviously not up to us to decide. Any historical or theological truth, controversial by its very nature, is closed to us—our aim is a certain dramatic truth. This is why we have chosen to keep the two faces of Krishna that are in the original poem, and to emphasize their opposite and paradoxical nature. (1988: xi)

The result is an unavoidable blandness.

The erasure of context also implies that there are no indications as to what motivates major characters like Kunti ('who suffers with stoic calm'), Gandhari ('monolith of endurance'), and Draupadi (erasure of her sexuality, pain, defiance). Bharucha brings detailed discussions of the depiction of these characters. He rightly points out that the contradictions inherent in them need, on the one hand, a more textured, multi-levelled text and, on the other, more sensitive direction. Only some actors such as Helen Patarot, survive Brook's handling of character.

Bharucha similarly makes an attempt to reclaim and retrieve the figure of Gandhi as portrayed in Philip Glass' opera *Satyagraha* (1980), which deals with Gandhi's life and experiences in South Africa, before he rose to become a Mahatma and a national figure in Indian politics. It is a reading of Gandhi's beliefs and tenets, as retrospectively interpreted by himself in his *Satyagraha in South Africa*. The libretto is composed of passages from the Bhagavadgita, and in that it is sung by figures from his political life, it is coupled with the narrativization of Gandhi's struggle in Africa. It has then both some claim to historicity, though there are obvious and deliberate anachronisms (such as the presence of Sarojini Naidu in this early phase), and some claims regarding the authenticity and validity of the message conveyed by this particular juxtaposition. Bharucha concentrates his fire on two aspects of the depiction of Gandhi, both of which form a central concern: the dehistoricization and the consequent idealization of the figure of Gandhi. Here it must be emphasized that Bharucha is discussing the 1981 Brooklyn Academy production in New York, and what he says holds true of that, more than for the totality of the Glass composition. It is here that Gandhi, as played by Douglas Perry, appears as a messianic figure, 'standing centre-stage and barely looking at the world around him, lost in a trance inspired by the Bhagavadgita, which provides the libretto for the opera' (Bharucha 1990: 87). Perry radiates peace, an 'uncomplicated guru at peace with the world rather than a relentlessly questioning man who suffered and fought for the dignity of his fellow men' (ibid.: 88).

Bharucha criticizes the choice of the Bhagvadgita for the libretto. As it is in Sanskrit, there is obviously no expectation of the words being understood; it is more a question of sound than meaning. This he finds particularly inadequate, since the grandiloquence of the sound seems to bypass Gandhi's pragmatic approach to the issues of the day. Instead, there is something like a cult of personality in operation, coupled as it is with the presentation of luminaries such as Tolstoy, Tagore, and Martin Luther King. Whereas there are obvious links to Tolstoy and King, it is well known that Tagore and Gandhi disagreed on several key issues. The naive interpretation of history is further extended by the 'Oriental aura of the spectacle'. Gandhi, who chose to dress as a fakir in his Indian political life, is according to Bharucha hardly the right object for such an opulent form (ibid.: 92). Bharucha comes to the conclusion:

It is one thing to feel an aura of peace; it is another to think about the possibilities of peace in our world. Satyagraha, however, is not ultimately concerned with our world or the historical significance of Gandhi. It is concerned with itself. For as long as it lasts, history is temporarily forgotten as it fades into oblivion. The world outside of time triumphs in a void. (ibid.: 93)

Bharucha's protest is legitimate, since the historicity of the sequence of episodes invoked by Glass himself seems dehistoricized by deliberate anachronism, such as the projection of the text of the Bhagvadgita, which came to acquire such significance in Gandhi's life later, into the South African years. This further contributes to an uncritical idealization of the figure.

In conclusion, and bearing in mind the discussions at the symposium in Bad Homburg, where I was also a participant, I should like to draw attention to the two strands of inter-culturalism that, I believe, allow themselves to be clearly distinguished: the 'national' traditions which make selective use of material gleaned from other traditions, and Western experiments with Eastern forms which are made in the name of a global culture. Both the reductivist tendency as well as the rhetorics of universalism are characteristic of 'national' traditions, as well as of those brands of inter-culturalism that make use of individual aspects of the theatres claimed by these nations, though thereby the interest of the inter-culturalists is to concoct a mixture which is to transcend all national categories. Inter-culturalism is a term of Western coinage, it seems to answer to a very 'Western' need. Its usage should profitably be restricted to the work of Western—European and American—theatre practitioners, as instanced in the very different works of Robert Wilson, Ariane Mnouchkine,[14] Brook, and Barba. If at one level inter-culturalism in the West can be seen as an attempt to come to terms with the urban, post-industrial, as a search for the Asiatic within,[15] it is an attempt, which is based on a process of simplification, of dichotomization, and of the use of essentialist categories, which project the difference, often consisting of all that has been marginalized in one's own culture, on to the other, pre-empting thereby any real effort to understand and represent with any degree of responsibility the cultural referent thus invoked. Assuming that inter-culturalism still remains a legitimate exercise at one level, for formal and thematic appropriations have been practised at all times and in all cultures, it becomes exploitative the moment it begins to subsume and represent these cultures with global authority. And it is here that the correspondence to the kind of Orientalism described by Said becomes the most marked. Then it only remains for the cultures thus represented to voice dissent, to become querulous in matters of detail—whether this or that is essentially Indian or African, and even so discerning an author as Wole Soyinka is provoked into such response—to thus participate in the kind of discourse where the terms of debate have been set by the appropriators. The Nigerian theatre critic, Biodun Jeyifous, has pointed out the pitfalls of this essentially *reactive* response. First and most important, the binarism is retained, one continues to operate within a scheme that essentially retains even the projected dichotomies, though these are corrected in matters of detail. Second, the methodological and thematic cues continue to be drawn from the very discourse that is sought to be replaced (Jeyifous 1990: 245). The task does not really end with questioning the localization of the East as seen by the West, the question is one of self-location, as well as of some attempt to ground the work of the inter-culturalists in its own context. In the next section, I shall try to pinpoint the areas that in my opinion, need further reflection and even some self-questioning.

THE MODALITIES AND PITFALLS OF COUNTERING INTER-CULTURALISM

1. Essentialist Positions

To insist on differentiation, once the inter-culturalists have made short work of complex issues, is an effort to reclaim lost ground, to question the claim to authenticity. Yet here one is venturing on tricky terrrain. If one wishes to avoid relapsing into essentialist positions oneself, it becomes necessary to take stock at each stage of one's own vantage point. Unfortunately, in such encounters, the mechanisms of the debate often determine one's response to such an extent that one begins, while protesting against indiscriminate appropriation, in explicating traditional forms, to speak from a traditionalist position oneself, equating this position almost involuntarily with the Indian tradition at large. Though he explicitly points to the regional diversity of traditions in the country,[16] Bharucha's pioneering essays do not entirely escape this pitfall. This is particularly marked where the provocation is strong, such as in Brook's interpretation of the Mahabharata. Brook claims to represent the Indian ethos at large and it seems legitimate to question the authenticity of this, yet Brook does not really equate his work with any traditional Indian narrative or performative tradition. Bharucha's statement then insists on a standpoint that is not Brook's own: 'I respect his (Brook's) decision to create his own idiom of theatre and acting, but I regret that it has not absorbed some of the fundamental *principles* underlying traditional narratives in India. Without an understanding of these principles, I don't believe that the narratives make much sense' (Bharucha 1990: 105). Of course, the narrative has been reconceived in Western terms, for Brook has created his own idiom of theatre and acting. However, once Bharucha concedes this position, it appears to be little more than quibbling to question the radically different notion of time that underlies the reconceptualization of the narrative.

Perhaps Brook could have been more inventive in the juxtaposition of scenic sequences, yet can it be expected of the play, with its immensely dense narrative, that it have a different scheme of time, 'a sense of time that transcends chronology, time that stretches into infinity'? In Brook's play '(t)ime is truncated into blocks of action, acts and scenes that have definite beginnings and end' (105). Brook's repeated references to Shakespeare should however have alerted us to the theatrical lineage.[17]

The time scheme of traditional forms such as kathakali could only be transferred in a situation where the audiences were familiar with the rest of the cluster of episodes grouped around a particular sequence in the Mahabharata, only then would it be feasible to elaborate on a section of the narrative, on the micro-sequences that this in turn consists of, at any length. Further there is the question of the cyclicity that Bharucha sees as being characteristic of the Indian notion of time. The time scheme of traditional storytelling in other parts of the world and the epic construction of episodes have always had their own conventions, and these have been anything but linear, as the studies on oral epics, at least since the time of Parry and Lord, have conclusively shown. Though the scheme of rebirth does lend another dimension to the Indian concept of time, and here it is possible to generalize to some extent, the cyclicity is not peculiar to India alone. To posit then a peculiarly Indian sense of cyclical time is to relapse into the kind of binarism, with its insistence on a 'we', that a certain variety of Orientalism has always luxuriated in.[18] It is merely the other side of the coin.

In Bharucha's polemical piece on Grotowski's present paratheatrical work, there is similarly a strong 'we' while addressing him, which in its broad sweep, seems to shoot beyond the mark:

We are still in touch with our bodies without making an issue out of it.... It is still possible to meet a stranger and make him your friend. We don't think about these things, but I have a strong feeling that what you're talking about with so much (perhaps unintended) mysticism, is actually a very normal part of our every day lives in India. (ibid.: 61)

Now even though Bharucha is speaking of dailiness, the terms of his description are such that it is impossible to bypass the suspicion that some idealization and exoticization are at work here, though these are the very qualities that he criticizes in Grotowski's recent work.

When protesting about the idealization of Gandhi by Glass, there seems to be a similar inadvertent counter-idealization at work. The complexities of Gandhi's motivation, regarding non-violence, his concept of satyagraha, his insistence on cleanliness, notwithstanding his own statements regarding their constitution, have called forth much pyschological and psycho-analytic comment in recent years. Bharucha's reading seems largely to accept Gandhi's self-representation at face value. This occurs when for instance he speaks of

his unfailing need to mingle with people. Not only did he eat their food and comfort them, he unhesitatingly assumed menial tasks like sweeping the floor and cleaning the toilet. These actions were not made by him to set himself apart from men. On the contrary, they were made primarily to *undifferentiate* himself from other men. Just as he attempted to lose his will in the will of God, he endeavoured to immerse his actions in the action of men. (ibid.: 86)

The Mahatma saw himself very much as a leader of men, as his practice in the many *ashrams* he founded testifies. Similarly in his delineation of the principles of satyagraha, a leader was always called for. Satyagraha itself was a complex principle, which in practice was modified incessantly, in spite of the definitive statement he attempted in his *Satyagraha in South Africa*.

Thus there seems to be some inadvertent idealization at work when Bharucha makes the following comments: '*Satyagraha* may have inspired other political leaders, but it was never implemented by them with the uncompromising simplicity of Gandhi. He alone fully understood and exemplified his strategy of dealing with violence. Many of his own countrymen failed to accept the validity of *satyagraha*; they were aware of its potential to cause violence despite Gandhi's reiteration that *Satyagraha* was totally opposed to 'injuring the opponent' (ibid.: 90–1). Though his perception of the characters of the *Mahabharata* is penetrating and full of insights, there is some similar idealization: 'An actor playing Krishna should be more human than any other actor on stage, and yet, evoke a spiritual order of being; he should fill the stage with his energy, and yet, remain curiously detached' (ibid.: 107).

2. The Need to Re-contextualize

Bharucha makes an important point when he says that since India has so many living traditions, 'a director of any traditional literature related to India has both the advantage and *the responsibility* to confront traditional performances within their own aesthetic context'. And this, not in order to imitate, but so that it can 'inspire significant points of departure' (ibid.: 103). Brook seems to have failed to live up to this challenge. Yet Bharucha's response becomes problematic when he asks that the work, since it is so significant in its original habitat, continue in this new interpretation to have 'some bearing on the lives of the Indian people for whom the Mahabharata was written, and who continue to derive their strength from it' (97). Brook's Mahabharata is practically irrelevant if not incomprehensible for Indian viewers, though it may gratify the needs of a handful of Western-oriented viewers, for, as Bharucha's own analysis demonstrates so conclusively, the production was designed for the needs of Western audiences. What, however, can be expected of such a well-informed observer of the inter-cultural scenario as Bharucha, is some indication of the context in which Brook recreates the Mahabharata. What needs of Western audiences does it cater to, since it was such a towering success? There is more to the production than the visuals alone, as Bharucha suggests. Brook himself clearly states the context of his reading of the epic:

In the heart of the *Mahabharata* is destruction. When it starts, the *Mahabharata* is only about the gods, giving us the impression of an imaginary enchanted world which really doesn't concern us. But little by little, the mythical characters 'descend', they get involved with conflicts of ambition, love, jealousy, pride. The myth becomes theatre—a theatre of war. We are faced with the truth of violence and suffering, the same war as always. The *Mahabharata* is of our time. (in Schechner et al. 1986: 62)

The perspective is provided by the European view of war and destruction, coloured of course by Brook's own vision of human suffering—the kind of 'despondent nihilism' that Kenneth Tynan, in a perceptive interview many years ago, saw as being typical of Brook's work.[19] If it is despondent nihilism that Brook once again offers, it is in a new packaging: using the phraseology of 'New Age' which has almost become a part of everyday vocabulary, operating with concepts taken from 'Oriental' religions that sound familiar, well known, but that are deliberately left vague (Sebald 1988). They tend to mystify while at the same time holding out the promise of some kind of betterment to be achieved through an understanding of the inner depths of human beings. Despondency and diffuse hope: an extremely potent mixture. On the one hand, then, the violence and suffering reflect the European experience of war, address the real fears and apprehensions that people live with, on the other there is an offer of hope, associated with the diffusely articulated message of the Bhagavadgita, as further corroborated by Brook's own reading:

In the *Mahabharata* there is an appeal to a positive attitude. The *Mahabharata* tells a history that is as sombre, tragic, and terrible as our contemporary situation.... What does 'positive' mean? It is a word that takes us back to our starting point. And very concretely, that brings us to the heart of the *Bhagvad Gita*: do you stand back, do you act, or what? The question 'or what' is every one's question today, and to it the *Mahabharata* gives no answer. It simply gives immense nourishment. (in Schechner et al. 1986: 71)

The diffuse vocabulary used is compensated by the speed with which the episode is dealt with, since the whole is pressed into the five minutes Bharucha mentions; in the printed version it lasts through one and a half pages. Though he speaks of taking concrete recourse to the Bhagvadgita, Brook in fact has absolved himself of the responsibility of providing any concrete answer, he merely leads the viewer/reader into believing that there is one, somewhere, inherent in Krishna's teaching. Krishna leads Arjuna through *the tangled forest of illusion*. He begins to teach him the *ancient yoga of wisdom* and the *mysterious path of action.* He leads Arjuna through all the *fibres of his spirit.* He shows him *the deepest movements of his being* and his true battlefield where you need neither warriors nor arrows, where each man must fight alone. It is the most *secret knowledge.* He shows him *the whole truth;* he teaches him *how the world unfolds* (in Schechner et al. 1986: 160, my emphasis). With the use of this phraseology, evocative and imprecise, since it is nowhere explicated or used in a context that could further locate its significance, Arjuna's illusions and apprehensions are taken care of. This 'intellectual shallowness' (again a phrase coined by Tynan 1977) is obviously extremely effective, since it makes no excessive demands on the understanding, while catering to the needs of which the New Age movement is also one expression. Conceived on a vast popular scale and coupled with the impressive visuals that are also a hallmark of Brook's theatrical craft, the impact of the play is undeniable and deserves serious consideration.

I have dealt with the play at some length, because I believe that in order to be effectively unravelled, it is not enough to register protest about the inauthenticity of the Indian components alone. I believe that it needs to be understood and, if necessary, dismantled in its own context as well.

In the same vein, I should briefly like to take up Glass's opera again. First, there is the question of the appropriateness of the form, whether Gandhi in his insistence on asceticism is a fit subject for a form as opulent as opera. I believe that here Brecht's critique of opera is applied without adequate consideration of the terms of Glass's composition. The insistence on historicization cannot be laboured beyond a point. If satyagraha operates with symbols and signs, it would be necessary to gauge their depth and consistency. It is well to recall that a thinker as radical as Brecht, for all his polemics, had asked that as a result of the unreality that music contributes to real processes on stage, the effort be made to create a third reality on stage. This complex third reality was to be distinguished from the everyday reality of the world; this could in its turn have very real effects.[20] The historicity of the figure of Gandhi, in order to retain its effectiveness, would not need to be exactly reproduced. It could be heightened, foregrounded in a number of ways through the musical score. Thus, even according to a theoretician as stern as Brecht, the operatic form in itself could well cope both with the asceticism and the historicism of the figure. Gandhi's asceticism was ideologically grounded, it was not based necessarily on any actual paucity of means. It was even considered by some to be carefully groomed. It was, as all else connected to him, a highly self-conscious projection of an image. There is really no reason why opera as a form should not further highlight this image. Glass's musical score is anything but sweet and mellifluous, it has a nervous energy; motifs which sound serene emphasize the more the tremulous, threatening, gasping rhythms they are set against.[21]

It is, of course a question of how the whole is finally staged. Achim Freyer's Stuttgart production (1984) projects Gandhi as one figure among many, or even as a lonely figure, who is visualized as struggling against forces that almost overwhelm him, forces that seem more apocalyptic than paradisical. The libretto then, the *shlokas* from the Bhagvadgita, if at all one cares to follow the translation, wins additional dimensions once it is regarded not so much as a message, as triumphant proclamation of ends already achieved, but as a programme of ends still to be achieved. Though one could find fault with the pathos of ending the opera with Krishna's promise of incarnating himself again and again in times of destruction, in the American context it has some significance. In the civil rights movement, and specifically for Martin Luther King, Gandhi was avowedly a model, and invoking him in the early 1980s, when civil rights no longer played any significant role in public discourse, could even be considered an act of some political significance. We might not agree with this conceptualization of Gandhi, but the Americanization of Gandhi also has its own history, which needs to be considered in its own context. As Mark Juergensmeyer has retraced it, the powerful image of Gandhi as an almost Christian saint, 'a perfect combination of religion and social concern', was established early in the West.[22] His almost naked figure, clad sparsely in home-spun, his ascetic diet, his abstinence from sex, evoked strong religious associations.[23] This image of the Christian saint might not have been shared by his immediate followers in India, but notwithstanding Juergensmeyer's proposition to the contrary, the Mahatma was sanctified early in India also (cf. Amin 1984).

Given the widespread idolization of Gandhi, what Glass attempts seems in comparison to be even somewhat of an understatement, and his effort to couple it in some way with the American civil rights movement at that point in time could even be interpreted as a fairly radical gesture.

The two points I have tried to make here are then, first, that inter-culturalist inauthenticity cannot be answered back with 'authenticity' alone, because in doing so the very dichotomization that is to be resisted is validated, even reinstated. The 'we' cannot be entirely resisted, but it is important not to fall back into generalizations; it is imperative that we qualify incessantly the statements which do have to be made. Similarly the 'West' cannot be regarded as a monolith. Even if it is not possible to do away with the category, there are internal differentiations that need to be made, contexts which need to be worked out. The response that the Mahabharata evoked needs to be viewed not globally, then, as valid for all of the West; instead it might be fruitful to consider the response of single countries. I know for instance that many in Germany viewed it as reflecting their own experience of the devastation and futility of the Second World War. The dramatization by Brook and Carrière needs, in its turn, to be historicized as well.

ALTERNATIVE MODALITIES

Even though the inter-culturalist encounter can entrap the most wary into taking 'essentialist' stands, Bharucha certainly cannot stand accused of not being aware that both Indian and 'traditional' theatre are most complex entities. In the following I recapitulate briefly an encounter with 'traditional' theatre in its modern-day setting: the performance of *Krishnattam* on the temple premises of Guruvayur in Kerala. Here Bharucha creates a narrative that beautifully demonstrates how well the aesthetics of performance can blend with its history and ethnology.

In his study of Krishnattam, appropriately entitled 'Preparing for Krishna', Bharucha offers a specimen of the approach that he considers an alternative to both the Western fascination with structure and technique alone, as also to the Indian tendency to amass facts in scholarly terms, to draw upon the terminology of the *Natya Shastra*, and then refine upon it endlessly; which last seems to fix the form in changeless stasis. Bharucha's own approach is multi-layered, as befitting the multi-layered texture of the performance itself. He manages, while conveying a good measure of the experience of the play—the aesthetics and erotics of the performance—to interweave—manipulate the perspective as he calls it—his narrative with historical, ethnological, and social information; this in order to view the play as a socio-historical continuum, rather than as fixed in time. I shall touch very briefly on the piece, only indicating its method and approach, since its eminently literary quality cannot be reproduced, nor the information it contains be adequately summed up in an essay.

Bharucha distinguishes thereby between the dramatic text, the Sanskrit *padam*s and shlokas of the *Krishnagithi*, which were created by Manavdevan, the Zamorin of Calicut (who reigned from 1655 to 1658), and the performance text, which has evolved since that period, even independently of the Manavdevan's text, to which it does not always adhere. The recent, somewhat pedantic, Sanskritizing tendency followed by the younger gurus, has been to establish a closer correspondence between the narrative and the choreography. There was, according to Bharucha, possibly a social reason for the separation between song and dance. The Sanskrit text of the song could only be recited by the Brahmans and the Ambalavasis, the temple-serving caste; the other castes, including the Nairs, could only act and dance. So the two were separately learned activities. (In *koodiyattam* the performers are mostly Chakyars, the highest-ranking Ambalavasis, thus the close correspondence between narrative and choreography in this kind of theatre.) Of the fifty-six members of the present troupe, thirty-seven are Nairs.

Krishnattam has a ritual framework; it is rooted in devotion, 'The actors offer themselves to Krishna through their performance, which in turn serves as a medium through which the spectators can direct their devotion' (Bharucha 1990: 225). Yet as an offering it has clearly pragmatic functions as well. Devotees donate a performance, as a payment of fees to the temple authorities, in accordance with the family occasion that they wish to celebrate. Though the performance can be expensive, the troupe is booked out for weeks in advance.

The play is restricted to performance by a single troupe, which is now no longer under the patronage of the Zamorin but operates instead under the surveillance of the temple bureaucracy. Correspondingly the performance now no longer consists of a series of presentations in the temples between Calicut, where the troupe was formerly housed, and Guruvayur, but is confined to the premises of the temple in Guruvayur. It may have been the Sanskrit of the text which restricted the spread of the form, as against the Malayalam kathakali, which was adopted by a number of troupes. On the other hand, both unlike kathakali and koodiyattam, the gestures are not strongly codified, so that it retains a popular character, *lokadharmi*, as Bharucha terms it, and remains therefore easily accessible to the audience of devotees. The whole consists of blending together of the performance of an ensemble, rather than of any star or virtuoso performer operating in isolation. Yet the performance as well as the troupe are held together by Krishna. 'It is the child in Krishna who gives Krishnattam its naive wonder' (ibid.: 240).

Bharucha gives a vivid description, one amongst many such, of the episode when the heron-demon Bakasura is killed, the fanciful gear of the demon, the springing hopping movements which accompany the narrative rather than illustrate it. Bharucha's description of the *raskrida* forms the climax of the piece. It is at once lyrical and pragmatic in its registration of the interplay of the reality of the actors and the reality of performance.

One cannot hide behind rationality and scholarship, one has to open oneself to experience. It might seem fanciful, but the writer of Krishnattam has to be a gopi in spirit, a participant in the field of desire where there is a reciprocal play between lover and god, man and woman, spectator and actor. (ibid.: 246)

That in this circular dance around the god, the *gopi*s, as well as Radha are played by males, serves further to emphasize the androgynous nature of the erotics of Krishna worship. Though the movements off-stage are casually male, the costumes of the gopis are so designed as to cover all signs of maleness, and the one blends into the other. Through the slow, graceful movements of the looping dance of the gopis around Krishna, through the tender dalliance of Radha with her god, the audience, consisting largely of women and children, becomes a participant in the 'field of desire' as well.

If at all I would question any aspect of Bharucha's presentation, it would be to ask that terms taken from the *Natyshastra*, themselves not static in their functionality, be more precisely located in their present usage. There is, I would agree, a problem in taking over terms current in Western performance theory. I would also agree that when Schechner uses terms such as 'score' and 'flow' (Bharucha 1990: 43), they have a cover-up function, rather than any explicatory value. Yet the problem is obviously not solved by replacing these with indigenous terms. Essentially of course, there is no reason why technical terms from the *Natyashastra* cannot be reused and relocated in contemporary writing; that it is as valid an exercise as for instance using the vocabulary created by Bakhtin, which is also not invalidated simply because it stems from the West, but in each case the terms would need to be used with some precision. The two key concepts that Bharucha uses are *lokadharmi* and *natyadharmi*. Even if the English translation can only remain inaccurate, so that the terms are to be explicated by their usage 'in a specific performance context (necessarily culture-bound)' as he proposes to demonstrate in the context of Krishnattam, the usage alone cannot by itself convey, as he maintains 'a precise meaning and resonance' (Bharucha 1990: 248). In effect, his usage of lokadharmi covers a variety of functions, it does amount to something like 'resembling the gestures of daily life', 'realistic', 'popular', 'improvised', meanings that he resists as inadequate, when used by other interpreters. The problem of devising an adequate conceptual apparatus is a very real one, perhaps only approximations can be aimed at. Yet it needs to be addressed and the various easily used terms such as 'lokadharmi' be more precisely defined in their current usage.

Through Bharucha's observations, brilliant, scintillating, and provocative, initiated a discussion almost two decades ago, the issues that he raised have yet to come up in broader public discussion. What does 'Indian' signify in the early twenty-first century? Have we ceased to essentialize in projecting ourselves and in resisting the projections of others? And most of all, have we ceased to see Hindu India as all of India?

Notes

[1] Fischer-Lichte et al. (1990: 5). See also the special double issue on interculturalism of *Performing Arts Journal*, 33/34.

[2] Bharucha has written extensively on the political theatre of 1970s Bengal (1983).

[3] Cited in Bharucha (1990: 22).

[4] Cited in ibid.: 17.

[5] Cited in ibid.: 71.

[6] In this connection, Barba's workshop production in Salente, Italy, of Goethe's *Faust* (1987) is of considerable interest, a production in which the Japanese *buyo* dancer, Katsuko Azuma, and the Indian odissi dancer Sanjukta Panigrahi, played Faust and Mephisto respectively. As Patrice Pavis in his singularly perceptive analysis of the play pointed out: 'The function of this adaptation is also to erode codified theatrical or choreographic forms that are too specifically honed to a single culture and performance tradition, the better to adapt to the audience's universalizing demands. Thus, the human and dramatizing situation becomes immediately comprehensible, without the mediation of an artistic code and specific theatrical forms. This flattening is the price paid for the spectator's comfortable reception of what Barba calls the pre-expressive, what we might call an ideology or universal psychology.' The transcultural values, striving, temptation, fall, which then emerge are diluted and very general. Pavis (1989: 48).

[7] As against Schechner's theories regarding transportation of ritual, Bharucha (1990) emphasizes the difference between authentic and fabricated ritual. Apart from lack of skill, accuracy, belief, the travesty of ritual must lead to a loss of the significance of the original. It is thus not only a question of misrepresentation, the performance of rituals outside their own context can lead to commodification, even of such powerful, potent rituals as death rituals (44–5).

[8] Quoted in Bharucha 1990: 39.

[9] Nationalist discourse tended, for all its resistance to imperialism, to integrate the Orientalist construction of the classical tradition into its own conceptualization of tradition, as we saw in the last chapters. Post-colonial elites show little hesitation in adopting much of this rhetoric, which was taken over by the inter-culturalists, on occasions such as for the production of publicity material for the Festivals of India organized by the Government of India in the 1980s and 1990s.

[10] One can borrow, extract, transform, but there remains the question, as posed by Bharucha, of the committment to the cultures, from which these borrowings are made. For certain aspects of the kind of 'barter' practised by Eugenio Barba for instance, egalitarian in themselves, Bharucha can have unqualified admiration. This kind of barter was born when an improvised

performance by the Odin Teatret in an open square in Lecce, Italy, prompted the spectators to sing songs in exchange. Yet Barba's International School of Theatre Anthropology has become an established institution, with the power to alter perceptions of theatre, so that the position from which exchange is effected is obviously different from the one a decade ago (1990: 82).

[11] Brook was asked in an interview by Ananda Lal:

Have you read Rustom Bharucha's essay criticizing your 'blatant appropriation of Indian culture?' Brooks' answer would seem legitimate enough: 'We're telling the story of the Mahabharata. We are not becoming spokesmen for Indian culture. We're approaching this as part of the common heritage of man, like Shakespeare; one could make the same comment on every part of the world where non-English people do Shakespeare. Certain geniuses like Shakespeare make works that belong to mankind. This work of course could not have existed without India any more than Shakespeare could have existed without England (Ananda Lal 1992: 301).

But, as pointed out above, no Shakespeare production in the non-West, would claim to have produced an authoritative version of Shakespeare. Further, as Ananda Lal pointed out in his own essay on the production:

Therefore to ask Brook why he chose the Mahabharata and not the *Iliad* or the *Odyssey* (epics nearer to this cultural ethos) is, to use his own words, a 'false question'. He has merely supplied the world with his own reading of our epic.... The trouble arises when he tries to pass off his Mahabharata as the Mahabharata. Explicitly credited to Carrière and himself though it may be, the very fact that it is to date the only Western production of the Mahabharata gives it a sort of fake authenticity that may need debunking (ibid.: 203).

[12] As Carrière himself specifies in an interview: 'I was so immersed in the poem, so familiar with it, that I discovered relationships betwen the characters and things that nobody realized. The familiarity enabled me to imagine scenes that don't exist in the poem but that are possible. Once you know the characters, you play with them. You make this one meet that one—almost half the scenes don't exist in the original text' (Schechner et al. 1986: 74).

[13] Bhattacharya (1992: 285–6). The review had appeared originally in *Mother India*, Pondicherry.

[14] I miss a discussion of her work in this otherwise exhaustive analysis of the Western use of Indian theatre.

15 Franz Norbert Mennemeier in a short sketch of the development of the European interest in the East, points out that the 'eternal Orient', a phrase first coined by Schlegel, had no precise topography. The respective visions of it and their incorporation into the arts were 'a way of transcending the well-known own element in order to go back to the wild and shocking foreign, the "other" element within the own' (Fischer-Lichte et al. 1990: 25).

16 'It is only by respecting the specificities of our "regional" cultures that we in India can begin to understand how much we have in common.... At this stage, it seems that the particularities are being prematuraely dissolved in larger, nebulous categories like the Euro-American tradition, not to mention the "Indian" tradition' (Bharucha 1990: 48–9). This insight is not always integrated into his own analysis.

17 The change of genre from epic narrative to drama is one important factor that also needs to be considered with reference to the time scheme. A good example from the Sanskrit drama tradition would be Bhasa's *Karnabhara* which assembles, for purposes of dramatic density, episodes from different parts of the epic and puts them into a new and much tighter chronological time sequence. The time scheme of forms like kathakali and even of *kudiyattam* with its 'flashback' technique—does not appear 'cyclical' or 'summary' but stresses sequence within the episodes selected from the epic. These have distinctive beginnings and ends. The episode as part of the whole works out a particular aspect of the latter and in so far also reflects the whole.

18 In statements such as the following: 'Can a story be separated from the ways in which it is told to its own people? We Indians are known for our circumlocutions. When we are describing a family quarrel or the plot of a Hindi film, we never get to the point. Always, the elaboration is more important than the thrust of the narrative. There is no steady progression in our narratives from exposition to complication to climax to dénouement, as in the well-made play. For us, the climaxes are at the very beginning, while the complications invariably stimulate new beginnings. Time never seems to matter—a story lasts for as long as there is need for it' (Bharucha 1990: 106). Apart from the fact that plot-construction rules are very precisely laid down in manuals such as *Dasharupaka* (*Arambha, prayatna, praptyasha, niyatapti, phalagama*), in making these generalizations about the Indian sense of time, Bharucha seems to be falling back on stereotypes of the East.

19 Analysing Brook's early work, Tynan made the following pertinent observations, which seem applicable to the present work as well:

Lear, which very much impressed me at the time, was, of course based very much on Jan Kott's view of the play and its connection with Beckett and *Endgame*. I think the connection with Beckett, and the philosophy behind him, gave Peter a justification for the world view which was later to become dominant in his work. Now, if I could sum up the world view, it would be this: that human beings, left to themselves, stripped of social restraints, are animals, and are inherently rotten, and destructive. You might call it a ritualistic misanthropy: and it has been the driving force behind Brook's work from the early sixties onwards (1977).

[20] Even though Brecht polemicized against the culinary effect of the opera of his day, he was careful not to ask for the more obvious kind of historic realism in its stead. As he specified in the notes to the opera *Mahagonny* (1927), for which Kurt Weill composed the music, and where he first formulated his theory of epic theatre, music made for its own complex kind of realism (Brecht [1967] 1976 vol. 17, 1007).

[21] His music is based on the extended repetition of brief, elegant melodic fragments that weave in and out of an aural tapestry. Listening to this music is something like watching a challenging painting that initially appears static, but seems to metamorphose slowly as one concentrates. Compositional material is usually limited to a few elements, which are then subjected to a transformational process. One shouldn't expect Westernized musical events—sforzandos, sudden dinuendos—in this music; rather... a sonic weather that surrounds, twists, turns, develops. Glass prefers to speak of his work as 'music with repetitive structures.' His busy, tonal, aggressively rhythmic compositions would seem to mark a spiritual break with the spare, atonal and largely arhythmic world of the 50's and 60's *avant-gardists*. (Page 1980).

[22] See Hawley (1987). Further material in Gatfield (1976).

[23] He reminded Willy Pearson, who visited Gandhi along with C.F. Andrews in South Africa in 1914, of St Francis of Assisi. As John Haynes Holmes, an American clergyman, wrote in 1921: 'When I think of Gandhi, I think of Jesus Christ. He lives his life; he speaks his word; he suffers, strives, and will some day nobly die, for his kingdom upon earth.' This avid and vociferous following was to keep up a stream of publications through the 1930s and 1940s.

LERdhi as Mahatma. Gorakhpur District, Eastern U.P.CES*

Amin, Shahid. 1984. 'Gandhi as Mahatma. Gorakhpur District, Eastern U.P. 1921–1922', in *Subaltern Studies III*, Ranajit Guha (ed.). Delhi: Oxford University Press.

Bharucha, Rustom. 1983. *Rehearsal of Revolution: The Political Theater of Bengal.* Honolulu: University of Hawaii Press, Calcutta: Seagull Books.

——. 1990. *Theatre and the World: Essays on Performance and Politics of Culture.* Delhi: Manohar.

Bhattacharya, Pradip. 1992. 'Brook's *Mahabharata*—The Film', in *Vyasa's Mahabharata*, P. Lal (ed.). Volume 2.

Brecht, Bertolt. 1976. *Gesammelte Werke* [Collected Works]. 20 volumes. Frankfurt: Suhrkamp.

Carrière, Jean Claude. 1988. *The Mahabharata.* Translated from the French by Peter Brook. London: Methuen.

Elam, Keir. 1980. *The Semiotics of Theatre and Drama.* London and New York: Methuen.

Fischer–Lichte, Erika, et al. (eds.) 1990. *The dramatic touch of difference: theatre, own and foreign.* Tübingen: Gunter Narr.

Gatfield, Charles. (ed.) 1976. *The Americanization of Gandhi: Images of the Mahatma.* New York and London: Garland Publishing,

Gillespie, Marie. 1990. 'The Mahabharata: From the Sanskrit to Sacred Soap. A Case Study Exploring the Reception of Two Contemporary Televisual Productions of the Mahabharata'. Paper presented at 40th International Communication Association Annual Conference, June 1990, Dublin.

Hawley, John Stratton. 1987. 'Saint Gandhi', in *Saints and Virtues*, John S. Hawley (ed.). Berkeley: University of California Press.

Jeyifous, Biodoun. 1990. 'The reinvention of theatrical tradition: Critical discourses on inter-culturalism in the African Theatre', in *The dramatic touch of difference*, Fischer-Lichte et al (eds.).

Lal, Ananda. 1992. 'From Sagar to Brook,' and '"All Theatre Lives by Surprise": Peter Brook interviewed by Ananda Lal', in *Vyasa's Mahabharata*, P. Lal (ed.), Volume 2.

Lal, P. (ed.) 1992. *Vyasa's Mahabharata: Creative Insights.* In 2 volumes. Calcutta: Writer's Workshop.

Mennemeier, Franz Norbert. 1990. 'The Own and the Foreign Orient.

Schlegel, Nietzsche, Artaud, Brecht: Notes on the process of a Reception', in *The dramatic touch of difference*, Fischer-Lichte et al. (eds.).

Page, Tim. 1980. 'Satyagraha: The Sense of Peace', in the booklet accompanying the disc: *Satyagraha*. Produced by Kurt Munkacsi and Michael Riesman. Performed by the New York City Opera and Orchestra. Dir. Christopher Keene. CBS Masterworks. E3M39672.

Pavis, Patrice. 1989. 'Dancing with Faust: A Semiotician's Reflections on Barba's Inter-cultural Mise-en-scène', in *TDR* 33/3 (T123) Fall 1989.

Performing Arts Journal. 1989. Special double issue on inter-culturalism. 11/3, 12/1.

Said, Edward. [1978] 1985. *Orientalism*. Harmondsworth: Penguin Books.

Schechner, Richard and Mathilde La Bardoonie, Joel Jounneau and George Banu. 1986. 'The Mahabharata. Talking with Peter Brook'. Interviews by Schechner et al in *TDR*, 30/1 (T109), Spring.

Sebald, Hans. 1988. 'New-Age-Spiritualität', in *Kursbuch 93*, September, 105–22.

Tynan, Kenneth. 1977. 'Director as Misanthropist: on the Moral Neutrality of Peter Brook', in *Theatre Quarterly*, 8/25.

'I Am a Hindu'
Assertions and Queries

At the close of the twentieth century, the fixed assumptions on which IPTA enthusiasts had once operated, had long since ceased to be regarded as affording a sound base for theatre with any political intent. Nationalism had been hijacked by the Hindu Right and Indianness debased by its commercialization in the global market. The 'masses' that IPTA had once set out to address had been consigned to a folksiness, which prettified rural arts in order to serve as the backdrop to urban needs. Even this folksiness was to give way to the theatre of 'roots', which subsumed folk traditions once again under the larger umbrella of the 'traditional' and relegated them to the subterranean. And lastly, the space created by the radical feminist movements of the 1970s and 1980s was coming, at least partially, to be occupied by the firebrand rhetoric of Right Wing Hindu women ideologues, who assimilated the emancipatory idiom under the old heads of 'wife' and 'mother', allowing for some agency that could, however, only move within the well-defined parameters of Hindutva (see Sarkar 2001).

However, brittle or not, the labels, nation and nationalism, tradition and roots, Hindutva and Hindu woman, enjoyed wide circulation and in the hands of demagogues could at all times serve vital mobilizing functions. The challenge of prising open the categories in circulation, of questioning stereotypes and the very basis on which they operated, was taken up by a set of women directors, largely concentrated in Delhi and the North, acquainted with each other, yet working autonomously and in very different experimental idioms. I shall discuss their work briefly, tracing the range of operational modes and the converging and diverging strands, before focusing on one production, an adaptation of Rabindranath Tagore's novel *Gora* (1910) which engages with notions of identity and gender, particularly with Hinduness, at a crucial period in the subcontinent's history: the mounting communal tension of the late 1980s which would lead to the destruction of the Babri Masjid.

IPTA had, as in so many other spheres, played a pioneering role in paving the way for women to play a crucial role both as artistes and directors in the performing arts by making culture a broad-based nationalist concern. Shanta and Dina Gandhi (later Pathak) had played a leading role in the Association's activities, as also Zohra Sehgal, and from the 1950s, directors such as Sheila Bhatia had worked in Delhi; Bhatia called her peculiar mix of rural and urban 'Punjabi Opera'. Joy Michaels was director of Yatrik, one of the most active English-language theatre groups in the capital. In Bengal, there were at least two well-known women directors, Usha Ganguly, foregrounding social concerns in the best IPTA lineage, and Saoli Mitra, known all over India for her brilliant solo performance, as director and sole actress in *Nathabati Anathabat*, which dramatized the plight of Draupadi, who in the last instance was left to fend for herself, in spite of her five husbands. And Vijaya Mehta was to play a pioneering role in combinng the folk traditions of the region with the modern in a broad range of plays in Bombay from the 1960s on.

WOMEN DIRECTORS OF THE 1990s

It was from their midst that the avant-garde work of women directors of the 1990s emerged. It took up the many strands that had evolved through the post-Independence decades, the folk, the classical, Western high bourgeois, but also the feminist and the cinematic, to weave together into a self-reflective modernist idiom. The particular focus as also the idiom differed vastly. Kirti Jain, who had served as director of the National School of Drama, working in the liberal tradition spawned by IPTA, dramatized works such as Urvashi Butalia's *The Other Side of Silence*, relating the experience particularly of the women and children, who had survived the trauma of Partition. In Chandigarh, Neelam Man Singh, who had worked with B.V. Karanth in Bhopal and was to enter into long-term collaborative work with him, reverted to the folk idiom in a novel way, working with the performance traditions of Punjab, but in an ensemble made up of urban and rural artistes, who pooled together their knowledge of a range of performance traditions, to explore the multiple facets of female sexuality, of womanhood, and of motherhood. Words, music, movement formed their own texts that clashed or came together in the dissonances of a heightened everyday. The musical score of Man Singh's plays was generally composed by Karanth; the compilation of the play script, reworked and adapted from novels as much as from plays, was often in collaboration with the well-known Punjabi poet, Surjit Singh Pattar. If Neelam Man Singh turned to the folk repertoire in her explorations, Maya Rao, brought the intense grace and versatility of the highly codified kathakali, of which she was a trained performer, to create angular modernist performances that ranged from abstract symbolism to political cabaret. She transported the gestural language of kathakali onto the bare modern stage, and shorn of costume and make-up, the performance gained another kind of power, at once expressive and impassive.

Anamika Haksar, trained in the erstwhile Soviet Union, with her deep insight into Stanisklavskian modes of exploring interiority and its externalization in narrative, and her subsequent, equally formative training in the National School of Drama under B.V. Karanth, dramatized works as different as the Tamil epic *Silappadhikaran*, and Dostoyevsky's *The Idiot*, to explore the overlapping selves of wife and courtesan, ascetic and madman. The range was immense. If Tripurari Sharma, playwright and director, elected to work with marginalized groups, peasants, factory workers, slum-dwellers, most often women and children, to produce and direct plays about and sometimes with them, Amal Allana worked most often with the monumental. She staged a spectacular *King Lear* with veteran character-actor Manohar Singh in a memorable performance as the king. But she also cast Manohar

Singh as *Himmat Mai* in the play of the same name, a Hindi adaptation of Brecht's *Mother Courage*. She dropped standard Hindi to use the regional languages of the Hindi belt, but with the kind of deliberation that had come a long way from the folksy dialect adaptations of the 1980s. She has described the process of discovering the format she and Manohar Singh finally found for a Brecht play that had acquired canonical status in the classic performance by an actress as powerful as Helene Weigel.

Manohar Singh was beginning to evolve the 'gestures, postures, gait and stance' of a woman performing domestic tasks. However, in order to ensure that he did not disappear into the role, it was decided that his voice remain unchanged. Yet it was an awkward fit. He sounded more like a eunuch than like a man playing a woman. Allana's casual suggestion that he speak like a woman from his native Himachal changed the whole cast of the play. With the musical sing-song of Himachali, 'a certain feminine quality seemed to seep in through the words, now spoken with a peculiar rhythm and lilt', locating the character firmly in a specific landscape and shifting the location of the entire play to the northern mountains and central plains. Manohar Singh, who had been an eminently 'male' actor, could recur creatively to his Himachali past; his father had been a female impersonator, though he based the figure of Himmat Mai as it evolved on his mother. The Hindi broadcaster and translator Neelabh, who was writing the script, was asked to transfer it from Hindi to Himachali, interspersing it with Haryanvi, northern Punjabi, and Bhojpuri, the regions through which Himmat Mai would pull her covered wagon; a broad language belt, 'encompassing the much vaster sense of territory, which helped to give the play a certain epic dimension' (Allana 2002: 176–8).

Allana also experimented with shifting gender identities, of being a woman, becoming a woman, in her next play: the Hindi version of Satish Altekar's Marathi play, *Begum Barve*, in which an old actor who had once played bit parts, enacts the grand roles of the Marathi stage performed by Bal Gandharva, the legendary female impersonator of the Marathi stage.

There was a sense of whimsical innocence in Manohar Singh's portrayal of Barve, a certain transparency and guilelessness to this old actor's yearning to play female roles and through them live out his deepest fantasies. In visually trying to represent the male-female aspects of his divided self, we clothed him in a wispy, shredded, skin-toned kurta–dhoti which, in a sense, became a statement of his nakedness and vulnerability, both actual and metaphoric. On this was planted, in the second half of the play, a practically clown-like painted female face. The foundation was whitish-pink (generally used by folk performers to appear fair, upper caste or as divinities), bringing into sharp contrast the lurid bright red lips, pink cheeks and kajalled eyes. (183)

It is impossible to do justice in this brief survey to the range of experiment in the theatre work of this last decade and a half, which is by no means confined to women directors alone.[1] But they figure prominently therein and their work does have certain features in common. It slits open the certainties of gender roles, of the stereotype of wife, mother, and courtesan, and it dissolves the boundaries between public and private, between outer and inner selves. The old definitions of character no longer hold. As Anuradha Kapur, whose work I will introduce in the following discussion, points out,

This is in a sense a rejection (especially via Bertolt Brecht) of essence, of psychological characterization, which is often seen as making what it is—without which that something would have been something else—as constituting unique individual identity.... In order to highlight the idea of character as a product, a focal point of forces (desire, loss, fulfillment, plenitude among others) rather than a sum and substance of basic nature, an intact and impervious and determined agent, the cultural aggregation that the world makes sense, is overturned and replaced by a condition in which words and actions can be incompatible, creating their own inner logic, resilient patterns, unpredictability. Consequently in some feminist work, plot is frequently circular, and refuses any resolution, character can change status, personality, and even gender, crossing society's often artificially maintained boundaries of gender roles; and objects can bring about social relationships, realities and imaginary landscapes (as in Neelam Mansingh and Anamika Haksar's work). Thus coherent structures, traditional plot devices, and a dependence on dialogic communication are derailed and called into question in order to unsettle expectations of portrayals. (Kapur 2001: 6–7)

These layered portrayals are then again viewed from multiple perspectives. The body of the play is not constituted by words alone, thus the importance of gesture and gestus, of music and visuals, which serve as parallel texts. The choreography of the whole is a collective process, the parallel texts 'put in place a different set of authorial and professional relationships' (5). This layerdness has particular significance for the performance of gender:

If the body is a social script then the performance of gender is a social act governed and engineered by codes that are embedded in prevailing social structures. Women directors are concerned to surface and make visible this process of gendering: the process of showing, after Judith Butler, how bodies are 'materialized as sexed': how men and women are made. Shifting the elements of gender, of the social codes of masculinity and femininity, would mean destablizing them and refocusing on them. This destablization has a modernist history; Bertolt Brecht's *Good Person of Sezuan* comes immediately to mind as a strongly ideological restructuring of the elements of gender. Lately life scripts such as these [Mother Courage: *Himmat Mai*, Manohar Singh] are not authored alone or singularly—these are social scripts formed by communities and individuals alike and may be full of contradictions that might not be resolved or brought together in a powerfully coherent or focused narrative. (Kapur 2001: 10–11)

The Vivadi Collective

Anuradha Kapur is director and coordinator of the plays staged by the Vivadi Collective since the late 1980s. Kapur is an unusual combination of a finely analytical and articulate theatre scholar, who has written an extensive study of a traditional form, the *Ramlila* of Ramnagar, as also an avant-garde director, who has not shied away from taking risks. She has worked since 1989 with Vivadi, an artiste's collective of which she is a co-founder, to produce plays which range from Tagore to Brecht, from a late-nineteenth-century Urdu novel to the autobiography of Jaishankar Sundari, a famed female impersonator of the early twentieth century. A play that has gratified a large number of audiences has been the fresh interpretation of an old favourite: *Umrao*, the dramatization of a famous turn-of-the-nineteenth-century Urdu novel, the first-person narrative of a famous *tawaif*, courtesan, of Lucknow.[2] In the novel, Umrao had reminisced in old age, acquiring the figure of youth as her narrative progressed from girlhood to full-fledged womanhood. In the play, it was the process of ageing, of age, which was present throughout. Kapur chose to cast the middle-aged Uttara Baorkar, one of the most versatile character-actresses of the Hindi stage, in the leading role. Her lack of coquetry as Umrao was a figuration crucial for the self-understanding sought while reminiscing: it was her middle-aged body that went back in time to inhabit the world of ephemeral youth. Umrao herself was seen from multiple perspectives:

This emphasis on point of view produces a character with dissolving contours, a character that appears, if you like, frame within frame. Just as Umrao sees people in many personae, so do *they* see her from many perspectives. The coherent constitution of *tawaif* is dispersed, to be located in many subjectivities. This delicate balance of constructing a subject which is itself made up by a crisscross of subjectivities requires flexibility with respect to performance. (Kapur 2001: 8)

The changing skies of the beautiful set of images recalling miniature painting, which could be wheeled in and out, were conceived and painted by well-known artist Neelima Sheikh.

The script was a literary transcreation by Geetanjali Shree, avant-garde Hindi novelist and short-story writer. Geetanjali Shree's first novel, *Mai*, was a nuanced portrayal of the mother written with an honesty and intimacy as yet untried in Hindi, and the second, *Hamara shahar us baras* (Our town, that year), was a deeply troubled and finely honed reading of communal antagonisms and violence in a university town in north India. Geetanjali Shree's handling of the *Umrao* script was an open and multi-layered process:

Her readings are aggregates, as it were, for performance, as they question the nature of subjectivity. Subjectivity is not seen as unified sovereign rational consciousness but as something that is discursively produced, encompassing unconscious and subconscious dimensions of the self and implying contradictions, process and change. (8)

Music in Vivadi productions is an integral part of the narrative, it was particularly so in *Umrao Jan*, woven as it was around the life of a poet and dancer-singer of high calibre. It was chosen and rendered by Vidya Rao, a performer known most of all for her rendition of *thumri*, the form honed to such high perfection in courtesan culture.[3]

There was similar cooperation of art forms, visual and performative, in *The Job* (1997), a deeply moving dramatization of a short story by Bertolt Brecht, with immediate political implications in an economy industrializing at a brutally fast pace. A man long unemployed finds a job as a watchman only to die of ill health on his way to the factory where he is to work. These are the years of the Great Depression and his family hovers on the brink of starvation. His wife decides to slip into his role to take up his position as a watchman. Her disguise is discovered when she is injured in a factory accident. The set consisted of an extensive installation by well-known artist Nalini Malani. There were a series of objects:

food jars which are inverted and contain plastic foetuses, grains and other food stuff, are akin to the subversion of the nurturing function of the breasts, These lead to what Malani terms the 'memory membrane'—a film which reveals like a subtext, the inner space of the woman. The sepia on the screen deepens, then becomes bound by black, then erased like a continuous flux of emotions and identity. On the other side is a peep-show and a silver tent, which is a kaleidoscope, zooming in on the woman, sewing mechanically. Heaped cardboard cartons form the walls of the theatre space in which the large pistons, painted by Malani, are suspended...made of acrylic sheets, these cylinders are painted in reverse, each carrying images provoked by the story.[4]

Malani worked with the acute awareness of the live performance which would once again transform the objects she had assembled: 'I've tried to work a presence into various objects—including the sets and costumes. In fact, many of the things I've planned will come alive only because of the performance.'[5]

This intensely interactive process of creation contributes to the subtle layeredness which has become characteristic of Vivadi's very different creations, which range from the creative ingenuity of a woman factory worker masquerading as a man to the process of artistic creation itself, as in *Sundari: An Actor Prepares* (1998). The actor Jaishankar Sundari (1889–1975) acquired the name after he played Sundari (Desdemona) in an adaptation of *Othello*. Vivadi's play was in its turn an adaptation of Sundari's autobiography, once again by Geetanjali Shree, focusing on his most active years (1901–32) as female impersonator in the Gujarati Natak Mandali, and working within the conventions of the Parsi theatre, then at the peak of its popularity. Kapur has written about the multi-layered composition of the narrative:

The visual narrative is layered, so the narrative of the auto/biography is layered by presenting thirty years of Sundari's performing life in three parts, three different bodies, three presences, three sexualities that describe a career from childhood, to young adulthood, to middle age. The child Sundari is almost ungendered and so is the middle-aged one. They are the brackets within which the youthful Sundari glides. Both man/woman and woman/man, he pulls towards himself the desire of both men and women. These three stylisations code femininity equally in skill, costumes, deportment, convention and fantasy. (Kapur 2001: 104)

I reproduce here a part of the interview held with three central figures in this production, Anuradha Kapur, Geetanjali Shree, and Vidya Rao, since it so vividly illustrates the collective creative process and leads up to my own discussion of *Gora*:

GEETANJALI SHREE: The way we collaborate is quite special. I don't think there is a hierarchy of one script over another. Scripts run parallel to each other and come together to make the play. At some point as I start writing, Vidya works on the music and Nilima works on the sets. Very soon, we are exchanging ideas with each other. Each of us has her own strong parallel script and we might be deliberately taking different directions.

ANURADHA KAPUR: The decision to work on a script is more or less collective. As Geetanjali says, most of the scripts choose us. For example, we chose Tagore's *Gora* in 1991, as we felt it was an apt text at that time when national and regional identities were discussed and questions of purity of identity were being focussed upon. Generally, we begin working with our individual scripts after initial discussions. I begin working with the actors, at the same time as Geetanjali and Vidya are working on their written and music texts respectively. At some stage in this process we look at each other's text. Input from the actors is very important and after watching the rehearsals, Geetanjali might even substantially change the script, or Vidya might suggest a break in the scene with an introduction of music. Or, I might improvise a scene with the actors on which Geetanjali and Nilima are already working. So the whole process is extremely complex and entails a good deal of work and emotional energy. Even the actors are very good about it.

VIDYA RAO: Sometimes a word or an idea that Geetanjali may be using may suggest a certain kind of musical form to crystallise. (in Subramanyam 2002: 236–7)

Nalini Malani had felt that it was the performance which brought her installations to life. But the director and the performer could as well have said, given the nature of the collaborative creative process, that it was the installations that gave the performance life. Word, image, music, and choreography of movement coalesce, then, in a process that does not attempt to cover the jagged edges of the pieces which come together to make the whole.

NATION AND RELIGIOUS IDENTITY: TAGORE'S *GORA* 1907–1909

The Vivadi Collective has turned twice to the novels of Tagore for major productions. Both *Gora* and *The Home and the World* are novels that revolve around similar themes: public and private spaces, nation and religion as identity markers, and the subjectivities of women relegated to serving as public and private icons. In the following brief discussion which will form a prelude to an excerpt from the text itself, I shall focus on Vivadi's production of *Gora*. The novel is of particular interest since it questions notions of identity, anticipating and deconstructing the ideologies of Hinduness which would be fully articulated only in the 1920s. The novel's political concerns acquired new significance in the early 1990s, as Hindu–Muslim tensions were brought to an escalation, which was to peak in the destruction of the Babri Masjid.

Gora had been serialized in the journal *Prabasi* from 1907 to 1909 and published in book form in 1910. It was a critical period of transition for Tagore. He seriously questioned the claims of the Brahmo Samaj to be sole arbiter of truth and its arrogantly virulent rejection of Hinduism. At the same time, he questioned the radical Hindu enthusiasts who claimed in their turn, that Hinduism was the sole repository of values eternal, *sanatana dharma*, and chose to demonize the West. Tagore critiqued both positions. And he showed little patience with the mindless rejection of the West. Western traditions had filtrated Indian thinking, they could no longer be thought away:

The time has come now to discuss this change because an element of doubt has certainly crept in. We seem to be sitting undecided at the crossroads of ancient India and modern civilization. Even a few years ago our educated people had no genuine hesitation. Whatever the nationalists might have professed verbally, their faith in Western values was unshakeable. The emotional effusion generated by the French Revolution, the effort to abolish slavery, and English poetry written at the dawn of the nineteenth century had not yet subsided. Western civilization seemed to proclaim an inclusiveness for all humanity irrespective of race and colour. We were spellbound by Europe. We contrasted the generosity of that civilization with the narrow-mindedness of our own, and applauded the West.[6]

And thus it was that he drew fire from all sides, from Brahmos, Sanatani Hindus, and nationalists at large:

In late 1911 and early 1912, he was particularly oppressed by his countrymen. Orthodoxy—Hindu and Brahmo—was up in arms about *Gora*, his satirical play *Achalayatan* and a lecture to Brahmo sectarians in which Tagore stated provocatively: 'How can we utter this great lie that only what is dull and lifeless is part of Hinduism, whereas its ideal and its striving toward freedom are things which belong to the world but not to the Hindus?' And jealousy of his position as a writer, recognized by a unique fiftieth birthday reception for him at Calcutta's Town Hall in January 1912, added fuel to the attacks of the bigots (Hindus and Brahmo). (Dutta and Robinson 1995: 160–1)

But the most controversial of his publicly expressed opinions was his stand on the exuberant nationalism, *Swadeshi*, which was ready to trample over all other interests, particularly of the impoverished peasants of East Bengal, Hindu and Muslim, though the latter were clearly in the majority. 'A movement predominantly of upper caste Hindu bhadralok who tended to have rentier interests in land cultivated, in the main, by lower caste Hindus and Muslims, Swadeshi often sought mass contact through a highly emotional Hindu revivalism, particularly as it turned militant or extremist.' And further, 'Swadeshi nationalism simultaneously exalted and subordinated womanhood' (Sarkar 2002: 118, 132). Tagore publicly parted ways with the Swadeshi movement when Hindu–Muslim riots broke out in several East Bengal villages in 1907. The riots called for a serious revision of his own thinking, which had gone along with the revivalist stream up to this point, also with respect to the problematic deification of women. He delivered a series of lectures attacking nationalism on his lecture tours through Japan and the USA which were later published in book form as *Nationalism* (1917). Ashis Nandy has quoted from these lectures in writing of Tagore's decisive turn away from this uncritical brand of nationalism:

Not merely the subject races, but you who live under the delusion that you are free, are every day sacrificing your freedom and humanity to this fetish of nationalism.... It is no consolation to us to know that the weakening of humanity from which the present age is suffering is not limited to the subject races, and that its ravages are even more radical because insidious and voluntary in peoples who are hypnotized into believing that they are free.[7]

Tagore did not resort to the invocation of 'tradition' as the antidote to 'this fetish of nationalism'. He sought to go beyond nationalism, not regress to some utopia which had preceded it. Tagore was a convinced modernist—Nandy has duly noted this in his important study (1994: 1). Yet in his subsequent reading of *Gora*, Nandy tends to take recourse to his familiar anti-modernist positions. He sees the reaction to the narrow Hindu nationalism which Gora represents as resting on his mistaken reading of Indian tradition. The truly Indian traditions that tolerate plurality rest, for Nandy, in the positions taken by Paresh Babu and Anandamayi, both of whom disregard the narrow confines not only of caste but of orthodox Hinduism and Brahmoism respectively:

Four persons play crucial roles in this [Gora's] self confrontation—Binay, Paresh, Anandamayi and Sucharita. Of the four, Paresh provides the metaphysical and moral fulcrum for the story and is the main agent of change in Gora's personality. But it is Anandmayi who emerges as the most powerful presence in the narrative....

    That shared moral universe, Tagore suggests, is a universal one and, if Anandamayi can so effortlessly make it her own and defend it, it is in continuity with Indian traditions. What Paresh has acquired through self-discipline, Anandmayi has acquired through everyday womanliness, by being herself. (Nandy 1994: 40–1)

Nandy elaborates further on this mode of being which is 'in continuity with Indian traditions' and which in another place he calls 'the inner strengths of the Indian tradition' (47). He views this tradition as an organic state to which persons such as Anandamayi and Paresh have natural access:

Anandamayi, whose resistance is the deepest and most 'natural'. She fathoms the inauthenticity of Gora's nationalism from the beginning.... In Tagore's world, motherliness questions the dominant consciousness and resists it more radically and effectively than does conjugality. Hence, when Gora goes through his climactic transformation to arrive at a political position that anticipates the Gandhian worldview in significant ways, his first reconciliation is with his mother and childhood nurse. (49–50)

In idealizing Anandamayi's position as naturally given and as setting forth tradition rather than renewing it, Nandy bypasses a major concern of the novel and indeed of the phase through which Tagore was passing. As Sumit Sarkar has noted: 'Revivalist nationalism was often associated with certain conceptions of ideal Hindu womanhood that, once again, Rabindranath had briefly shared, but then came to very sharply repudiate. *Gora* is marked by the signs of this second debate, possibly as one not yet decisively resolved' (2002: 119).

This debate takes place primarily between Gora and Vinay. Considering that Gora himself is an aggressive propagator of orthodox Hindu values, but that both he and Vinay[8] are attracted to Brahmo women, Sucharita and Lalita, who seem radically progressive in their ways, it is natural that there are never-ending discussions about the ideal women they seek:

The two friends, Gora and Benoy, endlessly argue about the true nature of womanhood. For the major part of the novel Gora aggressively upholds a home/world type of disjunction as authentically national, and also as a thing of beauty and grace by itself. Benoy is much more critical, and even suggests at one point a homologue between the confinement of women to purely domestic functions and the bhadralok tendency to categorise peasants and other plebian folk by their service to their social superiors alone. The conversations of the two Brahmo girls, Sucharita and Lalita, go much further.... But the men still seem quite far from any recognition of the autonomous subjectivity of women.... The figure of Anandamoyi, quintessentially maternal but free of all social taboos and prejudices, helps in a way to smooth over an unresolved debate. Gora's peroration denouncing all sectarian barriers remains silent about gender. (Sarkar 2002: 133–4)

Even if they seem far removed from any theoretical recognition of the autonomous subjectivity of women, the very fact that both Gora and Vinay come together with Brahmo women without demanding sacrifices from them would show that a journey's end has indeed been reached. Yet if being Hindu or Brahmo determines social identity, on what foundation is religion, dharma to be based? Birth? Hard upon the heels of his realization that he is truly *gora*, a white man of Irish birth, comes the radical reversal in Gora's thinking. He is freed from the constraints of caste Hinduism. He tells Paresh Babu, 'I am not a Hindu,' which means, 'no longer do I need to fear that I shall fall away from caste or be defiled. I shall no longer have to look at the ground at every step to avoid pollution' (Tagore [1910] 2003: 474). By this definition, a person *is* a Hindu by birth, and *being* Hindu consists of observing caste mores, which are seen as universally applicable. Yet, living in a manifestly diverse social situation, maintaining this illusion means inhabiting an imaginary universe, a Hindu India that exists primarily, but no less dangerously for that, in the minds of Gora and his friends and allies. There is thus much violence involved in keeping the image of this Bharat intact:

How much I have struggled against forces all around me in order to build in my mind a Bharat that was without problems or distortions, and hold my devotion safely within that impregnable fort. Today in a matter of moments that imagined fort has vanished like a dream. I have been released completely and find myself in the midst of a vast truth. The good and the bad, the joys and sorrows, the wisdom and follies, of all of Bharatvarsha have suddenly come very close to my heart. At last I have gained the right to serve, and my true area of work has appeared before me. It is not an area of my mind—it is the area outside where the welfare of twenty-five crores is to be served....

Can you follow what I am saying? That which I sought day and night to become but could not, today I have indeed become that. Today I am Bharatiya. Within me there is no conflict between communities, whether Hindu or Muslim or Krishtan. Today all castes of Bharat are my caste. Whatever everybody eats is my food. (475)

Gora's passionate pledge of allegiance to a Bharat devoid of the notion of difference marks his swing of opinion from one extreme to what almost seems like another extreme. For there are indeed differences to be negotiated and a process that needs to be undergone in order to do so. It is true that his cumulative experience as an activist undergirds his new conviction, but the complete reversal of his original position is nevertheless sudden.

Gora has, by the end of the novel, ceased to be a Hindu and has become Bharatiya or Indian instead. Yet what if one were to remain Hindu? And marry a Brahmo girl who remained Brahmo? Vivadi's dramatization of the novel focused not only upon Gora but also on Vinay, the less spectacular figure, who had to struggle with the Hinduness into which he was born in order to overcome its Brahminically interpreted bounds and marry a Brahmo girl.

'HINDU' IN THE AGE OF HINDUTVA: *GORA* (1991)

The decision to turn to Tagore's *Gora* in summer 1991 had been taken in the wake of the mounting communal tension in the country. The melodramatic *rathyatras* staged by the Hindu Right, the cross-country processional expedition in a chariot mounted on a Toyota van, had generated the kind of mass agitation which was hurtling towards its gory conclusion at the end of the year: the demolition of the Babri Masjid and the Hindu–Muslim riots that would follow. As Geetanjali Shree relates it, *Gora* was chosen because it dealt with notions of belonging, of inclusion and exclusion. The idea was, in fact, not to restrict it to the Muslim question alone, but address wider issues of modern communitarian identities.[9] The script was written by Geetanjali Shree, working with S.H. Vatsyayan's beautifully rendered Hindi translation, which was then constantly reworked in the course of rehearsals. As Anuradha Kapur elucidated in the 'Director's Note' to the production brochure, the novel brought 'several debates centre stage, about the meaning of nation, nationalism and national identity'. While retaining a sense of its history—the action of the novel is placed in the late 1870s—the play made no hale of the fact that the tussle with identity, so closely related to choosing life partnerships, was being enacted in another time and in another medium; the re-enactment of these tussles could not exhaust itself in a reproduction of Tagore's 1910 positions:

While the audience knows that Gora is a white man, Gora himself struggles with the question 'who am I' posed in tandem with the question 'what makes a nation?'. Gora sees his friend Binay moving away from Hinduness. Meanwhile, the main woman protagonist, Sucharita, who is an enlightened Brahmo Samaji, moves away from the Samaj, but further complicates issues by questioning religion. This production attempts a strategic repositioning of the characters of Vinay and Sucharita.... Gora is torn between orthodox Hinduism, Western education and the colour of his skin. His whiteness has metaphoric implications, suggesting both the presence of the white colonialist and the incorporation of his alien presence into the social body of India. Whether Gora will follow a path similar to that of Vinay is left unresolved in this production. Indeed how we construct the meaning of the word citizen in today's India is a vexed question.[10]

The focus was on characters who reflect on their given identities, thus on Sucharita, who was to come to see the limitations of Brahmo progressivism and on Vinay, who would be brought to probe what he meant when he proclaimed 'I am a Hindu' to affirm and negate it, only to revise his position and then revert once again to being Hindu. How could one 'be' a Hindu? Could it be a process rather than a received notion?

Though the individual roles were carefully cast, the attempt was to let characters emerge in the interaction; the person was a changeable entity, often caught in the very process of change. The lines of the characters were often spoken by the chorus, which was also not a fixed set of people. Rather, the lines spoken by the chorus were also redistributed amongst the characters present on stage. The chorus was thus not a single impersonal voice or a collective, which voiced approval or disapproval. The mode of staging was then deliberately decentred, constructing a modernist stage vocabulary without resorting to essentialist notions of 'Indianness'.[11]

The play fleshed out spoken and unspoken clashes, the conflicts and ideas suggested by the novel. If Sucharita, still caught in the Brahmo world, insists that Vinay must convert before he can marry Lalita, she herself has, at the same time, begun to anticipate a state of affairs where such conversions will be seen as accoutrements that can be dispensed with. Implicated as she is in their deliberations, the course of her future action does indeed hang in the balance and will be affected by the decisions taken in the Vinay–Lalita conflict involving dharma and Samaj:

Sucharita:	Baba, whatever happens, Lalita and Vinay must get married.
Paresh:	But you were just insisting that without initiation....
Sucharita:	It is necessary for Lalita's happiness.
Panu:	Do you want them to set a precedence?
	(Vivadi script)

Panu, fanatic Brahmo and self-interested advocate of conversion into the Brahmo fold, hopes to marry Sucharita and coerce her into a more submissive role. He plays the devil's advocate in the debates that follow. He insists on the need to conform, while Paresh Babu takes the much more nuanced stance and advises caution in the matter of conversion. He is clearly modernist in the intensely reflexive stance he adopts; he sees partnerships based on choice as the coming together of two souls leading to a state higher than any other in individual life, which can transcend difference. As he proclaims: 'Only love can tolerate difference.'

However, the truly radical modernist stand is that taken by Anandamayi. She is a caste-Hindu who does not observe caste. She remains within the walls of her hidebound Hindu household, resisting and bypassing the thousand dos and don'ts laid down by her husband and her son Gora. She has adopted a white child, left orphaned in the 1857 uprising, and has had subsequently to bear all the consequences of taking in a *mleccha* who does not know that he is one and regards himself as purer than the pure. She has learnt through suffering and experience. As the Chorus says: 'She seems more modern than Paresh Babu to me. One by one, she has managed to transcend all societal bounds. For her, God and truth now reside in the human being, in his soul (*atma*). No Samaj, no dharma is greater than that.'

But what can being Hindu signify to an intellectual such as Vinay? Can it be more or less than social habitus? Vinay confesses that Hindu rites have never meant much to him and that he does not possess the knowledge to expressly agree or disagree with dharma precepts. In the switching to and fro from the one to the other on this slim basis, from Hindu to Brahmo to Hindu again, in the interest of his union with Lalita, there dawns the realization that he does not need to change his Hindu social identity in order to marry Brahmo Lalita. The realization emerges in the course of his conversations with Anandamayi and Paresh Babu.

Though Paresh Babu advises caution in the matter of conversion, he asks Vinay to throw himself into stormy waters, to not rest in given belief systems but to tussle with them. A Hindu or Brahmo identity can be an outer shell, in which case it would, of course, be possible to step out of it. But there can be tolerance of difference, if being either one of them, Brahmo on Hindu, involves a search for inner truth. As Paresh Babu sees it, truth has also to prove itself, it has also to stand the test of time, for no truth can congeal into dogma.

Vinay has then to realize that being Hindu in this sense can equally give freedom. He need neither leave Hindu society nor take an oppositional stand. It is quite another matter if Hindu society decides to excommunicate him. But then Anandamayi had once told him that the Hindu Samaj has made space for a myriad faiths. Perhaps it would create space for a wife from the Brahmo Samaj?

In an almost parallel process and in the course of these very conversations, Sucharita is also made to realize the narrowness of Brahmo beliefs. Would the world around her really fall apart if the wedding ceremony were indeed performed according to Hindu rites? The presence of a *shaligram* could neither hold a marriage together nor keep it from breaking apart. The shaligram could be present; it could, as well, not be present. The final scene in the play concludes with the question: is it necessary to identify oneself as Hindu? In a given historical and political juncture designating oneself 'Hindu' as an exclusive identity marker could become a manifest act of violence. In 1991 it was no longer possible to proclaim that one was a Hindu in any 1910 sense, as yet unburdened with the subsequent misuse and manipulation of the term. It had by this time become tarnished and tainted with the tawdry paint of the chariots employed in the rathyatras.

In a tense political situation, Vivadi's *Gora* could not be received other than with some reserve. Once again, an extraordinarily talented set of artistes had come together for the production. Vivan Sundaram had designed the stage set. The all-pervasive luminous blue screen lightened and darkened the stage to create night or day. A golden *thali* glowed within it, to become the sun but also to serve as platter that stood for food, for purity, as much as for pollution. Purity and pollution were the themes of the heated debates between Anandamayi and Gora, who would not eat in her rooms because she employed a Christian maid. The white, ochre, and red costumes against the blue and the gold were startlingly beautiful.

Both Sucharita and Anandamayi sat on the swing at crucial moments. The swing was a quotation from Satyajit Ray's film *Charulata*, swinging to and fro, weighing and balancing ideas and personas. The music provided its own text. While rehearsing *The Merchant of Venice* scene, the music changed from the haunting Baul music of the Bengal countryside to the ironic citation of a popular Mozart played by the Cambridge Buskers. Portia's famous speech, 'The quality of mercy is not strained', acquired an absurd note: the Brahmo elite performing Shakespeare at the house of District Magistrate Brownlow for an after-dinner function, which would be graced by the presence of the Lieutenant Governor and the Commissioner, a bucolic idyll held in blissful disregard of a ravaged countryside and an exploited peasantry.

Vibha Chibber gave a radiant performance as Anandamayi, 'a fluent character, resolved by modernity, not by tradition'.[12] Lines such as 'But who wants to marry the Brahmo Samaj? No, Vinay?' could then be delivered in an easy, tranquil, mode. Sima Biswas as Sucharita was a much more agitated, riven character, in the process of resolution. Her brisk modern walk revealed the tension of unresolved conflict: a new, individualistic 'love' and desire for romance in partnership which pulled in a direction other than the socially sanctioned. Both Gora and Sucharita pulled in opposite directions even as they sought to converge. Jitu Shastri as Gora was warm, passionate. He convinced Sucharita with the intensity of his beliefs and he kept Vinay in tow. He had a noisy footfall. Deepak Chibber as Vinay had the physical mannerisms, the gait of a Brahmo, though his ostensible position was that of a Hindu. He sought to align his exterior with his interior, to overcome its disjunction; he entered always with a book. He was already 'modern', rational in a style of debate that was as impassioned as it was reserved.

As conclusion to this chapter and to this book I cite in full the last scene of Geetanjali Shree's *Gora* in English translation, which dramatizes the conflict involved in retaining a social-political identity as Hindu or Brahmo while seeking a marital partnership with the other. The resolutions exist alongside questions that are left deliberately open.[13] The text is preceded by a series of photographs which serve as a parallel text.

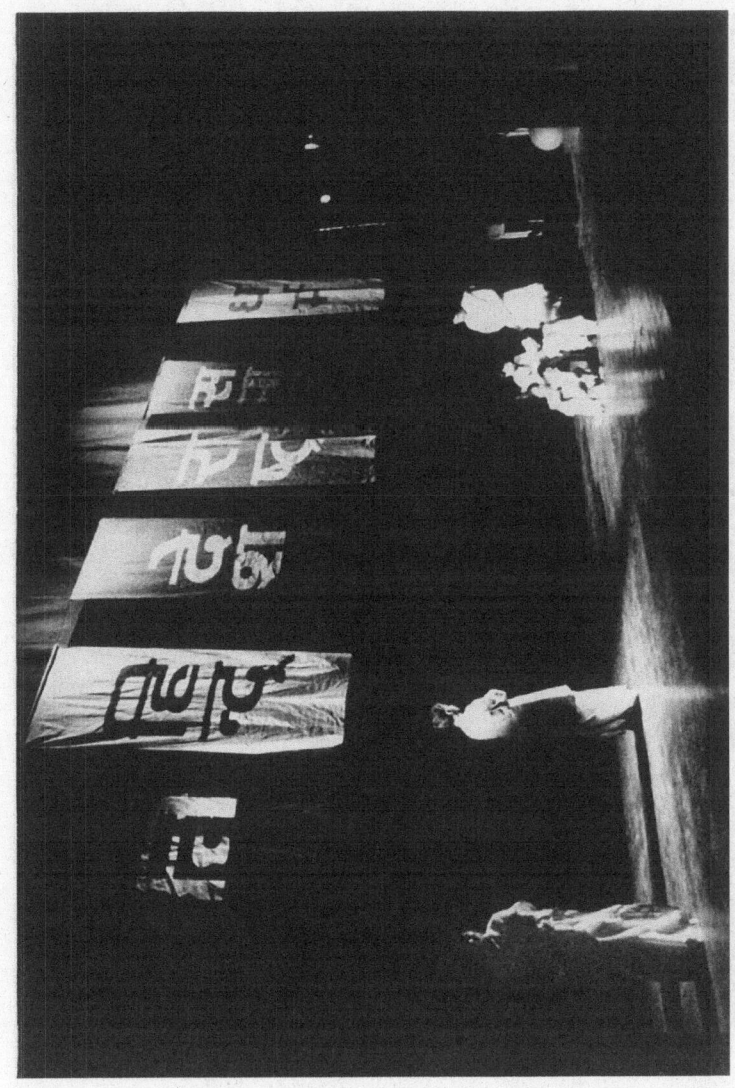

Post-Brecht Reformulations: Anuradha Kapur's production of Tagore's *Gora* (1990s)

Inter-dining

Debate

Community

Soliloquy

Recasting

'I AM A HINDU'

Vinay:	I am a Hindu.
Chorus:	Is this a statement or a query?
Panu:	Of course you're a Hindu and you won't leave your Samaj. Why on earth are you going around spreading rumours about these girls?
Chorus:	Well, and what about you? You and your friends dash off article after article, proclaiming that the Brahmo Samaj is in danger. Its members have begun to wonder: once this marriage takes place, will they come to be considered part of the Hindu Samaj again?
Panu:	What makes you go in and out of this house constantly?
Chorus:	Paresh Babu's drawing room.

Sucharita's small clock is ticking away on the writing table. It's around nine-thirty, the hubbub in the lane has subsided. Embroidered sofa covers. Deerskin spread before the armchair, Lalita has yet to come back.

She was just sitting on the cane chair. The curtain behind it is still swaying gently.

It seems to Vinay as if Lalita just went past. She must have swished past that curtain.

Chorus:	Where could she have gone?
Chorus:	To Anandmayi. Paresh Babu sent her there; go to her, he said, you'll find some peace of mind there. Lalita is sick of it. The same disputes, day in and day out. Ugly articles in the press. Sometimes, that a renegade Hindu youth is out to trap an innocent Brahmo girl. Sometimes, that a fast Brahmo girl is bent upon debasing the dharma of a devout Hindu boy. Paresh Babu has asked her to go speak to Anandmayi.
Chorus:	Anandmayi has asked Vinay to go talk to Paresh Babu.... When she saw Vinay looking bothered, she said, go pour out your heart to him.
Chorus:	But before he could do so, Panu Babu spotted Vinay at the street corner. And he landed there to play the wet blanket.
Chorus:	Sucharita is also here. Why wouldn't Panu Babu show off now?
Panu:	Our Samaj is going to make life difficult for these people.

Vinay:	That's something your Samaj should be ashamed of.
Panu:	While you bear no responsibility for that?
Vinay:	Someone in the Samaj is choosing to make a mountain out of a molehill. Do you expect me to hold that in check?
Panu:	And which Samaj will tolerate that a young man, alone with a young girl, in the dark of the night....
Paresh:	Can we equate an external incident with internal transgression? If we were going to indulge in such practice, did we need to leave the Hindu Samaj to join the Brahmo Samaj.
Panu:	Paresh Babu, philosophizing is hardly going to help now. We'll have to take action.
Vinay:	I've said, haven't I, that I am ready to marry Lalita?
Panu:	You, a Hindu....
Vinay:	Yes, I, a Hindu....
Sucharita:	Could you leave your Samaj?
Vinay:	You put that question to Anandmayi just yesterday.
Paresh:	What did she say?
Chorus:	The same as what Vinay is saying now.
Vinay:	Let the Hindu Samaj throw me out, why should I leave it?
Sucharita:	But how can a Brahmo marry a Hindu? What are you saying Vinay?
Panu:	We won't allow this to happen.
Chorus:	Paresh Babu? (looking at him)
Chorus:	He is silent. He is concerned. His beliefs take shape slowly within him. This is the first time that he's been challenged by a situation outside himself. He's also being tested.
Chorus:	It's also a test for Vinay, a confrontation with dharma and with the Hindu Samaj, a test of his forgotten dispositions and beliefs. It's easier to cross the limits of the Samaj in the mind than in deeds.
Chorus:	But you love Lalita, isn't that what it's about, you're keeping that under cover.
Chorus:	Place it right at the centre and look at it. It's Anandmayi's main concern and because it's there, it's only right to engage with both dharma and the Hindu Samaj.
Chorus:	Anandamayi seems more modern than Paresh Babu to me. One by one, she has managed to transcend all societal bounds.

For her, God and truth now reside in the human being, in his soul (*atma*). No Samaj, no dharma is greater than that.

Chorus: She has attained her release (*moksha*) by breaking bounds and adopting Gora. She says that again and again. Once Paresh Babu's gone through some such experience, he'll also speak up fearlessly.

Sucharita: Baba, why don't you say something?

Panu: He's upset. His children regress, they don't progress.

Paresh: Who's progressing, who's regressing? Only the Supreme One knows. I want my children to be happy and I want their reputation to grow. That's my one concern.

Chorus: This marriage will surely bring happiness. But reputation?

Chorus: Anandmayi is not unhappy even though she's already acquired a bad reputation. Gora won't drink even a sip of water in her room. Does that make her happy?

Chorus: Well, will this marriage happen or not?

Chorus: Of course it'll happen. The boy's party will set out from Anandmayi's house.

Chorus: What! So is Vinay going to marry Shashi after all?

Chorus: It's Vinay and Lalita; she has shifted to Anandamayi's because even her mother won't help her out. So Anandamayi will represent the girl's side also.

Chorus: Oh, is that why Lalita's gone there?

Chorus: But there's still a problem, no initiation, no marriage....

Chorus: Initiation? Who's taking initiation?

Vinay: May I be permitted to ask, why Lalita can't become a Hindu?

Sucharita: Our Samaj is founded on belief, whereas yours is bound by social custom. It'll be less bothersome for you to leave the Hindu Samaj than for Lalita to leave hers....

Paresh: (to himself) Can dharma be socially determined? Doesn't it come rather from personal striving (*sadhana*)?

Sucharita: Did you say something Baba?

Paresh: You'll have to be larger than the Samaj, if you want to cross its bounds.

Panu: Which is impossible.

Paresh: At your age, we had cast off our moorings and plunged our boat into stormy waters. And we haven't lived to regret it. One

	makes mistakes, runs aground, and suffers, but one doesn't just wait. One struggles for whatever one considers right.
Panu:	One loses all sense of direction if one opposes the Samaj.
Paresh:	One can't test truth without opposing it. Truth has always been tested. In each age, truth needs to renew itself; it has to overcome obstacles, only then can it stand its ground as truth.
Panu:	If you plan to give men so much freedom....
Paresh:	It's the pain caused by this freedom that will show us which truth is eternal and which the illusion of the moment. Herein lies the good of society.
Vinay:	Baba, then....
Paresh:	Think it over well, Vinay....
Vinay:	That's precisely what I find I cannot do.
Paresh:	Speak to your mother.
Vinay:	She says I should speak to you.
Paresh:	No, she is not as assailed by doubt as I am. If she were here she would dispel all doubt, honestly and clearly.
Chorus:	She comes here.
Chorus:	She came, but she left after meeting the girls.
Chorus:	She didn't appear in front of Paresh Babu?
Chorus:	If there'd been need to come before him, she would have done so, she wouldn't have thought twice about it.
Chorus:	There was need, wasn't there? In this matter of initiation?
Chorus:	The matter was resolved slowly. The girls went to her house, then they talked to Paresh; Vinay also....
Chorus:	But it took a long time. Just suppose she were here today, would it have taken quite so long?
Chorus:	She is so clear about this matter; she would never have given in.
Chorus:	Firmness rather than obstinacy.
Chorus:	Of course.
Chorus:	How quickly she would have resolved everything, if she'd come here today.
Chorus:	She'd say, look, dharma and Samaj....
Chorus:	Never, she'd say 'namaste' and cover her head with the sari.
Chorus:	No, she would not, and everyone would be shocked.

Sucharita:	Ma ji.
Vinay:	You?
Anandamayi:	Paresh Babu, do you recognize me? I know you well.
Paresh:	I know you well too, though I've never met you. Vinay speaks of you with such respect....
Anandamayi:	He'd write such a wonderful biography of me, if I died right now.
Paresh:	We won't let you let you off quite so easily.
Vinay:	Is everything alright?
Sucharita:	Here...meet Panu Babu.
Anandamayi:	Bless you. Lalita has come to me.
Panu:	Was there any need for her to do that?
Anandamayi:	She came with Sucharita.
Sucharita:	Where did she go? She went upstairs right away.
Paresh:	She must have felt better after talking to you.
Panu:	Is there a special recipe for making people feel better?
Anandamayi:	Panu ji, we older people have seen life and understood some things about it.
Sucharita:	Have you started using the handbag?
Anandamayi:	Are you happy now? See, Sucharita has made it for me. But where on earth would I go swinging such a handbag, at this age?
Vinay:	And what's that?
Anandamayi:	It's for sister Baradasundari.
Sucharita:	Ma, you....
Anandamayi:	Why can't we allow two people to come together? Because their belief systems clash? Do human beings meet in belief systems (*matvad*)?
Panu:	It's wrong to force the Samaj to bend this way or that.
Anandamayi:	Son, it's wrong to force people to bend this way or that.
Panu:	Is there call for this kind of controversy here?
Paresh:	There *is* call for this kind of controversy here. Please feel free to speak!
Anandamayi:	Will your Brahmo Samaj forbid human being to meet human being? Will the Brahmo Samaj continue to hold them apart even if the Lord created them the same from inside?

Panu:	The Lord is not discrete from the Samaj.
Anandamayi:	What are you saying, son? Do you want to swallow the Lord whole?
Panu:	Our dharma....
Anandamayi:	Paresh Babu, will man (*insan*) continue to battle the Lord? Do we form a Samaj for that reason?
Paresh:	A Samaj which doesn't take note of petty difference, which draws people into vaster harmony....
Vinay:	Is it possible to craft such a Samaj?
Anandamayi:	Wasn't this the ultimate goal of the Brahmo Samaj?
Panu:	I, Baradasundari, Sucharita, and Paresh believe that Vinay has to take initiation into the Brahmo Samaj. Only then can the Brahmo Samaj begin to consider the matter of this marriage.
Anandamayi:	But who wants to marry the Brahmo Samaj? No, Vinay?
Panu:	Forgive me, but Vinay will have to become a member of the Brahmo Samaj. We'll have to exert pressure.
Sucharita:	Even Lalita....
Anandamayi:	Forgive me, but pressure won't work here.
Chrorus:	Her resolution stunned them into silence.
Chorus:	Paresh Babu, why are you listening so intently? Have you seen his shining eye?
Chorus:	Because all that he tries to suppress he hears Anandmayi say openly. Look, he speaks.
Paresh:	Vinay, you don't have to play Lalita's saviour.
Anandamayi:	Absolutely, that would be most unfair to her.
Vinay:	I can't bear it, because of me, you people....
Paresh:	People don't have a long memory. They'll stop talking, if not tomorrow, then the day after....
Vinay:	That will be my good fortune....
Chorus:	Stuttered words, why can't he admit that this has nothing to do with being her saviour, that he loves her?
Vinay:	I love Lalita with all my heart....
Anandamayi:	And she cares for you.
Sucharita:	Yes, I know Lalita's mind.
Panu:	Then you'll have to take initiation into the Samaj.
Sucharita:	You used to say that you appreciate the Brahmo Samaj.

Vinay:	On the other hand, I ask myself whether I mean nothing to the Hindu Samaj. Baba, what do you think?
Sucharita:	Baba, why don't you speak?
Paresh:	Anandmayi, you speak so clearly, why don't you tell us?
Anandamayi:	That's why I've come here, quite uninvited. I feel removed from the rules and regulations of my house, but that doesn't stop it from being my house. Why should I stop calling it my own? I'll think about what to do, if at some point in time they cast me out.
Vinay:	No, Ma, I won't allow yet more blame to be heaped upon me.

They leave.

Chorus:	And they both leave. But you were saying that if Anandamayi were to come, the decision would be taken like this (snaps fingers).
Chorus:	Do you remember how long they took to resolve this in the book?
Chorus:	In the book Anandamayi did not come in the nick of time. We just supposed that if she were to come, she would take care of the matter in no time....
Chorus:	Now, think of all that could happen. Once Mother and son left, what would these people have done?
Chorus:	Panu smiles when he hears Vinay's words of defeat.
Chorus:	Sucharita is getting more and more restless.
Sucharita:	Baba, whatever happens, Lalita and Vinay must get married.
Paresh:	But you were just insisting that without initiation....
Sucharita:	It is necessary for Lalita's happiness.
Panu:	Do you want them to set a precedent?
Paresh:	Vinay is a good person of course.
Panu:	We've been hearing that a traditionally dressed person comes here everyday to initiate you into the Hindu Samaj.
Paresh:	Tell Gora to come here also. The two houses are so near each other.
Sucharita:	He came last evening; he wanted to meet you. I brought him here.
Paresh:	But you were by yourself.

Sucharita:	You were doing puja. Gora bowed and went away silently.
Paresh:	Why didn't you ask him to wait?
Panu:	Yes, yes, why didn't you ask him to wait?
Sucharita:	I'll go to Vinay again tomorrow.
Paresh:	This room is so cold.
Panu:	Vinay is running back. What's up, brother? Someone called out from the window in the upper storey. Did someone stop you from going away?
Vinay:	Paresh Babu, I've come back.
Paresh:	Whatever happened?
Vinay:	Paresh Babu, I'll take initiation from you.
Panu:	Hey?
Vinay:	I break one or the other ritual prescriptions of the Hindu Samaj every day.
Paresh:	After much reflection, these things....
Vinay:	I respect the Brahmo Samaj....
Sucharita:	Are you saying this to reassure yourself....
Vinay:	The truth is that I cause hurt to each Samaj. The truth is that I cannot in all honesty accept the ritual prescriptions of any Samaj fully.
Paresh:	Regarding the dharma of the Brahmo Samaj....
Vinay:	Baba, dharma has yet to bear any fruit in my life. I've never been particularly attached to dharma.
Panu:	Are you listening?
Sucharita:	Then you were being needlessly partisan about the dharma of your own Samaj?
Vinay:	Which dharma is truer? I never gave the matter particular thought, I never felt any particular need for dharma.
Panu:	But you indulged in very subtle analysis of dharma in your articles, in your discussions.
Vinay:	Perhaps I have a head for debate.
Panu:	And you are indulging in just that now?
Vinay:	There's no debating this time around. Paresh Babu, I'll take initiation from you this coming Sunday.
Paresh:	I can't do it.
Sucharita:	Why?
Panu:	Which way does the wind blow now?

Paresh: I can't perform an initiation from which I stand to gain. Write to the Brahmo Samaj.

Vinay: Write to all the people who are raking up such muck about us? Who...how'll I be able to write.... They'll all read it...my head (bows it).

Paresh: Don't allow your head to hang. Does Anandmayi know that you want initiation? Why did you come back?

Chorus: Does she know?

Chorus: How should I know what happens next if we are not following the sequence given in the book?

Chorus: Then try and imagine it. Just suppose he'd told Anandmayi of this before coming here.

Chorus: She would have said you're doing something absolutely wrong. Think for yourself.

Chorus: Does she really believe there's a way out for these two, without one or the other kind of initiation?

Chorus: Don't you remember, she once said to Vinay that there was space for a million belief systems within Hindu dharma. Won't there be space for just one more?

Chorus: She said that in a particular context. She believes that it's possible for people of different belief systems to marry.

Chorus: Anyway, Vinay has another problem. He is confused about being aligned to any dharma, not just Hindu dharma.

Chorus: Does he place himself outside dharma? He'll have to find out, won't he? The question at the moment is whether the marriage took place or not.

Chorus: It took place and without the initiation. Without the presence of the shaligram. For two human beings to come together, it was necessary neither to leave the Samaj nor dharma.

Chorus: But Vinay left after he heard Paresh Babu's words about his initiation.

Panu: He'd come to take initiation. To pollute that pure moment for the sake of his love. We would never forgive you, if the chronicles of the Samaj recorded that you were responsible for its downfall.

Sucharita: Who can tolerate condescension and pity? People are used to being assaulted by you.

Paresh:	Only love can tolerate difference.
Chorus:	But remember, Baradasundari made Vinay put down in writing that he was willing to become a Brahmo Samaji. The condition was that she would speak to the secretary so that he undertake the initiation without any fuss and bother.
Chorus:	That letter suffered the only fate that could befall it once it got into the hands of a person as self-respecting as Lalita.
Chorus:	The letter torn into shreds? The shreds scattered? Well then, Vinay and Lalita decided to do what Anandmayi had considered proper right from the start.
Chorus:	But Vinay decided to do all this because of personal love?
Chorus:	What is that supposed to mean? One way or the other, he would have worked it out at some point in time, when something else came in his way.
Chorus:	Hmmm...well, the marriage did take place. Anandmayi gave the bride away and Paresh Babu was the bridegroom's party. As for Gora, he stayed away entirely.
Chorus:	It just occurs to me. Vinay doesn't go to Gora for advice any longer, for the old question-and-answer sessions.
Chorus:	Who knows where he is, even if Vinay does go to see him. Meanwhile, Gora and Sucharita meet almost every day.
Chorus:	Then after the wedding....
Chorus:	The wedding hasn't taken place. It will take place.
Chorus:	Tell me, has Vinay remained a Hindu?
Chorus:	I don't really feel like asking him. Can't one let this question be?

NOTES

[1] See the important programmatic essay by Kapur (2001) and the survey by Jain (2002).

[2] The novel inspired the Pakistani (1976) and the Indian (1981) films. The Indian film was to become an all-time favourite. See Dar (2002) for an analysis of the respective cultural constructions of the figure of the Lucknow courtesan in the two films.

[3] See Rao's sensitive analysis of thumri (1996). I am grateful to Nalini Delvoye for drawing my attention to this essay.

[4] From a review of the play by Yashodhara Dalmia (1997).

[5] Note in the production brochure.

[6] *Rabindra Rachnabali* (vol. 6: 702). Cited in Meenakshi Mukherjee's introduction to the English translation of *Gora* (2003: x).

[7] *Nationalism* [1917] Reprint Madras: Macmillan (1985: 18), cited by Nandy (1994: 6).

[8] The alternate forms are Binay and Benoy. I have consistently used Vinay.

[9] Conversation with Geetanjali Shree and Anuradha Kapur on 28 November 2003.

[10] 'Director's Note', production brochure.

[11] Conversation with Anuradha Kapur on 21 November 2003.

[12] This phrase, as also many of the terms used to describe the various roles in the play in the following paragraphs, stem from Anuradha Kapur (conversation on 21 November 2003).

[13] There are two key terms, '*samaj*' and 'dharma' which need to be glossed, since I have often left them untranslated. Samaj comes from the Sanskrit [prefix *sam* with the root *aj*] and carries a wide range of meanings: 'to bring or collect together', as a masculine noun it means 'meeting with, falling in with'. It later came to mean 'congregation, meeting, assembly, conclave, society, company, association, collection'. From the early nineteenth century on, it was used for 'society, community, religious community'. When 'samaj' is used in the larger, more comprehensive sense, I have used 'society' so that the translation reads better. 'Samaj' as in Hindu Samaj has the sense of societal, social, social customs and so on, and is clearly a translation of the English term, society. In conjunction with Brahmo, it acquires the sense of religious congregation, surely inspired by English compounds such as the Bible Society and the like. Sucharita says 'Our Samaj is founded on belief, whereas yours is bound by social custom.' These are two different conceptions of samaj. One has to do with exclusionary belief, the other with social custom. Brahmo Samaj is founded on belief, Hindu Samaj is seen as a conglomeration of belief and social custom, where custom outweighs. Hindu Samaj then, as it defines itself in this new period, recurs to its most structured stratum, which is the Brahminical and also seeks to become more exclusionary; it needs to be oppositional in order to define its own contours. This is the position represented by Gora and his father. 'Dharma' also has several meanings; it can mean social status, social and moral *varna* and *jati* expectations, but also stage in life. But most of all, in later usage 'dharma' has come to mean religion

in the modern sense that includes belief systems. Thus Sucharita is only half right when she distinguishes between Brahmo and Hindu Samaj on the basis of belief. Hindu Samaj has increasingly sought to portray itself as also founded on a shared belief system.

REFERENCES

Allana, Amal. 2002. 'Gender Relations and Self Identity', in *Muffled Voices*, L. Subramanyam (ed.).

Dalmia, Yashodhara. 1997. 'Creative Fusion' review of Vivadi's adaptation of Bertolt Brecht's *The Job*, in *The Express Magazine*, March 9.

Dar, Huma. 2002. *Islamizing the Tawa'if or Tawa'ifing the Muslims: The Lucknow Courtesan Partitioned*. M.A. Thesis. University of California, Berkeley.

Dutta, Krishna and Andrew Robinson. 1995. *Rabindranath Tagore: The Myriad-minded Man*. London: Bloomsbury.

Geetanjali Shree 1991. *Gora*. Hindi manuscript of the play.

Jain, Kirti. 2002. 'In Search of a Narrative', in *Muffled Voices*, L. Subramanyam (ed.).

Kapur, Anuradha. 1990. *Actors, Pilgrims and Gods: The Ramlila of Ramnagar*. Calcutta: Seagull. Paperback, 2004.

_____. 2001. 'A Wandering Word, an Unstable subject...' in *Theatre India*, May, 5–12.

_____. 2003. 'Actors Prepare', *Body, City: Contemporary Culture in India*, Indira Chandrashekhar and Peter C. Seel (eds.). Berlin: Haus der Weltkulturen, Delhi: Tullika.

_____. 2004. 'Impersonation, Narration, Desire, and the Parsi Theatre', in *India's Literary History: Essays on the Nineteenth Century*. Delhi: Permanent Black.

Nandy, Ashis. 1994. *The Illegitimacy of Nationalism: Rabindranath Tagore and the Politics of the Self*. Delhi: Oxford University Press.

Rao, Vidya. 1996. 'Thumri and Thumri Singers: Changes in Style and Life-Style', in *Cultural Reorientation in Modern India*, Indu Banga and Jaidev (eds.). Shimla: Institute of Advanced Study, 278–315.

Sarkar, Sumit. 2002. *Beyond Nationalist Frames: Postmodernism, Hindu Fundamentalism and History*. Bloomington and Indianapolis: Indiana University Press, Delhi: Permanent Black.

Sarkar, Tanika. 2001. 'Aspects of Contemporary Hindutva Theology: The Voice of Sadhvi Rithambhara', in *Charisma and Canon: Essays on the Religious History of the Indian Subcontinent*, Vasudha Dalmia, Angelika Malinar and Martin Christof (eds.). Delhi: Oxford University Press.

Subramanyam, Lakshmi. 2002. 'In Their Own Voice: In Conversation with Anuradha Kapur, Geetanjali Shree and Vidya Rao', in *Muffled Voices: Women in Modern Indian Theatre*, Lakshmi Subramanyam (ed.). Delhi: Shakti Books.

Tagore, Rabindranath. [1910] 1976. *Gora*. Translated into Hindi by Satchidanand Hiranand Vatsyayan. Delhi: Sahitya Akademi.

____ [1910] 2003. *Gora*. Translated into English by Sujit Mukherjee. With an introduction by Meenakshi Mukherjee. Delhi: Sahitya Akademi.

Index